Asian Islam in the 21st Century

Asian Islam in the 21st Century

EDITED BY

JOHN L. ESPOSITO

JOHN O. VOLL

OSMAN BAKAR

OXFORD
UNIVERSITY PRESS

2008

OXFORD
UNIVERSITY PRESS

Oxford University Press, Inc., publishes works that further
Oxford University's objective of excellence
in research, scholarship, and education.

Oxford   New York
Auckland   Cape Town   Dar es Salaam   Hong Kong   Karachi
Kuala Lumpur   Madrid   Melbourne   Mexico City   Nairobi
New Delhi   Shanghai   Taipei   Toronto

With offices in
Argentina   Austria   Brazil   Chile   Czech Republic   France   Greece
Guatemala   Hungary   Italy   Japan   Poland   Portugal   Singapore
South Korea   Switzerland   Thailand   Turkey   Ukraine   Vietnam

Published by Oxford University Press, Inc.
198 Madison Avenue, New York, New York 10016

www.oup.com

Oxford is a registered trademark of Oxford University Press

Library of Congress Cataloging-in-Publication Data
Asian Islam in the 21st century / coedited by
John L. Esposito, John O. Voll, and Osman Bakar.
   p. cm.
Includes bibliographical references and index.
ISBN 978-0-19-533302-2; 978-0-19-533303-9 (pbk.)
1. Islam—Asia—21st century.   2. Islam and state—Asia—
21st century.   3. Islam and politics—Asia—21st century.
I. Esposito, John L.   II. Voll, John Obert, 1936–   III. Bakar, Osman.
BP63.A1A75 2007
297.095'0905—dc22   2007007819

9   8   7   6   5   4   3   2   1

Printed in the United States of America
on acid-free paper

Acknowledgments

This volume owes much to many talented and generous people. First, I want to thank my colleagues, coeditors and long-time friends John Voll and Osman Bakar. The chapter authors have patiently revised and updated probably more than they might have anticipated! Clare Merrill, former assistant director of the Prince Alwaleed bin Talal Center for Muslim-Christian Understanding, and Lesley Sebastian, executive assistant, were key players in the organization and logistics of the original conference in Hawaii in December 2003, at which these chapters were presented. Clare then followed up with authors through a series of revisions. Huma Malik, current associate director of the center, has been a major driving force in assuring that this manuscript would see the light of day, from motivating my colleagues to get that one last revision done to reviewing, editing, and suggesting revisions. Preparing this volume like so many before has been enjoyable because of my long-time editor at Oxford University Press, Cynthia Read. Finally, as with all my work over the years, Jeanette Esposito, my wife and life partner, has always been there with advice and encouragement.

John L. Esposito

Through this book I wish to honor the memory of my parents, Obert and Ruth Voll, who maintained an interest in religion in Asia throughout their lives.

John O. Voll

Contents

Contributors, ix

1. Introduction: Islam in Asia in the Twenty-First Century, 3
   John L. Esposito

PART I Religion and Politics in Muslim
          Majority Societies

2. Islam in Indonesia in the Twenty-First Century, 11
   Fred R. von der Mehden

3. Pakistan after Islamization: Mainstream and Militant
   Islamism in a Changing State, 31
   Vali Nasr

4. Islam, State, and Society in Bangladesh, 49
   Mumtaz Ahmad

5. Malaysian Islam in the Twenty-First Century: The Promise
   of a Democratic Transformation? 81
   Osman Bakar

6. The Trifurcated Islam of Central Asia:
   A Turkish Perspective, 109
   M. Hakan Yavuz

7. A Provincial Islamist Victory in Pakistan: The Social Reform Agenda of the Muttahida Majlis-i-Amal, 145
Anita M. Weiss

PART II Religion and Politics in Muslim
Minority Societies

8. Muslims in Post-Independence India, 177
Steven I. Wilkinson

9. Islam in China, 197
Jacqueline Armijo

10. The Effect of 9/11 on Mindanao Muslims and the Mindanao Peace Process, 229
Eliseo R. Mercado

11. Thai and Cambodian Muslims and the War on Terrorism, 245
Imtiyaz Yusuf

12. Conclusion: Asian Islam at a Crossroads, 261
John O. Voll

Index, 291

Contributors

Mumtaz Ahmad is professor of political science at Hampton University in Virginia. He received an M.A. in political science from the University of Karachi in Pakistan, an M.A. in development administration from the American University of Beirut in Lebanon, and his Ph.D. in political science from the University of Chicago. He has been a Research Fellow at the Brookings Institution in Washington, D.C.; a Senior Fulbright Research Fellow in India, Pakistan, and Bangladesh; and a U.S. Institute of Peace Fellow in Sudan, Pakistan, and Malaysia. In addition, he has been a Fellow of the American Institute of Bangladesh Studies and the American Institute of Pakistan Studies. He was a member of the Islam and Social Change Project at the University of Chicago, and the Fundamentalism Project of the American Academy of Arts and Sciences. He is the current president of the South Asian Muslim Studies Association and coeditor of the journal *Studies in Contemporary Islam*. He has published eight books, numerous book chapters, and encyclopedia and journal articles on the politics of South Asia and the Middle East and the politics of Islamic resurgence. He is currently working on the pedagogy and politics of madrasa education in Muslim South Asia.

Jacqueline Armijo is assistant professor of international studies at Zayed University in the United Arab Emirates. She received her Ph.D. from Harvard University and has taught at the Hong Kong University of Science and Technology, Cornell University, Clark

Atlanta University, and Stanford University. She has spent more than seven years living in China, working and carrying out research on Muslims there. Her research focuses on Islam in China, both the early history and the recent revival of Islamic education among Muslim communities. This research has also examined the effect of growing numbers of Chinese Muslims who are seeking to continue their Islamic studies overseas in countries such as Saudi Arabia, Pakistan, Syria, Egypt, Malaysia, and Iran, along with their role in Muslim communities on their return to China. Her research has also focused on the active role played by women in the revival of Islamic education in China and the influence of Islamic education on Muslim girls. Her teaching interests include women and Islam (with a focus on women outside of the Middle East), Chinese studies, and Muslim minorities. Her publications include articles in *Encyclopedia of Women and Islamic Cultures, Encyclopedia of Islam in the Muslim World, American Journal of Islamic Social Sciences, Journal of Asian Studies,* and *Harvard Asia Quarterly.* She is a founding member of the editorial board of the recently inaugurated *Journal of Middle East and Islamic Studies in Asia.*

Osman Bakar, formerly Malaysia Chair of Southeast Asian Islam at the Prince al-Waleed Center for Muslim-Christian Understanding, Georgetown University, Washington, D.C., is currently professor of Islamic thought at the International Institute of Islamic Thought and Civilization (ISTAC), Kuala Lumpur. He is also Emeritus Professor of Philosophy of Science, University of Malaya, and Senior Research Fellow at the university's Center for Civilizational Dialogue; and Visiting Research Fellow, Center for Interdisciplinary Studies of Monotheism (CISMOR), Doshisha University, Kyoto, Japan. He is author of thirteen books and more than 200 articles on various aspects of Islamic thought and civilization, particularly Islamic science and philosophy and Islam in Southeast Asia. He is a member of the Council of 100 Leaders of the West-Islamic World Initiative for Dialogue founded by the World Economic Forum, Davos, Switzerland.

John L. Esposito is University Professor of Religion and International Affairs and Islamic Studies and is the founding director of the Prince Alwaleed Bin Talal Center for Muslim-Christian Understanding at the Edmund A. Walsh School of Foreign Service at Georgetown University. Prior to moving to Georgetown University, he was Loyola Professor of Middle East Studies, chair of the department of religious studies, and director of the Center for International Studies at the College of the Holy Cross. A consultant to the Department of State, as well as corporations, universities, and the media worldwide, he specializes in Islam, political Islam, and the effect of Islamic movements from North Africa to Southeast Asia. He has served as president of the Middle East Studies Association of North America and the American Council for the Study of Islamic Societies and is currently president of the Executive Scientific Committee for La Maison de la Méditerranée's 2005–2010 project, "The Mediterranean, Europe and Islam: Actors in Dialogue." He has been appointed to the World Economic Forum's Council of 100 Leaders and to the High Level Group of the U.N. Alliance of Civilizations. He is a recipient of the American Academy of Religion's 2005 Martin E. Marty Award for the Public Understanding of Religion and of Pakistan's Quaid-i-Azzam Award for Outstanding Contributions in Islamic Studies. In 2003, he received the Georgetown University Award for Outstanding Teaching in the School of Foreign Service. He is editor in chief of *The Oxford Encyclopedia of the Modern Islamic World* (4 vols.); *The Oxford History of Islam*, a Book-of-the-Month Club and History Book Club selection; *The Oxford Dictionary of Islam*; and *The Islamic World: Past and Present* (3 vols.). His more than thirty books include *Unholy War: Terror in the Name of Islam*; *What Everyone Needs to Know about Islam*; *World Religions Today* (with D. Fasching and T. Lewis); *Geography of Religion: Where God Lives, Where Pilgrims Walk* (with S. Hitchcock); *The Islamic Threat: Myth or Reality?* and *Islam: The Straight Path*. His books and articles have been translated into Arabic, Persian, Urdu, Bahasa Indonesia, Turkish, Japanese, Chinese, and European languages.

Eliseo R. Mercado, or Father Jun as he is fondly called, is a man of dialogue in the southern Philippines. In his younger years as a missionary, he lived in four municipalities of Maguindanao Province in southern Philippines that are predominantly Muslims. There he was able to become a friend to the Muslims, including the two Moro Liberation Fronts. Because of his friendship with the Muslims and his expertise in Islam, he continues to influence the peace process in the southern Philippines. From 1996 to 2000, he was given the mandate by the Republic of the Philippines and the Moro Islamic Liberation Front to chair the Independent Ceasefire Monitoring Commission that supervised the compliance of government and the MILF to the 1997 Agreement on the Cessation of Hostilities. From 1992 to 2002, he was president of Notre Dame University in Cotabato City, the only Catholic university in the autonomous region in Muslim Mindanao. During his time as president, the university developed an education paradigm on peace education.

Vali Nasr is professor of international politics at the Fletcher School of Law and Diplomacy, Tufts University; an Adjunct Senior Fellow at the Council on Foreign Relations; and Senior Fellow at the Belfar Center of the Kennedy

School of Government, Harvard University. He is the author of *The Shia Revival: How Conflicts within Islam Will Shape the Future* (2006); *Democracy in Iran: History and the Quest for Liberty* (Oxford University Press, 2006); *The Islamic Leviathan: Islam and the Making of State Power* (Oxford University Press, 2001); *Mawdudi and the Making of Islamic Revivalism* (Oxford University Press, 1996); *The Vanguard of the Islamic Revolution: The Jama'at-i Islami of Pakistan* (1994); and an editor of the *Oxford Dictionary of Islam* (Oxford University Press, 2003). He has been the recipient of grants from the John D. and Catherine T. MacArthur Foundation, the Harry Frank Guggenheim Foundation, and the Social Science Research Council. He was a Carnegie Scholar for 2006.

John O. Voll is professor of Islamic history and associate director of the Prince Alwaleed Bin Talal Center for Muslim-Christian Understanding at Georgetown University. He taught Middle Eastern, Islamic, and world history at the University of New Hampshire for thirty years before moving to Georgetown in 1995. He graduated from Dartmouth College and received his Ph.D. from Harvard University. He has lived in Cairo, Beirut, Jerusalem, and Sudan and has traveled widely in the Muslim world. The second edition of his book *Islam: Continuity and Change in the Modern World* appeared in 1994. He is coauthor, with John L. Esposito, of *Islam and Democracy* and *Makers of Contemporary Islam* and is editor, author, or coauthor of five additional books. He is a past president of the Middle East Studies Association and of the New England Historical Association. He has served on the boards of directors of the American Council of Learned Societies, the New Hampshire Humanities Council, the New Hampshire Council on World Affairs, and the Sudan Studies Association. He was the chair of the program committee for the 1999 annual meeting of the American Historical Association. In 1991 he received a Presidential Medal in recognition for scholarship on Islam from President Hosni Mubarak of Egypt. He has published numerous articles and book chapters on modern Islamic and Sudanese history.

Fred R. von der Mehden, Albert Thomas Professor Emeritus at Rice University, received his Ph.D. at the University of California, Berkeley, in 1957. He then taught at the University of Wisconsin–Madison until 1968, where he became professor of political science and director of East Asian studies. Since 1968, he has been at Rice University. He has written widely on religion in Southeast Asia. Among his books and monographs are *Religion and Nationalism in Southeast Asia* (1963), *Religion and Modernization in Southeast Asia* (1986), *Two Worlds of Islam: Interaction between Islam in Southeast Asia and the Middle East* (1993), and *Radical Islam in Southeast Asia* (2006).

Anita M. Weiss, professor of international studies at the University of Oregon, received her Ph.D. in sociology from the University of California at Berkeley. She has written four books on social development and gender issues in Pakistan, including *Walls within Walls: Life Histories of Working Women in the Old City of Lahore* (Oxford University Press, 2nd ed., 2002), and, with Zulfiqar Gilani, *Power and Civil Society in Pakistan* (Oxford University Press, 2001), as well as numerous articles on culture, women, and development in Pakistan. She is a member of the editorial boards of two journals, *Citizenship Studies* and *Globalizations*, and is on the editorial advisory board of Kumarian Press.

Steven I. Wilkinson is associate professor of political science at the University of Chicago. He has research interests in ethnicity, ethnic violence, and the institutional legacies of colonialism. His book *Votes and Violence: Electoral Competition and Ethnic Riots in India* (2004) explores the ways in which electoral competition drives and constrains ethnic violence in India. The book was corecipient of the American Political Science Association's 2005 Woodrow Wilson prize for the best book in government, politics, or international relations published in the previous year. He also coedited *Patrons, Clients, and Policies* (2007) with Herbert Kitschelt, his former colleague at Duke University, on patterns of patron-client party competition throughout the world. His current book project is on colonization, democracy, and conflict. It examines, among other issues, how colonial patterns of political decentralization and ethnic favoritism in the military and administration have influenced postindependence patterns of democratic consolidation and ethnic conflict.

M. Hakan Yavuz is an associate professor of political science at the University of Utah. He received his early education in Ankara, Turkey, and graduated with a B.A. from Siyasal Bilgiler Fakultesi, Ankara. He received his M.A. from the University of Wisconsin–Milwaukee and spent a semester at Hebrew University, Israel (1990); in 1998, he received his Ph.D. from the University of Wisconsin–Madison in political science. He has written a number of books: *Islamic Political Identity in Turkey* (Oxford University Press, 2003/2005); with John Esposito, *Turkish Islam and the Secular State* (2003); and *The Emergence of a New Turkey: Democracy and the AK Parti* (2006). He also carried out extensive fieldwork in Fergana Valley, Uzbekistan, to examine the relationship between Islam and nationalism and the preservation and dissemination of Islamic knowledge under socialism. He is an author of more than forty articles on Islam, nationalism, the Kurdish question, and modern Turkish politics. He has written articles published in *Comparative Politics*, *Critique*, *SAIS Review*, *Journal of Muslim Minority Affairs*, *Central Asian Survey*, *Journal of Islamic*

Studies, and *Journal of Palestine Studies.* He is an editorial member of *Critique, Silk Road,* and *Journal of Muslim Minority Affairs.*

Imtiyaz Yusuf is currently head of the department of religion in the Graduate School of Philosophy and Religion, Assumption University, Bangkok, Thailand. His academic and research specialization is in the area of religion with a focus on Islam in Thailand and Southeast Asia. He has contributed to the *Oxford Encyclopedia of Modern Islamic World, Oxford Dictionary of Islam,* and *Encyclopedia of the Qur'an.* His recent publications are "Dialogue between Islam and Buddhism through the Concepts of *Tathagata* and *Nur Muhammadi*" in *International Journal of Buddhist Thought and Culture; Understanding Conflict and Approaching Peace in Southern Thailand* (2007); *Faces of Islam in Southern Thailand* (2007); and *Doing Cross-Cultural Dawah in Southeast Asia* (2007).

Asian Islam in
the 21st Century

I

Introduction: Islam in Asia in the Twenty-First Century

John L. Esposito

At the dawn of the twenty-first century, Islam is the second largest of the world's religions. The 1.3 billion Muslims of the world are spread across more than fifty-six Muslim majority countries and in a matter of decades have become a significant presence in Europe and America, where Islam is the second and third largest religion, respectively. Despite its global profile, Islam in the popular imagination—and often in the media—still tends to be disproportionately identified with the Arab world or the Middle East. Yet, in fact, the vast majority of Muslims are in Asia and Africa.

Islam in Asia in the twenty-first century has a dynamic and diverse presence in regional and global politics. Its multifaceted significance in all areas of life and society is only now beginning to be appreciated. The Muslims of Asia constitute the largest Muslim communities in the world. In this context, Asia, especially South and Southeast Asia, enjoys special importance. First, Asia accounts for 49.7 percent of all Muslims.[1] Indonesia, Pakistan, Bangladesh, and India have more Muslims than the entire Arab world. A rich diversity of Muslim discourse and politics stretches from the Taliban of Afghanistan to the more modern cosmopolitan societies of Malaysia and Indonesia. Second, in the last century, Asia has produced some of the most prominent and influential intellectuals in the Muslim world: from South Asia's Muhammad Iqbal and Abul A'la Al-Mawdudi to Southeast Asia's Nurcholish Madjid and Abdurrahman Wahid. Third, Islam has been used to legitimate self-proclaimed

Islamic governments in Pakistan and Afghanistan and to mobilize armed opposition in Central Asia and the southern Philippines. At the same time, Asian countries like Malaysia, have achieved considerable economic development and a measure of political democracy, while emphasizing their Islamic roots and culture. Fourth, many Asian Muslim countries are multireligious and multiethnic societies with a history and legacy of religious and political pluralism and tolerance. In recent years, communal conflicts have challenged and threatened that legacy.

With the effects of globalization and the communication revolution, the flow of ideas and people within the Islamic world has vastly increased. Consequently, Muslims in Asia are affected by what is happening in the Arab Middle East and the Western part of the Islamic world. Thus, the Asian scene reflects the ideological and philosophical trends prevalent in the Western Muslim world. Similarly, extremist trends, some with affinity with groups such as al-Qaeda, exist in Asia and have been responsible for violent acts such as the bombings in Bali in October 2002 and for militant groups like Abu Sayyaf in the Philippines. For several decades, religion has become a more visible and potent force in Muslim politics. Contemporary Islamic revivalism has manifested itself in both personal and public life. Military rulers, kings, ayatollahs, Islamic organizations, and terrorist groups have justified their actions in the name of Islam. Iran, Sudan, and Afghanistan established new Islamic republics or governments; governments and opposition movements appeal to Islam to enhance their legitimacy and mobilize popular support; Islamists or Islamic activists (sometimes popularly referred to as fundamentalists) engage in political and social activism. Some have won elections as mayors and parliamentarians and served in cabinets and as prime ministers. Others have created strong social movements that are effective institution builders. They have created new institutions in civil society, offering education, along with legal and social welfare services, and they have established Islamic banks, insurance companies, publishing houses, newspapers, and websites. A small though deadly minority of religious extremists use violence and terrorism in attempts to destabilize or overthrow regimes.

The influence of political Islam in Asia reveals the fullest picture of the diverse roles of Islam in public life, both the best and the worst. The heroic image of the Afghan mujahideen as freedom fighters whose resistance movement overcame Soviet occupation gave way to a Taliban-imposed Islamic state that many in the international community regarded as a pariah. The example of the Taliban embodies for many the threat of fundamentalism with regard to global terrorism and intolerance, especially toward women and minorities. Pakistan, Bangladesh, Malaysia, and Indonesia in diverse ways reveal the multiple roles that Islam takes in their movements toward democracy, from elected to military, and from government manipulation of Islam to religious and ethnic communal conflicts.

This book is a successor to the first volume edited by John Esposito, *Islam in Asia: Religion, Politics, and Society*, published by Oxford University Press in 1987. For many years, the faculty of the Prince Alwaleed Bin Talal Center for Muslim-Christian Understanding has paid special attention to developments in Asia and how they have affected the character and praxis of Asian Islam. The center has held a series of conferences in recent years in Kuala Lumpur, Bangkok, Singapore, and Hawaii, at which the effect of the terrorist attacks of September 11, 2001, were viewed within long-term sociopolitical and cultural developments in Asia. As a result, in *Asian Islam in the 21st Century*, terrorism and its effects are placed within the broader context of the evolution of Islamic political activism and how Islamic ideals and movements, mainstream and extremist, have shaped the developments of Muslim societies both in Muslim majority countries and in countries where there are Muslim minorities.

Asian Islam in the 21st Century is divided into two sections: religion, politics, and society in major Muslim majority countries (Indonesia, Malaysia, Pakistan, Bangladesh, and Central Asia) and ethnic and religious politics in Muslim minority communities (India, China, Thailand, and the Philippines).

Part I begins with chapter 2, "Islam in Indonesia in the Twenty-First Century," in which Fred R. von der Mehden analyzes the ramifications of September 11 and the effects of Islam on democracy in the country. He argues that "although some radical Islamic groups oppose the idea of democracy, the majority of significant Islamic parties and organizations support it." However, the occupation of Iraq and deteriorating conditions in Afghanistan detract from the indigenous democratic experiment in Indonesian politics.

In chapter 3, "Pakistan after Islamization: Mainstream and Militant Islamism in a Changing State," Vali Nasr discusses the ways in which politics in Pakistan are undergoing a redefinition in relations among Islamist groups and the military in terms of domestic politics. In the post–September 11 environment, the Pakistani military cracked down on the very groups it relied on earlier for political gain in Afghanistan and Kashmir. As a result, the Islamist groups also realize that their future is not in jihadi activism but in mainstream politics.

In chapter 4, "Islam, State, and Society in Bangladesh," Mumtaz Ahmad argues that the rise in the influence of Islamist ideology in Bangladeshi politics is a consequence of the country's political culture and not, as he demonstrates, a consequence of foreign intervention. In gaining independence, Bangladesh has neither abandoned Islam nor lost it to secularism. In fact, the Muslim masses find no "contradiction between their Islamic identity on the one hand and their struggle for socioeconomic justice and political rights on the other."

Osman Bakar looks at the process of democratization in chapter 5, "Malaysian Islam in the Twenty-First Century: The Promise of a Democratic Transformation?" Bakar argues that Malaysia is currently witnessing a major shift from Malay identity to an ethnic distribution and issues that more accurately represent Malaysia's pluralistic society.

Islam has been part of the process of nation building in Central Asia and the Caucasus and part of the game of power politics by domestic and international actors. The Muslims of Central Asia were transformed from weak minority communities in a very large state under Soviet rule, into Muslim majority societies, when the Soviet Union collapsed. This created challenges and opportunities as Islam became a major contending source in the newly created or newly emerging Muslim majority states of Central Asia. In chapter 6, "The Trifurcated Islam of Central Asia: A Turkish Perspective," Hakan Yavuz analyzes Islam's role in the development of political movements in Central Asia and how the perceptions of Western and Russian Islam inflate the threat that Islamic political activism poses. He explains that Islamic revivalism in Central Asia is not a "major threat to the stability of the region" but rather, a reclaiming of Islam from the control of the state and turning it into a "source of morality and identity."

South Asian history and politics have been profoundly affected by the role of Islamic activist movements whose Islamist ideology has influenced and been influenced by the Middle East. The situation in South Asia reflects the continued influence though a shifting landscape of Islamist ideology and groups. Anita Weiss in chapter 7, "A Provincial Islamist Victory in Pakistan: The Social Reform Agenda of the Muttahida Majlis-i-Amal," examines the long-term ramifications of the political victory of Pakistani Islamist political parties. She demonstrates how activists in the country structure their behavior in ways that are possible in a Muslim majority society.

Part II examines the extraordinarily diverse ethnic and religious politics in Muslim minority communities. Muslim minorities in Asia, as in other parts of the world, struggle with issues of faith and identity, such as how to maintain communal identity in the face of pressures for cultural and political assimilation, as well as political development. In some Asian countries, Muslim minority populations are inextricably linked with issues of minority movements for greater socioeconomic recognition, cultural rights, and, in some cases, total autonomy. This is the situation in Thailand and in the Philippines and, to some degree, among the Chinese Uighur Muslim minority.

India is the home of the largest Muslim minority community, and the fourth largest Muslim community, in the world. Chapter 8, Steven Wilkinson's "Muslims in Post-Independence India," discusses the experience of the Indian

Muslim minority and its dynamic interaction with the majority society. Such efforts of lessening intercommunal conflict are key to strengthening the Indian Muslim community. Wilkinson argues that, despite the wave of anti-Muslim sentiment in India since the early 1990s, the increase in political competitiveness among Indian states has positively affected Muslims' security—in exchange for political support—and economic prospects.

In contrast, Chinese Muslims have less corporate identity and leverage than Indian Muslims, with correspondingly stronger pressures for assimilation. China's Muslims face their second millennium under Chinese rule, a millennium in which issues of identity, integration, self-determination, and autonomy remain important and often politically explosive issues. Though many Muslims initially supported early communist calls for autonomy, equity, and freedom of religion, China's Muslims have more often been the objects of antireligious and antiethnic nationalism: from the closing of mosques to widespread persecution and executions. In chapter 9, "Islam in China," Jacqueline Armijo discusses the diverse religious and political influences that have made for coexistence and conflict. Islam in China is the product of strong external influences from the Middle East and broader Muslim world—from reformist ideas and movements (in particular Wahhabi-inspired reform movements) to Sufi orders. China's Muslims continue to be influenced culturally, religiously, and, at times, politically by ideas and movements from the Middle East and Central and South Asia. While the Hui remain the largest of Muslim nationalities and have accommodated to Chinese culture, Uighur separatism has resulted in clashes and conflicts that have been countered by government repression of what it sees as its Islamic threat, a fear exacerbated by events and fear of influence from Afghanistan and Central Asia.

Other activist and militant movements, like those in Mindanao and Thailand, however, are shaped by their contexts as representing movements of advocacy for minority rights. This ties them more closely to local ethnic identities, and they become similar to separatist movements rather than following too closely the modes of actions of mujahideen groups. In chapter 10, "The Effect of 9/11 on Mindanao Muslims and the Mindanao Peace Process," Eliseo R. Mercado discusses the cultural dynamics of Muslim ethnic identities and how they relate to the emergence of activist groups in southern Philippines. He examines the cultural processes within the Lumad (indigenous people), the Bangsamoro (Muslim groups), and the migrant Christians to address the intricacy and predicament of the peace process. Chapter 11, Imtiyaz Yusuf's "Thai and Cambodian Muslims and the War on Terrorism," analyzes Islam in the context of ethnoreligious developments in the southern part of the country, arguing that this conflict is the product of the merging of an ethnically Malay

Islamic viewpoint with a puritanical interpretation of Islam acquired from abroad.

Finally, chapter 12, John Voll's "Asian Islam at a Crossroads," concludes the volume with an overall examination of Asian Islamic states and assesses Islam's role in the changes that are taking place in secular and civil societies. He notes the competition among a wide range of groups who are attempting to determine the nature of states and societies in the Muslim world of the future. This competition involves defining appropriate Islamic education and the changing nature of the mass media and popular culture, as well as the more visible conflicts involving efforts to control political institutions in the contexts of globalization and religious resurgence. He concludes that whatever the outcomes of these competitions, Islam will have an important role in the transformations of state and society.

NOTE

1. *2007 CIA World Factbook* (http://www.cia.gov/library/publications/the-world-factbook/index.html).

PART I

Religion and Politics in Muslim Majority Societies

2

Islam in Indonesia in
the Twenty-First Century

Fred R. von der Mehden

Domestic and international forces have transformed Islam in Indonesia
significantly since the early 1980s. In this chapter, I assess the nature
of these changes and the influence that framed them. Special attention is given to the effect on Islam of two major events since the year
1999: the reemergence of democracy in Indonesia and the ramifications of 9/11 and its aftermath. I consider the implications of these
changes on the relation of Islam to democracy, pluralism, the growth
of religious radicalism, and reactions to the "war on terror" among
Muslims in Indonesia.

Before focusing on the major points, let me underscore an
important caveat. To talk about "Indonesian Islam" is to oversim-
plify a highly heterogeneous religious mosaic. Islam in Indonesia
has long been characterized by its considerable variations in belief
and practice. On one level, there are differences framed by the influence of pre-Islamic beliefs, such as Hinduism and animism. Historically, this Hindu heritage has been particularly powerful on
Java, the country's most populated island. On another level, there is
a wide range of local and regional influences that help determine
religious belief and behavior. A review of the multitude of village
studies throughout the archipelago would quickly provide illustra-
tions of this pattern. On still another level, Indonesian political history
reflects divisions among the country's Muslim-oriented organizations. From prewar conflicts between Islamically oriented nationalist parties such as Sarekat Islam and Partai Nahdatul Ulama to

postindependence competition between Masjumi, Nahdatul Ulama, and other Islamic parties, there has been no consistent common agenda. As discussed later in this chapter, this divisiveness continues today.

Important differences about the role of Islam in society and the state are reflected in contemporary religious organizations. There is an increasing consensus that the public dialogue on Islam can be divided into four major categories.[1] Modernists, with their roots in the early twentieth century move- ment in Egypt, have long had a considerable following in Indonesia. These include members of the first mass nationalist movement, Sarekat Islam, and the Muhammadiyah, the largest Muslim organization in the country. Today, the Muhammadiyah rejects official political participation, although parties with a similar agenda form the largest Islamic bloc in Parliament. Contemporary groups are committed to democracy and nationalism.

The so-called traditionalists include those who follow a variety of traditional customary values and practices. This group presents great diversity, but the majority supports implementation of the Sharia and obedience to Muslim clerics. Politically, their platforms vary from pluralist to anti-minority positions. The other large Islamic association in Indonesia today, Nahdatul Ulama (NU) is in this category. The NU as an organization has abandoned party politics, although its leadership formed the National Awakening Party. Generally sup- portive of democracy, the leadership of this category remains suspicious of those who are seeking a more secular state.

The neo-modernists have a more nearly universal view of the role of Islam, rejecting narrow interpretations of the Sharia and the formation of an Islamic state. Rather, they see in Islam a source of motivation and inspiration. Neo- modernist discourse does not support the development of Islamic institu- tions but emphasizes personal ethical and pious behavior. The neo-modernists strongly support a pluralist perspective with attention to human rights, includ- ing women's rights, and democracy. A number of well-known Muslim intel- lectuals are in this group.

Finally, there are the Islamists who include within their ranks a range of violent and nonviolent elements. While not united on issues, they generally tend to seek the imposition of the Sharia throughout the country, as well as the establishment of an Islamic state, and they expound anti-Christian and anti- secular sentiment. They remain a minority and do not have significant official representation in Parliament. However, parts of their agenda resonate in the general public.

Often, the lines between the adherents to these categories are not clear-cut, but the existence of all of these variations makes it difficult to generalize about Islam in Indonesia.

In addition to these Islamic groups, there are those who support Islam Jawa (Javanese Islam), the syncretic mystical belief system based in East and Central Java. Members of this community provided the elite core to the Suharto regime and make up the base for former President Megawati Sukarnoputri and her Indonesian Democratic Party of Struggle. In debates in Parliament over the implementation of Islamic agendas, the party has tended to promote a more secular position.

Another important point is that considerable change has taken place in the character of public Islam since the 1980s.[2] In part, this has been due to external forces. The world oil crisis in 1973 provided the money that allowed Middle Eastern states such as Saudi Arabia and Libya to fund religious activities in many countries, including Indonesia. More important, the Iranian revolution galvanized political Islam. There was admiration for Iran's stand against the West, although this was not part of a Shia reaction, given Indonesia's Sunni population. Nor was there strong support for copying the clerical government instituted in Iran.

The ensuing years brought a major influx of literature from the Islamic resurgence into the country, as translations of Sayyid Abu al-Ala Mawdudi, Hassan al Banna, Sayyid Qutb, Seyyed Hossein Nasr, Sayyid Naguib al-Attas, Ali Shari'ati, and a range of other writers were increasingly available to the public. There has also been a rising interest in Sufism,[3] even though Sufi influence has been present since the introduction of Islam into the archipelago. Indonesian writing on Islam began to display a wider appreciation of contemporary Muslim literature, and the number of publications on Islam in Indonesian grew appreciably. In addition to the traditional role of scholarship by Indonesians trained at Middle Eastern institutions such as Al Azhar, a significant number of young scholars began to receive their Islamic education at Western institutions in the United States, Australia, the Netherlands, Canada, and the United Kingdom. Those returning to Indonesia brought with them new perspectives and methodologies that broadened Indonesian Islamic thinking. Often the writings of influential Muslim authors, such as Murtaza Mutahhari and Fazlur Rahman, were translated into Indonesian from English.

There were also important changes taking place in the character of Indonesian Islam resulting from domestic factors. The process of development with its concomitant increase in mass communications and mobility brought traditionally rural Muslims into contact with modern Western activities and values. This not only reinforced secularist influences but also brought negative reactions from many Indonesians who sought the support of traditional religious values. The institutionalization of Islamic religious training in public schools and the growing influence of indigenous Muslim educational institutions helped homogenize the understanding of Islam in the republic. The number of Islamic colleges and madrasas has increased greatly in recent years. This has tended to diminish previous "un-Islamic" perceptions of young Indonesians.

All these factors have been reflected in the public face of Islam in society. For example, these decades saw the marked increase in the number of women wearing what was once derided as "Arab dress." Those going to Mecca for the pilgrimage increased. The number of banks offering Islamic banking (non-interest-based banking) grew markedly. Even the marketing of products began to employ more Islamic motifs. The media gave greater attention to Islamic subjects.[4] Indonesians, particularly those from Hindu-influenced places like Java, had historically been quite lax in pursuing religious practices such as prayer and fasting during Ramadan. But in the latter decades of the twentieth century, they began to recognize the need to follow these requirements. Polls taken in 2001 and 2002 found a strengthening of support for Muslim rituals such as prayer and a weakening of un-Islamic practices such as burning incense and seeking advice from a shaman.[5] The number of people going to the mosque and involving themselves in religious organizations grew considerably, particularly among the country's youth. And the number of those who agreed with the establishment of an Islamic government increased significantly.

During these years, students were attracted to a wide range of Islamic ideas that interacted with their negative reactions to the undemocratic government of President Suharto and his "New Order." Factors such as Suharto's policies, in conjunction with reactions to the Iranian revolution, and the influence of the Islamic revival abroad, gave strength to liberal and even radical Islam on the country's campuses. Most prominent in influencing these students was a combination of the Iranian revolution, the Egyptian Muslim Brotherhood, and Wahhabi (or Salafi Islam) ideas supported by Saudi government agencies in Indonesia. All of these contributed to the intellectual religious ferment in the nation in the 1980s and 1990s.

There was one area where Islam did not display an increasing role in society—politics. Through most of the latter years of former President Sukarno's dominance and during the first twenty-five years of the Suharto regime, the Indonesian government sought to diminish the role of political Islam. Suharto's New Order would not allow political parties to present an Islamic agenda, and all political organizations were forced to accept a national ideology, the Pancasila, which was anathema to many Muslims (they argued that it was agnostic and gave equal weight to Islam, Christianity, Buddhism, and other faiths). It was only in the early 1990s that President Suharto had a change of heart, and the government attempted to capture the image of a supporter of Islam. Suharto personally attempted to project himself as a devout Muslim, and the government sponsored the Islamic organization, the ICMI or Association of Indonesian Muslim Intellectuals. While criticized by some as a tool of the regime and as a supporter of modern rather than traditional Islam, the ICMI did include a number of well-known and legitimate leaders of Muslim organizations and did increase the Islamic dialogue in the country. However, because of their religion, Muslims remained unable to compete politically.

Return of Democracy and Islam

Two events in the period 1999–2006 have profoundly affected the public character of Islam in Indonesia; these are the return of democracy to the republic, and 9/11 and its aftermath. Indonesia last experienced a competitive democratic system in the 1950s, after which the country faced Sukarno's Guided Democracy, which eschewed Western liberal democracy, and then the façade democracy that characterized Suharto's New Order. In the latter case, although there were elections and much of the public paraphernalia of a democratic system, the military and its allies actually determined the decision-making process. Within this system, as noted, political Islam had no recognized place. But all of this changed when the economic debacle that Indonesia faced in the late 1990s threatened the continuance of the Suharto regime. The end result was the first truly competitive national elections since 1955 and the reestablishment of democracy in Indonesia.

This new democratic system helped frame the public role of Islam in twenty-first-century Indonesia in several significant ways. First, it allowed the reemergence of political parties with Islamic agendas. The 1999 parliamentary elections to the Dewan Perwakilan Rakyat (People's Representative Council; DPR) did not provide the Islamic parties with a majority.[6] Islamically oriented parties took 38 percent of the legislature's 462 elected members (in addition, the military chose 38 members), while the secular and Christian parties gained the rest, with 62 percent of the popular vote. The Muslim parties not only could not garner a majority of the DPR, but their adherents badly split their votes. The 1999 elections again illustrated the split between Indonesian Islamic traditionalists and modernists, a condition that continues to this day. Neither of the largest Muslim organizations, the modernist-oriented Muhammadiyah and the more traditional Nahdatul Ulama, could get their supporters to rally around one Muslim party, although the latter finally supported one party that garnered 12.6 percent of the vote. To be sure, the leaders of both organizations did not attempt to present themselves simply as spokesmen for the *ummah* (community) and made an effort to appeal to non-Muslims, as well as their natural constituencies. In addition, together, the major Muslim parties appeared unable to present a coherent Islamic platform, and the larger parties could not agree on how to implement the establishment of an Islamic state or Sharia law. This situation did give Muslims an institutional voice and sufficient power to affect both policy decisions and the choice of government leadership, however. Thus, there were a number of key offices held by Muslims, including Abdurrahman Wahid (Gus Dur), the first president of the republic after the elections, and Hamzah Haz, the second vice president. Both were chosen by the DPR in conjunction with the largely appointed Peoples Consultative Assembly (MPR). In addition, Amein Rais, long-time leader of the Muhammadiyah, became the speaker in the MPR, and the minister of justice was a member of the Muslim PPP (Partai Persatuan Pembangunan) party.

Finally, while the other parties did not present an Islamic agenda, their members were well aware of the power of certain issues that were important to their own Islamic constituencies. This lack of institutional power by political Islam was not as apparent at the informal local level where popular attitudes lent support to Islamic ideas. Thus, a majority of the Parliament has supported several foreign and domestic policies central to the platforms of the Islamic parties.

The 2004 elections to the DPR (this time without an appointed military bloc) resulted in a similar pattern of fragmentation within both the secular and the Islamic party blocs. In fact, Indonesia faced the greatest legislative fragmentation in its history, with seventeen parties represented in the DPR. The new DPR again had only a minority of Islamic parties, although they were favored by the weighting of votes in areas where they were strong.[7] Once more, they were split in terms of policies and leadership and with one exception lacked year-round local organization. The presidential elections that followed later in that year found two secular candidates facing one another in the run-off, as Islamic candidates were defeated in the initial votes. Susilo Bambang Yudhoyono (SBY), promising reform and anticorruption policies, defeated President Megawati Sukarnoputri decisively, obtaining over 60 percent of the popular vote.

The events of 9/11 and their aftermath, including the attack on Iraq and "the war on terror," also have had a major influence in framing public Islam in Indonesia. Perhaps most important was that the Coalition conflicts with Afghanistan and Iraq and the attacks on Islamic militants (combined with the continued prominence of the Israel-Palestinian conflict) galvanized the sense of Islamic identity within Indonesia's Muslim population. These attacks reinforced previous beliefs within much of the general public that the West was on a crusade against Islam. In addition, the actions of the United States, Israel, and their perceived allies facilitated the radicalization of elements of the

Muslim community and helped form a sense of sympathy for their goals and actions among many Indonesians.

Certainly, both the general public and politicians from a range of parties reacted negatively to the American attacks on the Taliban and on Iraq. After the invasion of Iraq, some 100,000 people, sponsored by parties from the radical left to conservative Islamic, took to the streets of Jakarta to protest. Speeches referred to the U.S. president as "evil" and "Satan." Polls found overwhelming popular rejection of American actions and the explanations for them. One poll showed that 80 percent of Indonesians wished that the Iraqis had fought better. Negative perceptions of the United States in the Indonesian public grew from 36 percent in 2002 to 83 percent just one year later. These negative numbers declined following American aid to tsunami victims and have not reached the earlier highs in recent years. However, when asked in 2003 how worried they were that the United States could endanger their country some day, some 74 percent said "very" or "somewhat."[8]

At the elite level, there has been strong condemnation of Western actions against Afghanistan and Iraq from both Islamic leaders and spokespeople for more secular organizations. Before the United States entered Afghanistan, the Council of Islamic Ulemas called for jihad if the United States attacked that country; later, the council demanded that Indonesia cut ties with the United States. When the United States did act, a variety of political and religious leaders condemned the attacks. MPR Speaker Rais called Israel the real number one terrorist state. Then Vice President Haz wanted an end to the attacks and questioned the amount of evidence against Osama bin Laden. Islamic organizations from the more radical Islamic United Front to the modernist Muhammadiyah also opposed the U.S. policies in Afghanistan.

Sometime later, Hassan Wirayuda, the Indonesian foreign minister under Megawati, argued that the American unilateral approach in Iraq had failed. Although these objections have reached across party lines, some have argued that Muslim politicians looked to the 2004 parliamentary elections and hoped that taking a position opposed to U.S policies could attract potential voters. For example, Vice President Haz was vocal in his remarks, calling the United States the "king of terrorists." Objection to Coalition activities have continued and were joined by condemnation of Israel's actions in Lebanon and of U.S. support of Tel Aviv.

In the rest of this chapter, I analyze the present and future role of Islam in Indonesia in three major areas: (1) support for pluralism within the society, (2) the maintenance of democracy in the republic, and (3) dealing with radical elements in the archipelago and Muslim views toward the "war on terror."

Pluralism

The traditional description of Islam in Indonesia is that of a "flexible" and peaceful system that eschews the rigid interpretations of the religion and the intolerance of many other Muslim societies. There is no question that in most parts of Indonesia this has been true and that among the Javanese, in particular, there was a tendency toward laxness in religious practice and eclecticism in belief. Even before the recent well-publicized violent actions by radical Islamic groups, however, this characterization of Islam in Indonesia as tolerant and nonviolent was overly simplistic. It ignored major movements in the postindependence era that showed some elements of the country's Muslim community that were prepared to employ violence in the name of Islam and were highly critical of other religious and ethnic minorities. Even before independence, there was deep-seated antagonism against other minorities. The first Muslim nationalist organization, Sarekat Dagang Islam, formed before the eruption of World War I, had its impetus in anti-Chinese sentiments among East Javanese Muslim merchants. There was also considerable antipathy in colonial days against the Christians, who were seen as supporters of the Dutch.

Two prominent examples of violence involved Islamic groups after independence. First were the actions of Darul Islam, an organization that called for an Islamic state and confronted the Indonesian state in the late 1940s, after World War II. Second was the involvement of Muslims in the mass killing of Communists and their allies in 1965 and 1966, when Muslim youth elements aided the military.[9] Also receiving considerable press in the 1980s and 1990s were cases of bombing of churches and shopping centers and the dramatic and violent actions of small, and at times, colorful groups like Kommando Jihad.

In the decade before the 1998 fall of Suharto, Indonesia experienced increasing anti-Christian and anti-Chinese sentiment within the government and among some Muslim organizations. Suharto's flirtation with Islam had led to the sacking of Christian ministers, and there were reports of members of the armed forces aiding radical Muslims. More extreme elements of the Dewan Dakwah Islamiyah Indonesia (Dakwah Council, formed in the 1980s), following a traditional anti-Christian missionary view of the group, appeared to join with the anti-Christian, anti-Jewish KISDI (Indonesian Committee for Solidarity with the Islamic World) in the 1990s. These actions appeared to take place with the tacit acceptance of the Suharto government. In addition, anti-Chinese expressions portrayed the Chinese as allies of the Christians. Other groups joined in during the 1990s, and anti-minority rhetoric became more vitriolic. These expressions were part of a wider set of attitudes. Martin van Bruinessen has argued that "solidarity with Palestine is only part of the story; the words 'Jew' or 'Zionist' refer to the whole range of internal enemies and such threats as secularism, cosmopolitanism, and globalization, as well, as the inseparable evil pair of Capitalism and communism."[10] Not only fringe groups expressed anti-Christian sentiment; there were also supporters within major Muslim organizations, including the Muhammadiyah. In 2005, within the general public, 38 percent had an unfavorable view of Christians and 76 percent saw Jews negatively

Certainly, in contrast, there were prominent spokesmen for tolerance and religious pluralism. The two major Muslim organizations—the Muhammadiyah, representing the modernist wing of Indonesian Islam and the more traditional Nahdatul Ulama presented leaders who appeared as supporters of pluralism. The best known of these individuals was Abdurrahman Wahid, leader of Nahdatul Ulama. Both before and after his rise to the presidency of the republic, Wahid and some of his colleagues regularly called for dialogue and religious tolerance. But many in Nahdatul Ulama and other conservative Islamic groups were not in agreement with Wahid's willingness to deal with Israel, his position on women's rights, or his liberal interpretations of Islam.[11] Other spokesmen for religious pluralism and democratic values included a new class of Western-educated intellectuals such as Nurcholish Madjid, former leader of the Muslim Students Association, and the late Harun Nasution, former rector of the Jakarta State Institute of Islamic Studies.

The new democratic era has not seen a major diminution in ethnic and religious tension, although, as always in Indonesia, it is often difficult to disentangle the two. Attacks against the Chinese during the economic crisis of the late 1990s brought international condemnation, particularly from Chinese-populated states such as China, Taiwan, and Singapore. These activities were not primarily based on religious factors, but they may have played a subtle role in reinforcing antagonism against religion.

Since the fall of Suharto in 1998, there have been a series of clashes between Muslims and Christians: bombings of churches, attacks on mosques, violent confrontations between believers, reported forced conversions, and other examples of religious intolerance. While these events have taken place in many parts of the archipelago, the worst incidents have been on Sulawesi and in the Maluku. Both of these areas have large Christian populations, a history of separatism, and long-term economic divisions.[12] The conflict in Maluku reportedly left over 5,000 killed and 500,000 displaced. However, levels of violence have declined since the early 2000s, although it continues to be a serious problem.

The history of the major perpetrator of this violence, Laskar Jihad, provides a useful tool for understanding the complex nature of this problem of religious pluralism. It emerged publicly in 2000 and disbanded in 2002 after declaring its job done (although pressure from Islamic leaders was also a factor). Although some have characterized Laskar Jihad as simply an anti-Christian terrorist organization, its agenda had its roots in the belief of many Indonesian Muslims that Christians were targeting them in Maluku, in fears of antiseparatist sentiment, and in efforts to rally conservative Muslims after the 1999 elections. Laskar Jihad did not simply recruit disaffected rural Muslims; it especially proselytized among university students rather than the general Muslim community. Its leader, Ja'far Umar Thalib, had studied in Saudi Arabia, and he and many of his original followers were strongly influenced by conservative Wahhabi Salafy beliefs. While the organization failed to gain the support of large-scale Muslim organizations or the more modern parties in Parliament, there was public and private backing from conservative Islamic groups and elements of the Indonesian armed forces. There were charges of direct military support from the army, including training.[13] In a sign of his relationships, after his arrest, then Vice President Haz and other Muslim leaders visited the leader of Laskar Jihad in prison.[14]

Issues of religious pluralism in Indonesia are far more complex than these violent activities. They also include questions about the acceptance of other "marginal" religions, the right to practice one's faith freely, apostasy, and the role of women. To be sure, many limitations on religious freedom have existed in Indonesia for many years and do not necessarily reflect contemporary Muslim pressure. Thus, it has long been required that a person declare a religion if he or she wants an official identity card. It is not new to find that the dissemination of religious literature to members of other faiths has been banned, missionaries have found some difficulties in obtaining visas, and marginal religious groups may find it hard to obtain marriage licenses, and so on. There has also been some relaxation of limits on other faiths—for example, in 2002, the ban on Jehovah's Witnesses was ended.

Indonesia has historically not experienced the enforcement of religious laws by the state, with exceptions in more conservative provinces like Aceh. There have been fatwas by the National Ulemas Council against marginal elements, but the government has often not made the effort to implement them. Thus, a 1994 fatwa banning the Ahmadiyah sect was renewed in 2005, and the minister of religion recommended that its members join another religion. Darul Arqam, Jamaah Salamullah, and many traditional sects (*aliran kepercayaan*) have also been banned, and there have been violent demonstrations, particularly against the Ahmadiyah. State authorities have not always enforced the bans. Also, the state makes proselytizing other faiths illegal but tends to use these laws only with regard to efforts to convert Muslims The draconian state laws against apostasy that exist in many other Muslim states do not exist today in Indonesia where the law allows conversion. Yet, this laxness in implementing laws has another side, as the military and police frequently have not protected minorities against violence or arrested the perpetrators. In fact, in many cases, their members participated in the attacks.

Islamic groups also have lobbied Parliament to further implement the parts of the Sharia and other elements of their religious agenda. In 2002, there were large demonstrations for the incorporation of the Sharia into the constitution. To this point, only Aceh has seen the official establishment of a provincial Sharia court, but many local jurisdictions have enacted Sharia legislation. Muslim organizations did have a victory over more secular parties and the Christian opposition when the DPR passed the education bill in 2003. This legislation required non- Muslim schools to hire Islamic teachers to teach the religion to their Muslim students. The government has been slow to implement this legislation. Muslim parties have also pressed for laws against extramarital sex, sodomy, and homosexuality, as well as witchcraft.[15] Other failed legislation has forbidden doctors from tending to members of other religions, banning support of any faith that did not accept one God, and forcing adherents to obey religious teachers. Recent polling has also found a decline in the percentage of Indonesian Muslims who support harsh religious punishments, and one 2006 survey found a strong majority who opposed cutting off the hands of a thief or the death penalty for apostasy.[16] In addition, Islamic parties were unable to implement the original 1945 Jakarta Charter on which the republic is based. It had called for a "Belief in the One Supreme God with the obligation to carry out Sharia for adherents of Islam." There is obvious worry among Christians, other minority faiths, and secularists that pressure will lead to further efforts to enact laws adversely effecting non-Muslim interests.

The general public supports the idea of a more Islamically oriented state but does not generally accept the use of the government to enforce religious regulations. Thus, a 2002 survey found that 67 percent of the respondents agreed that an Islamic government is best for Indonesia, and 70.8 percent of those thought that the state should require Muslims to obey the Sharia.[17]

Historically, Indonesian culture has given women a freer role than in most other Muslim countries, although there have been exceptions in highly conservative areas like Aceh, and paternalism is alive and well in rural areas. Women's organizations have long been active in the republic and helped in implementing the marriage law in the 1970s, which gave wives more protection, particularly with regard to divorce and polygamy. The economic problems of the late 1990s gave impetus to women's organizations in a variety of areas.[18]

There is still no equity in many sectors, however; women have a larger burden of proof in divorce, and polygamy still exists. However, it is legally (if not always in reality) required that a husband obtain the first wife's permission for another wife, and there are restrictions on polygamy for government workers. At the same time, some municipalities have attempted to enforce the use of the headdress, and conservative religious groups have argued for limits on women's rights. However, the prescriptions on women vary across the republic, and generalizations are difficult.[19] Cultural and religious attitudes can be seen in negative views expressed by many Islamic organizations and religious leaders regarding the presidency of Megawati Sukarnoputri because of her gender. Women's organizations today are more active and influential than in most Muslim countries, although, like so much else in Indonesia, there is no agreement on the basic paradigm that should guide the movement.[20]

As noted, religious intolerance was not absent before the reestablishment of democracy, and it has continued since. Some have looked at this as a typical problem of a failed state, but that determination is premature. There is no question that the present democracy, like the last one, is fragile and that the New Order had the advantage of more centralized authoritarian power. The Suharto regime found it easier to control unruly factions and manipulate the system to its advantage. The fragmented multiparty character of the legislature, combined with two presidents with weak leadership capabilities, made it difficult to maintain order. Political parties are poorly organized at the national and local levels. There is the additional problem of a historically poorly disciplined military and police that have frequently either "overlooked" or even joined in ethnoreligious violence. The inability of the system to solve many of Indonesia's economic and social problems has further exacerbated tensions and led to targeting scapegoats. Without strong leadership and agreement among the political parties, this messy democracy is not likely to be able to control ethnic and religious intolerance in the near future. Although this new democracy is less than ten years old, it has held two successful parliamentary elections and Indonesia's first popular presidential vote.

Dealing with Radical Islam

Laskar Jihad has not been the only radical Islamic organization to develop since the reemergence of democracy, but its violent anti-Christian activities made it somewhat different from the others. As noted, the general tenor of Indonesian politics has been secular or moderately Islamic in its orientation, and extremist Islamic organizations are small. However, the need for the Indonesian government to deal with more radical Islam is important on several fronts.[21] Radical Islam has apparently grown since 1995, reinforced by both domestic and foreign factors. In many ways, it reflects the inability of the system to deal with basic needs, including security. It also tends to color foreign perceptions of the country and could affect its economy. Certainly, acts like the Bali and Marriott Hotel bombings have adversely affected tourism in the islands. Combined with violent outbreaks, particularly those targeting foreigners, this is probably why poll results show that formerly favorable views of Indonesia among Americans have plummeted since the start of the Iraq conflict.

Other Islamic groups described as radical have not been as tied to violence or as large as was Laskar Jihad. A number of small groups accused of extremism have risen, however. While emphasizing the moderate nature of Indonesian Islam, the U.S. government has listed as coercive, violent, and extremist the Hizbullah Front, Laskar Mujahidin, the Campus Association of Muslim Students, Laskar Jundullah, Islamic Youth Movement, Surakarta Islamic Youth Forum, and Islamic Defenders Front.[22] More recently, the multinational Jemaah Islamiyah (JI) has come to the forefront because of its supposed ties to al-Qaeda and acts of violence. While it has lost some of its popular support, become more fragmented, and come under severe attack from the authorities, the JI remains active. Many of these organizations are small and ephemeral.

Two groups, other than Laskar Jihad, have received considerable press. The Islamic Defenders Front is frequently described as a primarily criminal group with a religious façade. Originally closely tied to Islamic-oriented elements in the military, it is now acting more independently and has clashed with the authorities from its base in Jakarta. In 2004, elements of the front were accused of attacks on those seen as breaking the fast during Ramadan. The Majelis Mujahidin Indonesia (MMI) includes conservative intellectuals, as well as a wing of violent extremists.[23] Its armed wing is Laskar Mujahidin. Prominent in the peaceful wing is the well-known Western-trained historian Deliar Noer. The organization was founded in 2000 to implement Sharia law throughout the nation. Among the extremists involved in the MMI are two targets of the U.S. anti-terrorist campaign: Abu Bakar Ba'asyir, termed Jemaah Islamiyah's spiritual leader, and Riduan Isamuddin, alias Hambali, who was arrested as an alleged key member of that organization. Because the extremist elements of the MMI have their roots in Darul Islam, they have not had the good relations with the police and military that other radical organizations have enjoyed.

There is also general agreement that contacts between most of these organizations and international "terrorist" elements are weak. However, both Laskar Jihad and the successor to Darul Islam, Majelis Mujahidin, take pride in experiences against the Soviets in Afghanistan. The head of Laskar Jihad stated that he had met Osama bin Laden, but considered him to be a poor Muslim. Disagreement exists regarding the degree of penetration of al-Qaeda into Indonesia.[24] There are allegedly closer ties between Jemaah Islamiyah and international "terrorist" networks than is true of other radical groups.

The more militant groups in Indonesia have become more fragmented and more subject to government scrutiny than in previous years. Remnants still exist, and madrasas known for teaching more radical Islamic ideology are still operating. While weakened, these militant groups are still capable of mounting violent actions.

Perhaps more interesting and long-lasting have been the views of nonviolent conservative Islamic organizations. There has been a significant increase in Wahhabi influence, and its puritan emphasis fits well with popular rejection of what is seen as the immorality of Western influences. While reflecting only a small minority, Wahhabi ideas have found support from those educated in Saudi Arabia and Yemen, as well as among other intellectual groups. Adherents to these beliefs can be found in both radical violent and purely intellectual circles.

Neither the general public nor most Islamic parties have come forward with a clear program as to how to implement an Islamic state. Those running for election to the DPR, with a strong Islamist agenda, have tended to be unsuccessful at the polls. At the same time, there is interest in implementing conservative Muslim policies, as illustrated by a manifesto of the first Congress of Mujahidin in 2000. Two major Islamic factions of the MPR later supported the basic principles of the statement. Among the articles was a call for the establishment of Islamic Sharia, intensive study of Islam at all levels of the public school curriculum, prohibiting non-Muslims from holding public office if Muslims would serve, combating all forms of secularism, combating all efforts to establish a relationship with Israel, and holding that every religious community should respect differences among faiths.[25]

Islam and Democracy

Any assessment of the relation of Islam to democracy in contemporary Indonesia must recognize the mixed nature of the relationship. On the positive side, the leaders of all the major Islamic parties have been supportive of a democratic state with free and open elections. Men like Wahid and Rais were active in seeking to establish the foundations of a democratic society during Suharto's regime and played a role in the regime's downfall. As noted, these men have supported a pluralist Indonesia and condemned the communal violence of recent years. During the 2004 elections, all the Islamic parties supported the democratic process and accepted the legitimacy of the vote. Jamhari takes a very optimistic tone by arguing that the new pattern of politics has aided democracy on three bases: (1) the variety of Islamic parties gives participation to a wide range of Muslims, thus limiting the possibility of one monolithic Islamic party and forcing them into coalitions; (2) the multiple parties prevent fundamentalism by keeping Muslims from feeling marginalized; and (3) all parties become more accountable to the people.[26]

The Indonesian public tends to see little conflict between religion and democracy. A 2005 Pew Research study found that 73 percent of those polled saw a growing role of Islam in political life, and 83 percent of that group considered this a favorable development. Even though 85 percent held that Islam played a large role in Indonesian politics, 77 percent believed that democracy could work in the country.[27]

The religious implications of democracy are a frequent topic of discussions and articles with a wide range of views. For example, on one hand, the president of the Muhammadiyah, Syafi Ma'arif, argued that the idea of democracy is implicit in the Islamic concept of *shura*, or consultation within the community.[28] At the same time, he has opposed a completely secular state. Nurcholish Madjid, on the other hand, earlier sought to contain political Islam and to delink Islam from political institutions. Islam, he argued, does not provide definitive formulations for temporal acts.[29]

In juxtaposition to the democratic ideology expressed by these leaders, there also have been the views expressed by more militant groups. Organizations with Wahhabi influences, such as Laskar Jihad, have tended to reject many of the fundamentals of liberal democracy. As previously noted, other radical and conservative groups with anti-Christian and antisecular agendas have not accepted some of democracy's pluralist foundations. The politics of exclusion displayed in the Mujahidin Manifesto and some statements of the Council of Ulema are not conducive to the maintenance of a democratic system.

Mark Woodward and others have raised the question as to whether the broad mass of Muslims in Indonesia is prepared to accept the "give and take" of democracy or to accept nonreligious bases of policy.[30] Polls and studies of public attitudes in other democracies, including the United States, have shown a disjunction between the popular acceptance of the broad definitions of democracy and the people's willingness to agree to the specific application of its principles. It would be surprising if the Indonesians were any different.

The problems faced by democracy in Indonesia today are not primarily related to Islam. Instead, it is necessary to look at the fragmented nature of political parties and the weakness of national leadership. The parties have not paid sufficient attention to the development of their own cadre and grassroots organizations. Party platforms are underdeveloped. Money is increasingly important in influencing internal party activities, and corruption remains a serious issue at the local and national levels. With all of these problems, at this point Indonesia can take pride in refuting the frequently declared view that Islam and democracy are not compatible.

Islam and Dealing with "Terrorism"

All of the factors discussed heretofore, including issues related to pluralism, the reestablishment of democracy, and the growth of radical Islam, have come together in the debates over how to deal with the "war on terror." First, from the point of view of some external observers, a number of forces have hindered Indonesia's efforts to deal effectively in this conflict. Elements of the military and police have been accused of aiding radical Islamic groups through providing training, personnel, and arms. Significant numbers of members of the armed forces are believed to have joined groups like Laskar Jihad. There are also accusations that the authorities were slow to arrest those responsible for violent acts against Christians and Chinese and later did not act aggressively against alleged "terrorists" with international connections. However, there is general agreement that Indonesian authorities acted more effectively and seriously after the Bali bombings. More recent statements by American officials, including President George Bush during his visit to Indonesia in October 2003, have lauded the country's efforts in this area.

Second, mainline Islamic organizations, their leaders, and their constituencies have questioned the strength and even the existence of Muslim "terrorist" elements in the Republic. There had been cooperation with regard to common religious agendas between alleged extremists in organizations such as the MMI and other Islamic associations. In the words of Abu Bakar Bashir of the extreme wing of the MMI:

> The MMI is an institution where a lot of people from a lot of Muslim groups including the NU and Muhamidya gather at one table to discuss how to get our vision of sharia implemented into national laws.... The long-term strategy is to get Indonesia 100 percent based on sharia. As long as Muslims are the majority, the country should be ruled by sharia.[31]

Western criticism of Jemaah Islamiyah has brought many statements in the defense of that organization or counterarguments that it is a tool of the United States. Thus, Hasyim Muzadi, leader of Nahdatul Ulama, stated that attacking the JI was part of the American strategy to force "Islam into a corner." Sola-huddin Wahid, a human rights activist and brother of former President Wahid, said that JI members were trained in the United States and foreign agencies were "steering" the police in the case.[32]

The broad majority of Indonesian Muslims simply do not believe the proclaimed foundations of the "war on terror." Polling shows that Indonesians are divided almost equally between those who see Islamic extremism as a danger to the country and those who do not. There are serious questions among Indonesians as to those responsible for 9/11. We can question the methodology and reliability of some of the public opinion polling in Indonesia, but the re-sults show a remarkable consensus on Indonesian popular attitudes regarding the "war on terror." A poll by a secular news magazine, *Gatra*, found that the largest percentage of respondents (46.43 percent) stated that the attacks were by "the American people themselves."[33] A poll of readership in a modernist publication often unfriendly to U.S. foreign policy found that the respondents believed the 9/11 actions were by anti-U.S. forces (42.7 percent), radical Jews (34.4 percent), Osama bin Laden's group (10.4 percent), domestic terrorists (10.3 percent), and the Red Army of Japan (2.2 percent).[34] The views of the Indonesian public in this matter are not very different from those expressed in other Muslim countries.

There is also a pattern of disbelief regarding foreign explanations of radical Islamist activities in Indonesia. A *Tempo* poll found that 60 percent of its respondents did not believe that the Bali bombing was by "local groups," as stated by the United States, and 70 percent considered these allegations to be part of a conspiracy to define Indonesia as a terrorist nation. Another poll shortly after Bali had 72 percent of the respondents saying that the bombing involved the CIA. Some 52 percent thought that the JI was a creation of the Americans.[35] Other polling and interviewing shows a prevailing view that the "war on terror" is in reality a war on Islam. This assessment is not only found among the members of radical and conservative organizations but also is an overwhelming perception of the Indonesian public.

The Indonesian public and major Islamic parties and their leaders do not support violent acts such as the Bali bombing. However, they do question the source of these and other acts at home and abroad and the American rationale for the "war on terror." Like their new president, they reject any relationship between Islam and terrorism.

Conclusions

Any assessment of the character of Islam in Indonesia at the beginning of the twenty-first century must recognize its decidedly mixed nature. On the one hand, there are currents of thought and action that worry outside observers. There has been an increase in ethnic and religious divisiveness, although there are historic roots to the conditions that need to be understood. Small extremist elements have carried out violence against Christians, foreigners, Chinese, and others in the name of Islam, and the authorities have been known to either abet these acts or ignore them. While there are important advocates of religious pluralism, there also exists deep-seated animosity between Christians and Muslims in parts of the republic. Western, and particularly American, policies and rhetoric dealing with the Middle East and the "war on terror" have galvanized radical Islam and given Indonesian Muslims a sense that they are the targets of a war against Islam. At times, this has led to a degree of denial with regard to some of the domestic roots of violence in the country.

For good or bad, there is little agreement on a common agenda among Islamic political and social organizations. The divisions that were apparent in the prewar and postindependence years remain today. This heterogeneity provides Indonesians with a broad spectrum of ideas and programs, and some observers, like Jamhari, argue that it has thwarted the rise of monolithic "fundamentalism." Others argue that it weakens the ability of Muslims to promote those parts of their agenda on which there is agreement.

On the other hand, there is a new vitality and sense of religious identity. A plurality of Indonesians see themselves as Muslims first and national citizens second. For the first time in decades, there are Islamic political parties whose leaders have played important roles in national governing institutions. Muslim religious schools, banks, and media outlets have proliferated. Muslims practice their religion with greater attentiveness, and there is a decline in the acceptance of un-Islamic elements such as shamans, the worship of saints, and a variety of Hindu and animist rituals. There is also a greater knowledge of the intellectual currents existing in other parts of the *ummah* and, at the same time, Islamic scholars in Indonesia are developing their own religious thinking. Although some radical Islamic groups oppose the idea of democracy, the majority of significant Islamic parties and organizations support it. Indonesia is the great counterargument to those who state that Islam and democracy are incompatible, although that democracy is admittedly fragile. Islam in Indonesia is probably more vital today than it has been for a very long time.

NOTES

1. For example, P. Riddell, "The Diverse Voices of Political Islam in Post-Suharto Indonesia," *Islam and Christian-Muslim Relations* 13:1 (2002), pp. 68–73, and M. Woodward, "Indonesia, Islam and the Prospect for Democracy," paper presented at the Southern Methodist University (SMU) Asian Symposium, Dallas, 2002. The groups described here do not necessarily use the names given for categories.

2. I have discussed this in considerable detail in Fred R. von der Mehden, *Two Worlds of Islam: Interaction between the Middle East and Southeast Asia* (Gainesville: University of Florida Press, 1993).

3. J. Howell, "Sufism and the Indonesian Revival," *Journal of Asian Studies* 60:3 (August 2001), pp. 701–29.

4. Riddell, "Diverse Voices of Islam," pp. 65–66.

5. Jamhari, "Indonesian Fundamentalism?" *Studia Islamika* 9:3 (2002), pp. 183–89.

6. A. R. Baswedan, "Political Islam in Indonesia: Present and Future Trajectory," *Asian Survey* 44:5 (September–October 2004), pp. 669–90.

7. Stephen Sherlock, *Consolidation and Change: The Indonesian Parliament after the 2004 Elections*, (Canberra: Centre for Democratic Institutions, 2004), and R. W. Liddle and S. Mujani, "Indonesia in 2004: The Rise of Susilo Bambang Yudhoyono," *Asian Survey* 45:1 (January–February 2005), pp. 119–27.

8. *New York Times*, June 3, 2003.

9. C. van Dijk, *Rebellion under the Banner of Islam: The Darul Islam in Indonesia* (The Hague: Nijhoff, 1981), and R. Mortimer, *Indonesian Communism under Sukarno* (Ithaca, N.Y.: Cornell University Press, 1974), p. 390.

10. M. van Bruinessen "Genealogies of Islamic Radicalism in post-Suharto Indonesia," *South East Asia Research* 10:2, 2002, pp. 117–54.

11. Sya'ban Muhammad, *The Role of Islam in Indonesian Politics* (New Delhi: Ajanta, 1999), p. 179.

12. P. Searle, "Ethno-Religious Conflicts: Rise or Decline? Recent Developments in Southeast Asia," *Contemporary Southeast Asia* 24:1 (April 2002), pp. 1–11; van Bruinessen, "Genealogies of Islamic Radicalism"; and M. Davis, "Laskar Jihad and the Position of Conservative Islam in Indonesia," paper presented at the Institute of Southeast Asian Studies, Singapore, 2002.

13. For an interesting analysis of Laskar Jihad, including illuminating interview reports, see R. Hefner, "Globalization, Governance and the Crisis of Indonesian Islam," paper presented at the Conference on Globalization, State Capacity, and Muslim Self-Determination, University of California–Santa Cruz, March 7–9, 2002.

14. U.S. Department of State, *Indonesia: International Religious Freedom Report 2002* (Washington D.C.: U.S. Department of State, 2002).

15. *Straits Times*, Singapore, September 30, 2003.

16. From a poll by the Indonesian Survey Circle noted in "Indonesians Reject Islamic Law Provisions," Angus Reid Strategies, August 27, 2006. Available at: www.angus-reid.com/polls/index.cfml/fuseaction=view/Item&itemID=12929.

17. R.W. Liddle, "New Patterns of Islamic Politics in Democratic Indonesia," in *Piety and Pragmatism: Trends in Indonesian Islamic Politics*, Asian Special Report, No. 10 (Washington, D.C.: Woodrow Wilson International Center, 2003), p. 9.

18. M. Budianta, "The Blessed Tragedy: The Making of Women's Activism during the *Reformasi* Years," in A. Heryanto and S. Mandal, eds., *Challenging Authoritarianism in Southeast Asia; Comparing Indonesia and Malaysia* (New York: RoutledgeCurzon, 2003), pp. 145–77.

19. M. Hooker, *Indonesian Islam: Social Change through Contemporary Fatawa* (Crows Nest, NSW: Allen and Unwin, 2003), pp. 122–56.

20. S. Blackburn, "Women and the Nation," *Inside Indonesia*, April–June 2001, pp. 6–8.

21. For a more detailed analysis, see Fred R. von der Mehden, *Radical Islam in Southeast Asia and the Challenge to U.S. Foreign Policy* (Houston: Rice University, Baker Institute for Public Policy, 2005).

22. U.S. State Department, *International Religious Freedom Report 2002*, p. 13.

23. Hefner, "Globalization," pp. 21–23.

24. Z. Abuza, "Tentacles of Terror: Al Qaeda's Southeast Asian Network," *Contemporary Southeast Asia* 24:3 (December 2002), pp. 427–59.

25. For the complete manifesto, see M. Woodward, "Indonesia, Islam and the Prospect for Democracy," paper presented at the Southern Methodist University Asian Symposium, Dallas, 2001.

26. Jamhari, "Islamic Political Parties: Threats or Prospects?" in G. Forrester, *Post-Soeharto Indonesia: Renewal or Chaos?* (Singapore: Institute of Southeast Asian Studies, 1999), pp. 186.

27. Pew Global Attitude Study, 2005. Islamic Extremism: Common Concern for Muslims and Western Public," available at: http://pewglobal.org/reports/display.php?ReportID=248.

28. United states-Indonesia Society Forum on "Islam and Democracy," Washington, D.C., April 8, 2002.

29. N. Madjid, "More on Secularization," in M. Hassan, ed., *Muslim Intellectual Responses to "New Order" Modernization in Indonesia* (Kuala Lumpur: Dewan Bahasa dan Pustaka, 1980), pp.199–211.

30. Hassan, *Muslim Intellectual Responses*, pp. 17–18.

31. Quoted in Abuza, "Tentacles of Terror," p. 451.

32. Greg Fealy, "Another Mindset," *Courier-Mail*, October 20, 2003. Fealy, a lecturer on Indonesian politics at the Australian National University, noted that "Jemaah Islamiyah" means Islamic Congregation, and thousands of largely informal and peaceful groups go under that name.

33. G. Barkin, "Indonesian Media Reaction to Terrorist Attacks in the United States," *Re: Constructions* (September 19, 2001). Available at: http://mit.edu/cms/re-consrtuctions/communications/indonesia.html.

34. Ibid.

35. Fealy, "Another Mindset."

3

Pakistan after Islamization: Mainstream and Militant Islamism in a Changing State

Vali Nasr

In 1999 the Pakistan military staged a coup that removed the government of Prime Minister Nawaz Sharif from office. The military justified its actions by claiming to be ridding Pakistan of corruption and the paralysis that constant bickering between politicians had produced. The military promised to bring to Pakistan the development that had thus far deluded it. The generals argued that democracy was too permissive to corruption and was open to influence by Islamists. Genuine development would only be possible under the aegis of the military, which could provide for a secular decision-making environment in which technocrats could run the affairs of the state free from the influence of politicians. The military's gambit has opened a new chapter in Pakistan's politics, one that would redefine the relations between the military, Islam, and civilian politics.

Since the 1970s, the separate and yet interdependent issues of democratization and civil-military relations on the one hand, and Islamization and Islam's relation to the state on the other, have shaped Pakistan's politics. In the 1980s, Islamism supported the military's rule over Pakistan. Between 1988 and 1999, the military, Islamist forces, and democratic parties have cooperated and competed with one another, jockeying for power and position in defining the rules of the game. Since 1999, the military has increasingly been at loggerheads with both democracy and Islamism in its attempt to dominate and shape Pakistan's politics. The case of Pakistan is instructive in what it reveals about the changing role of

Islamism in determining the balance of power in civil-military relations and about how democratization and Islamization—civil-military and Islamism-state relations—are influencing one another, deciding how Pakistani politics will unfold from this point forward.

The Islamist Factor in Pakistan's Politics

Islam has had an important role in Pakistan since the 1970s, providing the framework through which the country has defined its national interests and has provided cadence between its domestic and international politics.[1] Islam has also increased Pakistan's regional power by opening new foreign policy possibilities before Islamabad, most notably in using Islamist activism to deal with developments in Afghanistan and Kashmir.[2]

Mainstream Islamist parties such as the Jama'at-i Islami have been instrumental in defining the place of Islam in politics.[3] The Jama'at was particularly successful in articulating a coherent Islamic ideology that effectively organized social action around the struggle to attain an ideal Islamic state. This action would embody and implement the core values of Islamic ideology, as it solves sociopolitical problems and attains the goal of development,[4] the very issues that the military claim can be achieved through a combination of military rule, technocratic management of government, and secularism.

The Jama'at was successful in instituting many Islamist assumptions in popular political culture and also in framing key debates in an Islamist frame of reference. This success eventually helped weaken the grip of secular politics in Pakistan in the 1960s, contributing first to the fall of the Ayub Khan regime (1958–69) and later to the demise of Zulfiqar Ali Bhutto's experiment with socialism (1971–77).[5]

It was during the Zia ul-Haq era (1977–88) that the Islamist vision became the credo of the state.[6] The Zia regime initiated a policy of Islamization of laws, public policy, and popular culture, and it can be seen as a unique case of systematic propagation of Islamism from above.[7] The Zia regime's vision of the place of Islam in state and society drew heavily on Islamist ideology in order to shore up state power by ending its war of attrition with Islamism and to expand its own powers both domestically and regionally.[8] The alliance between Islamists and the military provided legitimacy to military rule, which then justified its suppression of democratic forces by claiming to be building an Islamic order; however, that alliance was fraught with too many inconsistencies and divergent interests of its key actors to ultimately survive.

The end of the Zia period in 1988 also ended the formal alliance between Islamism and the state. With the return of democracy and the growing power of civilian politics, the military and Islamists confronted diverse and divergent interests in a changing political context. Since 1988 and especially after the 1999 coup, Islamists, politicians, and generals have sought to manage relations between Islam and the state. The continuous negotiations, debates, and confrontations between them have changed the nature of both Islamism and Pakistani politics.

Islamism and Civilian Rule

The end of the Zia regime ushered in a period of transition in relations between the state and its allies among mainstream Islamists. The regime that was most closely associated with Islamization, and which had the most legitimacy to speak for and embody the growing Islamic identity in Pakistan, gave place to a more secular democratic order that was initially led by the most secular forces in Pakistan's politics, Benazir Bhutto and the Pakistan Peoples Party (PPP). The passing of the Zia regime had not occurred through political defeat, so the Islamic coalition that led Pakistan in the 1980s retained notable power. In addition, the continuation of the war in Afghanistan required Pakistan to remain true to its Islamic ideology.

As a result, the democratic period that followed the Zia years, 1988–99, was marked by struggles of power between the military and civilian politicians and between Islamist forces and secular political institutions.[9] The result was not only debilitating political crises that ultimately undermined democracy but a more subtle competition for the soul of Pakistan. Just as democratic forces sought to recalibrate Pakistan's ideology, moving it away from Islamization to better support development and modernization, the coalition of military forces and Islamic parties sought to resist this trend by ever more tightly weaving Pakistan's foreign policy and regional interests with Islam, and thus continuing to anchor domestic politics in the debate over Islamization.

Initially, the military cobbled together an alliance between the main pillars of the Zia regime, the Pakistan Muslim League (PML) led by Nawaz Sharif and Islamist parties, most notably Jama'at-i Islami and the two ulama parties, Jami'at-i Ulama-i Islam (Society of Ulama of Islam, JUI) and Jami'at-i Ulama-i Pakistan (Society of Ulama of Pakistan, JUP). Their alliance, Islami Jumhoori Ittihad (Islamic Democratic Alliance, IJI) was charged with containing PPP in the 1988 elections with the aim of ensuring that pro-Zia forces would have a voice in the democratic process and would use it to stymie PPP's progress.[10] In time, the military hoped IJI would become a more consolidated political force that could defeat PPP and reproduce Zia's Islamization order through the democratic process.

IJI was initially successful. It was able to limit PPP electoral success in the 1988 polls (and even win elections to the Punjab Assembly and form the government in that province).[11] It was also effective in using the open political process to defend the gains of Islamization to that time and to make it difficult for PPP to consolidate power and govern effectively. That success allowed the military to dismiss the PPP government in 1990. IJI won the subsequent elections and formed the government until disagreements with the military led to its fall from power in 1993.

Between 1988 and 1993, the struggle of power between PPP and IJI created a "crisis of governability" in Pakistan.[12] Divided parliaments, economic crises, corruption, and growing acrimony between Nawaz Sharif and Benazir Bhutto caused paralysis. In the meantime, continued interference with the democratic process by the military led to dismissal of two governments, first PPP's in 1990 and later IJI's in 1993. At the same time, Pakistan's economic growth slowed, and popular disgruntlement with government became more vociferous.

The military's continuous interference with the political process was successful in limiting the growth in PPP's power, as it weakened democratization to the advantage of the military. This success also resulted in a weaker IJI and, ultimately, broke up the alliance between right-of-center civilian politicians, gathered in PML, and Islamists—the alliance that had constituted the basis of the Zia regime and, later, IJI.

The democratic period opened new incentive opportunities before both PML and Islamist forces. Freed of the confines of Zia's military regime, both political forces began to see the opportunity to dominate Pakistan's politics to an extent that was not conceivable during the 1980s. Nawaz Sharif was the first to make this realization and to distance his party from the military. As a result, the machinations that first brought his party into government in 1990 toppled him in 1993.[13]

Jama'at-i Islami made the same realization. In the 1990–92 period, the party's leader, Qazi Hussain Ahmed, actively distanced his party from PML and supported the military in dismissing Nawaz Sharif's government in 1992. The Jama'at ran in the elections of 1993 on its own, with Qazi Hussain posing as the alternative to both Bhutto and Sharif.[14]

The military-PML-Jama'at alliance (the base of IJI) was now reduced to the military and the Jama'at. The two also had a close working relationship in Afghanistan and Kashmir, where the training camps, recruitment efforts, and many of the jihadi activities were organized by the Jama'at. Moreover, Gulbidin Hikmatyar, Jama'at's close ally was then also the military's main client in Afghanistan.

Soon after 1993, the picture began to change. The results of elections of 1993 suggested that Sharif had a strong appeal to the Islamic vote bank. Whereas PML did very well carrying the Islamic vote, the Jama'at performed poorly. The result suggested the emergence of a strong right-of-center party that would also represent the Islamic vote—rendering Islamist parties as irrelevant. This was the first time in the Muslim world that a democratic process had produced a brake to Islamism. The military was less concerned with limiting Islamism and more with constricting democratic parties, however, the military was shocked by these results. They had expected that the Jama'at would limit PML's electoral success and that, without Islamist allies, Sharif would fail to curry favor with the public. The result was a military-Islamist alliance that enjoyed little prominence in the political scene, along with an increasingly independent right-of-center party that portended to take control of Islamism away from the military.

The military was also growing impatient with Hikmatyar's inability to gain control of Kabul in the aftermath of the Soviet withdrawal from Afghanistan; increasingly, it saw the mainstream Islamism of Jama'at and its ilk as ineffectual in managing either domestic or regional issues. The Islamist force that had empowered the Zia regime was now viewed as a spent force. The military thus began to look elsewhere. The change, as discussed earlier, came about in 1994 pursuant to change of events in Afghanistan with the rise of the Taliban.

The rise of the Taliban introduced a new militant Islamist force to the scene. The military that was unhappy with both Hikmatyar and the Jama'at now turned to this new militancy to prop up its position in both Pakistan's politics and Afghanistan's civil war.[15] The rise of the Taliban meant giving free reign to the more militant forces in Pakistan that shared its ideology and provided recruits and resources. JUI used its position to ensure a seamless linkage between the Taliban and domestic extremist forces. The military also concluded that, just as the Taliban's brand of Islamism had proven more productive on the battlefield in Afghanistan, extremism was likely to serve the military's objective of controlling domestic politics more effectively. General Musharraf, in particular, proved adept at using extremist forces domestically and also Kashmir to undermine civilian governments.[16]

The PML government that came to power in 1997 sought to chart a new path for Pakistan to follow.[17] The elections of 1997 were the first since 1988 to give a party a clear mandate to rule. PML led by Nawaz Sharif won the majority of seats (63 percent) to the National Assembly.[18] The elections produced the smallest contingent of Islamist representation in the Parliament on record (a sharp contrast with the elections of 2002). The results permitted Nawaz Sharif to vie for controlling Pakistan's politics, defining the relationship between civilian rule and Islam, and creating a tenable relationship between Islam and the state—the first since the Zia period. To achieve this, he openly fashioned PML as, simultaneously, a modern democratic party that was committed to the development of Pakistan and the champion of the cause of Islamization. In effect, he positioned PML as a "Muslim democratic party" similar to European Christian Democratic parties.[19] Sharif, an industrialist from Punjab, was popular and was known to be a pious Muslim. He used his image to argue that he would deliver on the demands of Islamization, just as he would pursue development. PML was to form a stable right-of-center government that would not be beholden to Islamist parties and would be able to govern Pakistan with a strong claim to represent popular and national religious aspirations.

Sharif modeled PML after Malaysia's United Malays National Organization (UMNO), which, in the 1980s, had successfully coopted Islamic forces and advocated both Islamization and capitalist development. As a senior PML leader, Mushahid Husain, put it: "Nawaz Sharif will be both the Erbakan [leader of Turkey's Islamist Refah Party] and Mahathir of Pakistan."[20] PML's claim was bolstered by the fact that it had taken over seats that were once held by Islamist parties and had defeated those Islamist candidates who had participated in the elections. It argued that it could better serve the interests of the Islamic vote bank.

The military under General Musharraf (who became army chief in 1998) viewed Sharif's gambit as a threat. Had Sharif succeeded in establishing a viable right of center and Islamist coalition, he would have dominated the middle in Pakistan. If this had happened, it would have been a democratic party rather than the military that would have defined and controlled the nexus between Islam and the state.

The military under General Musharraf turned to extremist forces to undermine Sharif. Throughout 1998–99, sectarian violence raged across Pakistan, and militant activism in Kashmir grew in intensity.[21] There were two attempts on Nawaz Sharif's life by militant groups with ties to the military in the events leading to the coup of 1999.[22] By encouraging increasing radicalization of the Islamist discourse, and supporting the extremist forces, the military sought to destabilize the relations between PML and its constituency, and thereby more generally radicalize Islamism to the extent that a viable center-right coalition would not be feasible. The military also used extremist forces in Kashmir to undermine Sharif, most notably in Kargil in 1999, when an incursion by militants into Indian-held Kashmir brought the two countries to the brink of war and eventually greatly weakened Nawaz Sharif.[23]

Islam and the State since 1999

The growing tensions between the military and the PML, combined with political gridlock, contributed to Nawaz Sharif's unpopularity. This precipitated a
crisis of governability, which, in turn, aggravated other problems—notably,
economic stagnation and, in particular, growing corruption. Sharif sought to
deal with these problems by tightening his own hold on power, which only
intensified his confrontation with the military. Sharif sought to gain control of
the military by bringing a friendly general to the helm. This backfired, eroding
his authority, and eventually led to the military coup of 1999.[24]

The military regime that came into power initially purported to revamp
Pakistan's politics. Musharraf is a secular general, known for his drinking and
fondness for gambling. Some of his first pictures after the coup were with his
dogs, and his speeches were then peppered with terminologies such as "dou-
bling down" and "tripling down" (drawn from blackjack).[25] His persona could
not have been more different from that of Zia. He had spent some of his youth
in Turkey and had an admiration for Ataturk, and he looked positively on the
role that the military has in Turkey's politics—which is clearly at odds with how
the military has seen its own role in Pakistan.[26] The combination of Kemalism
and military rule differs greatly from Zia's formula of combining Islamism
with military rule. It appeared at face value that Musharraf's response to the
gradual melting away of the Zia alliance of military-PML-Islamism was to
anchor martial rule in a completely different ideological foundation.[27]

Musharraf sought to move beyond Zia's model to look to the Ayub Khan
era. His vision was one of allying the military with the modern middle classes
and "liberal" Muslims, and focusing Pakistan on economic development.[28]
What Musharraf proposed was a 1960s approach to development—a military
dictatorship claiming to be better able than civilian politicians to manage development. It was a model that had been in vogue in Latin America and Asia,
but which had long been discarded in favor of more pluralist approaches to
growth and progress. In Pakistan, it had been in place during the military
regime of General Ayub Khan (1959–69). However, Ayub's fall to a popular
social movement in 1969 and the subsequent secession of Bangladesh had
tarnished the appeal of the model. Its revival under Musharraf was therefore a
testimony to the continuation of certain kind of thinking in Pakistan military
about state and society, despite changes in Pakistan and the international environment over the preceding two decades.

Musharraf's approach was quickly marketed as a strategic measure that was
necessitated by the events of September 11 and the changes in the international

climate that followed it. Having realized that the military had lost the control of mainstream Islamism to PML, Musharraf saw no point in continuing to anchor the military's strategy in a political and ideological position over which it could not have direct control. The military would continue to use extremist forces, but extremism was merely a tactical and strategic tool akin to a weapons system. It did not provide the military with ideological legitimacy. Musharraf therefore saw no contradiction between a secular military cultivating and using Islamic militancy.

Musharraf also purged the military of pro-Islamist generals—confirming the military's new orientation.[29] The military would be committed to its strategic vision rather than any ideology. Musharraf was successful in loosening the grip of Islamists over the public sphere, reducing their ability to enforce morality on the public or to use "Qur'an-thumping" to set the tone for public debates. The new regime even encouraged more laxity in popular culture. Political Islam became a less dominant force in the public arena, especially in Punjab and Sind. Islamic observance did not decline, but compulsion in religious observance was tempered.

The events of September 11 had a momentous impact on Pakistan. Musharraf and the military decided to support the U.S. war against the Taliban and also the hunt for al-Qaeda in the Afghanistan-Pakistan corridor.[30] This meant clamping down on the militant jihadi groups that the military had used as strategic assets to control Afghanistan and manage conflict in Kashmir.[31] It also meant severing the military's last remaining overt tie with Islamism. That the military leadership that was undertaking this move was secular in outlook, and was doing so in alliance with the United States, was (and continues to be) politically problematic. However, the military understood that the alternative could be even more costly to its interests. External factors thus forced a break with militancy. The Pakistan military now became closely allied with the United States and openly at odds with the Islamist base of power in Pakistan.

The military was not able to compensate for the estrangement of Islamists by appealing to the modern middle classes, because they, too, were opposed to U.S. policies and, more important, objected to martial rule—even in the name of moderation and economic development. For this reason, the military began to relieve some of the pressure that it was putting on Islamists. With no discernable social base, the military decided to reduce the scope of its confrontation with Islam. For instance, the much vaunted reform of the curricula of madrasas that were held responsible for the jihadi culture in Pakistan came to naught. The government left reforms to the madrasas themselves and did not seek to reduce the scope of their social and educational activities.[32]

Elections of 2002

The dilemmas facing the Musharraf regime came to the fore in the national elections of 2002.[33] PML and PPP were greatly disadvantaged in these elections. Their leaders were barred from the country, and the parties were broken into different factions by the military. In addition, there were many irregularities in polling stations, putting into question some of the results. More important, in the name of improving the quality of parliamentary representatives, the military decreed that those getting into Parliament must hold higher education degrees—eliminating many political veterans from the race—and that certificates issued by madrasas (*ijazahs*) would be accepted as higher education degrees. These measures disadvantaged PPP and PML and conversely benefited Islamist parties.

The Islamist parties (Jama'at, JUI, and JUP, as well as smaller ulama and Shi'i parties) formed an electoral alliance: Mutahhidah Majlis Amal (United Action Front, MMA).[34] The alliance reflected the Islamic parties' frustration with the Musharraf regime, with the fall of the Taliban, and the war on terror. It also reflected the fact that with PML and PPP under pressure, Islamic parties now had the opportunity to reverse the losses they had suffered during PML's rise to prominence in the 1993–99 period. MMA also had the tacit support of the military—which is popularly believed to have helped put together MMA. Musharraf viewed PML and PPP as the main obstacles before the military's project of controlling Pakistan's politics. He was comparatively less concerned with Islamic parties, which he believed the military could always manipulate.[35]

In addition, a strong MMA would help the general manage Washington's expectations by presenting it with a zero sum choice between the military or the mullahs. At any rate, the military expected MMA to be fraught with internal conflict and, hence, easy to divide and rule. In essence, the secularizing general was back to cobbling together some form of military-Islamist alliance, except that, unlike in the Zia period, this alliance was surreptitious and was characterized by mutual distrust between the two sides. Unlike the 1980s, too, Islamic parties no longer looked to an alliance with the military as the only way in which their ambitions for power could be realized. MMA leaders such as Jama'at's Qazi Hussain Ahmed believed that MMA could fill in PML's shoes and that Islamist interests now lay in the political process. MMA could use the interim period of military rule to develop its organizational capabilities and develop stronger roots in key social and ethnic groups so that it would be a contender for power when democracy returns to Pakistan. Their strategy therefore became one of coexistence with military rule in the short run in order to prepare for the post-military period.

MMA was designed as a strong electoral alliance between the two most important Islamist forces in Pakistan—the Deobandi JUI and Jama'at-i Islami—to consolidate the hold over Islamic politics under an Islamist force. Although JUI represents the political muscle of MMA (with the largest parliamentary representation and control of the Northwest Frontier Province [NWFP] Assembly). the alliance's organizational design and political strategy are largely the brainchild of Jama'at's chief, Qazi Hussain Ahmed. Qazi conceived of MMA as the means to use the tug of war between the military and PML and PPP to the advantage of the Islamist parties. He believed that MMA would provide Islamists with the opportunity to wrest control of Islamism from lay and secular forces or institutions—the military and PML.

Qazi believes that JUI and the Jama'at have the potential to create a powerful mainstream political force.[36] JUI has a strong representation in rural and tribal areas; it is a main player in Pathan politics; and it still has strong resources among militant forces. The Jama'at, in contrast, has notable street power in urban Pakistan and has the political and administrative know-how to make MMA a credible political force. The goal is for MMA to become the dominant right-of center party in Pakistan—what PML was before the 1999 coup. It is for this reason that MMA has distanced itself from jihadi forces. Sipah Sahabah Pakistan (SSP), the largest of the sectarian forces that was banned after September 11 for its ties to the Taliban and al-Qaeda, did not join MMA, and its leader, A'zam Tariq, remained Musharraf's most prominent Islamist ally until his assassination in October 2003. In official trips to Delhi and Kabul in 2003, MMA Executive Secretary Mawlana Fazlur Rahman openly distanced MMA from jihadi forces in Kashmir and from the resurgent Taliban fighters in southern Afghnaistan. In Delhi, Rahman went as far as to endorse a cease-fire in Kashmir. As one senior Jama'at-i Islami leader noted, "the only jihadi force in Pakistan is the army."[37] Similarly, outside of NWFP—where there is strong demand for Islamization—MMA's political agenda has shied away from overt talk of Islamization and Shariat bills and instead focused on good governance and democracy.[38] MMA has become a de facto defender of democracy before the military regime, as well as a serious contender for providing the kind of clean and transparent government that Musharraf promised Pakistan after the coup. Since 2001, MMA has developed an organizational apparatus that ties its various parties together. That the MMA organization has worked for five years has gone a long way in creating bonds between its constituent parties and in defining Islamism's role in politics.

The alliance between Jama'at and JUI is also religiously significant. MMA is the coming together of erstwhile rivals: lay Islamists and ulama. However, political interest has for now overridden ideological differences. The Pathan factor has also been important in making the alliance possible. MMA's popularity reflects the frustrations of Pathans with developments in Afghanistan. The ties between the constituent parties of MMA have drawn a great deal on the common Pathan nationalist platform—what they agree on as opposed to Islamic doctrines where their views may diverge. It is important to note that of the founding leaders of the six parties that constitute MMA, with the exception of the late Mawlana Shah Ahmad Noorani of JUP, all were Pathans.

In 1999, Islamist parties in Pakistan also sought protection in numbers, especially JUI whose rank and file had been tied to the Taliban. The military's "betrayal" of the Taliban convinced JUI that its future rested in a larger Islamist alliance. In fact, the closer Musharraf got to Washington, the more JUI feared a "Taliban fate," and the more it sought refuge in a larger Islamic alliance.

The elections of 2002 produced a spectacular result for MMA, better than Islamic parties had achieved in any of the previous elections.[39] In national elections, MMA got only 3.19 million votes, or 11 percent of the total (in NWFP, MMA won 82 percent of the seats to the National Assembly), finishing fourth in the tally of popular vote, after PPP (with 7.39 million votes), PML(Q) (a pro-Musharraf faction of PML created by the military, with 7.33 million votes), and PML(N) (a pro-Nawaz Sharif PML, with 3.32 million votes). The numbers led Musharraf to continue to view PML and PPP as the main threats to the military's position.

In provincial elections, MMA too did well (winning 51 of 101 seats to the NWFP Assembly—where it formed the government—and 14 of 51 to the Baluchistan Assembly). However, in Punjab, MMA won only 8 out of 297 Provincial Assembly seats, and in Sind 11 out of 130—forming the city government in Karachi. One important outcome of the elections is that Punjab and Sind voted very differently from NWFP and Baluchistan. To be more precise, Pathans voted overwhelmingly for Islamism and MMA, and the rest of Pakistan shied away from MMA. This is the first time since the 1970s and the Afghan war that there was such a political divide between Pathans and Punjabis.

The results also indicated the extent to which Pathan politics has become Islamized—a "Talibanization" of Pathan politics in Pakistan. Talibanization in Afghanistan meant militant and jihadi activism. It also meant Islamization of Pathan nationalism. This trend began with the Afghan jihad and was later closely associated with JUI—the Deobandi ulama party that has a strong following in NWFP and Pathans in Baluchistan, and whose madrasas were important to the rise of the Taliban. However, MMA today is clearly not interested in militancy. MMA has concluded that the fall of the Taliban shows that jihadi activism will not serve Islamist and Deobandi interests. Rather, the future of Islamism and Deobandi politics lies in mainstream electoral politics.

Hence, it is the second meaning of Talibanization—Islamization of Pathan nationalism—that is what is at work in Pakistan. The rise of MMA suggests that Deobandis have completed their domination of Pathan politics and nationalism in Pakistan in the manner that the Taliban had done in Afghanistan. It took direct U.S. military action to free Pathan politics in Afghanistan of the Taliban—and still the United States has not managed to end the Taliban's control of Pathan nationalism in that country. The military may try to dismantle MMA's control of NWFP, but it cannot easily untangle Deobandis from Pathan politics. Pathan politics is now essentially Deobandi.

The Deobandi domination of Pathan politics has actually expanded after the fall of the Taliban. Until then, Deobandis competed with PML for control of Pathan politics in Pakistan. PML was able to remain relevant in mainstream Pathan politics. The demise of the PML opened the door for Deobandis to move beyond madrasas and jihadi groups to quickly fill the resultant vacuum. Consequently, the Deobandization—or "Talibanization"—of Pathan politics in Pakistan started in earnest after 1999 and became more prominent with fall of Taliban in Afghanistan and rise of MMA. The Deobandi ascendancy in NWFP and Baluchistan and Afghanistan has in effect created an Islamist-Pathan belt that stretches from Kandahar to Quetta and Peshawar.

The Military and MMA after the Elections

Since October 2002, two developments have been notable. First, MMA has retained its cohesion and has proved resilient in the face of the military's efforts to break it up.[40] Second, Musharraf has faced stiff resistance to his efforts to revamp the constitution to sanction military rule. The general has been criticized for seeking to formalize military involvement in politics, most notably for serving as both the president and Army chief. The resistance to Musharraf has been led by the rump of PML and PPP, but also by MMA.

MMA has benefited from Musharraf's rule. The general undermined PML and PPP to MMA's advantage, and he continues to be preoccupied with rooting out support for those parties. Regardless of the positive returns of the Musharraf regime for MMA, however, the alliance is eager to maximize its political interests and avoid becoming a tool of the military. As a result, MMA led the charge in the Parliament against Musharraf's tampering with the constitution, as well as his support for the United States in the war on terror.

Jama'at's leader, Qazi Hussain Ahmed, was at the forefront of opposition to the Legal Framework Order—the constitutional changes that Musharraf proposed to legitimize the military's control of the state—demanding that he "take-off his uniform" if he wished to remain president. In August 2003, the MMA and JUI leader, Mawlana Sami' ul-Haq, led some 200 ulama in signing a fatwa that declared sending of troops to Iraq to be *haram*, and forbidding any member of the ulama from performing funeral prayers for Pakistani soldiers that are killed there.[41] More recently, MMA organized strikes and demonstrations in defense of Abdul-Qadeer Khan, who was blamed for sale of Pakistani nuclear technology to Iran and Libya. Islamists—echoing nationalist sentiments—view Khan as a national hero and see the international pressure on Pakistan over the sale of nuclear technology as subterfuge for containing and eventually dismantling Pakistan's nuclear program. MMA joined hands with other nationalist voices in Pakistan to criticize Musharraf over his handling of the Khan issue, hoping to cast aspersions on his nationalist credentials and depict the military's close ties to the United States as a point of vulnerability for Pakistan.

Since the October 2002 elections, MMA has gained strength, both in NWFP by championing Pathan nationalism and in the center by standing up to the military. Growing tensions between the military and Pashtun tribes in South Waziristan that followed extensive military operations in that region in order to capture al-Qaeda activists has benefited MMA. South Waziristan operations have pitted Pakistan military against local tribesmen in skirmishes that have cost many lives on both sides. This has drawn a wedge between the military and local Pashtun nationalism. MMA has protested military operations in South Waziristan and used the military's falling out with Pashtun tribes to strengthen its own position in NWFP.

MMA poses a challenge to the Musharraf regime. Ideologically Musharraf seeks to institute a moderate and apolitical Islam in Pakistan—what he refers to as "Jinnah's Islam." However, he is at loggerheads with secular political parties that have traditionally represented that approach to Islam. The general continues to view PML and PPP as the greater threats to his regime. The confrontation with those parties has alienated the moderate Islamic vote and the modern middle classes from the military regime. This became clear when the civilian partner that the military had put together from the rump of PML and PPP, named PML(Q), began to falter. In summer 2004, the general dismissed the PML(Q) prime minister, Zafarullah Khan Jamali, and appointed a technocrat, Shaukat Aziz. Aziz was a banker who had been managing the economy as minister of finance. Musharraf hoped that Aziz could both expedite economic reforms and more directly appeal to the middle class. It was an admission on the part of the military that it was at a disadvantage at the game of democracy, and that its best bet was to deliver on the promise of development. This, however, meant moving even further away from democracy, which made it possible to build its political platform around a combination of demand for Islam and democracy as the foil for the military's authoritarian secularism.

In effect, the outcome leaves MMA as the only viable civilian partner for the military. In fact, it is said that Musharraf favors MMA as the "Military-Mullah Alliance."[42] The formal agreement with MMA created a modus vivendi between the military and MMA. In the wake of the agreement, Benazir Bhutto's PPP and Nawaz Sharif's PML remain as the only overtly anti-Musharraf forces. As the principal chasm in Pakistan's politics becomes the one between the generals and civilian politicians of PPP and PML rather than between the military and Islamists, Musharraf is compelled to abandon his secularist pretense and hand over substantial powers to MMA.

The issue is important in understanding where Islam fits in Pakistan's politics. In the international arena, the military has been the chief sponsor of jihadi activism. It has viewed militancy as a strategic weapon to maximize foreign policy interests. Although international pressure, along with the scale of attempts on Musharraf's life in December 2003 and on his prime minister, Shaukat Aziz, in July 2004,[43] has forced the military to abandon jihadi activism and reign in militant organizations, the military's thinking on its foreign policy imperatives and the value of jihadi activism to realize it has not changed.

In the domestic arena, Islamism continues to be an important force, but it has been able to project greater power since 1999 only because democratic forces have been undermined by the military. The military has not been the bulwark against Islamism but its liberator from its nemesis, PML. It is through the military's assault on the political process, and as an intended or unintended consequence of the struggle for power between the military and democratic forces, that Islamism has gained ground.[44] Its growth in power in the current form feeds on the instability of the political process. The fundamental issue in Pakistan's politics remains civil-military relations and not the stand-off between Islamism and the state. In fact, growing tensions between the generals and civilian politicians has brought the military closer to Islamists.

The relationship between Islamists and the military is fraught with tensions, however. First, Islamist forces would like to avoid new elections and to keep the civilian parties out of the political process, but they do not wish to get too close to the Musharraf government. MMA has already faced a decline in its popularity since it made an agreement with Musharraf over the Legal Framework Order (LFO) issue. More important, the military is finding it difficult to maintain its modus vivendi with Islamist forces in the face of developments in Afghanistan and the international pressure on Islamabad over the war on terror, instability in southern Afghanistan, conflict in South Waziristan, and the Khan and nuclear proliferation issue.

During the Zia period, the alliance between the military and Islamists was anchored in a shared Islamic nationalist ideology. Musharraf's regime is not Islamic, and the aforementioned issues are also sapping it of its nationalist pretensions. Since 2001, but increasingly so in 2007, Genaral Musharraf has found himself at odds with the Islamic nationalist sentiment that MMA, its intended civilian partner, is firmly rooted in. This makes Musharraf's strategy for managing the domestic political scene more tenuous.

The new constitution in Afghanistan is unpopular in Pakistan—and especially in MMA's base of support among the Pathans in NWFP and Baluchistan. The constitution concentrates power in Kabul under a government that is viewed as both pro-India and biased against Pathans. MMA has been critical of developments in Afghanistan and is likely to openly break with Musharraf over Islamabad's Afghan policy if Pathan unhappiness in Afghanistan precipitates conflict in that country and if that unhappiness spills over into Pakistan.

Similarly, MMA has refused to support General Musharraf in his attempts to deal with the nuclear proliferation scandal surrounding the sale of nuclear technology to Iran, Libya, and North Korea by Abdul-Qadeer Khan's laboratory. MMA has spearheaded criticisms of the government's handling of this issue in the Parliament and has orchestrated demonstrations in the streets. Qazi Hussain Ahmed has called on Musharraf to resign and to refer the matter to the Parliament for consideration.[45] The nuclear proliferation issue goes to the heart of the Musharraf government's dilemma of balancing its ties with Washington with its dependence on Islamist forces. The public censure of Khan has been depicted by MMA as surrender to Washington on an issue that is critical to national security. That the sale of nuclear technology to Iran and Libya were portrayed by some quarters as General Mirza Aslam Beig's (the fiercely nationalist army chief in the late 1980s) strategy to create a Muslim nuclear bloc to stand up to the West has made Khan more of a hero than a villain.

MMA's position on both the Afghanistan and the nuclear proliferation issues are in tune with the nationalist sentiment in Pakistan, which resonates with many in the military. The assassination attempts on Musharraf in December 2003 and on Shaukat Aziz in July 2004 were remarkable in their degree of sophistication and access to critical intelligence, enough to suggest complicity on the part of elements within the military and other security apparatuses. Notably, the Christmas Day attempt on Musharraf's life came three days after it was revealed that Khan would be questioned by the authorities for the activities of his laboratory.[46] Subsequent investigations identified al-Qaeda sympathizers among the lower ranks of the military, among whom religious sentiments run high, and there is great deal of sympathy for the anti-Americanism of al-Qaeda. The apparent secularism of the top brass means that Islam is no longer the glue that binds the military together. This has made it more difficult to maintain unity in the ranks in the face of mounting challenges.

The South Waziristan imbroglio has increased tensions within the military. The conflict created widespread consternation in the military, 15 percent of whose officer corps is Pashtun. In addition, the specter of conflict between the Punjabi-dominated military and the Pashtun tribesmen directly threatens the military's strategic interests, domestically as well as regionally.

The pressures on the Pakistan military to maintain its unity in the face of domestic political challenges and international pressures is considerable. Musharraf's foreign policy enjoys little support domestically at a time when the military's political status compels it to be sensitive to public opinion. The challenge facing Musharraf is how to avoid isolation in the domestic political arena while fulfilling the international demands on the Pakistan state. With little ideological leverage with which to manage the domestic political scene— and its most obstreperous elements—the general faces an uphill battle. How General Musharraf addresses this problem will be decisive not only for his regime but also for the future of Pakistan.

As pressures mount, the military—Pakistan's single most important political actor—will not likely remain politically active without fueling Islamism. The notion of a secularizing military has become a contradiction in terms. As the military faces stiff resistance to its authority, it is likely that it will give in to MMA, returning to the framework of relations that governed military-Islamist relations in the 1980s. This time, however, the military lacks ideological commitment to Islamism, and MMA will not be content with playing a secondary role in the alliance. The balances of ideology and power are very different, although the need for cooperation remains the same. This may well present Islamists with the first serious opportunity to emerge as a viable mainstream political actor.

NOTES

1. Seyyed Vali Reza Nasr, *Islamic Leviathan: Islam and State Power* (New York: Oxford University Press, 2001).

2. Marvin Weinbaum, *Pakistan and Afghanistan: Resistance and Reconstruction* (Boulder, Colo.: Westview, 1994); and Rasul B. Rais, *War without Winners: Afghanistan's Uncertain Transition after the Cold War* (Karachi: Oxford University Press, 1994).

3. Leonard Binder, *Religion and Politics in Pakistan* (Berkeley: University of California Press, 1961).

4. Seyyed Vali Reza Nasr, *Vanguard of the Islamic Revolution: The Jama'at-i Islami of Pakistan* (Berkeley: University of California Press, 1994); and Ishtiaq Ahmed *The Concept of an Islamic State: An Analysis of the Ideological Controversy in Pakistan* (New York: St. Martin's, 1987).

5. Mumtaz Ahmad, "Islam and the State: The Case of Pakistan," in Mathew Moen and Lowell Gustafson, eds., *The Religious Challenge to the State* (Philadelphia: Temple University Press, 1992), pp. 239–67; and Seyyed Vali Reza Nasr, "Islamic Opposition in the Political Process: Lessons from Pakistan," in John L. Esposito, ed., *Political Islam: Revolution, Radicalism, or Reform?* (Boulder, Colo.: Lynne Rienner, 1997), pp. 135–56.

6. Shahid Javed Burki and Craig Baxter, *Pakistan under the Military: Eleven Years of Zia ul-Haq* (Boulder, Colo.: Westview, 1991).

7. Afzal Iqbal, *Islamization of Pakistan* (Lahore: Vanguard, 1986); Lawrence Ziring, "From Islamic Republic to Islamic State in Pakistan," *Asian Survey* 24:9 (September 1984), pp. 931–46; Charles Kennedy, "Islamization and Legal Reform in Pakistan, 1979–89," *Pacific Affairs* 63:1 (Spring 1990), pp. 62–77; and Charles Kennedy, *Islamization of Laws and Economy: Case Studies on Pakistan* (Islamabad: Institute of Policy Studies, 1996).

8. Nasr, *Islamic Leviathan*.

9. Vali Nasr, "Democracy and the Crisis of Governability in Pakistan," *Asian Survey* 32:6 (June 1992), pp. 521–37.

10. Nasr, *Vanguard of the Islamic Revolution*, pp. 206–18.

11. Tariq Isma'il, *Election '88* (Lahore: Maktabah-i Nawa'-i Waqt, 1989).

12. Vali Nasr, "Democracy and the Crisis of Governability in Pakistan," *Asian Survey* 32:6 (June 1992), pp. 521–37.

13. Mohammad Waseem, "Pakistan's Lingering Crisis of Dyarchy," *Asian Survey* 32:7 (July 1992), pp. 617–34; and Anwar H. Syed, "The Ouster of Nawaz Sharif in 1993: Power Plays within the Ruling Establishment," in Rasul Bakhsh Rais, ed., *State, Society and Democratic Change in Pakistan* (Karachi: Oxford University Press, 1997), pp. 45–75.

14. Tahir Amin, "Pakistan in 1993," *Asian Survey* 34:2 (February 1994), p. 195.

15. Ahmed Rashid, *Taliban: Militant Islam, Oil and Fundamentalism in Central Asia* (New Haven, Conn.: Yale University Press, 2001); Peter Marsden, *The Taliban: War and Religion in Afghanistan* (London: Zed, 2002); William Maley, *Fundamentalism Reborn? Afghanistan and the Taliban* (New York: New York University Press, 1988); and Larry Goodson, *Afghanistan's Endless War: State Failure, Regional Politics, and the Rise of the Taliban* (Seattle: University of Washington Press, 2001).

16. Hassan Abbas, *Pakistan's Drift into Extremism: Allah, the Army, and America's War on Terror* (Armonk, N.Y.: M. E. Sharpe, 2005).

17. Nasr, *Islamic Leviathan*, pp. 154–56.

18. Vali Nasr, "Pakistan at Crossroads: The February Elections and Beyond," *Muslim Politics* [Council on Foreign Relations] 12 (March/April, 1997), pp. 1–4.

19. On this issue, see Vali Nasr, "The Rise of Muslim Democracy," *Journal of Democracy* 16:2 (April 2005), pp. 13–27.

20. Off-the-record interview in 1997.

21. Vali Nasr, "International Politics, Domestic Imperatives, and the Rise of Politics of Identity: Sectarianism in Pakistan, 1979–1997," *Comparative Politics* 32:2 (January 2000), pp. 171–90.

22. Owen Bennett Jones, *Pakistan: In the Eye of the Storm*, 2nd ed. (New Haven, Conn.: Yale University Press, 2003), pp. 22–23; and Abbas, *Pakistan's Drift into Extremism*, pp. 209–10.

23. Ibid.

24. Jones, *Pakistan*; and Mary Anne Weaver, *Pakistan: In the Shadow of Jihad and Afghanistan* (New York: Farrar Straus Giroux, 2003).

25. "The Reign of a Compulsive Gambler," *Tanzim-i Islami* web edition; available at: http://www.tanzeem.org/resources/articles/articles/abidullah-the%20reign%20of%20a%20compulive%20gambler.htm.

26. Ilene R. Prusher, "A Turkish Path for Pakistan?" *Christian Science Monitor*, January 24, 2002, web edition; available at: http://www.csmonitor.com/2002/0124/p01s04-wosc.html.

27. Zafar Afaq Ansari and Abdul Rashid Moten, "From Crisis to Crisis: Musharraf's Personal Rule and the 2002 Elections in Pakistan," *Muslim World* 93:4 (July/October 2003), pp. 33–90.

28. Pamela Constable, "Pakistan's Predicament," *Journal of Democracy* 12:1 (January 2000), pp. 15–29.

29. *Herald*, Karachi, October 2003, pp. 44–47.

30. C. Christine Fair, "Militant Recruitment in Pakistan: Implications for al-Qaeda and Other Organizations," *Studies in Conflict and Terrorism* 27:6 (November–December 2004), pp. 489–504.

31. Stephen Philip Cohen, "The Jihadist Threat to Pakistan," *Washington Quarterly* 26:3 (Summer 2003), pp. 7–26.

32. International Crisis Group, "Madrasas, Extremism and the Military." Asia Report No. 36 (Brussels and Islamabad, 2002).

33. Ian Talbot, "Pakistan in 2002: Democracy, Terrorism, and Brinkmanship," *Asian Survey* 43:1 (January/February 2003), pp. 205–207.

34. *Herald*, Karachi, November 2002.

35. Interviews, October 2003.

36. Interviews, May and October 2003.

37. Interview with Chaudhri Aslam Salimi, Deputy Amir of the Jama'at, Lahore, May 2003.

38. Interviews with MMA leadership, October 2003 and January 2004.

39. Ansari and Moten, "From Crisis to Crisis," 373–90.

40. *Newsline*, Karachi, October 2003, pp. 19–28.

41. *Pakistan Political Perspective*, Karachi, 12:9 (September 2003), pp. 47–48.

42. The term was coined by Najam Sethi of the *Friday Times of Lahore* and was used in a number of his editorials in 2003; see also Zafar Abbas, "The Military-Mullah Alliance," *Herald*, Karachi, January 2004, p. 50.

43. Abbas, "Military-Mullah Alliance," pp. 38–42.

44. Alfred Stepan and Aqil Shah, "Pakistan's Real Bulwark," *Washington Post*, May 5, 2004, p. A29.

45. See Jama'at's web site: www.jamaat.org (posted February 4, 2004).

46. Abbas, "Military-Mullah Alliance," p. 82.

4

Islam, State, and Society in Bangladesh

Mumtaz Ahmad

Unlike many other Muslim countries identified with Islamic resurgence or Islamic radicalism where this phenomenon emerged as a gradual process, or was anticipated by observers as an incremental development of long-term socioreligious and political trends, Bangladesh entered the world of Islamic radicalism with a bang.[1] In August 2005, Bangladesh made international headlines when bomb blasts occurred simultaneously in sixty-three of sixty-four districts of the country, throwing the government and the people in utter chaos and panic.[2] Only one outside observer had seen what was coming: in April 2002, a cover story in the *Far Eastern Economic Review* by Bertil Lintner described—in a rather sensational tone—this second largest Muslim country in the world as a "cocoon of terror" and showed pictures on its title of look-alike bin Ladens springing to life.[3] The *Review* article warned:

> A revolution is taking place in Bangladesh that threatens trouble for the region and beyond if left unchallenged. Islamic fundamentalism, religious intolerance, militant Muslim groups with links to international terrorist groups, a powerful military with ties to the militants, the mushrooming of Islamic schools churning out radical students, middle class apathy, poverty and lawlessness—all are combining to transform the nation.[4]

The report talked about the "impending threat of Talibanization" of Bangladesh and claimed to have "discovered" links between Bangladeshi extremist groups and their Pakistani, Afghan, Chechen, and Southeast Asian counterparts with the blessings from Osama bin Laden. The same author published another story in the *Wall Street Journal* in which he singled out the Bangladeshi military establishment for mobilizing Islamic extremist groups for purposes of terrorist activities in Bangladesh and abroad.[5]

The *Review* story was picked up by several Indian publications, one of which listed thirteen "militant" organizations with international linkages that were said to be active in Bangladesh.[6] A pro–Awami League Bangla newspaper from Dhaka went as far as to claim in 2003 that "more than 100,000 militants are now active" in Bangladesh.[7] No wonder that Indian Deputy Prime Minister K. L. Advani and Foreign Minister Yashwant Sinha, under the Bhartia Janata Party (BJP) government, suggested that Bangladesh had become a sanctuary for al-Qaeda and Taliban fugitives.[8] This image of Bangladesh as a hotbed of Islamic militancy was further strengthened by the sporadic—and later, in 2005, systematic—terrorist activities by the two clandestine Ahl-e-Hadith groups, Jamaat-ul-Mujahidin Bangladesh (JMB) and Jagarta Muslim Janata Bangladesh (JMJB), led by Sheikh Abdur Rahman and Siddiqul Islam (popularly known as Bangla Bhai), respectively.

In this chapter, I examine the dynamics of the interaction between the state, politics, and Islam in Bangladesh within the context of both domestic and international developments since its inception in 1971; and I identify the factors that have contributed to the salience of Islam as an important player in the politics of a nation that was established to uphold the ideals of secularism, Bengali nationalism, socialism, and democracy. I examine the developments that precipitated the shift, within less than a couple of decades, from the total exclusion of Islam from politics to the emergence of Islamists as major power brokers in national politics. In order to situate Islamic political developments within the larger societal context, I examine how Islam—in its diverse manifestations—is embedded in the Bangladeshi society. Finally, I look into the roots and the magnitude and influence of Islamic radicalism in Bangladeshi politics and society.

I argue that neither the salience of Islam in Bangladeshi political discourse nor the sporadic militant actions of some clandestine groups such as Jamaat-ul-Mujahidin Bangladesh (JMB) necessarily leads to the conclusion that religious extremism has also become a principal mode of domestic politics or that Bangladeshis will soon join the ranks of international terrorist groups.[9] The current popularity of Islamic elements and Islamic discourse are shaped by Bangladesh's own national particularities and, as Ali Riaz has observed, can be described as "nationalization of Islamism" in Bangladesh. Thus, the rise of Islamic forces as prominent legitimate political actors in Bangladesh is a product of Bangladeshi political culture and is not symbolic of "a sympathetic gesture to any extraneous organization or ideology."[10]

That there is violence in Bangladesh is no news—more people are killed in Bangladesh in confrontations between the two rival secular political parties and their student wings than in religious conflicts.[11] The frequent clashes between rival political groups, including those associated with some religious organizations, may indicate a "primitive stage of democracy"[12] but certainly do not prove the rise of radical fundamentalism, jihadi Islam, Talibanism, and Bin Ladenism in Bangladesh, as has been frequently described in some quarters.

Islam and the State in Bangladesh

Bangladesh started its career as an independent state in 1972, with a constitutional commitment to uphold the principles of "nationalism, socialism, democracy, and secularism."[13] The Awami League that spearheaded the movement for an independent Bangladesh was a secular political party that championed Bengali nationalism and Bengali language as the raison d'être of the new state and rejected religion as a basis of state formation and nationhood.[14] The Awami League's aversion to Islam in public life was based both on its view that religion plays a divisive role and on its experience of the blatant exploitation of Islam by West Pakistani military and bureaucratic rulers in suppressing East Pakistan's demands for political participation and economic equality. Thus the 1972 constitution of Bangladesh not only declared secularism as one of the fundamental principles of state policy but also sought to (a) abolish all forms of "communalism," (b) ban all political activities and parties in the name of religion, (c) prohibit all forms of exploitation of religion for political ends, and (d) make it illegal to discriminate on religious grounds.[15] The Awami League leader and the founder of the new nation, Sheikh Mujibur Rahman, banned all Islamic political groups—Jamaat-e-Islami, Nizam-e-Islam Party, Muslim League, and Jamiyat-e-Ulama-e-Islam—and embarked on a path of neutralizing the role of Islam in public affairs.[16]

The anti-Islamic campaign of the secular zealots and the left-wing militants in the Awami League government during the early phase of the Mujib era was so fervent that it provoked a backlash, not only from the religious establishment but also from the petit bourgeois and rural peasant social support base of the Awami League itself. Thus we see a gradual shift toward a more accommodating attitude toward Islamic symbols in the latter years of Mujib's rule.

The fundamental shift in the state's ideological orientation came when General Ziaur Rahman (Zia) came to power in the aftermath of the assassination of Sheikh Mujibur Rahman in 1975. Zia dropped secularism as one of the four pillars of the state's policy, withdrew the ban on Islamic political parties, and replaced Bengali nationalism with Bangladeshi nationalism (that is, Bengali nationalism with an Islamic content) and started recitation of the Qur'an on radio and television, as well as in official ceremonies. President Zia also strengthened Bangladesh's relationships with Pakistan and the Middle Eastern Muslim countries, emphasizing Bangladesh's integral links with the world Islamic *ummah.*

The first symbolic gesture of Zia toward the "Islamization" of the constitution was to insert "Bismillah-ar-Rahman-ar-Rahim" (In the name of Allah, the Beneficent, the Merciful) in the beginning of the preamble. Also, Article 8 of the constitution that mentioned secularism as one of the fundamental principles of the state policy was amended to read in place of secularism "absolute trust and faith in the Almighty Allah." Article 12 that talked about the measures to implement secular ideals was completely deleted, adding a new clause in Article 25 to say that the state will stabilize, preserve, and strengthen "fraternal ties with the Muslim states on the basis of Islamic solidarity." Also, the word "socialism" in the preamble was defined to mean "social and economic justice." Besides these constitutional changes, President Zia also undertook a series of symbolic measures to emphasize the salience of Islam in public affairs: radio and television programs on Islam were increased substantially; Islamic holidays and special occasions (Miladun Nabi, Muharram, Ramadan, and Jummatul Wida') were celebrated officially; and special government transport arrangements were made to facilitate the annual "Biswa ijtema" of the Tablighi Jamaat. At the administrative level, two other important measures were taken: a new government department of religious affairs was created to coordinate policies and activities pertaining to Islam and other religions; and the previously dormant Islamic Academy was upgraded into the Islamic Foundation, Bangladesh, with generous funding from the government to promote Islamic research, education, and *d'awa* among Muslims.[17]

The trend toward Islamization at the state level was further strengthened by the next military ruler, General Hussain Muhammad Ershad, who ruled Bangladesh from 1982 to 1990. Ershad made Islam the state religion of Bangladesh, patronized Islamic religious activities, declared Friday instead of Sunday as the weekly holiday, and doled out generous government funds to religious institutions, including *maktabs* (elementary schools) and madrasas (religious schools). Despite his personal life style, considered "hedonistic" by many of his countrymen,[18] President Ershad was most ostentatious in public display of his Islamic credentials. He also established a Zakat Fund for the collection and distribution of the Islamic obligatory charity under his own supervision and emphasized the teaching of Islam and the Arabic language in public schools.[19]

On the face of it, it would appear that Bangladesh made a 180-degree turn in its ideological orientation from a secular state to an "Islamic state" in only ten years of its history. But one should not read too much into the pious phrases of constitutional changes introduced during the Zia and Ershad periods: these changes have remained mostly symbolic and have never been invoked, either in substantive public policies or in any of the major constitutional or legal cases that have come up to the apex courts in Bangladesh. Neither the insertion of "Bismillah" nor the "absolute trust and faith in Almighty Allah," nor the proclamation that "the state religion of the Republic is Islam" have any operational significance for law making in Bangladesh.[20]

The most substantive effect of these constitutional changes and symbolic measures was the re-legitimization of Islamic political parties and their participation in national politics. The Jamaat-e-Islami and other Islamic political groups were able to stage a comeback into the national political mainstream only as a result of the legal changes that were introduced by the Zia government. Also, these measures created an environment in which invocation of Islam in public debates was no longer considered a taboo.

Several Bangladeshi writers have explained the Islamic policies pursued by Zia and Ershad as a cynical exploitation of Islam to gain legitimacy for their military regimes.[21] This tired and rather simplistic explanation itself begs an explanation: Why Islam? Rulers exploit only those sentiments that already have a great deal of resonance in the masses. The fact that it was Islam that was instrumentally used by the rulers to legitimize their regimes—and not any other ideology or sentiment—only shows that the rulers were, in fact, responding to something that already had a strong popular base of support. Otherwise, the whole exercise must be seen as counterproductive. Thus, the "legitimacy" argument as an explanatory variable for the "return" of Islam at the state level not only requires its own explanation but also does not tell the whole story. One can identify several other factors that contributed to the ideological shift of the state from secularism to Islam.

First, of course, is the fact that Islam remains central to the lives of the overwhelming majority of Bangladeshi Muslims, and it would not be a pragmatic policy on the part of the state to continue to remain hostile toward Islam or to marginalize its role in public life. Second, the abysmal failure of the ideology of secular nationalism that culminated in 1975 in the one-party dictatorship in the name of "Mujibism" and widespread corruption and cronyism also opened the doors for Islamic alternative. Third, there was a pervasive perception of the large number of Bangladeshis that a secular Bangladesh was too close to India for comfort and that only a reassertion of Bangladesh's Muslim identity could justify its separate existence from its fellow Bengalis in the Indian Bengal. Fourth, there was the factor of Bangladesh's growing cultural and economic relations (read: aid and labor export) with the oil-producing Middle Eastern Muslim countries and Malaysia that spurred the state-sponsored Islamic activities with the generous official financial assistance from Saudi Arabia, Kuwait, and the United Arab Emirates (UAE). This funding was supplemented after the mid 1970s with large amounts of money from private Arab philanthropists and semi-government and private Islamic nongovernmental organizations (NGOs) that went to finance social welfare activities, as well as to build mosques and madrasas.

Diversity of Islamic Expressions in Bangladesh

At the sociocultural level, Islam is central to the life of most Bangladeshis; as in other Muslim societies, however, Bangladesh does not present a monolithic structure of Islamic beliefs, practices, and interpretations. There is considerable variation in the ways people articulate, interpret, and practice their faith and work out its implications in their individual and collective lives.[22] For analytical purposes, one can discuss the religio-intellectual situation of Islam in Bangladesh with reference to at least six distinct categories: orthodox Islam; Sufi Islam; reformist/liberal Islam; revivalist/fundamentalist Islam; "Islamic patriotism"; and a nascent postmodern, nonestablishmentarian Islam.

Orthodox Islam

Orthodox Islam is represented by the ulama, who are regarded as guardians of the Sunnah of the Prophet and of the socioreligious institutional structures developed under the guidance of the classical jurists. Included in this category are three schools: the orthodox Deobandi school[23] (the product of the Quomi madrasas), which constitutes the largest group among the traditional ulama in Bangladesh; the Sufi-oriented Barelvi school,[24] mostly the product of Alia madrasas; and the extreme right wing Wahhabi school of Ahl-e-Hadith, the smallest in number in Bangladesh but most active in radical politics in recent years.

The ulama, as the bearers of the legal and political tradition of the late Abbasid period, have four primary concerns: the unity and integrity of the Islamic *ummah* as a universal religious community; the integrity of the orthodox beliefs and practices of Islam as represented by 'Asha'ari theology and the consensus (*ijma'*) of the classical jurists; the implementation of the Sharia under their supervision, especially in matters pertaining to family law and religious rituals; and the preservation and dissemination of the Islamic religious sciences under their guidance. As the interpreters of the divine law, they resolve religious disputes and issue fatwas, providing the faithful with religious guidance on all kinds of issues. As religious functionaries, they organize and lead congregational prayers, supervise the celebration of Islamic religious occasions and festivals, and conduct marriage ceremonies and burial rituals.[25]

The persistence of orthodox Islam as a living and lived religious tradition and as a powerful mode of Islamic religious discourse is nowhere more salient than in the two central Islamic institutions, mosques and madrasas, which constitute the base of the legitimacy, power, and authority of the ulama. A recent government survey estimated that there were more than 200,000 mosques of various sizes in Bangladesh, staffed by approximately 350,000 religious functionaries: imams (prayer leaders), *khatibs* (preachers), and *khadims* (caretakers).[26] Unlike most Middle Eastern Muslim countries, the network of mosques and madrasas in Bangladesh operate outside state control and retain considerable autonomy, despite several half-hearted moves by the state to weaken their independence. In many small towns and cities, where there are no public halls or similar civic facilities, the mosque is not only a place of worship but also a forum in which to discuss public issues. A typical town will have at least four or five major mosques (Jami'ahs) and at least one small mosque for each *muhallah* (neighborhood). These small neighborhood mosques are managed and funded by their local congregations and are thus closely linked with the everyday lives of the faithful.

Madrasas have long been the centers of classical Islamic studies and the guardians of orthodoxy in South Asian Islam. There are two kinds of madrasas in Bangladesh: Quomi and 'Alia.

Quomi madrasas—estimated at more than 6,500 at the secondary, intermediate, and tertiary levels, with about 1,462,500 students and 130,000 teachers—are a legacy of the spectacular resurgence of Islamic religious education in India during the late nineteenth century.[27] Since then, the madrasa system has played an important historical role by preserving the orthodox tradition of Islam, training generations of Islamic religious scholars and functionaries, providing vigorous religio-political leadership, and, most important, reawakening the consciousness of Islamic solidarity and the Islamic way of life among the Muslims of South Asia.[28] The Quomi madrasas in Bangladesh teach a curriculum known as Dars-i-Nizami, a standard course of study in all Sunni madrasas of India, Pakistan, and Bangladesh. It consists of about twenty subjects, broadly divided into transmitted sciences (al-'ulum al-naqliyah) and rational sciences (al-'ulum al-'aqliyah). The Quomi madrasas are private, receive no financial support from the government, and are supported by religious endowments (*awqaf*) or by Zakat, Sadaka, and donations from the faithful. This financial autonomy of the mosques and madrasas has been a major source of the independent religio-political power base of the ulama in Bangladesh. It has also been responsible for resisting the efforts of state authorities to introduce reforms into the Quomi madrasa system and to bridge the gap between the traditional system of Islamic education and the modern, secular system.[29]

The other category is the government or 'Alia madrasa system, a unique system of Islamic religious education that has no parallel in the Muslim word. Divided into four distinct levels—Dakhil (SSC), 'Alim (HSC), Fazil (B.A.), and Kamil (M.A.)—these madrasas teach all the required modern subjects like English, Bangla, science, social studies, math, geography, history, and so on, along with a revised and an abbreviated version of Dars-i-Nizami. Although they are privately owned and managed, the government of Bangladesh spends 11.5 percent of its total education budget on madrasa education.[30] The government pays 80 percent of the salaries of their teachers and administrators and a considerable portion of their development expenditure as well.[31] These 'Alia madrasas are registered with, and supervised by, the government-appointed Bangladesh Madrasa Education Board, which also prescribes their curriculum and syllabi and conducts examinations. In 2006, the BNP government of Prime Minister Khalida Zia decided to recognize 'Alia madrasa degrees as equivalent to comparable general education degrees. According to the Madrasa Education Board, there are 6,906 nongovernment 'Alia madrasas in Bangladesh, with the largest number, 4,826, at Dakhil level. The total number of teachers in these madrasas is 100,732, and the number of students at all four levels is 1,879,300. Unlike the graduates of Quomi madrasas, whose degrees are not recognized by the government and who pursue their careers in religious establishments and private businesses, a large number of the graduates of 'Alia madrasas merge into the general stream of education by continuing their education in colleges and universities.

There has been a phenomenal growth in the number of both the 'Alia and Quomi madrasas since the early 1990s. Data on the rate of growth in the Quomi madrasas is not generally available, but anecdotal evidence suggests at least 25 percent growth during 1995–2005.[32] 'Alia madrasas also registered substantial growth during this period. In fact, the number of general educational institutions in the public sector increased only 9.74 percent during 2001–2005 as against 22.22 percent growth in the 'Alia madrasas during the same period.[33] It is interesting that the number of madrasa students in the 'Alia sector increased at a much higher rate (58 percent) during the secularly oriented Awami

League government (1996–2000) than during the centrist-Islamist coalition government (2001–2005) of BNP, which was only 10 percent.[34]

Then there are elementary-level madrasas, known as Ebtedayee madrasas, first formally approved by President Ziaur Rahman in 1978. The Madrasa Education Board has approved only 5,150 of all independent Ebtedayee madrasas, with 23,176 teachers and 377,749 students. However, another report suggested the existence of 18,000 independent Ebtedayee madrasas, with 85,000 teachers and close to 2 million students.[35] This figure should be closer to reality since a 1992 Ministry of Education estimate puts the total number of Ebtedayee madrasas at 17,279. In any case, the Ebtedayee madrasas have provided elementary education in areas where no government primary schools are available, and they are now acting as feeder institutions for both the 'Alia and Quomi madrasas. It is estimated that more than 50 percent of students in the Quomi madrasas and more than 70 percent of students in the 'Alia madrasas come from an Ebtedayee background.[36]

A more graphic picture of madrasa education in Bangladesh is presented in table 4.1, showing the magnitude and expanse of the civil society space that is occupied by the religious sector in Bangladesh.

Although the ulama have vigorously resisted state efforts to introduce changes in traditional religious practices, Muslim family law, and madrasas education, they are not, contrary to the general perception, frozen in legal, theological, and intellectual rigidity. The ulama have shown a remarkable flexibility in adapting to changing socioeconomic and political conditions, as is evident in the important changes in the social organization of madrasas education. The 'Alia madrasas system is one spectacular example of how the modern and traditional systems of education were combined, notwithstanding its well-known inadequacies. But what is not widely known and appreciated are the important changes that have been introduced in Quomi madrasas since the 1970s: Bangla has replaced Urdu and Arabic as the medium of instruction, English has been

TABLE 4.1. Profile of Madrasas in Bangladesh, 2004–2005

Type	Number of Schools	Number of Students	Number of Teachers
Quomi madrasas	6,500	1,462,500	130,000
'Alia madrasas	6,906	1,878,300	100,732
Ebtedaee madrasas[a]	5,150	377,749	23,176
Total	18,556	3,718,549	253,908

[a]Government-approved.

Source: Data collected from publications of the Bangladesh Madrasa Education Board, four major Quomi Madrasa Wafaqs (federations), and Bangladesh Ministry of Education documents.

introduced in most Quomi madrasas at the elementary level, some important changes have been made in the curriculum and textbooks, management practices have been bureaucratized, and the examination system has been centralized.

The only major attempt by the state to reorganize madrasa education in postindependence Bangladesh was made in 1972 when Sheikh Mujibur Rahman appointed a Commission on National Education under the chairmanship of Muhammad Qudrat-i-Khuda. The commission nominated a special committee on religious education to suggest reforms in the madrasas. The general perception that a large number of madrasa students and teachers had collaborated with the Pakistan military during the war of liberation had already created a hostile political environment for the madrasas. A group of Awami League intellectuals petitioned to the commission that these madrasas would keep on producing "Dallals" (Pakistani agents and collaborators), which would undermine the spirit of Bengali nationalism—the ideological basis of the newly independent state of Bangladesh. They asked the commission to recommend that the madrasa education be abolished and integrated into the general education.

Although the commission ignored the political aspects of the madrasa education, they lashed out heavily at the outdated and "reactionary nature" of its curriculum. The commission stated that madrasa education needed radical change and should be reconstituted according to the demands of the modern age. The main thrust of the commission's recommendation was to gradually integrate madrasa education with the general education stream and bring all education under state control.[37] What prevented the Awami League government from implementing the Qudrat-i-Khuda Commission report on madrasa education was the opposition, not only from the traditional religious sectors but also from the modern educated elites. When the commission sent the questionnaire to elicit public opinion on madrasa education, 75 percent of the respondents among the modern educated elite favored religious education, and about 90 percent wanted to retain madrasa education in some form.[38]

Although the Quomi madrasas system of education remains an exclusive, and relatively isolated, phenomenon, there are, nevertheless, powerful, social, economic, and political forces and institutions that cut across socioeconomic and cultural strata and tend to create new linkages, however weak, between the traditional and modern sectors. These processual and institutional changes have become more significant in the post-1971 era, as the changed political context has created a series of symbolic and institutional linkages—shared religious symbols; government and private-sponsored Islamic educational and cultural activities, as well as projects and advisory institutions; political parties and elected assemblies; and communication media, particularly the growing vernacular press—that facilitate increasing interaction between the ulama and the modern educated elite.[39] There have been several recent attempts to establish "modern-type" madrasas that may pave the way for some integration, even at a very small level. One such example is Madrasas Darur Rashad in Mirpur, Dhaka, which gives admission only to college graduates and has a condensed five-year course of Islamic sciences. Then there is the Dhaka Cadet Madrasa, which combines all subjects of college education along with the usual Islamic sciences, with English as the medium of instruction for general subjects and Arabic for Islamic religious subjects. Dhaka alone has at least five major English medium secondary and higher secondary level schools that combine Cambridge and London universities "A" and "O" level curricula with traditional Islamic subjects. In Sylhet, a major Quomi madrasa has introduced modern subjects, as well as compulsory English language, for its Dars-e-Nizami students. Market forces, it appears, have done something here that the governments couldn't do, in that these madrasas have emerged in response to the increasing demand for the English-speaking, modern-educated ulama who can act as imams and *khatibs* in the United Kingdom and North America. The Sylhet-based Quomi madrasa, Jamiatul Madina, alone has trained more than 100 graduates who are working as imams and *khatibs* in Bangladeshi neighborhoods in various cities in the United Kingdom.[40]

Although the top leadership of major Quomi madrasas is active in politics, especially in Dhaka, most of the teachers and students are not included in a unified voting bloc. Anecdotal evidence suggests that a majority of madrasa students and graduates voted for the BNP during both the 1991 and 1996 elections, but some of their votes went to the Jatiya Party of General H. M. Ershad and the Awami League, especially when the candidate was personally known for his religiosity, but hardly any for the Jamaat-i-Islami, since the Jamaat, in the view of most Deobandi ulama, represents a *firqah-i-batyla* (deviant sect). The 'Alia madrasa teachers and students, in contrast, are the backbone of the Jamaat-i-Islami's central and regional leadership and social support base. The Islami Chhatra Shibbir, the student wing of the Jamaat-e-Islami, dominates the campuses of an overwhelming majority of the 'Alia madrasas. However, a good number of 'Alia-associated teachers and students are BNP supporters as well.

Sufi Islam

Sufi Islam in Bangladesh is represented at two levels. The first is the folk, populist Sufis of the rural masses, associated with unorthodox religious rituals and practices, belief in supernatural powers of saints, a binding spiritual relationship between the *pir* (master) and *murid* (disciple), and visits to and veneration of shrines: Shah Jalal in Sylhet and Shah Makhdoom in Rajshahi, for example. Sufi religious communities of Bauls, wandering from village to village and singing devotional Sufi songs, enjoyed enormous popularity among ordinary Bengali Muslims in the premodern period. This tradition has been preserved in puthi songs, a genre of Bengali poetry composed by fakirs and dervishes, representing the best in Sufi devotionalism.[41] Muhammad Abdur Rahim lists the names of sixty-two prominent saints (both mythical and historical) whose shrines in different parts of today's Bangladesh attract hundreds and thousands of pilgrims every year.[42] Asim Roy describes three distinct features of *pirs* in Muslim Bengal: (1) the term *pir* in Bengal includes not only saints and spiritual guides but also "apotheosized soldiers," pioneering settlers, and "metamorphosed Hindu and Buddhist divinities and anthromorphized animistic spirits"; (2) the institution of *pirs* came to represent a folk religious transmutation of Islamic orthodoxy; and (3) the *pirs* became "a binding force of authority, stability and assurance in largely unstable physical and social situation" marked by the "ferocity of nature and anarchical conditions in the active delta."[43]

Quite a large number of Muslims in Bangladesh identify themselves with some *pir*, living or dead, and seek his spiritual guidance or his intercession for the solution of their worldly problems. The *pirs* in Bangladesh exercise enormous spiritual, but not much political, influence over their followers. Many prominent *pir* families have tried their luck in electoral politics by forming their own political parties in recent years but have failed to mobilize their spiritual disciples for political gains. They are also known for their shifting political alliances, moving from Awami League to BNP from election to election. What is common among all the *pir* families, however, is their intense hostility toward the Islamist Jamaat-e-Islami. Besides the established *pir* families of Bangladesh—Sarsina Sharif (former Pakistani President Ayub Khan's *pir*), Athrassi *pir* (former Bangladesh President H. M. Ershad's *pir*, who established the Zakir Party), the Pir of Charminai (leader of the Islamic Constitution Movement), and the Pir of Dewanbagh ("reviver of Muhammadi Islam")—there have emerged in recent years several new *pirs* in major urban centers, with a large following among military officers, government officials, college and university teachers, and businessmen and politicians. A Pakistani *pir* from the Northwest Frontier Province—the elder brother of the former Chief Minister of NWFP—has the largest following in the Chittagong area, which he visits every year and from which he collects millions of taka from the rich business community of Chittagong.

The other strain is the scholastic or intellectual Sufism, also a recent phenomenon based in urban areas and becoming increasingly popular in educated circles. Influenced by the writings of Abu Hamid al-Ghazzali and the spiritual experiences of the masters of the Suharwardiyah and Naqshbandiya orders, these modern educated Muslims are rearticulating Islamic metaphysics as an answer to Western materialism. For them, Sufism is the heart of Islam, and Islamic revival means nothing if it does not begin with the spiritual reawakening of individual Muslims. They believe in an integral Islamic tradition and, hence, are critical of both Islamic modernists and Islamic revivalists. In recent years, this trend toward intellectual Sufism was popularized by the late Seyyed Ali Ashraf and was strengthened by the writings of the Iranian scholar Seyyed Hossein Nasr, the French Muslim thinker René Guénon, and Martin Lings and Frithjof Schuon, all with their penetrating discussions of the metaphysical questions of Islamic gnosis.

Revivalist Islam

Revivalist Islam in today's Bangladesh is represented by two distinct and opposing streams: the politically activist revivalism is represented by the Jamaat-i-Islami, and the quietist, nonpolitical *d'awa*-oriented revivalism is represented by the Tablighi Jamaat.

JAMAAT-I-ISLAMI BANGLADESH. Regarded as one of the most effectively organized religio-political movements, the Jamaat-i-Islami has staged a remarkable comeback, despite the enormous liability that its leadership carries from the 1971 experience when it sided with the Pakistani forces and fought against the independence of Bangladesh. It was banned, along with the other Islamic political groups, after the liberation of Bangladesh. Soon after its reemergence on the national political stage in the late 1970s, however, the Jamaat became the most powerful Islamist group in Bangladesh.[44] Compared with fewer than 2 percent of the votes polled by all Islamic parties, the Jamaat candidates received 12.13 percent and 8.63 percent of votes during the 1991 and 1996 parliamentary elections, respectively. In the October 2001 parliamentary elections, the Jamaat-i-Islami participated as part of a center-right coalition and won seventeen seats in Parliament. The Jamaat-i-Islami was given two positions in Prime Minister Khalida Zia's cabinet, which was quite a transformation for a nation that came into being in the name of Bengali nationalism, secularism, and socialism.

The majority of the Jamaat leadership consists of those educated at modern institutions of higher learning, as well as of 'Alia associated graduates and semimodern-educated lay Muslims, who came to revivalist Islam via Maulana Abul Ala Maududi's writings. Its support base is lower-middle-class Muslims from both the traditional petite bourgeoisie and the lower echelons of the more modern economic sectors of Bangladeshi society. Its student's wing, Islami Chhatra Shibbir (ICS), claims a large following among students in major campuses all over Bangladesh, except Dhaka University, which is regarded as the bastion of secular/nationalist student politics in Bangladesh.[45]

The Jamaat seeks Islamic revival through the establishment of an Islamic state with the Qur'an and Sunnah as its constitution and the Sharia as its law. It regards Islam as a comprehensive way of life that provides guidance in all human activities. Its political struggle, since its reemergence in the early 1980s, has focused primarily, through shifting political alliances, to relegitimize itself in the new political context of postindependence Bangladesh. During the early 1990s, it formed a political alliance with its archenemy, the Awami League, to launch a joint movement against the BNP government of Prime Minister Zia. But then in 2001, it joined the BNP-led coalition to oppose the Awami League government of Sheikh Hasina Wazed. Having thus gained political legitimacy in the eyes of both major political forces, the Jamaat-e-Islami has emerged as an important power broker in Bangladeshi politics. The Jamaat has also recently tried to build bridges with the Deobandi ulama through its contacts with the Islami Oiyko Jote (IOJ), "a potpourri of traditional-orthodox Islamic groups."[46]

The Jamaat is also reaching out to the modern educated sectors of Bangladeshi society through its concerted efforts to develop contacts with college and university faculties, establish its own colleges and universities, organize seminars and conferences on public policy issues, and establish "think tanks." Nevertheless, in the course of its intense ideological and political battles against secular liberalism and Islamic modernism, the Jamaat, along with the ulama, still remains a major spokesman of Islamic conservatism in socioreligious matters in contemporary Bangladesh.

TABLIGHI JAMAAT. The Tablighi Jamaat is one of the very few, and probably the most important, grassroots Islamic revivalist movements in contemporary Islam. Founded in 1926 as a *d'awa* movement in Mewat near Delhi, with a few dozen disciples of Maulana Muhammad Ilyas (1885–1944), the Tablighi Jamaat today claims to have influenced millions throughout the Muslim world and the West. Its growth and popularity in Bangladesh has been most spectacular: Its annual conference, called Biswa Ijtema, is held in Tongi near Dhaka and is attended by about 1.7 million Muslims; it is the second largest congregation of the Muslim world after Hajj.[47]

The success of the Jamaat in Bangladesh, as elsewhere, owes much to the dedicated missionary work of its followers; its simple noncontroversial and nonsectarian message; and its direct, personal appeal to and contacts with individual Muslims. Instead of publishing books or addressing large gatherings, Jamaat members go door to door and invite people to join their ranks and spread the word of God. Their program of asking Muslims to leave their families, jobs, and hometowns for a time and join in a system of communal learning, worship, preaching, and other devotional activities has proved enormously effective in building community-type structures with close personal relationships and mutual moral-psychological support. Because the basic message of Tabligh is simple enough to be imparted by anyone willing to volunteer, it is ideally suited for ordinary Muslims with little or no pervious Islamic education. The Tablighi's reliance on lay preachers, rather than on ulama, has helped it reach and attract the Muslim masses in rural communities and small towns. But the Jamaat is equally popular among the educated classes in the urban areas. In fact, in recent years, it has attracted a large number of senior military officers (both active-duty and retired) and highly placed civil servants, as well as engineers, doctors, professionals, and paraprofessionals in Bangladesh. In terms of its ideological appeal, it is the only Islamic movement that seems to cut across socioeconomic class barriers.

From its inception, the Tabligh movement has deliberately stayed away from politics and political controversies. The Jamaat has rigidly maintained this nonpolitical posture and has scrupulously observed its founder's ban on political activities by refusing to take positions on political issues. This nonpolitical stance has helped it recruit followers from the military and civil service and has spared the movement from the vicissitudes of the conflicting ideological orientations of various political regimes in Bangladesh. Indeed, all presidents and prime ministers of Bangladesh have made a point of being seen (or reported in the press) attending the Biswa ijtema. As a general argument, the Tabligh movement justifies its repudiation of politics on the ground that, compared with much more important concerns, political involvement is a low-level activity and hence not worthy of the time, efforts, and energy of a religiously motivated person. But the politics of the Tablighi Jamaat's antipolitics has led to a situation in which the Tabligh movement's nonpolitical approach to Islamization of society has posed a serious challenge to the Islamic legitimacy of the politicized alternative offered by the Jamaat-i-Islami in Bangladesh.

Reformist/Liberal Islam

Reformist or liberal Islam in Bangladesh, as in India and Pakistan, owes its origin to the writings of the following: Sayyid Ahmad Khan (d. 1898), who emphasized the role of rational thinking in understanding the purposes of Sharia; Sayyid Ameer Ali (d. 1928), who argued for the essential compatibility between Islam and Western liberal values; and the poet-philosopher Muhammad Iqbal (d. 1938), who vigorously pleaded to reactivate the "principle of movement" in Islam—*ijtehad*—to reinterpret the fundamental legal principles of Islam in light of modern conditions and ideas, and to work toward the reconstruction of Islamic religious thought. In Muslim Bengal, the major exponents of Islamic modernism were Nawab Abdul Latif (d. 1893), Maulana Karamat Ali (d. 1873), and Sayyid Ameer Ali.[48] The Islamic modernist tradition was further strengthened by the modern educated Muslims, largely the product of Muslim educational renaissance in Bengal, especially after the establishment of Dhaka University.

The Islamic liberal/modernist alternative remained a viable alternative up until 1960s but seems to have eclipsed as an intellectual movement since the 1970s. Today, it remains the weakest link in the chain of Islamic religio-intellectual alternatives in Bangladesh. Modern, Western-educated Muslim intellectuals in the recent history of Bangladesh, both from the humanities and social sciences, have rarely, if ever, expressed their creative genius through their sustained interventions in the debates that currently engage Muslim intellectuals elsewhere. There is no dearth of polemical writings—mostly journalistic—that seek to belittle the significance of Islam as a focal point of public life in Bangladesh or to cast aspersions on some orthodox Islamic practices—à la Taslima Nasrin[49] and Shamsur Rahman—but a serious and sustained critique of the foundational structures of Islamic orthodoxy and its intellectual inadequacies has yet to come from either the secularists or Islamic liberals/modernists.[50]

"Islamic Patriotism"

Among the senior intellectuals, both institutional and noninstitutional, one can also witness a rediscovery of their Islamic identity, which, not surprisingly, has come through a route that, in earlier formulations, was considered antithetical to Islam: that is, nationalism. In the late 1940s, Hamilton Gibb was among the first Western scholars who were perceptive enough to foresee the eventual transformation of nationalism in Muslim societies to what he aptly called "Islamic patriotism." This, he argued, could happen as a result of reaction to external forces, as well as of the inner dynamics of Islam.

In the case of Bangladeshi intellectuals, two factors have contributed enormously to this generalized sense of Muslimness. First, the articulation of the hyphenated "Muslim-Bangladeshi" nationalism was as much a result of a conscious attempt to affirm moral-psychological alienation from India as it was an effort to relink the historical roots of the new nation with the struggle for freedom of Muslim Bengal, which was often parallel to, and juxtaposed with, those of the Hindus. The vacant space in the ideological divide of the 1970s and 1980s between, what Sufia M. Uddin described as "secular nationalists" and "religious nationalists," has now been occupied by "Muslim nationalists." In other words, "the primacy of Islamic traditions and sentiments, cast aside" by secular Bengali nationalists, "subsequently returned...as a broader quest for Muslim identity."[51]

But the second factor is no less important. This is what I call the "CNN Factor," CNN, of course, serving as a metaphor for the global media that bring closer to our homes the events of far away places. In this connection, one can mention several milestone events in the Islamic world—the plight of the Palestinian people; the Israeli invasion of Lebanon in 1982 and then in 2006; the Gulf War of 1991; the decade-long economic sanctions against the Iraqi people; the genocide of Muslims in Bosnia, Kosovo, and Chechnya; the Afghan war of 2001; and the invasion of Iraq in 2003—that caused a great deal of anguish and reawakened among the modern educated intellectuals of Bangladesh, as elsewhere in the Muslim world, both emotional and political-cultural solidarity with the historical community of Islam.

What awakened these intellectuals to rediscover their Muslim identity and solidarity with the Muslim causes was, first, the West's feverish and indiscriminately hostile reaction to the worldwide resurgence of Islam in the wake of the Iranian revolution; second, the destruction of a Muslim capital, Beirut, and the massacre in Sabra and Chatila during the Israeli invasion of Lebanon; third, the capture of another Muslim capital, Baghdad (the citadel of Islamic civilization and political glory during the Abbasid period), and the decimation of Iraq, killing of innocent people, and bombing its socioeconomic infrastructure during the 1991 and 2003 wars; and, finally, the initial indifference of the Western powers toward the ethnic cleansing of Muslims in Bosnia and the genocide of Chechen Muslims since the mid 1990s.

I call these Bangladeshi Muslim intellectuals "CNN Muslims"—only metaphorically, of course—for two reasons, based on their interpretations of the following: (1) CNN (as well as BBC television) provided the horrible scenes of massacres, concentration camps, and death camps of Muslims in Bosnia; showed the real-time destruction of the West Bank and Gaza cities and towns by Israeli bulldozers; and brought the pictures of Abu Ghraib prison to living rooms, showing in strong and vivid pictures the plight of their co-religionists. (2) The Western media allowed subtle, and often not very subtle, biases against Islam and Muslims to be demonstrated in the coverage of these events. Most of the writings of these senior intellectuals—university professors, retired diplomats, civil servants and military officers, journalists, and professionals—are found in daily and weekly newspapers, in both Bangla and English. Unlike the ulama and the Islamists, they know that they cannot be accused of having any sympathy with the Taliban or other international Islamic extremist groups. In fact, an overwhelming majority of them in the recent past were identified with the secular/nationalist political groups in Bangladesh.

It appears that recent international Islamic developments have tended to erode the so far "deliberate and sometimes scornful distancing" of Bangladeshi secular intelligentsia from their Islamic moorings.[52] Will these shifting attitudes toward Islam and Muslim solidarity engender a new trend toward a shared Muslim consciousness that is compatible with Bengali cultural sensibilities and Bengali nationalism, and will they open up new intellectual spaces that provide a wide audience with common interpretive framework of meaning? The answer to this question will depend not only on how the new Islamic voices cross the boundaries between secularism and Islam—or else make these boundaries interpenetrative—but also on whether the established ideological core of Islamists is willing to redefine the Islamic public space in more pluralistic terms.

Only a few of these intellectuals, however, have yet been engaged in a sustained articulation of what their new Islamic experience means and implies for debate on the role of Islam in Bangladesh.[53] There are visible elements of progressive, liberal Islamic thought in their orientations, but a full-fledged and public articulation of Islamic/Muslim elements in their ideas has been constrained by the political context of Bangladesh that still tends to bracket Islam, Muslim identity, and "Pakistani collaborators" in a single conceptual and political category.

A Postmodern Islam?

The last category consists of a nascent and amorphous group of young Muslims, mostly from the middle class and with a good grasp of the English language, who are trying to find their own religio-intellectual niche at a distance from both the traditional orthodoxy and the established Islamist groups. Although many of them had some previous connections with the Islamists, most of these young Muslim men and women seem to have rediscovered their Islamic identity independent of the established Islamic groups in Bangladesh and in an intellectual environment free of political combativeness. Their wellsprings of intellectual inspirations are quite diverse, eclectic, and mostly non-South Asian thinkers. There is no identifiable founder or domestic mentor of this group of young Muslim intellectuals, although some of them had some association with the late Seyyed Ali Ashraf during his brief tenure as vicechancellor of Darul Ahsan University.

All in all, it is a spontaneous movement rooted in deep yearning for Islamic intellectual renaissance, but it is equally engendered by dissatisfaction with the current state of Islamic scholarship among the known Islamic groups in Bangladesh. These young people are writing fiction, poetry, and literary criticism, and they describe themselves as postmodernist Islamic writers. Their favorite reading list consists of Edward Said's anti-orientalism, Malek Bennabi's Islamic self-criticism, Muhammad Arkoun's Islamic deconstructionism, Seyyed Hossein Nasr's and Seyyed Ali Ashraf's Islamic neo-traditional mysticism, and Yusuf al-Qardhawi's *ijtehadic* legal thought. One can also see elements of 'Ali Shariati in this generation of young Bangladeshi Muslim intellectuals, as is evident in their liberal use of diverse philosophical streams, their eclecticism, and their intellectual activism; their scholarly pursuits burst with passion.

Their movement, if one calls it a movement, privileges *ijtehad* over *taqlid*, pietistic Sufism over institutionalized rituals and legalistic hair-splitting, Muslim-Bangladeshi identity over Bengali nationalism, and tentativeness over predetermined and fixed meanings of the texts. Much of their intellectual production takes place in the forms of open discussions, study circles, and discourse workshops rather than in formal and written texts. "We are practicing Islam aesthetically, not ideologically," one of them said.[54]

This new Islamic discourse in Bangladesh is not only contributing toward the fragmentation—and subversion—of traditional religious authority but is also forcing Islamist intellectual thought to engage itself with the issues that it had neglected in the past: issues of gender equality, social justice, the environment, human rights, rights of religious minorities, and acceptance of the legitimacy of diverse Islamic religious experiences. What is most important in their eclectic approach is their willingness to extend the boundaries of Islam to encompass a wide variety of sensibilities, aesthetics, imaginaries, and practices—in the tradition of Sufis—as long as they do not explicitly conflict with Islamic Sharia.

Ahl-e-Hadith and Islamic Militancy in Bangladesh

Ahl-e-Hadith in Bangladesh, who are mostly concentrated in northern districts, largely remained unheard of until a mystery man, popularly known as "Bangla Bhai" (Bengali brother), a hitherto unknown Ahl-e-Hadith activist, hit the headlines of Bangladeshi newspapers in 2005. Bangla Bhai, whose real name is Siddiqul Islam, founded an underground militant organization, Jagarta Muslim Janata Bangladesh (JMJB) in northern Bangladesh to counter the increasingly violent activities of some Marxist groups and some powerful local gangs. Initially, Bangla Bhai received the full support of the local law enforcement agencies, as well as of some influential politicians. Once he gained some popular support because of his vigilante activities, Bangla Bhai extended his murderous operations to target government officials that he considered not sufficiently Islamic. Then, in February 2005, the Bangladesh government announced the arrest of Asadullah Ghalib, chair of the Arabic department at Rajshahi University and president of the largest and most well-organized Ahl-e-Hadith group in Bangladesh, Ahl-e-Hadith Andolan Bangladesh (AHAB), on charges of possession of explosives and bomb blasts. But the worst was yet to come: in August 2005, bombs exploded in sixty-three of sixty-four districts of Bangladesh at almost around the same time in crowded market places, government offices, and public transport points. This time it was another Ahl-e-Hadith activist, Sheikh Abdur Rahman, the chief of another underground militant outfit, Jamaatul Mujahidin Bangladesh (JMB), who claimed the responsibility for these well-coordinated terrorist attacks.

What was common between Siddiqul Islam alias Bangla Bhai of JMJB, Asadullah Ghalib of AHAB, and Sheikh Abdur Rahman of JMB was that all three belonged to the Ahl-e-Hadith school; all three had worked in the same Ahl-e-Hadith organizations at one time or another; all three had developed, directly or through the local Islamic NGOs, "Middle Eastern" connections; all three had close contacts with the veterans of the Afghan jihad; and their religio-political and ideological paths had frequently crossed each other.

Ahl-e-Hadith operated primarily as a religious group after the establishment of Bangladesh as an independent state. The Jamiyat-e-Ahl-e-Hadith East Pakistan did not take any formal position on the issue of the separation of the Eastern wing of united Pakistan, but many prominent Ahl-e-Hadith ulama, like the ulama of other schools of thought, were not sympathetic to the idea of independent Bangladesh since, in their view, it hurt the cause of Muslim unity. Unlike the Jamaat-e-Islami, which vigorously opposed the break-up of Pakistan and fought side by side with the Pakistan military against the Mukti Bahini—the guerrilla army created for the liberation of Bangladesh—the Ahl-e-Hadith rank and file remained low-profile during the entire period of the civil war. Throughout the 1970s and 1980s, the leadership of the Ahl-e-Hadith remained firmly in the hands of academicians who steered their group safely and unscathed from the then political controversies and turmoil. Nevertheless, deeply concerned about the secular-nationalist shift in politics in the postliberation rule of the Awami League under Sheikh Mujibur Rahman, they rallied their forces with the ulama of other schools of thought to oppose the proposed move by the Awami League government to do away with, or restrict the autonomy of, the private (Quomi) madrasa system. Noted academician Abdul Bari, who had done his doctoral research at Oxford in the early 1950s on the comparative study of the Wahhabi movement in Arabia and the Islamic reform movements of nineteenth-century India, served as president of the JAHB until the mid 1980s. A writer of great erudition, who was highly respected by his peers, as well as by the ulama of all schools of thought, Bari served as the vice-chancellor of Rajshahi University.

The transition from Bari to Ghalib to Rahman is a move from scholarly defense of the dogma, to metaphorical jihad, to literal jihad. Bari and other mainstream Ahl-e-Hadith ulama of the 1950s to the late 1970s were concerned primarily with the preservation and preaching of the Ahl-e-Hadith doctrines and also with the vigorous defense of the doctrine in the wake of sectarian assaults from the Hanafis (Brevlis). The old guard of the Ahl-e-Hadith in Bangladesh had steered the movement unblemished by partisan politics and had vigorously guarded it against the vicissitudes of Bangladesh's tumultuous politics during the Pakistan period and after the liberation. They were vigilant against the efforts by the zealots in the movement either to engage in sectarian confrontation with other sects and schools of thought or to politicize the movement by taking sides in political controversies.

The central, or intermediate, figure in the transition of the Ahl-e-Hadith in Bangladesh from the quietism and nonpolitical orientation of Abdul Bari to the militancy and terrorism of Abdur Rahman and Siddiqul Islam (Bangla Bhai) is then-sixty-year-old Asadullah Ghalib, amir (president) of the Ahl-e-Hadith Andolan, Bangladesh, and principal and chief administrator of Al-Markaz-ul-Islami, Nawdapara, Rajshahi, the largest Ahl-e-Hadith educational establishment in Bangladesh. In jail since February 23, 2005, on charges of involvement in militant activities, Ghalib, a graduate of Madina University in Saudi Arabia, has been described by his Rajshahi University colleagues as "an ardent sectarian," "politically ambitious," and "a religious entrepreneur."[55] Ghalib was not satisfied with the slow growth and low-key posture of his predecessors, and he wanted the Ahl-e-Hadith to assert their distinct religious (read: sectarian) identity and then translate this religious identity into an organized political movement with a clear religious agenda. Because the Ahl-e-Hadith constitute a considerable majority in many northern districts of Bangladesh, Ghalib's political ambitions were not unrealistic, if only the majority of his sectarian brothers and sisters could be mobilized on a single religio-political platform. Ghalib wanted the Ahl-e-Hadith to emerge as a major, if not the most influential, regional power broker in northern Bengal and thus be able to wield political influence in national politics. His model in this respect was the Jamaat-i-Islami, which had emerged as a power broker between the two main contenders for power—the Awami League (AL) and the Bangladesh Nationalist Party (BNP). While other religious groups—the Jamaat-e-Islami, the *pirs* (the

Brelvi-oriented spiritual leaders), and the Deobandi ulama (who were organized as Khilafat Majlis and Khilafat Andolan)—had established a niche in
national politics, Ghalib didn't want the Ahl-e-Hadith to be left behind and
serve merely as cheerleaders for them.

It was this dream that drove Ghalib to establish his own separate organization known as Ahl-e-Hadith Andolan, Bangladesh, in 1994.[56] A skillful
institution-builder, Ghalib soon developed a network of mosques, madrasas,
publishing houses, NGOs, and dozens of other Ahl-e-Hadith–affiliated organizations, including the Ahl-e-Hadith Mohila Sangstha (Ahl-e-Hadith Women's
Association) and Sonamoni, a network of clubs for Ahl-e-Hadith children.
Ghalib also took full advantage of both the domestic political environment
created by then-president General Ziaur Rahman's pro-Islamic policies and the
international political environment created by the Islamic revolution in Iran
and the subsequent Saudi policy of patronizing the anti-Shia salafi groups in
South Asia and elsewhere in the Muslim world. Ghalib also used his Saudi
contacts to send a large number of Ahl-e-Hadith madrasa graduates for higher
studies at Medina University; they came back with a strong dose of Wahhabi
indoctrination and, in many cases, with a reinvigorated jihadi spirit.

Ghalib's efforts to consolidate his hold over the Ahl-e-Hadith movement,
ulama, madrasas, and NGOs were greatly facilitated by the generous funds he
was able to collect from his Saudi and Kuwaiti contacts—both official and
private. From Saudi Arabia, he received "donations" for his madrasas and the
NGOs controlled by his organization, AHAB, through the Rabita-al-'Alam
al-Islami (World Muslim League)—a Saudi government-funded organization
to promote Islamic activities around the world—and through Al-Harmain
Foundation, a Saudi-based international NGO that has since been blacklisted
by the U.S. Treasury Department for its funding of militant groups in many
countries. Other major donors for Ghalib's various outfits were the Kuwait-
based Al-Jamiyat-ul-Ahyah-asaurah al-Islami (Revival of Islamic Heritage Society) and Al-Jamiyat-ul-Ahya-assunnah (Society for the Revival of the Sunnah
of the Prophet), which provided him generous funds to build mosques, establish and run madrasas, and organize Islamic NGOs in the field of education
and social welfare to neutralize the influence of secular, and especially the
Christian missionary-sponsored, international NGOs.[57]

The second person in the Ahl-e-Hadith radical circuit is Sheikh Abdur
Rahman of Jamaatul Mujahidin Bangladesh (JMB), now awaiting death by
hanging in a Dhaka jail, pending his appeal for clemency before the president
of Bangladesh. His early recruits for his JMB were the Bengali veterans of the
Afghan Jihad from Rajshahi and Sylhet regions: young, unemployed Ahl-e-
Hadith madrasa graduates, who had already been radicalized by Ghalib's

rhetoric about the imminent warfare between the forces of good and evil—although Ghalib was always careful to add that this "metaphorical warfare" does not imply engagement in actual, physical violence.

Both the JMB and the JMJB leaders seem to have been influenced immensely by the experience of the Afghan jihad, both through direct participation, and through its legends. They believe that an Islamic state can only be established after overthrowing the present political system through an armed struggle (jihad). Their model of an Islamic government is that of the Taliban rule in Afghanistan with its literal interpretation, and strict enforcement, of the Qur'anic injunctions, prophetic teachings, and Sharia rules. Another model that inspired them was that of Saudi Arabia where the Salafi-Wahhabi ulama exercised near monopoly of power over religious/Sharia matters.

Beyond their great fascination for the Taliban rule and the Saudi example, both Abdur Rahman of JMB and Bangla Bhai of JMJB had no clear vision or detailed blueprint of an Islamic government. Their half-baked ideas on Islamic revolution are contained in a few pamphlets—some of them are not even more than four pages long—that were being clandestinely circulated in mosques around the country during 2004–2005. Ghalib also rejects the modern democratic system as un-Islamic because "it is based on the idea of popular sovereignty and majority opinion," but he says that there is nothing wrong with elections if both the voters and the candidates for public offices are practicing Muslims and fulfill the condition of public trust as prescribed by Islam. But if democracy means following the desires of people who have no Islamic knowledge or Islamic commitment, then they are more likely to vote for candidates "who would support casinos, alcoholic drinks, bars, free mixing of sexes, prostitution, usury, etc. In other words, all these vices can be legalized if you can get 51 percent of votes in the parliament. It is this risk in democracy that we Muslims cannot take."[58]

Ghalib is not in favor of violent overthrow of the present system, nor does he advocate subversion of the system through clandestine tactics. According to a booklet he wrote in Bangla two years ago,[59] d'awa (call, preaching) and educational efforts by an organized movement—such as his own, AHAB—will eventually lead to the transformation of society on Islamic principles, and an Islamic society will then culminate in the establishment of an Islamic state based on the model of the Prophetic state in Medina and the early, rightly guided caliphate. In this publication, Ghalib rejects violence as a means of Islamic change and argues for a peaceful, "educational jihad" to transform society and to press rulers to attend to their Islamic duties.

Despite their ability to stage a spectacular scene of terrorist violence in August 2005, however, the JMB and the JMJB have no power. These organizations lack any social embeddedness in the larger Bangladeshi society, and they have been roundly condemned by an overwhelming majority of the ulama and religious political groups.[60] The mainstream Ahl-e-Hadith organizations, including Ghalib's Ahl-e-Hadith Andolan, have disassociated themselves from the terrorist violence perpetrated by the JMB and the JMJB. Most observers of Bangladesh politics agree that religiously inspired violence as witnessed in the early 2000s may continue in some small measure as an irritant and a nuisance for the authorities, but it is doomed to extinction in a sociopolitical environment as inhospitable as that of Bangladesh. As Talukdar Maniruzzaman, arguably the most prominent political scientist of Bangladesh and an acute observer of his country's development, noted: "A fish, in order to survive, needs ocean, or at least a pond. The JMB fish has no water to swim . . . no popular support. They have made a few splashes and that's it; they will have no impact on Bangladesh society."[61] Ahl-e-Hadith, with its theocratic particularism and a highly exaggerated notion of its own role as a puritanical, religious reform movement, will continue to remain an important part of the religious landscape of Bangladesh. However, a section of the Ahl-e-Hadith's stint in politics, and especially radical politics and militancy, has turned out to be both short-lived and disastrous for the rank and file of the community. The mainstream Ahl-e-Hadith community and leadership have now awakened to the need for wresting the leadership of the movement from the radicals and refocusing their activities on their traditional religious concerns.

Conclusion

The predominant trend in the official historiography of postindependence Bangladesh has emphasized the role of an all-inclusive Bengali nationalism over Islam and Muslim identity. Islamic developments have been studied by scholars of this school within the context of the conflict between the religious and ethnonational identities of Bengali Muslims. But while it is true that Bangladesh was created in the name of modern, secular nationalism and a deep sense of a separate Bengali identity—as was articulated in the original 1972 constitution that identified Bengali nationalism, secularism, socialism, and democracy as the four pillars of national ideology—it was, nevertheless, dependent on the religious experience of Bengali Muslims. With the creation of Bangladesh, ethnonationalism apparently triumphed, but not necessarily at the cost of a permanent damage to Islam. At the popular level, the overwhelming majority of Muslims in former East Pakistan did not see any inherent contradiction between their being good Muslims and their demand for political, cultural, and linguistic autonomy. In fact, the West Pakistani elite and the Pakistani military establishment asserted that (a) East Pakistan's continued unity with West Pakistan is imperative for the future of Islam in South Asia, and (b) by abandoning Pakistan, East Pakistanis would have abandoned Islam as well ("Agar Pakistan ko chhora to jaisey Islam Ko chhora"). Obviously, this was a convenient formulation to obfuscate the structural crisis of the state with the normative cloak of Islam. To be sure, the vanguard secular intellectuals in postliberation Bangladesh proclaimed precisely the same formulation when they asserted that (a) liberation of Bangladesh from Pakistan had affirmed the triumph of secularism over Islam, and (b) by abandoning Pakistan, the people in Bangladesh seemed to have abandoned their Islamic identity as well ("Pakistan sey alag hooe, to Islam sey bhi alag ho gaey").

Irrespective of the motives, ideas, and interests of the intellectual and political elites who sought to articulate a secular and, at times, deliberately de-Islamization policy framework for the new nation, there is ample evidence that the overwhelming majority of the Muslim masses did not see any contradiction between their Islamic identity on the one hand and their struggle for socioeconomic justice and political rights on the other. In their perception, to seek justice and affirm their political rights—either within a united Pakistan or by carving a new, sovereign state of their own—did not, in any way, adversely affect their commitment to Islam. Bangladesh, as M. Rashiduzzaman has noted, soon returned to its "center," defined both by Islam and Bangladeshi nationalism.[62]

Recently, Bangladesh became a focus of international attention because of the terrorist activities of certain clandestine Islamic groups during 2002–2005. It is, therefore, befitting that I conclude this essay by examining the factors, both domestic and international, that created a conducive religio-political environment for the rise of Islamic militancy in Bangladesh. Notwithstanding the rhetorical outbursts of some Deobandi ulama, Islamic militancy in the form of violent activities in recent years has been confined primarily to the Ahl-e-Hadith group, which, in its earlier phase, was mainly engaged in nonpolitical, peaceful religious activities. The transformation of the Ahl-e-Hadith in Bangladesh from political quietism to political activism to militancy—that is, from Abdul Bari to Asadullah Ghalib to Sheikh Abdur Rahman and Siddiqul Islam, was caused by multiplicity of factors:

1. Internal dynamics within the Ahl-e-Hadith movement in Bangladesh that first factionalized the movement and then led to the radicalization of the splinter groups
2. The gradual weakening of hold over the movement by the old guard

3. The political environment of Bangladesh during Ziaur Rahman's and Ershad's periods that encouraged Islamic political activities to counter the influence of the secularly oriented Awami League

4. The rise of the Jamaat-e-Islami and the Deobandi-oriented religio-political parties in 1980, which showed to the politically ambitious elements within the Ahl-e-Hadith movement that they, too, could become a political force to be reckoned with

5. The international environment created by the Islamic revolution in Iran that prompted the Saudis to counter the Iranian influence in Muslim South Asia, and elsewhere, by mobilizing and patronizing their natural, doctrinal allies, the Ahl-e-Hadith, through generous funds, both from official and semiofficial sources

6. The culture of political violence in Bangladesh that seems to have encompassed all political spectrums—from religious to nationalist to secular

7. The internecine conflict between the two main political parties, the Awami League and the BNP, which seems to have paralyzed the administrative structures, thus creating a fertile ground for militants

8. The almost total ideological disorientation, and the lack of social embeddedness and a well-defined class base of the Bangladeshi state, that creates a space for militant ideological and political alternatives

9. The existence of a large number of unemployed young men, mostly madrasa graduates from poor families, who have no prospects for any productive employment but are, at the same time, witness to highly ostentatious display of wealth and prosperity by corrupt officials, unscrupulous politicians, and *nouveau riche* businessmen

It is this large army of the poor, unemployed young men, many of them religiously motivated as well, who were most vulnerable to the radical ideas of the JMB and JMJB—those ideas that promised them a quick solution to their existential problems, as well as justice in a cruel world.

NOTES

I acknowledge with thanks the financial support from the American Institute of Bangladesh Studies (AIBS) for field research in Bangladesh. The moral support, administrative assistance, and intellectual inspiration from Dr. Mizanur Rahman Shelly, director of the Centre for Development Research, Bangladesh (CDRB), was indispensable during my several visits to Bangladesh. I have rarely met a foreign scholar of Bangladesh who was not in debt to Dr. Shelly's generosity. I am also grateful to Professor Talukdar Maniruzzaman and Professor U. A. Razia Akter Banu (both in the political science department), Dhaka University; Professor Tajul Islam

Hashmi of the Asia-Pacific Center of Security Studies, Honolulu, Hawaii; and Mr. Shah Abdul Hannan, former deputy governor of the Bangladesh Bank, for sharing their insights. Thanks are also due to Dr. Iftekhar Iqbal in the history department, Dhaka University, for his continued and valuable assistance over several years.

1. Among all major Muslim societies, Bangladesh remains the most under-studied in the literature on Islamic revivalism, Islamic resurgence, and Islamization in the contemporary world. Among the twenty-eight major anthologies published in the West in recent years on the experience of Islamic revivalism and Islamization in the Islamic world, only two have included chapters on Bangladesh. In the earlier phase of the worldwide Islamic resurgence, several observers described Bangladesh, as Imtiaz Ahmad did in the case of Indian Islam, a "surprising isolation," in that it had remained untouched by hectic Islamic developments in Iran and Pakistan, as well as in other countries of the Muslim world in the 1980s. It was then maintained that Islamic revivalism in other parts of the Islamic world did not strike a sympathetic chord among Muslims in Bangladesh. Although a latecomer to the world of Islamic radicalism, Bangladesh seems to have more than compensated for its long absence from the "Islamic" headlines of international media.

2. 459 Blasts in 63 Districts in 30 Minutes, *Daily Star* (Dhaka), 18 August 2005, p. 1.

3. Bertil Lintner, "Beware of Bangladesh—Bangladesh: Cocoon of Terror," *Far Eastern Economic Review* (April 4, 2002), pp. 14–18.

4. Ibid.

5. Bertil Lintner, "In Bangladesh, as in Pakistan, a Worrisome Rise in Islamic Extremism," *Wall Street Journal*, April 2, 2002, pp. A-18.

6. *Frontline* (Chennai), October 11–24, 2003, pp. 00–00. Three of the organizations mentioned in this article were found to be neighborhood-based Muslim charity societies in old Dhaka with combined assets of not more than U.S. $500.

7. *Daily Prothom Alo* (Dhaka), June 23, 2003.

8. *Asia Times* (Hong Kong), December 17, 2002.

9. It is not surprising that most reports about Bangladesh becoming another/next Afghanistan and Bangladeshi Islamic groups developing extensive links with the Pakistani Inter-Services Intelligence (ISI) and some international terrorist groups based in South Asia and the Middle East have emanated from the Indian news media and from the South Asia Terrorism Portal, a front organization of the Indian intelligence agencies.

10. Ali Riaz, "God Willing: Politics and Ideology of Islamism," *Comparative Studies of South Asia, Africa and the Middle East* 23:1–2 (2003), pp. 301–20.

11. Forty-three people died in two weeks of violent political agitation by the Awami League against the newly appointed interim caretaker government in October–November 2006. Four Jamaat-e-Islami workers were beaten to death by the Awami League activists in broad daylight and in floodlights of television cameras during these agitations.

12. Guy Sorman, *The Children of Rifah: In Search of a Moderate Islam* (New Delhi: Penguin, 2004), p. 141.

13. Preamble to the Constitution of the Peoples Republic of Bangladesh (Dhaka: Government Printing, 1972).

14. Sufia M. Uddin, *Constructing Bangladesh: Religion, Ethnicity and Language in an Islamic Nation* (Chapel Hill: University of North Carolina Press, 2006), pp. 122–36.

15. Article 12 of the constitution.

16. Emajuddin Ahmed and D.R.J.A. Nazneen, "Islam in Bangladesh: Revivalism or Power Politics," *Asian Survey* 30:8 (August 1990), pp. 795–808. See also Muhammad Ghulam Kabir, *Changing Face of Nationalism: The Case of Bangladesh* (New Delhi: South Asia Publications, 1994).

17. Ahmed and Nazneen, "Islam in Bangladesh," pp. 796–97. The Islamic Foundation today has become the premier Islamic research and educational institution in Bangladesh, with branches in several cities and activities spread all over the country. The foundation has so far published more than 2,000 books on various aspects of Islam, both scholarly and *d'awa*-oriented. The foundation's major publications include a multivolume *Bangla Encyclopedia of Islam* and the Bangla translations of several of the classical and modern exegeses of the Qur'an, as well as of all the standard Hadith collections. It runs hundreds of libraries on Islamic subjects and free clinics for the poor in different cities and also conducts training programs for the imams and *khatibs* of the mosques.

18. Taj Hashmi, "The Root of All Evil," *Forum* (Dhaka), 1:2, December 2006 (http://svr87.edns1/com/~starnet/forum/2006/december/evil.htm).

19. Ahmed and Nazneen, "Islam in Bangladesh," pp. 795–808.

20. For a fascinating discussion of the legal implications of the "Islamic" amendments to the constitution by a leading Bangladeshi constitutional scholar, see A. K. M. Shamsul Huda, *The Constitution of Bangladesh*, vol. 1 (Chittagong: Signet, 1997), pp. 197–251.

21. For example, Ahmed and Nazneen, "Islam in Bangladesh," and Uddin, *Constructing Bangladesh*.

22. For an extended discussion on the diversity of Islamic practices in Bangladesh, see Asim Roy, *The Islamic Syncretistic Tradition in Bengal* (Princeton, N.J.: Princeton University Press, 1983).

23. For a pathbreaking and most perceptive study of the Deobandi school, see Barbara D. Metcalf, *Islamic Revival in British India: Deoband, 1860–1900* (Princeton, N.J.: Princeton University Press, 1982).

24. For an excellent study of the Brelvi school, see Usha Sanyal, *Devotional Islam and Politics: Ahmad Riza Khan Barelwi and His Movement, 1870–1920* (New Delhi: Oxford University Press, 1996).

25. For the multifaceted roles of the ulama in Muslim South Asia, see Muhammad Qasim Zaman, *The Ulama in Contemporary Islam: Custodians of Change* (Princeton, N.J.: Princeton University Press, 2005).

26. *Nautan Fikr* (Dhaka), May 2002.

27. Metcalf, *Islamic Revival in British India*.

28. For a detailed study of the madrasas in Bangladesh and Pakistan, see Mumtaz Ahmad, "Madrasa Education in Pakistan and Bangladesh," in Satu P. Limya,

Robert C. Wirsing, and Mohan Malik, eds., *Religious Radicalism and Security in South Asia* (Honolulu: Asia-Pacific Center for Security Studies, 2004), pp. 101–16.

29. Most previous reform efforts by various governments during the Pakistan period, as well as after the independence of Bangladesh, failed not only because of the resistance from the ulama but also because of the reluctance of the state authorities to undertake the huge financial "burden" of the proposed reform measures.

30. Madrasas Mushroom with State Flavour *Daily Star* (Dhaka), August 4, 2005, pp. 1.

31. In the FY 2000–2001 budget, for example, the government allocated Taka 491 crore (approximately US$82 million) for the salary support of the nongovernment 'Alia madrasas. This was in addition to providing funds for building 171 new madrasas in the 'Alia sector; *Daily Star* (Dhaka), June 9, 2000.

32. Interview with Maulana Mokhlisur Rahman, chairman, Misbah Foundation, Dhaka, January 7, 2005.

33. *Bangladesh Economic Review* (Dhaka: Government of Bangladesh, 2006).

34. Madrasas Mushroom with State Flavour, *Daily Star* (Dhaka), August 4, 2005, pp. 1.

35. *Daily Dinkal* (Dhaka), March 2, 1998.

36. These are rough estimates based on my interviews with the administrators and teachers of both the Quomi and 'Alia madrasas during field trips to Bangladesh in 2000, 2002, 2004, and 2006.

37. M. Mustafizur Rahman, "Development of Traditional Islamic Education in Bangladesh," in A. K. M. Ayub Ali, M. A. Aziz, and Shahed Ali, eds., *Islam in Bangladesh through the Ages* (Dhaka: Islamic Foundation Bangladesh, 1995), pp. 256–57.

38. Talukdar Maniruzzaman, "Islam in Bangladesh Politics," unpublished manuscript, p. 7.

39. It is rather surprising that these interactions (especially in the context of an increasingly mature democratic political process) has not so far created a measure of shared intellectual space and a common language of religious discourse between the ulama and the modern educated Muslim intellectuals in Bangladesh. More than 25 percent of the elected members of the parliament (2001–2006) were graduates of either the 'Alia madrasas or the Quomi madrasas. Similarly, the ulama sit in an advisory capacity with almost all the commercial bank boards of governors to advise them on Islamic banking.

40. Information collected by the author during field research, 2004 and 2006.

41. Uddin, *Constructing Bangladesh*, p. 7.

42. Muhammad Abdur Rahim, *Social and Cultural History of Bengal*, vol. 1 (Karachi: Pakistan Historical Society, 1963), pp. 72–150.

43. Roy, *Islamic Syncretistic Tradition in Bengal*, p. 50. For a critique of Asim Roy's and Richard Eaton's thesis on the role of the *pirs* (*The Rise of Islam and the Bengal Frontier, 1204–1760* [New Delhi: Oxford University Press, 1994]), see Akbar Ali Khan, *Discovery of Bangladesh: Exploring into Dynamics of a Hidden Nation* (Dhaka: University Press, 1996), pp. 104–16.

44. Uddin, *Constructing Bangladesh*, pp. 163–73.

45. The ICS dominates the campuses of Rajshahi University, Chittagong University, Jahangirnagar University, and the Islamic University in Kushtia. It has also considerable presence in several agricultural and engineering colleges and universities throughout Bangladesh (Interview with M. Zubairi, former president of the ICS, Sylhet, July 8, 2006).

46. Mohammad Omar Farooq, "America's War against Terrorism or War against Islam?" *Daily Independent* (Dhaka), December 15, 2002, p. oo Cannot find.

47. Mumtaz Ahmad, "Islamic Fundamentalism in South Asia: The Jamaat-e-Islami and the Tablighi Jamaat of South Asia," in Martin E. Mart and R. Scott Appleby, eds., *Fundamentalisms Observed* (Chicago: University of Chicago Press, 1991), pp. 457–530.

48. Muinuddin Ahmad Khan, "Muslim Renaissance in Bangladesh," in A. K. M. Ayub Ali, M. A. Aziz, and Shahed Ali, eds., *Islam in Bangladesh through the Ages* (Dhaka: Islamic Foundation Bangladesh, 1995), pp. 193–94.

49. For details on the controversial Bangladeshi writer Taslima Nasrin, see S. M. Shamsul Alam, "Women in the Era of Modernity and Fundamentalism: The Case of Taslima Nasrin," *Signs: Journal of Women in Culture and Society* 23:2 (Winter 1998), pp. 429–61; and M. Rashiduzzaman, "The Liberals and the Religious Right in Bangladesh," *Asian Survey* 34:11 (November 1994), pp. 974–90.

50. There are a few notable exceptions, however. Seyyed Anwar Husain of Dhaka University, Muinuddin Ahmad Khan of Chittagong University, the late Seyyed Sajjad Husain of Dhaka University, and Tajul Islam Hashmi have all made important contributions to the debates on Islam and secularism; Islam, modernity, and national identity; and Islam and woman. Among the younger generation of Bangladeshi scholars, Maimuna Haq, Sufia M. Uddin, Dina Mahnaz Siddiqui, and Elora Shahabuddin are making interesting interventions in the Islam-modernity debate from a social sciences perspective.

51. Rashiduzzaman, "Liberals and Religious Right in Bangladesh," p. 974.

52. Interview with Talukdar Maniruzzaman, professor of political science, Dhaka University, Dhaka, December 25, 2005.

53. One can mention, as an example, dozens of newspaper and magazine articles written during the 1990s by Mizanur Rahman Shelly, a retired civil servant and former cabinet minister.

54. Interview with Ashraf Hussain, director, Islamization of Knowledge Project, Darul Ahsan University, Dhaka, July 8, 2006.

55. Interviews with faculty members of Rajshahi University, July 7, 2006.

56. Interview with Ameer Muhammad Muslehuddin, acting president of AHAB, Dhaka, January 5, 2006.

57. Interview with Asadullah Ghalib, Rajshahi, June 2, 2000.

58. Interview with Ghalib.

59. Asadullah Ghalib, *Equamat-e-Din: Poth O Poddoti* (Rajshahi: Hadith Foundation, 2004).

60. See *The Dhaka Declaration Adopted at the Ulama Convention, 15 December 2005* (Dhaka: Misbah Foundation, 2005). The declaration, adopted in a conference attended by more than 200 ulama of all schools of thought, described the terrorists as "enemies of Islam" and offered the government their full support to fight extremism and militancy.

61. Interview with Maniruzzaman.

62. M. Rashiduzzaman, "History of Bangladesh: In Search of a Flexible Narrative," *Studies in Contemporary Islam* 1:1 (Spring 1999), pp. 82–86.

5

Malaysian Islam in the Twenty-First Century: The Promise of a Democratic Transformation?

Osman Bakar

Issues and Challenges for Malaysian Islam in the Twenty-First Century

In both geographical and demographic terms, Malaysia is not a big country. It is much smaller in physical and population size than many other Muslim countries. In the domain of modern nation building, however, this multiethnic and multireligious Southeast Asian country—with just 12 million Muslim inhabitants, who constitute barely half of the total population—is a "towering figure" in the Islamic world. From its architectural feat of having the tallest twin towers in the world to its political feat of championing global Muslim interests in international forums Malaysia,[1] especially under the twenty-two-year rule of controversial former Prime Minister Mahathir Mohamed, has attracted considerable attention from the worldwide Muslim *ummah*.[2]

Indeed, as Malaysian Islam enters the twenty-first century, it finds itself in an envious position to boast of a number of societal achievements that most Muslim countries can only dream of. To start with, it is one of the most stable and peaceful religious and sociopolitical orders in the Islamic world. It has enjoyed this remarkable feat over the past half-century. This feat has been made possible thanks largely to another acquired feature of Malaysian Islam that critics, however, say is not good in the long term for the country: of all nationally organized and administered Islamic beliefs and practices in the Islamic world, Malaysian Islam is perhaps the most monolithic and most state-regulated.

The state regulation is to all intents and purposes to ensure that only interpretations of Islam sanctioned by the state as recommended by the official religious establishments prevail. On matters pertaining to Islamic law (Sharia), these interpretations generally follow the ethical-legal teachings of the Shafi'i school of thought that have shaped and dominated the Malay-Indonesian religious outlook ever since Islam created its first state in the region in the thirteenth century. On theological matters, Malay interpretations have been largely guided by the teachings of the Ash'arite school of Sunni theology, especially as interpreted and synthesized by Abu Hamid al-Ghazzali whom the Malays generally regarded as the greatest Muslim theologian. This kind of homogeneity that has characterized Malay Islam for centuries[3] has helped to make Malaysia free of intra-Islamic conflicts. But it has also made the Malay Muslims untutored and inexperienced in the art of living together and sharing the public space with fellow Muslims from other schools of thought (madhahib), particularly with Shiites. In fact, they do not tolerate any form of acknowledgement of a Shiite presence in the Malaysian public square.

Malaysia's lack of experience in dealing with intra-Islamic pluralism within its borders has been compensated by its relatively successful management of ethnic pluralism that involves the Malay-Muslims in a sharing of political power with its various non-Muslim ethnic groups.[4] Its postindependence political stability owes much to this unique mechanism of ethnic power sharing, which, while ensuring Malay political dominance, allows the overwhelmingly non-Muslim non-Malays to continue to outclass the Malays in educational and economic achievements.

In the face of the formidable challenge posed to nation building and national unity by its ethnic and religious pluralism and diversity, Malaysia's well-tested formula of political stability has consistently linked Malay political dominance to economic freedom for the non-Malays. In its ambition to bring about a more equitable distribution of economic wealth among its ethnic groups, in 1970 Malaysia's government adopted a national policy that calls for a Malay-bumiputera (indigenous people) ownership of 30 percent of the country's wealth within three decades. On the surface, the target appears to be within practical reach, but until now, when the end of the twentieth century deadline for its realization has already passed, the target continues to elude the nation's policy makers, strategists, and implementers.

According to the Economic Planning Unit (EPU) of the Prime Minister's Department, the Malays have managed so far to secure only 18.9 percent of the nation's wealth. But recently, a Center for Public Policy Study (CPPS) of the Asian Strategy and Leadership Institute (ASLI), a respected independent think tank, claims the Malays and other *bumiputeras* now own 45 percent of the Malaysian equity. Since the study's findings have great political implications, its revelation to the public has sparked an uproar that has not yet subsided, with Malay government leaders, including Abdullah Ahmad Badawi himself, and other politicians defending the EPU's figures and dismissing the study as being based on "wrong assumptions and methodology." Apparently under pressure, ASLI's president, Mirzan Mahathir, a son of former Premier Mahathir Mohamad, withdrew the study's report. The lead researcher and author of the report, a former academic, who is also CPPS's research director, resigned "as a matter of principle, because he disagreed with the ASLI hierarchy's conclusion on the matter."[5] Now that views for and against the study are posted both in the print and electronic media, the public is confused as to who is telling the truth.[6]

Regardless of which figures are nearer to the truth, there are serious implications for the United Malays National Organization (UMNO), the dominant partner in the ruling coalition, Barisan Nasional (BN). If ASLI's findings are true, then Abdullah and the UMNO leadership have the moral duty to reveal to the public which groups of Malays and *bumiputeras* now own the 45 percent of the national equity, since the majority of these ethnic groups are still the nation's poorest. If EPU's figures are correct, then the failure of the UMNO-led government to achieve the target could have far-reaching political and perhaps even religious consequences for the country. It would provide strong ammunition for the Malay opposition, mainly from the Islamic Party (PAS) and the People's Justice Party (Keadilan Rakyat) to criticize UMNO as an incompetent party to deliver economic justice to the Malays.

Up till now, Islam as a source of inspiration for the economic salvation of the Malays has received very little attention of a serious nature from the ethnic community's political, economic, and intellectual leaders, either in the mainstream national discourse on the Malay relative underachievement in economic performance or in the implementation of sizeable economic programs. Although various strategies tried to achieve the target—and are still failing, despite the many institutional facilities provided by the government[7]—it is likely that, in the coming decade, Islam will feature more prominently in the nation's perennial debate on the economic plight of the Malays. For a growing number of well-educated Malays, Islam is now seen as the last savior to deliver Malay economic goals.

Notwithstanding the domestic interethnic rivalry for the national wealth, and the significant fact that the politically dominant Malay-Muslims are losing the economic race to the non-Muslim communities, Malaysia as a nation is quite economically advanced. Next to political stability and interreligious peace, an impressive economic development is Malaysia's most widely known item of national pride and achievement. Malaysia can boast of a world-class infra-structure of economic development. It is the seventeenth largest trading nation in the world. It has joined the information technology age, not just as con-sumers but also as producers. It has even launched the Multi-Media Super Corridor (MSC), its answer to Silicon Valley.[8] Viewed by its critics as extrava-gant, the nation's new administrative capital, Putrajaya, just outside the old city of Kuala Lumpur, boasts of a fully electronic government. Malaysia today is easily the most electronically wired country in the Islamic world. Its national vision for the twenty-first century, popularly known by its Malay term "Wa-wasan 2020" (Vision 2020),[9] formulated when Mahathir was in power, har-bors the dream of becoming the "Japan of the Islamic world"[10] and thus joining the world club of most advanced nations.

In short, Malaysia has entered the twenty-first century with a clear vision, fully equipped with well-defined national goals and objectives. In many re-spects, especially in the economic and technological domain, it appears to have made the necessary preparations for meeting the challenges of the new century. In the political, cultural, and religious spheres, the nation's leaders are hoping that they can still bank on the same traditional formulas of political stability, interethnic and interreligious peace, which prove to have worked relatively well all these years, to help steer the nation through the challenges and uncertainties of the new century. Domestic critics of government policies, however, are far less optimistic. In their contention, the nation's interethnic and interreligious peace is fragile, and therefore it needs a real strengthening. They see long-standing problems emanating from issues of ethnicity and religiosity that have not yet been satisfactorily tackled. Some critics even maintain that, far from progressing, ethnic relations have actually deteriorated, as might be observed among students in the nationwide college and university campuses.

There is also the often-heard critique that, despite the fact that Malaysia has practiced Westminster-style parliamentary democracy for half-century, the quality of its democracy has not made any visible progress since Mahathir assumed power in 1981. On the contrary, critics argue that his authoritarian-style leadership has caused the country's democratic space to shrink to an unprecedented low.[11] When he voluntarily left office in 2002, many Malaysians entertained the hope that under his hand-picked successor, Abdullah Badawi, Malaysia would usher in a new era of political liberalization. After nearly four years at the nation's helm, Abdullah has received mixed reactions to his achievement thus far in democratization. Later in this chapter, I take a closer look at the prospects for further democratization in the post-Mahathir era.

In an age of American-dominated globalization, issues current and dear to American society are bound to either freely overflow or be exported to the rest of the world. The Muslim world has begun to feel and also to talk about the impact of American and other Western discourses on the pet subjects of democracy and democratization, women and minorities' rights, and religious freedom. In fact, the impact has been felt to a much greater degree in the aftermath of September 11, as many American and European interests groups energetically pursue their purportedly "transnational" discourses right to the capitals of the Muslim world. In Malaysia, as in many other Muslim countries, the traditionally influential position of Islam in society has inevitably dragged the religion deeper into these discourses.[12]

Both new and older, more-established, Muslim groups have been discoursing or debating with each other on the place and role of Islam in society in the new century, be it in relation to democracy, rights of women and minorities, or religious freedom in the context of a religiously plural society. But there is also the perennial issue of the relationship between Islam and the state that is indigenous to Malaysia.[13] In deeds, if not in words, silently but visibly, Abdullah has abandoned Mahathir's Islamization policy[14] and his "Malaysia is already an Islamic state" stance in favor of a new policy, popularly known as "Islam hadhari" (civilizational Islam).[15] Later I discuss some of the major issues that are now at the heart of the national discourse on Islam and examine the possible long-term effect that present responses to these issues could have on the development of Islam in the country.

An Evolving Fellowship of Believers: From Malay to Malaysian Islam?

There is no doubt in my mind that the shape and contours of Malaysian Islam in the next few decades is going to be largely determined by the outcome of the country's responses to the issues and challenges just outlined. In the final analysis, however, it is the overall response of the majority Muslim community that is going to prove decisive. The Malay community in particular—the majority ethnic group within the majority multiethnic Muslim community—which has been regularly monitoring new challenges to Islam, is now reading their pulse on a good number of national screens, especially on the religious, political, economic, sociocultural, and demographic ones.

To begin exploring possibilities in the future terrains of Islam in Malaysia within the next several decades, we can look at a presently emerging growth pattern in the Muslim community that makes it more truly multiethnic in its composition. This changing terrain in the general demographic landscape of Malaysia is a good introduction to a discussion of possibilities within Malaysian

Islam in the twenty-first century. According to the most recent national census, the Muslim percentage of the population has increased from 55 percent to nearly 60 percent since the 1980s. Several demographic trends, if left undisturbed, would point to an even bigger Muslim percentage by the end of the first decade of this century. The most important of these trends is a significantly higher Muslim birth rate that has been registered in contrast to the non-Muslim one. Two other trends are minor, but nonetheless these are contributory factors to the relatively higher growth of the Muslim population. One is the growing number of foreign Muslims residing in Malaysia, particularly workers from neighboring Indonesia, who have been granted citizenship during the past decades, when the country was forced to recruit a large labor force from neighboring countries to serve its fast expanding economy. The other is religious conversion to Islam.

Because of its many implications and growing significance for Malaysian pluralism, both religiously and politically, the issue of religious conversion is what attracts us here the most. Although numerically speaking, new conversion to Islam in Malaysia is nothing compared to its corresponding phenomenon in the United States, it has become more visible during the last two decades, bringing about gradual changes to the identity pattern of the Malaysian Muslim community. An increasing number of ethnic Chinese, Indians, and non-Malay *bumiputeras* have joined the community of believers in Islam. Significantly, many of these converts are young and highly educated professionals. Converts who are academics and intellectuals are still few, but their number is on the increase, with several of them now nationally acknowledged as experts on different aspects of Islam.

Somewhat surprising in the case of the young ethnic Chinese converts is the revelation that most of them had made the spiritual passage to Islam through Christianity, not directly from one of their traditional religions: Taoism, Confucianism, or Buddhism. Many factors influence conversion, but three stand out as the most important: marriage, appreciation of Islam through acquaintance and friendship with Muslims at work places, and appreciation of Islam either through personal study or through Muslim missionary works. In Malaysia, there is a good reason for marriage to feature prominently as a factor of conversion. Islamic law in the land requires anyone who wants to take a Muslim spouse to embrace Islam. There are no exceptions to the rule, even when the Qur'an itself takes a contrary stand. At least, the Qur'an allows a Muslim man to marry a Christian or a Jewish woman without her having to embrace Islam. Clearly, in this case, cultural tradition prevails over scriptural prescription.

In the long run, however, it is the changing non-Malay perception of Islam, largely favorable to the religion, which might prove the most decisive in influencing the emergence of a cross-ethnic Muslim community. Its significance can hardly be overemphasized. Ethnic and religious pluralism in Malaysia is of a peculiar kind. Until recent times, the identification of religion with race and ethnicity is almost complete: the Malays with Islam, the ethnic Chinese with the traditional Chinese religions, and the ethnic Indians with Hinduism. This sort of religious-ethnic identification was to have unfortunate consequences for the progress of the Muslim community in the country. The Malays tend to communalize Islam by equating their ethnic interests with the interests of the religion itself. Thus, they help fortify the non-Malay perception of Islam as a Malay religion. As for the non-Malays, given this misleading perception, they tend to view Malay underachievement in development as attributable to the teachings of Islam itself.

As an ethnic group far more advanced than the Malays in modern education, business, trade, and so on, the ethnic Chinese fail to see any good reason why they should show interest in a religion that has been identified culturally with "an inferior ethnic group." Traditionally, the ethnic Chinese attitude toward Malay Islam has been largely one of indifference rather than of hostility. Conversely, the Malay attitude toward ethnic Chinese culture has been perpetuated through a lot of misunderstanding of its real Islamic worth. For example, the Malays had condemned the use of chopsticks when eating as un-Islamic, when, in fact, the custom was merely unacceptable to traditional Malay culture. This sort of value judgment on ethnic Chinese culture in the name of Islam certainly did not help the Chinese community to have a favorable impression of Islam. Moreover, with educated and successful Chinese nowhere to be seen embracing the Islamic faith, the community becomes more convinced that the religion of Islam is not meant for them.

But many of the traditional cultural barriers separating the Malays from the non-Malays have been broken down, interestingly thanks largely to Malaysia's modernization. As a result, a new social and cultural climate has been created, conducive to a better understanding of Islam among the non-Malays. A changing perception of Islam within the non-Malay communities is now discernible, leaving in its wake the first visible demographic changes. The Islamic faith has broken new grounds in its ethnic distribution, registering a growing representation in each one of the country's ethnic groups. With these demographic changes, the identity pattern of the Malaysian Muslim community becomes transformed from one that was exclusively of Malay ethnicity in character to one that is increasingly multiethnic.

One important factor that could help explain the changing perception of Islam within the non-Muslim communities during the last few decades is the worldwide Islamic resurgence that began in the 1970s. Non-Muslims in

Malaysia had their first major exposure to Islam through both national and international media coverage of events and personalities of the decade, relating primarily to political Islam but quite often also to Islam the religion and its history, culture, and civilization. Within Malaysia of the 1970s, two nongovernmental organizations (NGOs) had been more helpful than any other national organization in projecting a favorable impression of Islam to the non-Muslim communities. These were the Muslim Youth Movement of Malaysia (ABIM) and the National Awareness Current (ALIRAN), founded by Anwar Ibrahim and Chandra Muzaffar, respectively, two young, intellectual activists who were later to have an even greater visibility on the national and international stages.

ABIM and ALIRAN were instrumental in initiating and popularizing discourses on Islamic universalism and its relevance to plural societies, especially in colleges and universities.[16] For example, Anwar's presidential address to ABIM's 1977 annual conference was devoted to the theme of universal Islam as a major source of ideas and values for solving the delicate problems of Malaysia's ethnic and religious diversity and pluralism.[17] Attended by top political, religious, and youth leaders of the non-Muslim communities, the high-profile conference was indicative of their enthusiastic response to Anwar's exposition of the theme, as well as ABIM's dedicated work at reaching out to those communities. Widely viewed as an unprecedented move in Malaysia's history of interethnic relations, the conference, and Anwar's speech in particular, represented a bold departure from the kind of communal Islam with which both Malays and non-Malays have been acquainted for so long. To our knowledge, ABIM made a significant contribution toward a better perception of Islam among the non-Malays in the decades of the 1970s and 1980s, although its details remain to be studied.

Chandra, a Hindu convert to Islam, and his ALIRAN colleagues have sought through their writings and speeches to secure a space for Islamic universalism by criticizing both "Malayism" and "bumiputeraism,"[18] which they claimed could hardly be defended from the Islamic point of view. Chandra has proved to be an effective communicator of the universal message of Islam to the non-Malay audience, especially the educated groups.

Another important factor that positively influenced the non-Malay perception of Islam is the Malay involvement in interreligious dialogues. These dialogues help non-Muslims better understand Islam's attitudes toward other religions, providing evidence that Islam is an inclusive religion, far more than they had previously thought. A major breakthrough in Malaysian interreligious and intercultural dialogues occurred in March 1995, when the University of Malaya organized an international seminar on Islam and Confucianism.[19] The seminar was well attended, with a good representation from the Malay and Chinese communities. With excellent media coverage, thanks to its patronization by Anwar, who was then the second most powerful man in the country, the issue of Islam and Confucianism became a major topic of conversation in the country. The Malay organizers of the historic event had justified it on the basis of a new vision and understanding of Islam. Many Chinese responded in kind to the Malay initiative, welcoming the latter's new openness toward their religions and cultural heritage as a significant departure from the traditional position of communal Islam.

Yet another factor that must have influenced many Chinese to reassess their perception of Islam was the regular broadcast of Islamic religious programs in the Chinese language on government-controlled radio and television channels. Under Mahathir's Islamization policy, such programs had been intensified. These programs, featuring Chinese Muslim speakers, locals as well as guests specifically brought from China, proved effective in convincing the ethnic Chinese community that Islam is not just a Malay religion. What is more, they have come to realize that millions of Chinese outside Malaysia are believers in Islam. The message to them is clear: a Chinese could be a Muslim while remaining proud of his or her own ethnic culture, which is contrary to the hitherto popular perception that an ethnic Chinese who wishes to convert to Islam has to embrace Malay culture and custom as well. Religious and cultural contacts between Malaysia and Chinese Muslims in China have been on the increase since the 1990s. Private colleges and universities in Malaysia, including the well-known International Islamic University in Gombak, are now hosts to a growing number of Muslim students from China.

Now that non-Malay Muslims themselves are propagating Islam in their own ethnic communities, not to mention other favorable factors, one could expect to see a continuing expansion of the non-Malay component of the Malaysian *ummah*. For example, ethnic Chinese Muslims are getting better organized around the few small organizations they had established with the view of catering to the general welfare of their respective members,[20] as well as spreading the Islamic faith among the larger Chinese community. Although non-Malay Muslims still constitute a minority within their respective ethnic communities,[21] they have already made their presence felt in various ways, including in politics, business, and education. Even if conversion to the faith stays at the present rate into the coming decades, we could be witnessing the historic evolution of a Muslim community that is largely Malay in its ethnic composition and character into a multiethnic Muslim community that is more reflective of Malaysia's pluralistic character and more inclined to taking a noncommunal and universal approach to the country's ethnic and religious problems.

As a small minority living in a majority Muslim country in which ethnic consciousness is rather strong, non-Malay Muslims have to struggle hard to live as believers in the Islamic faith and as an integral part of mainstream Malaysian Islam, while yet proudly retaining their respective ethnic identities.[22] Fortunately, partly thanks to the new Malay openness in their general attitudes toward other cultures and religions, invaluable help and understanding is coming from various Malay-dominated organizations representing mainstream Islam. These organizations, such as ABIM, the Islamic Party (PAS), and the Malaysian Islamic Welfare Association (PERKIM), have opened their doors wide to non-Malay Muslims, especially new converts, to fully participate in their wide range of Islamic activities.

ABIM has succeeded in enlisting the services of non-Malay Muslim members to run and expand the interfaith activities of its Islamic outreach, which has been specifically established to explain Islam to the non-Muslim communities. As for PAS, its interest in securing a significant non-Malay Muslim membership has been motivated by its political strategy to portray itself as a Muslim political party with a new image that is both noncommunal and pro-pluralism. This strategy is also aimed at garnering political support among non-Malay voters. Toward that end, it had recruited Chinese Muslims as its members, with a few of them having run for political office through general elections at both state and federal levels.

One successful candidate from this closely watched group, Anuar Tan, is now a familiar figure both in PAS and on the national political scene. At the time of this writing, he is in his second term of service as a member of the PAS-led state cabinet running the state of Kelantan, the sole opposition-controlled state in Malaysia. Another Chinese Muslim, Kamal Koh, did not succeed in his candidature, but he has been made a member of the party's national leadership committee. An even more radical departure from its traditional party policy is its intention to invite non-Muslims to become associate members of the party. All these strategic moves by PAS, especially the high-profile role given to several of its Chinese Muslim members, have enabled it to score a psychological victory over UMNO, insofar as it deprives the latter of ammunition to continuously portray it as a political party incapable of working together with non-Malays.

Religious Conversion and Muslim Apostasy: The New Challenge

There is perhaps no other nation on earth where religious conversion to, or apostasy from, Islam could have such a major influence on interethnic relations as in Malaysia. Undoubtedly, the multidimensional effect of religious conversion in Malaysia has a lot to do with the country's peculiarly complex pattern of intertwining of ethnicity, religiosity, and power structure. The existing state structure was erected half -century ago on the basis of Malay political dominance. Malays have always dominated the country's multiethnic ruling coalition. Their religion, Islam, is the state religion, which, in the postcolonial period, has exercised an increasingly influential role in the public sphere.

The most fateful decision ever made in the foundation of the Malaysian state—at least from the point of view of its effect on the collective Malay stand on apostasy from Islam—was perhaps the complete identification of Malay ethnicity with Islam. The federal constitution defines "Malay" as a person "who professes the religion of Islam, habitually speaks the Malay language, [and] conforms to Malay custom."[23] Although this definition establishes and ensures an inextricable link between Islam and Malay ethnic identity, it would be incorrect, as some have maintained, to view this link as having originated with the constitution. The link had been fostered centuries earlier, dating back to the early Malay responses to European colonialism and imperialism in the region in the sixteenth century.[24] It is an entrenched belief in the modern Malay-Muslim consciousness that the Malays as a race and Islam as a religion have been destined to be mutual protectors. This close identification of religion with race has been both a source of strength and a source of weakness of Malaysian Islam.

Islam has helped the Malays forge a united front against colonialism and confront challenges posed to their postcolonial political dominance by pluralism, which is itself a product of Western colonialism. But this same phenomenon of ethnic and religious pluralism is now posing new challenges to the traditional political doctrine of identification of Malay ethnicity with Islam. One of these new challenges is the extremely small but increasing number of Malay-Muslim apostasy cases in recent years, which has raised considerable alarm in the Malay-Muslim community. Reactions from various segments of the community range from calls on the government to implement the *hudood* law on apostasy, which brings the death penalty, so as to discourage it, to attempts to raise the community's awareness of the dangers of apostasy to Malay-Muslim political power.

Another new challenge is the increasing uneasiness of non-Muslims with the phenomenal rise of conversions to Islam. Arguing that such conversions have often resulted in family disputes, breakups, and dislocations, especially when the convert at the time of conversion is legally married with young children but with the spouse refusing to go along with the conversion, non-Muslim organizations and community leaders have pressured the government to institute new laws to help spare non-Muslim families of converts from being burdened with unfavorable consequences of conversion. Many Muslims, however, see such moves by non-Muslim religious leaders as a clear attempt to make conversion to Islam more difficult. It is understandable that many Malaysians are increasingly worried about the interreligious feud that has begun to build up around the issue of religious conversion.

The problem is that religious conversion is on the rise. It is expected to be even more widespread in the days ahead. Living in a multireligious society like Malaysia, one is always open to the influence of religions other than one's own. Increased social interactions in the last three decades have led Malaysians to a greater awareness of each other's religious beliefs and customs. Such interactions have led to an increase in interethnic marriages and, consequently, religious conversions. For various reasons, however, particularly the strict Muslim views on apostasy and the legal provisions on mixed marriages that require non-Muslims to convert to Islam before they can take Muslim spouses, more Malaysians are entering than leaving Islam through such avenues.

If religious conversion of one individual could easily lead to societal tension with the possibility of even escalating into an open ethnic or interreligious conflict, it is because in Malaysia it is never simply viewed as a private matter between the individual convert and God. It also has a communal dimension that happens to be far more expressive in the Malaysian interfaith setting than anywhere else in the world. What is more, the legal dimension involves the state, through its administrative powers that govern religious conversions.

Issues arising from religious conversion have already proved to be sensitive and controversial, as well as difficult for the government to deal with to the satisfaction of all religious groups. These issues could strain ethnic and interreligious relations to the point of erupting into open sectarian conflicts. Both sides of the religious divide, Muslims and non-Muslims, have resorted to legal means and invoked the constitution to strengthen their respective positions on a wide range of issues pertaining to the place and role of Islam in relation to other religions and non-Muslim communities.[25] An open debate on these issues, which the government has recently suppressed, could even have the potential of causing cracks in the foundational structure of the country's pluralism, as recent controversies on constitutional matters pertaining to the respective jurisdictions of the civil and Sharia courts have amply demonstrated.

The state reacted to the religious controversy by suppressing public debates, but this official act alone could not help resolve the burning controversy. The role of the state in Islamic matters is extensive, but little explanation is offered to the non-Muslim public by the Muslim religious establishment on why the former has to accept this role and its implications for the life of non-Muslims. The nature and extent of state involvement in matters pertaining to the religion of Islam—not just religious conversion—appears to be both unique and potentially explosive. The judiciary has been structured to branch out into two distinct legal systems; one the Sharia and the other civil. The Sharia and civil courts are supposed to be mutually exclusive in their jurisdictions, with neither being able to claim superiority over the other. The Sharia courts administer Islamic laws; the civil courts, civil laws. This sort of legal arrangement put in place by a 1988 amendment to the federal constitution is both religiously and politically motivated.[26] It seeks to provide religious appeasement to the Muslim community, who, prior to the constitutional amendment, had long been disillusioned with the frequent decisions by the highest civil courts to overrule Sharia court rulings.

Muslims see interference by the supreme (civil) courts as acts of blatant disregard of their religious sensitivities and as a deliberate attempt to perpetuate the British colonial policy of subordinating Sharia courts to civil courts. Delightedly, they view the amendment as the fruit of a long struggle to secure a rightful and respectable place for Islamic laws and the Sharia court system in compatibility with the position of Islam as the official religion of the country. Understandably, they take seriously any attempt, especially by non-Muslim quarters, to revert to the pre-1988 legal status of the Sharia and civil courts.

The separate yet seemingly equal powers of the two court systems also seek to appease the non-Muslim communities, who do not want to live under the rule of the Sharia. Under the existing legal system, non-Muslims enjoy immunity from prosecution by a Sharia court if and when they are a party to a wrongdoing under Sharia law, in which case only the Muslim party is prosecuted.

Muslims seek to protect their religious interests through the Sharia courts, non-Muslims through the civil. But as recent debates have shown, as Malaysians begin to examine more deeply the interreligious issues that divide them, they have come to realize that the jurisdictional boundaries of the civil and Sharia courts are by no means clear. In theory, the constitution posits an equal status but separate powers for the two court systems. In practice, however, there have emerged new legal issues from the religious conversion controversy that point to the need for collaboration between the two court systems. Even though an absolute separation between them is simply impracticable, legal authorities and experts insist on identifying all legal issues as falling under the jurisdiction of either court but not of both. It now remains to be seen whether there is enough wisdom and courage in the country to deal with this new chapter in the history of conflicts between secular and religious laws by exploring the possibility of a common jurisdiction instead of affirming two mutually exclusive legal domains.

Malaysian Political Islam in the Post-Mahathir
Era: Trends and Possibilities

We define political Islam as that aspect of Islam that has to do with political
ideas, values, practices, and culture, including institutions. Political Islam may
be either directly connected to the religion of Islam or to Muslim political
history. In trying to predict the future of political Islam in Malaysia, we have to
rely on empirical facts pertaining to Malaysian politics. However, there are
empirical political facts that are transient in nature and that refer to just passing
phenomena. Then there are political facts that are more enduring in nature.
This latter category helps us better foretell a state's political future.

After more than twenty-two years in power, Mahathir voluntarily resigned
as prime minster of Malaysia on October 1, 2003. He was Malaysia's longest-
serving prime minister and also one of the best-known political leaders of the
Muslim world since the late 1980s.[27] With his exit from the corridors of power,
Malaysia enters a new political phase. In this new phase, a key role will be played
by the new prime minister, Abdullah Badawi, who, even in his first few months
in office, was already seen to be moving away from his predecessor's policies. He
has since then departed further and further away from his former boss, not only
in style and approaches but also in policies, so much so that the latter has
"disowned" him as his successor. Mahathir has publicly expressed his great
regret for choosing Abdullah as his successor, sidestepping Najib Tun Abdul
Razak, the current deputy prime minister, who has emerged as the most vocal
critic of Abdullah's policies. Abdullah justified his leadership by invoking the
strong mandate he received from the electorate in the elections of March 2004.

Since Mahathir's departure, there has been a great deal of discussion in
Malaysian political circles regarding limits on the prime minister's terms.
Many believe that the prime minister should serve only for two terms., and it
may be that the idea of term limits will translate into law. The real opinion that
counts in Malaysian politics is that of UMNO, however. Regardless of the
opinions of groups outside of UMNO, including its partners in BN, the outcome of any proposal on term limits will depend on Abdullah's own stand
on the matter. At the moment, Abdullah has not given any indication of his
inclination. What looks certain is that he will again lead UMNO and BN into the
next general elections, which must be held at the latest by 2008, to secure his
second-term mandate from voters. He is expected to easily win the elections,
albeit perhaps with a reduced majority.

In the post-Mahathir era—under Abdullah, as well as beyond—there are
strong reasons to believe that Islam will continue to be the most powerful and

most influential ideological force in Malaysia's political life. Political Islam is not going to lose much of its appeal, just because Abdullah and his administration, with the full backing of his state-controlled media, have diverted the national attention from "Islamic state" issues to his brand of civilizational Islam ("Islam hadhari"). Political Islam in the sense we have defined is not a fringe or peripheral political force. Rather, it has been part of mainstream Malay-Muslim politics for a long time, even during the British colonial period. Importantly, political teachings in the Qur'an and the prophetic hadiths will always be there to remind Muslims of the inseparable link between religion and politics. Furthermore, Malay political Islam has been dynamic—able to adapt to changing situations by taking on new forms and in the postindependence period to adjust to the requirements of a "pluralistic and democratic" political order.

The question, then, is not whether political Islam will emerge as a central force—since it is already so—but, rather, what shape will it take and how will it change in the coming years? How will the various domestic and international factors influence the shaping of political Islam in the context of Malaysian politics? UMNO's political Islam has been evolving through the decades of independence, just as PAS's political Islam has also been changing. For example, political Islam as pursued by Mahathir was certainly different from that accommodated by the three prime ministers before him (Tunku Abdul Rahman, Tun Abdul Razak, and Tun Hussein Onn).[28] Under Abdullah, a new Islam policy has been put in place. His "Islam hadhari" (civilizational Islam) policy deemphasizes the idea of an Islamic state, thus rejecting both Mahathir's Islamic state and PAS's version of it.

Why Political Islam Will Remain a Central Force

The continuing centrality of political Islam, first of all, may be inferred from both demographic and historical facts. Malay-Muslims who form the majority of the country's population would appeal to both facts in justifying their traditional position as the backbone of Malaysian politics. The first argument favoring Malaysian political Islam's persisting dominance is demographic. Demographic trends point to a bigger Muslim percentage of the population in Malaysian democracy, and demographic strength is translatable into political capital. Reacting to this development, as if sensing its political significance beyond Malaysia's borders, a Singaporean newspaper expressed in an editorial the concern that, with the growing Muslim population, support for the opposition Islamic Party (PAS) and its goal to turn Malaysia into an Islamic state is likely to increase. The opposition Chinese-dominated Democratic Action Party (DAP) has reacted to the swelling Muslim majority with similar sentiment. But such reactions appear to have been hasty. In the March 2004 general elections, the majority of first-time young Malay voters rejected PAS in favor of UMNO. One clear message from the election results is this: a significant increase in the numerical superiority of Malay-Muslims in the ballot box does not necessarily translate into support for PAS's vision of an Islamic state.

UMNO's electoral victory over PAS may be interpreted as the Malays' rejection of the latter's Islamic state agenda, but certainly not the defeat of political Islam. Rather, it should be seen as the victory of one brand of Malay political Islam over another. As earlier asserted, both parties are committed to their respective brands of political Islam. Ever since parliamentary elections were held in Malaysia in 1955, the Malay-Muslim electorate has been presented with the choice of settling for either UMNO's Islamic agenda or that of PAS. While both are committed to defending Islam as the official religion of the country, they emphasize and promise to deliver different Islamic programs for the Muslim community. PAS emphasizes the total implementation of Islamic law, and UMNO emphasizes physical and economic development and its greater creditability to govern a pluralistic Malaysia. In defending their respective brands of political Islam, both try their level best to find support in the teachings of the religion.

Another argument is historical. Because postindependence governments have been Malay-dominated until now, is it possible that a change in the ethnic makeup of the government would result in a new balance of power within the next ten years? Is it possible that, instead of the government continuing to be Malay-dominated, members of other ethnic groups could secure the highest political positions in the country, either as prime minister or deputy prime minister? The possibility of such change is premised on nonpolitical factors, which are not likely to materialize in the near future. Moreover, it is difficult to see how, with so many interests at stake, UMNO could allow that to happen as long as it remains in power. And PAS would also not allow it to happen, except for appointing non-Malays who are Muslims to the highest political posts.

While the traditional Malay political dominance is expected to survive for a still-considerable period of time, political realignments among the ethnic-based political parties might occur, especially if PAS succeeds in capturing more states. In other words, Islam as a political force is unlikely to vacate its center stage position, but the shape of Islamic politics and the rules of the political game may undergo significant changes. Even in the multiracial Peoples Justice Party (PKR) headed by Wan Azizah, Anwar Ibrahim's wife, we can expect Islam's influence to be considerable, though it is still not clear what the precise shape of this influence would be. Anwar's position as the party's chief advisor, his charisma and his well-known Islamic inclinations, all would help guarantee that influence. It is true, however, that at the moment, the party does not have a clear-cut Islam policy specifically packaged for public consumption. Many of Anwar's "Islamist" supporters outside the party are wondering how he is going to translate his Islamic ideals into a pragmatic political agenda and programs for his multiethnic and multireligious party.

Malaysian political realities would demand him, sooner or later, to articulate his Islam policy that would distinguish the party from both UMNO and PAS. In other words, PKR needs to have its own brand of political Islam to outwit the political Islam of UMNO and PAS. Anwar is known to be critical of PAS's Islamic state and its legalistic approach through *hudood* laws to solve social problems. He is also critical of Abdullah's "Islam hadhari" policy, not in its principles but because of government practices that he sees as blatantly contradictory to the core teachings of Islam.[29] For him, justice and anticorruption are the pillars of Islamic sociopolitical teachings. He sees no point in preaching about "Islam hadhari," if issues of social justice and corruption are not seriously discussed and resolved. Judging from his political speeches since his release from jail, one could say that he is leading PKR to embrace an Islam policy that would emphasize social justice (especially for the poor), anticorruption, and the virtues of democracy and civil society. He had an impeccable track record in championing all these issues. After all, he was jailed twice for speaking forcefully and leading street demonstrations against poverty and corruption in high places. Young voters may well be drawn to his brand of political Islam.

The final argument considered here is derived from the special character of Malay Islam. The destiny of the Malay identity is too closely tied up to religion, ethnicity, and the country's entrenched political institutions—both traditional, such as the monarchy, and modern. In consequence, political Islam is deeply structured in Malaysian sociopolitical life, thus guaranteeing its enduring influence. The two major characteristics that define Malay Islam are "Malayness" and a particular interpretation of Islam based on Sunni theology and the Shafi'i legal school of thought. For many Malays, race prevails over religion. Still, Islam is considered to be an important component of Malay identity since it defines and strengthens that identity. The Malay sense of belonging to a community is nurtured by their attachment to Islam, but the strong Malay ethnic consciousness also means that the Malays can be quite selective in their understanding and appreciation of Islam, thus preferring Islamic expressions that conform to the Malay psyche.

Despite the emergence of numerous civil rights groups and NGOs that argue for a universal rather than an ethnic approach to Islam and a multiracial

Malaysian politics, the dominant Malay mindset continues to favor a politics based on the marriage between ethnic "nationalism" and religion (Islam). This partly explains Abdullah's appeal to many Malays. In traditional Malay eyes, he is seen as a pious and devout Muslim, yet he is also regarded as a Malay nationalist loyal to Malay interests. He is surrounded by advisors who strongly believe in Malay political supremacy and a "moderate" brand of Islam, a factor that helped him become prime minister and win a resounding victory in the last general elections at the expense of PAS's political Islam.

What can best guarantee the continuing vitality of political Islam into the foreseeable future is the close intertwining of ethnicity and religiosity in the Malay identity. The pre-independence historical fact of this intertwining became enshrined in the constitution with independence. For both UMNO and PAS, the constitutional definition of Malay in Islamic terms has become a source of legitimacy and one of the pillars of their respective brands of political Islam.

Malay Political Islam: Stability and Change

Traditionally, Malay Islam manifests itself in politics mainly in the form of two political parties: UMNO and PAS. This has been the case since 1957. Structurally, this implies that political Islam in Malaysia has reached a certain level of maturity and stability. Within the Malay political universe, since 1957, Malays have known only a two-party system, and we do not foresee that this will change in the near future. Of course, since 1957, these two parties have produced offshoots, but they were marginal parties that did not survive. Good examples are Barisan Jemaah Islamiah Se-Malaysia (BERJASA), a breakaway from PAS, and Semangat 46 ("The Spirit of 46"), a breakaway from UMNO. A new political party that may yet break the postindependence Malay political tradition is PKR, which came into existence following Anwar's imprisonment by Mahathir in 1998. PKR has grown from being basically a political party of his former supporters in UMNO dedicated to keeping alive his political struggle and freeing him from prison to a more broad-based one.[30] With the party almost wiped out in the last elections, except for Wan Azizah's parliamentary seats—after many of its members returned to the fold of UMNO—many political observers predict the party will not survive. But others believe it is premature to write off PKR. They have a point. With Anwar now practically leading the party in his capacity as its advisor,[31] it has found a new surge of confidence and energy to face the coming general elections with better performance. But then, unlike UMNO and PAS, although Malay dominated, PKR is multiethnic and multireligious.

The fact remains that the political choices for most Malays continue to be limited to either UMNO or PAS. Most of the time, the majority of the Malays have given their support to UMNO. But when they have deep reasons to be disillusioned with UMNO's leadership, they tend to flock to PAS. This was the case in the 1969 elections, when Malays were disillusioned with Tunku Abdul Rahman's leadership, and in the 1999 elections, with Mahathir over the sacking of the popular Anwar as deputy prime minister and his expulsion from UMNO. Abdullah's resounding victory in the recent elections shows that most Malays have gone back to UMNO to give him a strong mandate to chart a new course for Malaysia, especially for Islam. It looks like the decades-old structure of Malay political Islam is not going to see any major change in the coming decade.

The historical developments of UMNO and PAS have shown that outside influences have often led to major changes within the respective parties. For example, PAS, which since its inception has been professing a political Islam that is wedded to ethnic nationalism, was deeply influenced by the Iranian revolution. It began to embrace the idea of the rule of the ulama. For nearly two decades, it was able to some extent to put the idea into practice, because it had leaders who were acceptable to members from among the ulama. After the death in 2002 of its former president, Fadzil Nor, however, the party faced a leadership crisis. In the 2003 party elections, while Hadi Awang, an ulama, was unanimously elected president to succeed Fadzil, PAS faced difficulty in finding someone from the rank of the ulama who was widely acceptable to become the number two leader. For the deputy leader's position, the party found itself in a dilemma whether to choose a popular and able candidate who comes from a secular background and therefore go against the party principle of the rule of the cleric, or to stand by the principle and settle for a candidate from the ulama but with "lesser leadership" qualities. Although the victory went to the ulama, generally viewed as more "progressive" than their predecessors, the party election results have revealed deep divisions within the party on the issue of the ulama leadership that throw doubt on the survival of the principle. PAS's poor showing in the last elections has undoubtedly placed the idea of ulama leadership under closer scrutiny by members, especially from the Western educated and professional groups.

The 2004 general elections results failed to generate any new realignment of non-Malay political forces that would influence Malay political Islam in any significant way. The only political development worthy of mention was the proposal by the Chinese-dominated DAP, which has ousted PAS as the biggest opposition group in parliament with twelve seats, for a merger with PKR. One of the grounds for merger, as cited by the DAP leader, Lim Kit Siang, was the need to stem the tide of political Islam and reaffirm Malaysia's secular democracy. Strong opposition from within both parties forced the merger proposal to be abandoned quickly.

Outside the domain of the political parties, however, some NGOs and cultural groups may have a significant degree of influence in shaping Malaysian politics in general and political Islam in particular. Both UMNO and PAS are well aware of the fact that each of them needs the support of such groups to strengthen its political power. Both parties know that they cannot be and remain in power without the cooperation of non-Muslim or non-Malay political parties and the support of the non-Muslim communities. More than UMNO, PAS is now under strong pressure to build new bridges to the non-Muslim communities. PKR's adoption of democracy, civil society, and social justice as its major platforms has brought it into a close rapport with civil society groups and NGOS.

The Near Future of Malaysian Islam: The Abdullah Badawi Factor

In the rest of the first decade in this century, it is a safe bet to claim that the pace of development of Malaysian Islam would be very much in the hands of Abdullah. Despite growing criticism of his style of leadership as "slow and indecisive" from many quarters, not least from Mahathir, Abdullah is still enjoying his reputation as "Mr. Clean" and his public image as a "good and moderate Muslim." But this aside, it is not easy to portray his real religious outlook, categorizing him as either a traditionalist or a modernist.

He had given some hints about his own religious inclination. Shortly after Mahathir stepped down, Abdullah, a graduate in Islamic studies, was asked in an interview about influences on his religious thought and life. Interestingly, he named al-Ghazzali (d. IIII) and al-Shafi'i (d. 820) as two Muslim religious scholars of the past who have inspired and influenced him most in his understanding and practice of Islam. Since these two scholars also happen to be the most respected by the Malay-Muslim community, Abdullah was probably sending a message to the community that he is a defender of traditional Malay Islam and the true ulama. To appreciate this particular stance of Abdullah toward Islam, we need only to remind ourselves of the fact that Mahathir alienated a large segment of the Malay-Muslim community because of his frequent criticism of the ulama, both past and present. But Abdullah was also directing his message to PAS, which, under the influence of the Iranian Islamic revolution, has been championing the political rule of the ulama, albeit in a Sunni context. By identifying himself with al-Ghazzali and Imam al-Shafi'i, Abdullah is telling the Malays these are the true ulama they should revere, not those of the kind of "propagandists of political Islam" whom PAS holds dear.

If Abdullah's long-term strategic goal on Islam is indeed to deemphasize fundamentalist and modernist political Islam among the Malays in favor of a more traditionalist political Islam, then his choice of religious advisors and core intellectual supporters seems to be consistent with that goal. The kind of Islamic minds he has brought into his confidence, and whom he has entrusted with the task of popularizing and implementing his Islam hadhari vision, may best be described as traditionalists and modernists belonging to what movement-oriented Muslim groups would regard as the politically conservative or conformist groups.

But there is another dimension of Abdullah's vision of Islam. While wooing the traditional Malay ulama who are opposed to the PAS brand of political Islam, he is also affirming his commitment to a "modern and progressive Islam." In asserting this kind of Islam, he has the support of intellectual activists like Chandra Muzaffar and the small but influential group of Muslim women human rights activists, the Sisters in Islam (SIS).[32] With his first term in office soon coming to an end, Malaysians are yet to see how his "two faces" of Islam—the cultural and legalistic Islam supported by the conservatives; and the modern, liberal, and progressive Islam supported by the secular educated activists—find reconciliation under his leadership.

A widely perceived problem afflicting Abdullah's Islam policy is its lack of direction, dynamism, and coordination. "Islam hadhari" is supposed to be a government policy, but in practice it does not appear to be one. The ten principles of "Islam hadhari" have been formulated and disseminated to the public, but their clear explanations are still forthcoming.[33] If we go by media coverage, then "the two Abdullahs" seem to be the only cabinet ministers talking about the subject.[34] Even the prime minister is seen as propagating the virtues of his "Islam hadhari" more widely outside Malaysia than inside the country. Critics, including those from UMNO, believe it was a mistake for Abdullah to give the job of overseeing the implementation of "Islam hadhari" policy to the Department of Islamic Development (JAKIM) within the Prime Minister's Department, a government agency noted for its bureaucratic practices.

In the March 2004 general elections, many of Abdullah's pro-Islam supporters were countering the PAS Islamic state agenda with the "Islam hadhari." Many believed "Islam hadhari" has contributed to his success in recovering the Malay support lost to the opposition in the previous general elections. But it is now questionable whether its appeal to the Muslim electorate is as strong as it was before. It looks like, in his battle for a second term in office, Abdullah has to bank on what survives of his greatest asset—namely, his image of a "good Muslim." Undoubtedly, in the last national polls, his moderate religious views proved to be appealing to ordinary Malays. There was then an extensive play of religious symbols by the government-controlled media, such as television coverage of Abdullah leading congregational prayers. It significantly affected the average Malay perception of his leadership, a fact that even PAS itself has acknowledged. We can expect a replay of such religious symbols favoring Abdullah. PAS may have lost badly in the last elections, but there are plenty of reasons to believe that UMNO and PAS will continue to be locked in a fierce political battle in which both sides would appeal to religion to gain public support.

Conclusion: The Future of Malaysian Islam

Abdullah's triumph at the 2004 polls has led some political commentators to prematurely predict the demise of political Islam in Malaysia and the decline of PAS as an Islamic political party. PAS's brand of political Islam may have fared worse in the 2004 than in the 1999 elections in terms of total electoral seats won, but the party has managed to increase its share of popular votes. In 1999, it was already regarded as having performed relatively well. PAS remains a formidable challenge to UMNO. This means UMNO has to energize its own brand of political Islam if it is to check new advances by PAS. We can therefore expect the debate on political Islam and the Islamic state to continue in the years to come. Critics of UMNO's victory have made the observation that, considering the various factors engineered to favor the ruling party, PAS, as a matter of fact, has not really lost support among the Malays. One of these factors was the redrawing of parliamentary and state constituencies that PAS in particular had criticized before the elections as deliberately intended to minimize its chance of retaining the seats it has held. The redrawing of constituency boundaries saw the creation of new safe seats for UMNO and the incorporation of non-Muslim voters into PAS strongholds that made it difficult for the opposition party to defend its seats.

PAS and the rest of the opposition directed their wrath at the Election Commission for what they perceived as its bias toward the ruling party, not only in its redrawing of constituencies but also in its conduct of the elections. Indeed, PAS and PKR refused to endorse the election results for the whole country after alleging widespread irregularities and foul play in the election process. They submitted a memorandum to the king asking for the formation of an independent royal commission of inquiry to probe the allegations. While the DAP demanded a fresh election for the state of Selangor, PAS and PKR demanded it for the entire country. As expected, Abdullah rejected the opposition demand for an independent inquiry. In light of their disgust at the conduct of the last general elections, we can expect the opposition to be putting more attention on the issue of the Malaysian democratic process, especially the issue of the independence of the Election Commission.

If the 1999 swing of voters to the Malay opposition and the 2004 swing back to UMNO signal the emergence of a new attitudinal pattern among independent and first-time voters, then in the coming decade we may see a greater fluidity in party preferences that will make Malaysian elections less predictable. What this means is that certain assumptions about voting tendencies, which proved to be true in the past, may no longer hold true in future elections. Abdullah cannot take for granted that his last big victory points to the Malays' ideological rejection of PAS's brand of political Islam, including its Islamic state project, and therefore he cannot ignore the issue altogether.

Abdullah is also facing a formidable challenge from Anwar's PKR. Anwar has been harping on the issues of rampant corruption, lack of democratization, civil society, and social justice. He is a master strategist at forging political alliances and striking rapport with the voters. He is expected to cement differences among the opposition parties and strengthen the Alternative Front (BA) in preparation for the coming polls. Even with the unmatched resources at their disposal, Abdullah and his BN will find the opposition this time around a much stronger foe. What Abdullah needs to do is to explain well to the public that his Islam hadhari is the best Islam policy for Malaysia. He has to convince voters that through his Islam hadhari he is able to provide satisfactory answers to many of the issues raised by the opposition.

Another development to watch in the area of political discourse on Islam in Malaysia is the kind of non-Muslim responses to political Islam that would emerge. In the last general elections, Chinese voters had put back into parliament well-known opposition figures such as Lim Kit Siang and Karpal Singh, because they wanted them to help check the tide of political Islam in the country. The two political veterans are well known for their rejection of the Islamic state, of both the PAS and UMNO types. Most Malays do not like to see non-Muslims participating in discourses on Islam. But the two veterans have shown they are ready to discourse on Islam whenever they feel that Islamic initiatives—whether coming from UMNO or PAS—are going to affect the lives of non-Muslims.

Will Abdullah tolerate or even encourage a freer public discourse on Islam in which non-Muslims can participate, at least on matters directly affecting them? Thus far, we have not seen encouraging signs. On the contrary, there are reasons for despair. Recently, the government suppressed public discussions of constitutional issues relating to Islam and other religious issues deemed sensitive, citing interreligious peace and public security as its justification. The suppression invited mixed receptions from the public. The majority of Malaysians, particularly Muslims, supported the move, but liberals and human rights groups criticized it, viewing the move as a deprivation of their democratic rights to freely discuss issues of individual religions. Abdullah is known to favor a controlled interreligious dialogue instead of open discussions of religious issues. A recent statement issued by the Prime Minister's Department insists such dialogues must be under the supervision of government authorities.

As expected, Abdullah has also given clear indications that he would be focusing more on human development and domestic issues like agriculture rather than on taking a more visible role in international politics. A major criticism of Mahathir's administration is that, though he was rather successful in modernizing Malaysia's economy, he had neglected human development issues, including issues of human rights, intellectual freedom, and liberty. Abdullah's major challenge is how to honor promises he had made after taking office, in regard to human development, while maintaining a growing economy, eradication of corruption, and the betterment of Malaysian democracy. On issues of corruption and democracy, the opposition political parties, as well as various independent groups, are far from being impressed with his performance, despite some encouraging signs. It seems a new era of democratization in Malaysia is still in the waiting.

NOTES

1. For a good introductory account of the place and role of Islam in Malaysian foreign policy since the 1970s, see Shanti Nair, *Islam in Malaysian Foreign Policy* (London: Routledge, 1997). On Mahathir's championing of global Muslim interests, see Mohamad Mahathir, *Islam and the Muslim Ummah* (Subang Jaya: Pelanduk, 2000).

2. On Malaysia's relations with the worldwide Muslim *ummah*, apart from the above-cited works, see Abdul Razak Baginda, ed., *Malaysia and the Islamic World* (London: ASEAN Academic Press, 2004).

3. For an excellent general introduction to various dimensions of Islam in the Malay-Indonesian world, from its beginning until modern times, and the picture of a theologically and legally homogeneous Malay Islam, see Peter G. Riddell, *Islam and the Malay-Indonesian World* (Singapore: Horizon, 2001).

4. For discussions of this aspect of Malaysia's success story, see, for example, Osman Bakar, "Islam, Ethnicity, Pluralism, and Democracy: Malaysia's Unique Experience," in M. A. Muqtedar Khan, ed., *Islamic Democratic Discourse: Theory, Debates, and Philosophical Perspectives* (Lanham, Md.: Lexington, 2006), pp. 63–83; and A. Rahman Embong, "Malaysia as a Multicivilizational Society," *Malaysia: Crossroads of Diversity in Southeast Asia, Macalester International* 12 (Autumn 2002), pp. 37–58.

5. For a critical review of the controversy surrounding the study's report, but sympathetic to it, see K. J. John, "A Truth Commission by Omission?" www .malaysiakini.com/columns/58309 (accessed October 17, 2006).

6. The mainstream media are mostly supportive of the EPU's official figures, but overwhelmingly with the politicians rather than the academics coming to its defense.

7. For a detailed discussion of "Islamic" strategies and programs implemented under Mahathir's Islamization policy, see Mohd. Norhashimah Yasin, *Islamisation/ Malaynisation: A Study on the Role of Islam Law in the Economic Development of Malaysia (1969–1993)* (Kuala Lumpur: A. S. Noordeen, 1996).

8. For a critical evaluation of the MSC, Malaysia's most publicized symbol of its entry as a global player into the Information Age, see Tim Bunnell, *Malaysia, Modernity and the Multimedia Corridor* (London: Routledge, 2004).

9. See Abdul Hamid Ahmad Sarji, *Malaysia's Vision 2020: Understanding the Concept, Implications and Challenges* (Subang Jaya: Pelanduk, 1993).

10. In early 1982, in his concerted attempt to turn this dream into reality, Mahathir launched his Look East Policy that encourages his countrymen to emulate the Japanese and the South Koreans, especially in their labor ethics, morale, and management. In his view, there has been a sharp decline of labor ethics in the West. For a critical discussion of this policy, see R. S. Milne and D. K. Mauzy, *Malaysian Politics under Mahathir* (London: Routledge, 1999).

11. For a critical evaluation of Malaysian democracy under Mahathir, see William Case, "Semi-Democracy in Mahathir's Malaysia," in Bridget Welsh, ed., *Reflections: The Mahathir Years* (Washington, D.C.: Johns Hopkins University Press, 2004), pp. 77–86.

12. On the general effect of the September 11 tragedy on Malaysian discourse on Islam, see Osman Bakar, "The Impact of the American War on Terror on Malaysian Islam," *Journal of Islam and Christian-Muslim Relations* 16:2 (April 2005), pp. 107–27.

13. For treatments of the issue of Islam and the state in Malaysia, see Hussin Mutalib, *Islam in Malaysia: From Revivalism to Islamic State* (Singapore: Singapore University Press, 1993); and Osman Bakar, "Islam and the State in Malaysia," paper presented at the Malaysia in the Twenty-First Century Conference, Washington, D.C., April 2–4, 2002; also Osman Bakar, "Islam and Political Legitimacy in Malaysia," in Shahram Akbarzadeh and Abdullah Saeed, eds., *Islam and Political Legitimacy* (London: RoutledgeCurzon, 2003), pp. 127–49.

14. In speaking of "Islamization" in Malaysia, there is a need to distinguish between Islamization understood in its general sense as referring to the spread, popularization, and intensification of Islamic teachings, practices, and institutions to which both the state and civil society groups have contributed and Islamization understood in its more specific sense as referring to Mahathir's government policy systematically pursued with the view of attaining certain political goals. For a well-researched study of Mahathir's Islamization policy, see S. Vali Reza Nasr, *The Islamic Leviathan: Islam and the Making of State Power* (New York: Oxford University Press, 2001).

15. On Abdullah's own vision of Islam hadhari, see his compiled speeches on the subject, published as Abdullah Badawi, *Islam Hadhari: A Model Approach for Development and Progress* (Singapore: Select Publishers, 2006).

16. On ALIRAN's early perceptions of universal Islam, see, for example, Chandra Muzaffar, ed., *Universalism of Islam* (Penang: ALIRAN, 1979). After leaving ALIRAN to found the International Movement for a Just World (JUST), which he still leads, Muzaffar continues to expound the Islamic core message of universalism and pluralism, both locally and internationally. One of his more recent writings dealing with this theme is *Pluralism and Civil Society*, www.islam21.net/pages/keyissues/key3–22.htm. ABIM's, and more specifically Anwar's early views on Islam's universalism may be gathered from its organizational mouthpiece, *Risalah*, popular among both students and intellectuals in the 1970s. See also the chapter on Anwar in John L. Espsoito and John O. Voll, *Makers of Contemporary Islam* (New York: Oxford University Press, 2001), pp. 177–98.

17. See ABIM's Newsletter, *Risalah*, 1977.

18. Muzaffar, *Universalism of Islam*; see also A. Ibrahim, S. Siddique, and Y. Hussain, compilers, *Readings on Islam in Southeast Asia* (Singapore: Institute of Southeast Asian Studies, 1990), pp. 356–61.

19. Papers presented at this historic conference have been published as a book: Osman Bakar and Gek Nai Cheng, eds., *Islam and Confucianism: A Civilizational Dialogue* (Kuala Lumpur: University of Malaya Press, 1997).

20. The biggest and most influential of them is the Malaysian Chinese Muslim Association (MACMA) with website address, www.macma.org.my.

21. Chinese Muslims are said to account for only 1 percent (about 60,000) of the nation's ethnic Chinese population of 5.35 million, compared with nearly 10 percent of them adopting Christianity: C. B. Tan, "The Religion of the Chinese in Malaysia," in K. H. Lee and C. B. Tan, eds., *The Chinese in Malaysia* (Kuala Lumpur: Oxford University Press, 2000), pp. 282–315.

22. For the few pioneering studies on the problems and challenges faced by Malaysian Chinese Muslims in their attempt to preserve both their ethnic and religious identities, see Rosey Wang Ma, "Shifting Identities: Chinese Muslims in Malaysia," *Asian Ethnicity* 6:2 (June 2005), pp. 89–107. See also Osman Chuah, *Chinese Muslims in Malaysia* (Kuala Lumpur: International Islamic University, 2001); Judith A. Nagata, "The Chinese Muslims of Malaysia: New Malays or New Associates? A Problem of Ethnicity," in G. P. Means, ed., *The Past in Southeast Asian's Present* (Ottawa: Canadian Society for Asian Studies, Canadian Council for Southeast Asian Studies, 1978), pp. 102–14; and Joy Y. Lam, *Religious Conversion and Construction of Identities: The Case of Chinese Muslim Converts in Malaysia*, Working Paper Series No. 74 (Hong Kong: Southeast Asia Research Center, City University of Hong Kong, 2004).

23. Federal Constitution, Article 160, on Interpretation, Clause (2).

24. For a philosophical-historical study of the relationship between religion and ethnicity in the formation of Malay-Islamic identity, see Osman Bakar, "Islam and the Malay Civilizational Identity: Tension and Harmony between Ethnicity and

Religiosity," in John J. Donohue and John L. Esposito, eds., *Islam in Transition: Muslim Perspectives*, 2nd ed. (New York: Oxford University Press, 2006), pp. 480–87.

25. A coalition of thirteen religious and human rights groups, calling itself "Article 11," was recently formed. It apparently derived the name from Article 11(1) of the constitution, which states that "every person has the right to profess and practice his religion, and subject to clause (4), to propagate it." Although its general aim is to educate Malaysians on their constitutional rights, especially religious rights, its immediate concerns include the highly publicized, controversial issue of a Malay woman, Lina Joy, who converted to Christianity. The country's highest court of appeal agreed that the civil high court was right in dismissing Joy's application to have the word "Islam" removed from her national identity card, on the ground that the matter falls within the jurisdiction of the Sharia court. Angry at Article 11 Coalition's road shows in the major cities to drum up support for Joy and its interpretation of religious freedom, which they see as challenging the position of Islam as the official religion, dozens of Muslim NGOs joined forces to form a countercoalition, "Pembela Islam" (Defenders of Islam). Their anti–Article 11 Coalition meetings drew big crowds in the thousands. Fearing a religious clash, Abdullah decided to ban all meetings purportedly held to discuss "sensitive" religious issues.

26. The new Article 121(A) ensures a dual legal system for the country with the civil and Sharia courts having separate jurisdictions.

27. For perhaps the earliest critical evaluation of Mahathir's administration since his resignation, see Bridget Welsh, ed., *Reflections: The Mahathir Years* (Washington, D.C.: Johns Hopkins University Press, 2004).

28. See Osman Bakar, "Islam and Political Legitimacy in Malaysia," in Shahram Akbarzadeh and Abdullah Saeed, eds., *Islam and Political Legitimacy* (London: RoutledgeCurzon, 2003), pp. 127–49.

29. Anwar's views on Abdullah's Islam hadhari may be found in his recent political speeches, which have been posted at his official website, http://anwaribrahim .com. Both Abdul Hadi Awang, PAS president, and Ashaari Muhammad, former leader of the banned Darul Arqam, have written critiques of Islam hadhari: Abdul Hadi Awang, *Hadharah Islam bukan Islam Hadhari* [Islamic Civilization Is Not Civilizational Islam] (Kuala Lumpur: Nufair Street Sdn Bhd, 2005); Mejar Abu Dzar Taharem, compiler, *Islam Hadhari menurut Ust. Hj. Ashaari Muhammad* [Islam Hadhari according to Ashaari Muhammad] (Rawang, Selangor: Penerbitan Minda Ikhwan, 2004).

30. Anwar was freed on September 2, 2004, after being acquitted by the Federal Court of a sodomy charge.

31. Anwar is barred by law from holding any political office until 2008 because of his previous imprisonment after the court found him guilty of corruption charges that many believe were politically orchestrated.

32. SIS was formed in 1988 and registered as a nongovernmental organization (NGO) in 1993. For the kind of issues with which SIS has been passionately engaged, see J. J. Donahue and J. L. Esposito, *Islam in Transition: Muslim Perspectives* (New York: Oxford University Press, 2006), pp. 197–202.

33. The principles in the order in which they have been listed in the official document are (1) faith and piety in Allah, (2) a just and trustworthy government, (3) a free and independent people, (4) mastery of knowledge, (5) balanced and comprehensive economic development, (6) a good quality of life, (7) protection of the rights of minority groups and women, (8) cultural and moral integrity, (9) safeguarding the environment, and (10) strong defenses. For an official clarification of the ten principles, see Government of Malaysia, *The Concept of Islam Hadhari* (Kuala Lumpur, 2005). See also www.pmo.gov.my/website.nsf/vIslamHadhari.

34. The "other Abdullah" refers to Abdullah Mohd Zin, a former university professor and administrator, who was appointed minister at the Prime Minister's Department in charge of Islamic affairs, following his victory in the 2004 parliamentary elections.

6

The Trifurcated Islam of Central Asia: A Turkish Perspective

M. Hakan Yavuz

After the collapse of the Soviet Union (USSR), many scholars focused on the role of Islam and Islamic movements in the newly formed southern tier states. The struggle over memory and suppressed identities, the tension between the center and the periphery, were all interpreted as the revival of Islam. Islam in general, and Islamic movements in particular, became the object of debate and sources of speculation. For instance, the events in the Fergana Valley in 1989, which resulted in the destruction of large numbers of Meskhetian Turks by mostly ethnic Uzbeks, the similar conflict between Uzbeks and Kyrgyz ethnic groups in Osh province of Kyrgyzstan in 1990, and the 1992–97 civil war in Tajikistan were all read as a struggle between modernity and Islamic fanaticism. In fact, a closer examination of these events indicates that their causes and public manifestations are not the same. The Tajik civil war was not primarily about the revival of Islam or creating an Islamic republic but was a struggle over resources between different regions of the country. Although the 1997 peace treaty restored a degree of order to that country, power struggles among different Tajik factions is still going on.

The evolving field of Central Asian studies very much deals with the old orientalist assumptions and themes. The current master concept, which is used to explain every issue in the region, is the "Islamic factor," or "Islamic fundamentalism." One needs to know the origins of this Islamic factor and what it purportedly entails. Is it an independent force that shapes social and political landscapes, or is it just a shared set of concepts and practices that provides common idioms of conversation to many Central Asian communities? During the Cold War, there was almost no information about Islamic practices, religiosity, or institutions in Central Asia. Soviet scholars treated Islam as an anachronism within the context of the Marxist-Leninist modernization theory. They echoed the worries of Soviet leadership about Islamic fundamentalism as a potential threat to the unity of the socialist project and scientific socialism. Such Islamophobia had deep historical and ideological roots in the Russian empire. Due to the Soviet view of Islam, some Western scholars welcomed the role of Islam, or the commonly known Islamic factor, as a potential force to destroy the communist "empire."[1] (This logic by the West led to the blind support of extremist Islamist, yet anticommunist, groups during the Cold War, with Afghanistan having become the focal point of U.S.-USSR confrontation, the post–Cold War ramifications of which continue to be felt today.) Though the Islamic factor was a welcome force for Western scholars and Western powers, because it could (and likely did) lead to the breakup of the Soviet Union, for Soviet scholars and policy makers, it was a destabilizing force that countered visions of international socialism.

The study of Soviet Islam was shaped by the works of Alexandre Bennigsen and his two students, S. Enders Winbush and Marie Broxup. Bennigsen developed an essentialist version of Islam as the primary source of identity and loyalty that governed the daily life of Central Asian Muslims. He argued that Islam makes it "impossible to assert that someone from a Muslim area who eschews the formal religious practice of Islam ipso facto ceases to be a Muslim."[2] In his examination of identities of Central Asia, Bennigsen stressed the role of pan-Islamic and pan-Turkish identity over "artificially formulated national" identities.[3] The second group of scholars had a more instrumental reading of Islam and insisted on competing loyalties in the region. This group was led by Martha Brill Olcott, Muriel Atkin, Teresa Rakowska-Harstone, and Mehrdad Haghayeghi.[4] They argued that religious knowledge in the region is basic, with people of the region not being deeply religious and their understanding of Islam shallow. Still, they stressed the conceptualization of Islam as a social but not a political force in the moral rejuvenation of Central Asians.

There are three dominant myths in the study of Central Asia:

Islam has been the dominant and unifying identity of the region.
Central Asian republics all internalized the nation-state identity, and
    Islamic identity has sought to destabilize these nation-states.
Soviet communism has had very little effect in the lives and cultures of
    the region.

I would argue that the anti-Soviet nationalist movements did not start in Central Asian republics because there was very little Islam left after almost complete scientific atheism in the region. Nazif Shahrani has examined the influence of this scientific atheism on Central Asian societies.[5] The Soviet legacy created a type of political culture based on fear and favor that undermined the emergence and functioning of civil society. Many scholars under the influence of modernization theory argued that the modernization process would eliminate religion and reason would replace God. They all expected the antimodernization challenge to come from the rural areas because of the conservative rural culture that is shaped by religion. In Central Asia, the modernization project (à la scientific atheism) had mixed results in terms of influencing the rural and the urban areas.

For any form of reform to succeed in Central Asia, one has to recognize Islam as a moral force that is capable of mobilizing the population. Islam is a powerful and constructive force for building new civil society and civic culture. Under Soviet policies, Islam was redefined as a cultural and moral legacy, but not as a religious force. Islamic ways of doing things helped Central Asians differentiate themselves from the non-Muslim Slavic population and colonialists. Under the Soviet system, Islam became an ethnic marker and a core for local nationalism in the region.

In examining the role of Islam in Central Asia here, I describe the basic religious landscape and the key sociohistorical factors. Next, I focus on the role of Turkey in the rebuilding of religious education and discuss local responses to Turkish initiatives. Finally, I examine the potential challenges to Islamic revivalism in Central Asia.

Context of Turkic Islam

The striking feature in the constitution of Islam in Central Asia is its geographic and environmental conditions. Central Asian history is shaped by nomadism and the settler peoples—especially of the Turkic population. The nomads populated the north (today's Kazakhstan and Kyrgyzstan) and the far south (Turkmenistan); the settler people primarily populated much of today's Uzbekistan and Tajikistan. Since water has always been scarce in much of the region, people usually either stayed where there was water or followed water where it could be found.[6] The culture of the region is a product of oasis agriculture and nomadic pastoralism. The urban centers developed in the south where water was more easily accessible. The epics and ballads are imprinted by the tension between these two lifestyles and cultures.

Central Asia has been the center for diverse cultural and cross-religious fertilization, as it is located at the crossroads of major empires and nomadic conquerors, including the armies that brought Islam to the region. As in many other parts of the world, Islam in Central Asia has been syncretic and organizationally fragmented. Islam coexisted with other religious traditions—Zoroastrianism, Manichaeism, Buddhism, and the Shamanist cults of the great steppe tribes. Syncretic versions of Islam, more than literal orthodoxy, have been the dominant understanding of Islam. One could explain this historical syncreticism in terms of the ongoing conflict between nomadic and sedentary populations over resources and cultural values. The caravan trade of the Silk Road allowed the evolution of more urban-based Islam with different religious and cultural traditions. These trade routes were also at the center of rich theological and artistic expressions of Islam. In Central Asian urban centers, a theologically rich version of Hanafi interpretation of Islam started to become dominant in the eleventh and twelfth centuries. The Hanafi teachings were revived under the new name of al-Maturidiyya.[7] Islam centered around major urban centers in what are today Uzbekistan and Tajikistan. Kazak and Kyrgyz tribes were less exposed to Islam.

This rich tradition began to change as maritime transportation opened new roads and opportunities in the greater world, thus shadowing the Silk Road. With the gradual collapse of the trade routes, Islam of the region started to become less independent and more dependent on developments in the Middle East. With British colonialism in India and Afghanistan and Russian colonialism in Central Asia, Muslims experimented with deep autocratization of Islamic institutions on the one hand, and Islam as a new ideology of resistance against colonialism on the other. Thus, two versions of Islam became dominant and constantly remained in conflict: traditional versus enlightened Islam.

The contemporary role of Islam in Central Asia was shaped by the three historical processes. First, Stalin's 1924 national delimitation policy created separate state institutions to invent competing national identities vis-à-vis Islamic identity and loyalty. The Kremlin pursued an aggressive policy to cleanse Islam from the public and private spheres through scientific atheism. Soviet scientific atheism totally destroyed higher religious education institutions, along with prominent religious scholars, the ulama, with many scholars having been purged or sent to exile. During the Stalinist purges, 25,000 mosques in Uzbekistan, 8,300 mosques in Turkmenistan, and all mosques in Kazakhstan were destroyed. The main target was the Muslim religious and charitable foundations (waqf). These waqf lands were the financial source of clerics and their independence from the state. These revenues were used to pay the salaries of the Muslim clergy or imams and to fund religious school buildings, educational expenses, and hospitals. In 1925, all *waqfs* were closed and Muslim courts were abolished. By 1927, both Sharia and customary law had been outlawed. As a result of socialist campaign, Muslim scholars were discredited, accused of financial corruption and ignorance.

Only with World War II, upon the initiative of the mufti of Ufa (the capital of Russia's Bashkortostan), Abdurrahman Rasulaev, did Stalin decide to "normalize" relations between Islam and the Soviet government by agreeing to establish four official administrations modeled on the Central Spiritual Directorate, created in Orenburg by Catherine II in 1783. The goal was to mobilize the Muslim population against the Nazi occupation. Four geographically based spiritual directorates were created. The first one was the Spiritual Board of Central Asian and Kazak Muslims (SADUM) in Taskent, with Uzbek as its official language; the process also reopened the Mir-i Arab Medrese in Bukhara in 1948 to train Muslim scholars. The second directorate was for Russia and Siberia, centered in Ufa, with Volga Tatar as its language. The third directorate was for Dagestan and the North Caucasus, centered in Makhachkala, with classical Arabic as its official language. The last directorate one was for Transcaucasia, with administration building in Baku, Azerbaijan, which covered all Shia communities of the Soviet Union. These institutions, however, were mostly used for the support of Soviet doctrine and creation of the Soviet version of Islam. Under the communist system, Islam was mainly reduced to an underground faith and its visible expressions were tightly controlled.

Second, Muslims of Central Asia did not experience what the Muslims under French or British colonialism experienced: some sort of democracy, rule of law, and capitalism. Rather, they were forced to experience the Soviet style of top-down modernization. Soviet colonial legacy is different from British or French colonialism. By invoking the leading theorist of subaltern studies, Partha Chatterje's *Nationalist Thought and the Colonial World: Derivative Discourse*, Nazif Shahrani argues that under European colonialism there was an autonomous "spiritual domain" in which people managed their personal affairs and preserved a code of ethics. This domain facilitated the formation of nationalism and a chart of moral code that provided a ground for civil society. There was little to no such autonomous spiritual domain in the Central Asian experience. Islam was a target of Russian suppressive policies. The Soviet state was very successful in the elimination of traditional Muslim society and, among other things, especially prohibited Islamic religious education. The lack of connection with the traditional centers of Islamic learning further isolated Central Asia and resulted in universal ignorance about basic religious education and practices.

Third, those Muslims who wanted to benefit from the Soviet system "abandoned" their faith or re-created Islamic practices and symbols as secularized and "national" cultural practices. Islamic identity turned into an ethnic marker to differentiate "natives" (Central Asian Muslims) from "outsiders" (Soviet Russians). The boundary between ethnicity and religion was blurred in the Soviet system. To be a Kazak or a Turkmen was to be a Muslim. Islam played an important part in the everyday life practices such as fasting during Ramadan, traditional weddings, circumcision of boys, and Islamic funerals and neighborhood meals for the deceased. These rituals helped mark the boundaries and distinctions between Russian colonialists and native populations. Islam became the constituting factor in the national heritage of the existing republics. Islam as a faith of "practicing and doing" more than believing creates its pattern of interactions. Under communist scientific atheism, these practices were reframed as "it is healthy to have circumscision" and "fasting is a way to clean oneself of toxins." Moreover, the social structure of Islam is more communal than individual. Thus, Muslim identity always presupposes a communal framework with neighbors and relatives.

Local and regional expressions of Islam are diverse forms of contextualization of Islam. In this case, one sees the process of the localization of universalistic principles of Islam that universal principles are not frozen and they are also not totally "plastic congeries of beliefs."[8] Islam can only be understood in the way in which ideals are contextualized and expressed in local situations. The constructive tension between ideal and real Islam provides a set of religious characters of specific practices.

One should not divide understanding of Islam in the south as "high" Islam and Kazak understanding as "low" Islam. These are two diverse processes of contextualization of a universal faith. Islam in the northern part of Central Asia is punctuated by Sufi shrines and cemeteries, evoking images of Muslim experiences. In Kazakhstan and Kyrgyzstan, Islam is not about religious knowledge per se but, rather, provides a religiously textured landscape that facilitates reproduction of the past. Islamic narratives and internalized conduct patterns function as the container of collective memory. The narrative story that is imprinted on the place makes it holy. Thus Islam is a narrative-based landscape religion for Kazaks and Kyrgyz. A narrative story that is textured on the landscape turns the place into a holy site.

Religion in Central Asia overall is a collective memory. Islam as memory is collectively constituted and perpetuated by the community through a rich culture of ways of remembering ancestors. These ways of remembering are very much "conflated" to the ways of Islam. Remembering ancestors by ways of Islamic practices and spirituality is the major mechanism in the maintenance of Kazak and Kyrgyz ethnic identities. It structures the conduct and daily reasoning of the people. In the north as much as in the south of Central Asia,

Turkic identity is a Muslim one, and these two identities are mutually constitutive; one leads the consciousness of the other. Islam in Central Asia is a collective memory, and it is more affective than cognitive. Maurice Halbwachs and
Frederic C. Bartlett argue that remembering is about creating a shared sense
or feeling and, subsequently, constructing the past in line with changing context. For instance, some commemorative events such as the Karbala incident
or the major wars cement social bonds in a given society.

In short, Islam of north Central Asia is less about textbook knowledge and
more about stories that are imprinted into the landscape. One could argue that
the case of Central Asia indicates that religion without theology could still exist
and stir up deep emotions. Due to communist oppression, the people of the
region learned to live Islam at an emotional and memory-habit (internalized
conduct) level. Thus, the past that is punctuated in the landscape of Central
Asia is not a literally constructed one, but it is selectively (mis)used to promote
diverse interests.

Many believers in Central Asia, especially the Kazak and Kyrgyz peoples,
have a deeper affection for Muslim shrines and cemeteries than for mosques.
For many of them, *ziyaret* (pilgrimage) at the shrine and not *namaz* (prayer) at
the mosque has more expression of religiosity.[9] *Ziyaret* brings the dimension of
memory and stirs up deep emotions. For instance, the Yasevi shrine of Turkistan is the largest shrine in Kazakistan and many Kazak visit it. There is also a
rich literature about the significance of the Yasevi shrine. Many of the Kazak
tried to maintain and perpetuate their faith through cemeteries and shrines due
to Soviet policies about worship, to their lack of economic means to build
mosques, or their ecological conditions. Most of the mosques in the region are
recently built. Through mosque building, people are reconstructing their version of Islam. Kazaks were, and still are, more attached to religious shrines than
mosques. If a mosque is attached to a shrine of a saint, it becomes important as
well. In addition to mosque and shrine building, Muslims of Central Asia in
recent years are also becoming closer to schooled knowledge and textbooks.
There is a gradual shift from a narrative-based "expressivist" way of Islam to
more "scripturalist" (mosque-, madrasa- and ulama-centric) Islam.[10] During
the Soviet period, very few homes had the Qur'an. With independence, however, not only Russian and Kazak versions but also several Turkish and Arabic
versions of the Qur'an all became available. Still, many people regard the
Qur'an as an audible word rather than a book to be studied. This new wave of
introducing Islam should be seen as a "second conversion" into textual Islam.

After the collapse of communism, there was an upsurge in building
mosques, opening religious madrasas, and printing books and magazines on
Islam. As a result of these three initial activities, there was an increased sense of

religiosity and people displayed it in different forms. People attended religious services in masses. But this upsurge of religiosity started to decline in the mid 1990s. The newly independent states tried to control or use this new sense of religious identity to consolidate their respective governments. The state sought to coopt Islam to serve its own needs. Almost all communist party leaders transformed themselves into "nationalist" leaders. Some made the pilgrimage to Mecca and Medina to signal a change in their newly discovered Islamic identity. Most of the governments of the region—especially the four heavily ethnic Turkic republics—used Turkey as a model to navigate relations between Islam and the state to create state-friendly pro-stability Islam. The institution building did not aim to free Islam from the political pressure or search for a better understanding of Islam but, rather, to control religious activities. Thus, each republic created its own national directorate of religious affairs. These new institutions tried to exert their control through religious education, formal examinations, and registration of religious scholars. Through registration of mosques and Muslim preachers, the state does not allow unregistered preachers to lead the mosque. Moreover, by providing the salaries of preachers, the state officialized Islam with the purpose of control. In other words, for the purpose of state control, the new republics established directorates of Muslim affairs and created a religious bureaucracy.

Islamic movements in Central Asia have no unified single goal. They are all shaped by local conditions, with global Islamic idioms and discourses of justice, democracy, political participation, and development. They are all critical of the oppressive nature of Central Asian states and the coopted Muslim hierarchy as corrupt and intellectually inept to address the religious needs of the people. These movements usually have several overlapping goals of rejuvenating moral life, connecting with the lost memory of Central Asia, and building more just political and economic systems. Some of these movements seek to reclaim Islam as a source of morality and identity. The reformist Islamic tradition of Central Asia, Jadidism, seeks to update Islamic idioms to meet modern challenges.[11] People seek to empower themselves, as well as their family, community, and nation, to control everyday affairs and construct their own shared language. Thus, Islamic knowledge is necessary—not only to build a civil society but also to lead to peaceful human interactions. In Islam, not the state but society is stressed.

The key concepts of these movements are faith (*iman*) and justice (*adalet*). In order to delegitimize these movements, the governments have often accused them of plotting to overthrow the governments and establish fundamentalist Islamic states. Almost all reactions against the oppressive governments of Central Asia are conveniently framed as "Wahhabi" movements, a generic term for all types of anti-state religious activism. These states often seek to criminalize all forms of dissent as Islamic opposition and carry out widespread witch hunts against opponents.

Exporting Islam to Central Asia

Islam is evolving from an ethnic definition to a shared moral code of conduct or a source of morality and personal identity. One sees more debate over Islam as a source of morality, along with debate over the inner self. The new debate is not about Islam as the tradition of forefathers but, rather, its "connectivity" with the global Muslim community and as the source of ethics.

Turkey, Saudi Arabia, Pakistan, and Iran have all been involved in a tense competition to shape the religious landscape of Central Asia. Before the events of September 11, 2001, the Saudis were in the forefront of constructing mosques and religious schools and distributing religious materials. They had also offered a number of scholarships to Central Asian students to study Islam in Saudi universities. In addition to such state-based activities, new waves of Muslim missionary activities were carried out by private organizations and individuals. These missionaries first attacked the "legendary" or "folk" Islamic practices as un-Islamic and encouraged the people to give them up in favor of more orthodox practices. This created anger on the part of the Central Asian Muslims, and state authorities began to raise concerns over these private Islamic missionary works. Uzbekistan was the first state to ban all Islamic missionary activities by the Saudis in 1992; the Turkish Nurcus followed in 1993.

In Turkey, after the War of Liberation, the modern Turkish Republic, under the leadership of Mustafa Kemal, pursued a new project of radical civilizational reorientation to transform the multiethnic and multireligious Ottoman society into a homogenous Turkish nation. In this top-down revolutionary project, the governing elite used secularism in accordance with the antireligious laicist model of the French revolution as a constituting and guiding principle. To create a homogenized secular and national-state, the government used various strategies to eliminate ethnic, religious, and economic differences. Any attempt to challenge this program was perceived as backsliding and was referred to as "reactionary."[12] The modern history of Turkey, therefore, is the story of a struggle between the state's efforts at social transformation to engineer a new society and traditional ethnic and religious movements. One of the ironies of the Kemalist project was that as it assaulted ethnic and religious loyalties it simultaneously stimulated ethnic and religious consciousness.

The foreign policy of Turkey has been subordinated to domestic identity politics. The republican elite's main goal was to anchor Turkey in the West in order to realize the goal of becoming a "civilized" (i.e., European) nation-state.[13] This elite quite brutally removed Islam and subregional identities from the public realm and replaced them with a linguistic and territorial-based Turkish nationalism.[14] Since the introduction of the neo-liberal economic policies of Turgut Özal and the collapse of the Soviet Union and Yugoslavia, the contradictions and tensions in the national orientation of Turkey have been further highlighted. This domestic and international conjuncture is crucial for understanding Turkey's ambiguous and competing policies toward Central Asia.

What are the connections between national identity and national interest in the formulation of Turkey's foreign policy toward the Central Asian republics?[15] The apparent Europhile Turkish elite, which determined official policy, and the Islamo-Turkish masses, who have a very different conception of the past, seek different heads for the ship of state. This duality of cultures and identities is at the center of the current foreign policy debate in Turkey, a duality that also manifests itself in Turkey's dealings with the Central Asian states.[16]

Since the collapse of the Soviet Union and the neo-liberal economic policies of Turgut Özal (1983–1993), Turkey has been struggling to redefine itself with or without democratic means. This crisis-driven identity debate in Turkey has greatly shaped its foreign policy toward Central Asia. The foreign policy of Turkey is greatly conditioned by the domestic fault line between the Kemalist establishment and the Turkish-Islamic population. To understand the shifting strategies and orientations of Turkish foreign policy, one needs to unpack the Turkish identity debate and examine its implications on foreign policy decisions. Identity politics explain the current disconcerting sense of betrayal among the ostensibly Western-oriented population and their endeavor to create a community of Turkic states to overcome Turkey's increasing isolation in the international system.

Next, by arguing that the foreign policy of Turkey has been shaped by the domestic identity debate rather than a given "national interest," I explore the power of identity (such as Islamic, Turkic, and European) to account for foreign policy orientation. I also analyze the role of Islam and Turkish nationalism in the constitution of Turkey's policy toward the Central Asian republics. The last section focuses on the role of Islam in Turkish–Central Asian relations. I argue that the most influential country in the reconstruction of Islamic knowledge in the Turkic world has been Turkey. The positive and negative trends of discourse relating to Islam in Turkey will mark the Islam of other Turkic communities.

THE TRIFURCATED ISLAM OF CENTRAL ASIA 119

Identity and Foreign Policy

Since identity is always a matter of interaction between the different sectors of society, it is not always easy to establish a causal link between identity and foreign policy. Here I demonstrate that identity and interest are mutually constituative. Identities are not given but are developed and transformed in interaction. Thus, one layer of identity is stressed in certain situations, depending on the identity of the "other" states or organizations. Alexander Went argues that a "world in which identities and interests are learned and sustained by intersubjectively grounded practice, by what states think and do, is one in which 'anarchy is what states make of it.'"[17] These intersubjective meanings evolve as a result of interactively constructed collective meanings. The identity of the state in Turkey shifted from an Islamically oriented foreign policy under Abdülhamid II to a national one, by acquiring a new identity that presupposes a set of new roles and expectations. Identities are significant because they help define interests.[18] These interests, in turn, shape Turkey's conduct in the Balkans and Central Asia. Therefore, the fluctuation in Turkey's foreign policy is related to the identity debate in Turkey.[19] As long as the transformation of this identity and these interests is not fully understood, one may not fully grasp Turkey's role in Central Asia, the Middle East, and the Balkans.[20]

I argue that Turkish state identity is constituted as a result of seismic international events that directly affected Turkey's perception of the "self" and the domestic transformation of elite politics. The historical legacy of the Ottoman state and the "culture of insecurity" are the two fundamental constraints in the evolution of state identity in Turkey. When external and internal interactions create conflicting intersubjective meanings, a crisis paralyzes the state elite's ability to determine its foreign policy orientation because the fundamental definition of self is very much in contestation. In turn, the way in which Turkish state perceives its self often depends on the perception of Turkey by foreign states, particularly the leading members of the Western bloc. The European Union's dismissive treatment of Turkey has affected Turkey's conception of self and this, in turn, is reflected in its foreign policy conduct. In addition to the self of the Turkish state, there is the self of Turkish nation. This latter is more dynamic and open to change than the official discourse of the state, which at the moment is held hostage by its own Kemalist ideology. Its Islamic and Turkic layers of identity have been stressed to overcome a deep identity crisis.

Identity is a matter of our minds picturing the way the world and our social interactions are organized in relation to other social groups. Political elites usually seek to mobilize or construct identities to promote specific interests. Therefore, identity becomes an instrument for the pursuit of interests. At the same time, the causal arrow between interest to identity could also run from identity to interest. For instance, Turkey uses religious, linguistic, and other cultural affinities to enhance its interest in Central Asia. At the same time, Turkish national interest is defined by how elites and populations view their identity. The national identity of Turkey has three layers: Islamic, Turkic, and European. These dimensions shape elite perceptions of interest and preferences, but the distinction cannot explain specific policy choices.

To understand contemporary Turkish foreign policy toward Central Asia, it is important to unpack the identity debate and analyze the competing identity-based elite factions that mold Turkey's foreign policies. The three layers of national identity of Turkey indicate contextual, relational, and multiple features of identity. Due to its multiple national identities, the Turkish state invokes different layers of identity on the basis of policy issues. During the crises of Bosnia and Kosovo, Turkey stressed its Ottoman and Islamic identity; whereas Central Asia stressed its Turkic layer of identity. These layers of identity are open to internal and external changes. There are three major identity-driven elite factions in Turkey:

1. The Kemalist elite have supported Turkey's full integration into the EU, as well as close ties with the United States. In terms of their ideology, they have professed to view their ties with Europe as based more on "civilizational" than on national interest. They have also been quite willing to denounce Europe and the U.S. Central Intelligence Agency (CIA) whenever pressure has been brought to bear on the Turkish establishment in terms of respecting democracy and human rights. They tend to treat the "new Turkish world" as a source of increasing Turkey's importance for Europe and in the international system and present Turkey as a "secular state model" for the new independent Muslim states.

2. The Muslim/Islamists elite have supported close ties with Muslim countries and subordinated ethnic identity to a religious one. This group is not inherently anti-Western and, instead, views Russia and the Orthodox world as its historic rival. Their view toward Central Asia is colored by Islamic solidarity; they also endeavor to present Turkey as a "protector" of Muslims in the Balkan and the former Soviet Union. They seek cooperation with the Turkic republics and the Balkan states to form the core of an Islamic bloc. The Islamists see Central Asia as part of an Islamic community.

3. The Turkic elite include groups who support cultural and political cooperation, and even integration, among Turkic states. This group includes some ultranationalists, who disagree with Turkey's full integration with the EU. This group seeks to form a Turkic world under the leadership of Turkey.

From Turkey *in* Europe to Turkey *and* Europe

Since the late nineteenth century, many in the Turkish elite have been reluctant to consider themselves as an integral part of the Middle East or the Islamic world. The demand for acceptance into Europe has been a constant aspect of Turkey's foreign policy. For instance, according to a recent survey, Turkish youth prefer that Turkey first become a member of the EU, then a member of a Turkic bloc, and finally a member of the Organization of the Islamic Conference and a Balkan regional bloc.[21]

Moreover, modern Turks measure their achievements through European acceptance of them as "European." There are two reasons that the Turks want to be a part of Europe. First, there is the Ottoman legacy. The Ottoman social, cultural, and political life was marked and oriented by the Balkan Muslims of Eastern Europe. The Ottoman Empire was a southeastern European empire more than an Anatolian or Middle Eastern one. The construction of the Ottoman state and Turkish identity took place in the Balkan frontiers rather than in the east; the Ottoman cultural and social networks were densest between the Danube and the Drina Rivers. Consequently, most of the governing elite and scholars came from the Balkans. There were more Ottoman mosques, cultural institutions, and architectural monuments in the Balkans than in Anatolia or other parts of the empire. Second, the identity of the modern Turkish population was molded and shaped during the disintegration of the Ottoman Empire between 1878 and 1921. The forced mass exodus of Muslims from the Balkans constituted the political elite of the modern republic.[22]

With the modernizing "reforms," Mustafa Kemal sought to Europeanize Turkish national identity, at least in its outward forms.[23] The reforms initiated a process of "becoming" European that was carried out by an ideologically committed elite who consolidated themselves by subscribing to a naive Kemalist version of Westernization—that is, positivism. The process of becoming European helps explain why Turkey joined the European Council (1949), the North Atlantic Treaty Organization (NATO) (1952), and the European Economic Community (EEC) with the Rome Treaty in 1963. The Cold War and Soviet threats further consolidated the elite's vision of joining all

European institutions. The ideological identity of the elite and the Soviet threat helped create a shared consensus in support of "full" Europeanization. In short, although Turkey's Western-oriented foreign policy was an outcome of its struggle to "become" European, the Soviet threat accentuated the process. During the Cold War years, Turkey's foreign policy became an extension of its relations with NATO. The anticommunist stand of most nationalist and Muslim groups helped consolidate the legitimacy of the homogenizing Turkish state. However, the Turkish Republic was never considered truly European for both its undemocratic and illiberal character and its Ottoman-Islamic heritage.

After Turkey's integration into NATO, a "European Turkey" became the dominant orientation of Ankara's foreign policy. The Cypriot crisis and other events opened a debate over foreign policy orientation in Turkey, but the fundamental course of foreign policy remained European in direction. The EEC's negative response to Turkey's membership application in 1989 constituted a turning point in the evolution of domestic identity and this, in turn, created a confused orientation in foreign policy.[24] Some in the Turkish elite realized the difficulty of integrating into the nascent EU in the late 1980s and decided to find solace in Central Asia and the Balkans.[25] Finally, Ankara later tried to overcome its exclusion from Europe by developing closer ties with the United States via Israel.

Turkey *with* the Turkic Republics

In the formative years of Turkish nationalism, "outside Turks" played an important part in its formulation and articulation.[26] Tatars developed the first indigenous bourgeoisie and intellectual class in the Turkic world to raise the Turko-Islamic consciousness. The leading Tatar intellectuals—Abdunnasir Kursavi (1771–1812), Sehabettin Mercani (1818–1889), Huseyin Feyizhani (1828–1866), and Kayyum Nasiri (1824–1902)—sought to reexamine Islamic teachings to raise religious and national consciousness. This was the first indigenous modernist movement in the Islamic world. Within the discursive tradition of Turkish nationalism, ethnic and religious forms have often been mutually constitutive due to the positive role of Jadid modernism.[27]

During the disintegration of the Ottoman Empire, there was a great popular desire to free captive Turks from the hegemony of Russia. Some of the most prominent theoreticians of Turkish nationalism were émigrés from "outside Turkish" communities in Russia, such as Ismail Gaspıralı, Yusuf Akçura, Abdürreşid Ibrahim, Ali Merdan Topcubaşı, Hüseyinzade Ali Bey, and Ahmet

Ağaoğlu.[28] This critical group of intellectuals stressed the mutually constitutive role of ethnicity and religion in the construction of Turkish nationalism. In short, protonational feelings of collective belonging to a shared Turkic language and religion were transformed into "national" Turkish identity.

The enthusiasm for developing close ties with "outside Turks" and freeing them from the Russian yoke came to an end when Mustafa Kemal decided to focus on domestic politics and established close ties with Bolshevik Russia.[29] Between 1923 and 1991, the governments of Turkey pursued a policy to "ignore" the presence of the Turkish world in Russia and remained indifferent to their plight.[30] However, at the societal level, interactions between the Central Asian diaspora communities in Turkey and those outside continued.

Although pan-Turkism became a motivating force for ultranationalists and this idea was institutionalized with the establishment of the National Movement Party (MHP), pan-Turkism never shaped Turkish foreign policy, and it remained a marginal movement.[31] With the participation of the MHP in the National Front coalitions in the mid 1970s, the "outside Turks" terminology was partially integrated into official Turkish discourse. Yet, neither the diaspora nor the MHP significantly influenced Turkish foreign policy toward the Soviet Union. For a while, any public debate or mention about the existence of outside Turks became a disapproved sign of ultranationalism. The Turkish governing elite either denied or ignored the existence of outside Turks. Turkey, therefore, has had very limited formal study of the Turkic world during the Republican Party period. Any interest or debate over the situation of the outside Turks was treated as backsliding from the Kemalist goal of Europeanization.

The idea of "Turkey *with* the Central Asian republics" is an outcome of the sudden collapse of the Soviet Union, the EU's exclusionary policies against Turkey, and rising Turkish nationalism. After 1991, Turkey sought to overcome its isolation and the sense of alienation in Europe and the Islamic world by searching for its Eastern roots in Central Asia.[32] Turkey's rediscovery of the Turkic world in the East has opened a new debate over its identity and foreign policy. This newly "discovered" Turkic identity punctuates Ankara's foreign policy and constitutes its self-esteem. This new discovery also affirms the core identity of the Turkish state as being "Turkish." When this core identity has been contested by Kurdish and Islamic voices, the foreign policy of Turkey has become embroiled in identity politics. Although the new world system has created "windows of opportunities" for the Turkish state, the Turkish population is experiencing a "formative moment," a time when its identity is under contestation and reformulation. Old identity frames are not useful for understanding new realities within and outside Turkey.

From Indifference to "Big Brother" (1991–1993)

When the Soviet Union started to collapse and the Turkic republics, starting with Azerbaijan in August 30, 1991, declared their independence, Turkey was taken by surprise.[33] The Bush administration encouraged Ankara to play an active role in Central Asia to counter the feared Iranian influence in the region. Ankara recognized nearly all the newly "independent" states with the blessings of the United States and without defining its short-term and long-term interests in Central Asia.

In 1991, many Western governments supported and even pushed Turkey to take a "leading" role in the newly independent Muslim states in Central Asia.[34] Turkey was expected to contain the Islamic Republic of Iran's penetration in the region and somewhat supplant the former role played by Russia in the region by offering a "Turkish model" of "secular democracy," market economics, and a pro-Western orientation for the new independent Turkic states to pursue.[35] The government in Ankara tried to use this opportunity to stress its "strategic" importance as an inevitable bridge between Asia and Europe to consolidate its position in Europe. By 1999, Turkey's foreign policy toward these new nations, especially the majority ethnic Turkic ones, was shaped by the mixed ideological and material interests that are at the center of the evolution of Turkey's Central Asian policy: (1) Turkey's search for a new identity in domestic politics and a new role in foreign policy; (2) Turkey's attempt to overcome its isolation in the West and in the Islamic world by developing a new Turkic grouping; (3) Turkey's attempt to have access to the rich oil and gas reservoirs in Central Asia; and (4) Turkey's search for new markets.

Özal was the first Turkish leader with a clear global vision to have a more activist role in Central Asia and the Balkans. He even argued that the "twenty-first century will be the century of the Turks."[36] He was in favor of creating an economic and cultural union with Central Asian Turkic states. Özal always treated shared cultural norms as the basis for "solidarity and cooperation among Turkic people." He argued that "our people are expecting regional cooperation among our countries because we are from the same origin. We are the branches of the same great tree and we are a big family."[37] He developed close ties with Central Asian leaders and did not hesitate to appeal to purported Islamic and Turkish bonds.[38]

Ankara's ultimate goal has been to create a forum for Turkic cooperation, not unity. Turkey took several measures to develop its relations with Turkish states. It first tried to anchor the new republics into the ECO (Economic

Cooperation Organization), which was founded by Iran, Pakistan, and Turkey, as a framework of cooperation. Then, in 1992, Turkey established the Turkish International Co-operation Agency (TIKA) to "coordinate, navigate and implement economic, cultural and social projects," especially in the Turkic republics of the former Soviet Union and neighboring countries.[39] The goal of this agency is to facilitate a transition to democracy and free markets by helping them in the areas of economic and legal reforms; improving education, transportation, and communication; and establishing small and medium-size enterprises. The first act of TIKA was to organize a Turkic summit by inviting the heads of the independent Turkic republics to Ankara for the celebration of the seventieth anniversary of the establishment of the Republic of Turkey on October 30, 1992.[40]

During the first summit, the presidents of the Turkic republics—Nursultan Nazarbayev (Kazkhstan), Askar Akayev (Kyrgyzstan), Islam Karimov (Uzbekistan), Safarmurad Niyazov (Turkmenistan), and Ebulfez Elchibey (Azerbaijan)–signed the Ankara Declaration. In the introduction to this declaration, the presidents stressed their common history, close lingual links, and shared culture as a basis for developing close cooperation between each other and Turkey. The Ankara Declaration was an expression of intentions to develop closer ties. These rediscovered affinities have not yet been fully translated into solidarity and action. On the basis of the Ankara Declaration, however, Turkey focused on promoting a common alphabet, language, and education to create shared feelings and understanding within the "Turkic world." Due to internal differences, it will take a long time to form a "security and peace community." The second summit took place in Istanbul on October 18–19, 1994. The third one was in Bishkek on August 28, 1995, and the fourth was in Tashkent on October 21, 1996. Although Turkey suggested a formal structure of Turkish cooperation, Kazakhstan and the other republics did not support this. These informal summits have been continuing as discussion forums without much formal results.

The most crucial step the Ankara government took in the early 1990s was establishing air links with most of the republics and Tatarstan. Ankara also helped these states establish their own independent digital phone systems; some of the states still use Turkish communication satellites. Furthermore, Ankara also used its limited resources to create a shared cultural language and consolidate the Turkish aspect of their shared history.[41] It introduced a transnational television channel, TRT Avrasya, to beam Turkish cultural and language programming to the region. Although TRT Avrasya sought to raise the consciousness of the people of Central Asia to realize their common heritage with the Turks of Turkey, it highlighted sociocultural differences. Moreover,

Ankara offered 10,000 university scholarships to students mostly from the Turkic republics to study in Turkish universities. In the 1996–2003 academic year, the distribution of such students in Turkey was as follows:

Azerbaijan	3,793
Kazakistan	2,178
Kyrgyzstan	1,804
Turkmenistan	2,102
Uzbekistan	538
Other Turkic groups in the Russian Federation	2,710
Balkan countries	3,396[42]

The Ministry of Education has opened eighteen high schools in the Central Asian republics and Azerbaijan, and a Turkish nongovernmental group, the community of Fethullah Gülen, a leader of the Nurcu movement, opened 129 high schools and several universities, mostly in (but not limited to) the Turkic republics and other autonomous regions in the Russian Federation.[43] The distribution of these schools and their students is shown in table 6.1. These schools have become very popular in the republics due to their bilingual pro-

TABLE 6.1. Turkish High Schools Established in the Russian Federation

Country	Number of High Schools	Number of Students	Personnel from Turkey[a]
Kazakistan	32	6,539	670
Azerbaijan	15	4,023	368
Uzbekistan	18	3,334	210
Turkmenistan	16	3,290	373
Kyrgyzstan	14	3,093	391
Tatarstan	6	2,802	267
Tajikistan	5	1,694	107
Dagistan	5	1,228	143
Baskurtistan	3	532	98
Siberia	4	438	101
Russia	5	786	63
Cuvasia	2	311	89
Crimea	3	518	97
Karacay	1	193	13
Total	129		

[a]Teachers and administrators.

Sources: *Yurt Dişinda Acilan Özel Öğretiim Kurumlari Temsilcileri Ikinci Toplantısı* (Ankara: MEB Yurtdışı Eğitim Genel Müdürlüğü, 1997); *Milli Eğitim Bakanlığ ı Istatistikler* (Ankara: MEB, 2004).

grams in English and local languages and high quality of teaching in the physical sciences.[44]

Although Turkey made some long-term investments in the field of education, a number of factors helped dissipate Turkish romanticism toward Central Asia. The year 1993 was critical, forcing the government to reexamine its ties with the region. Due to geographical connections and its linguistic and cultural affinity, Turkey developed close ties with Azerbaijan, and the relations were treated as a model for other Turkic republics.[45] However, Russia used all means to intervene in Azeri domestic politics to test Turkish resolve and demonstrate the weaknesses of the government in Ankara. The major setback to Turkey's rising influence was the Azeri-Armenian conflict, which highlighted the failure of Turkey to help Baku resist an Armenian invasion in 1993. The removal of the pro-Turkish Ebulfeyz Elcibey from power further demonstrated the limits of Ankara's abilities. Thus, the Azeri-Armenian conflict and its political consequences derailed the Turkish dream of becoming a "big brother" in the region.

After Turgut Özal, Süleyman Demirel, the most timid and subservient and least visionary Turkish politician, dominated relations with the Central Asian states. Demirel personalized the relations with the Turkic states. During the Demirel era, some of the Turkish approaches to the region were similar to the colonial attitude of Russia. It did not take long to realize that not Turks but, rather, Kazaks, Kyrgyz, and Uzbeks lived in this region and had their own perceptions of history and culture.[46] At the same time, many Turks became aware of the gap between the "imagined Turkish world" and the reality of six different sovereign nation-states with their own particular interests. Moreover, as Turkey insisted that they be renamed as "Türk," they insisted that a "Türk" meant a citizen of Turkey more than a generic name of the Turkic peoples of Central Asia.

From "Big" Brotherly Aspirations to Normalization (1993–present)

After realizing its limits and the differences within and between different Turkic states and regions, the government in Ankara pursued a more cautious policy. In what is still an unfolding and very dynamic region, its main goal is to create a Turkish space by applying economic and cultural factors. However, Ankara was confronted with a set of obstacles in consolidating its relations with Central Asia. The main internal obstacles are the domestic divisions and weak coalition governments, limited economic resources, and lack of proper information about the region; externally, Turkey's conduct in the region has been conditioned by the human rights question and Russian policies to restrict Turkey's influence.

Turkey's ties with the Central Asian states are not totally determined by the foreign ministry; they are also affected by sizeable and influential civic pressure groups. These diverse economic and social groups ask Ankara to meet their needs in the region. Moreover, there is a growing tension within different sectors of these pressure groups. The ideological and social fault lines of Turkey have been carried out to the region through the official and unofficial Turkish presence there. It is easy to find many competing and conflicting circles of Turkish interest groups, which range from pan-Turkish nationalists to pan-Islamists, and from short-sighted carpetbaggers to long-term investors. The diversity and complexity of Turkey has been reflected in the 1,616 Turkish firms and 134 Turkish associations in Central Asia. The Turkish "reality" with all of its complexity now exists in Central Asia.

By 1998, the Turkish Eximbank offered $1.2 billion in credits to develop trade between the Central Asian states (CAS) and Turkey. The trade between the CAS and Turkey is currently above $1 billion. Turkish construction firms have over $1.7 billion worth of projects with Turkic republics.[47] In addition to limited economic resources of Turkey, geographic distance and transportation problems have constrained the development of trade between Turkey and the Turkic republics.

One of the major external constraints, in addition to the human rights problems, is the Russian factor. For several reasons, Russia wants to develop close ties with Turkey. For example, Turkey is Russia's main trade partner in the Middle East. Trade between the two countries ranges between $11–12 billion a year. Turkish construction firms have been involved in major projects, and they even reconstructed the Duma, which was damaged in 1993 by an abortive anti-Yeltsin coup. Many Russian tourists are visiting Turkey, and they have rejuvenated the small goods trade in Istanbul. Turkey is the major purchaser of gas from Russia, and this encourages the powerful Gasprom conglomerate to promote Turko-Russian ties and promote better understanding between the two countries. Moreover, Russia is a new and unconditional source of military hardware since some European countries refuse to sell arms to Turkey due to the Kurdish conflict.

Alternatively, there are also sets of factors that create a constant tension between Turkey and the Russian Federation, such as the intense competition over gas and oil pipelines in the Caucasus and Central Asia. Turkey is lobbying for a Kazak and Azeri oil pipeline to go through Georgia to the Turkish port of

Ceyhan rather than the Russian port of Novorossisk via Chechnya. To prevent environmental damage and protect Istanbul, the government of Turkey is already regulating traffic along the Bosphorus and the Dardanelles. Russia has offered a new route through Bulgaria to Greece to avoid Turkey. The major source of tension, however, is Russian wariness of Turkey's support for the Chechen fighters and other ethnic Muslim groups in the North Caucasus. Due to the lack of centralized authority in Moscow, Russia has been pursuing conflicting policies toward Turkey.

As Turkey's economic ties with Russia are rapidly expanding, Ankara becomes more sensitive to Russian needs and influence in Central Asia. In other words, Turkey's identity and interest-based policies are in conflict as far as its policies toward Central Asia and Russia are concerned.

Sources of Identity Politics in Turkish Foreign Policy: Turkish-Islam

Islam and Turkic identity inhibits Turkey's behavior toward Russia and facilitates close ties with the Central Asian states. Turkey's policy toward the region evolves more slowly than we might otherwise expect since the role and meanings of Turkish identity are still contested at home. With its multiple identities, Turkey is acting differently in the international system. Turkified-Islamic identity, or Turkish-Islam, has been the most powerful cognitive identity map to define national interest and is used as a tool to promote the interest of Turkey. Turkish-Islam has three major differentiating characteristics among the five major zones of Islam: Arabic, Persian, Turkic, Malay, and African. These characteristics are Sufi oriented, state-centric, and more mixed with vernacular cultures.[48]

Although it was Arab invaders who took Islam to the region in the eighth century, the conversion patterns and sociocultural structure created its own vernacular Turkic-Islam. Saman and Kam, as legendary religious-charismatic leaders, converted and became Sufi dervishes, known as "baba" and "ata."[49] These individuals personified the old religion and became major agents of Islamicization in Central Asia. The new faith was internalized through vernacular narratives and the syncretization of older traditions. Islam, as a new faith, was regarded as a part of native culture due to its ability to enhance and build on important facets of the old shamanism.[50] This symbiosis between different cultures and religions in the region helped produce three major Sufi orders: Yeseviyye, Kübreviyye, and Naksibendiyye. Ahmet Yesevi, Sarı Saltuk,

Hacı Bektaşı Veli, and Bahattin Naksibend constitute the major cornerstones of Islam in Turkey.

Ahmet Yesevi (d. 1166), the founder of the Yeseviyye order, became very influential among tribes of Kazaks and Kyrgyz by reinterpreting Islam to accommodate nomadic lifestyles.[51] He did not seek to negate old customs and traditions but used them to disseminate Islamic teaching. His teachings were collected by his followers in a book known as the *Divan-I Hikmet*. This work heavily influenced the Anatolian Sufi poet Yunus Emre. This was one of the first literary Turkish works on Islam. Even though Yesevi knew Arabic and Persian, he wrote his work in the vernacular Turkic dialect to communicate with the people of the region. Many Central Asian Turks regard the teachings of Ahmet Yesevi as a part of their shared Turkic tradition. Yeseviyye became the intellectual origin of Kubreviyye, Naksibendiyye, and Bektasiyye in the Anatolian peninsula. Thus, Yesevi and his vernacularized understanding of Islam has been the dominant form of Islam in the Turkic world.

Since the first converts were the local khans and the population followed the top-down conversion, Islam has always been an ideology of power and social control. Some nomadic societies treated Islam as a conquering ideology of a sedentary population. Islam mixed with local customs (*adat*) set the parameters of social interactions in the Turkic world. One of the main characteristics of Islamization was the localization of religion in the region, and this created a powerful connection between local culture and Islam.

Between the sixteenth and nineteenth centuries, when the dynastic states weakened, Islam became the glue of civil society and social capital. This connection was then reproduced with the age of nationalism in the nineteenth century. Sufi orders became the major institutions for the reconciliation between local culture and universal Islamic norms. The same orders were at the center of an -ethnoreligious revival known as Jadidism in Russia and the Turkic world, which would greatly influence Turkish nationalism.

Against the colonial penetration of the elite, the Jadid movement sought to construct a Turkistani identity by reimagining a modernist Islam. The Jadid movement had a key role in the articulation of national identities. In short, Turkistani identity and local identities were reimagined within this spiritual domain of Islam. Turkic and Islamic identity were used interchangeably, and this, in turn, played a constitutive role in the formation of national identities of the new Central Asian states. Therefore, religious networks played an important part in Turkish relations with Central Asia.

Islam in Central Asia and Russia does not easily denote a religious category per se; instead, it is an ethnocultural category. Thus, the boundary between religion and ethnicity is blurred and in flux, just like in Turkey. The overwhelming population of the region is Sunni and belongs to the Hanafi school of law. Ethnic or cultural revival usually takes Islamic forms without necessarily being religious. As the engine of modernism, Jadidism, the Islam of Central Asia in the late nineteenth century, helped to highlight the "difference" between the Turkic groups and the dominant Russians.[52] Under communist rule, the people of the region created a sacred territory through imagined and invented holy places and cemeteries to maintain and perpetuate their conception of Islam. They also maintained their "distinctions" from the ruling Russian colonialism through circumcision, wedding, and burial rites. For these reasons, Russian academics and politicians frequently labeled all cultural revival and identity claims as "reactionary" and "fundamentalist."

From this symbiotic relationship between ethnicity and religion in Central Asia, the Soviet Union engineered a number of national identities to curb the potential unification of the region along Islamic or Turkistani lines. In the 1920s, Moscow divided the region into five independent republics, by highlighting ethnic and cultural nuancesand creating territorial national identities. Disparate dialects were made standardized national languages, and national histories were constructed in Moscow to be consumed by the elites of the region. Moreover, the construction of separate economies and administrative units helped consolidate separate national identities. In the 1980s, a weak and fragmented national "awakening" punctuated major sociopolitical events.[53] This "national" revival took Islamic coloring, and Islam became the language of opposition against the heavy-handed Soviet policies and the local Communist Party elites who sought to take over.

During the 1970s and 1980s, many Western scholars looked to Islam as the force that would undermine communist rule. In the study of the Soviet period, the scholarship of the Central Asian people was dominated by Cold War convictions and the field was dominated by Alexandre Bennigsen (1913–1988). He constantly presented Muslims as being the weakest integrated part of the Soviet system due to the role of Islam. They also presented these ambiguous Islamic loyalties as a form of "Muslim nationalism."[54] In 1982, Bennigsen argued:

> Soviet Muslims ... are likely to be influenced by the ideas (perhaps even by the political terrorism and guerrilla methods) adopted from the newly radicalized Middle East. These ideas, ranging from the most conservative religious fundamentalism to the wildest revolutionary, share one common characteristic: the potential for destabilizing Soviet Islam, thereby undermining the stability of the USSR itself.[55]

This orientalizing thesis dominated studies in the area. American scholar Michael Rywkin of the City University of New York popularized this view. A closer examination indicates that Islam did not play a significant role in the demise of the Soviet Union. The causes of this demise were those groups in the European part of the union rather than the Muslim borderlands of the Soviet Union. The Central Asian republics, dominated by cliques of notoriously corrupt nomenclatura, mostly voted to preserve the union. The conflicts between Uzbeks and Meskhetian Turks in 1989 and between Kyrgyz and Uzbeks in 1990 indicated that more narrow loyalties, not Islamic loyalty, are more dominant.[56] The modern revival of Islam in the Central Asian context means the "rebirth" and consolidation of ethnocultural identity, not the appropriation of Islamic "fundamentalism" from the Middle East.[57]

As the nations of Central Asia seek to construct their collective memories to consolidate their selfhood, Islam is used as a leading source. The Islam of Central Asia is a historical partner to nation building. However, with the collapse of the Soviet empire, the people of the region are searching for an "other" to consolidate their national identity. The people of the region have been trying to nationalize and parcel out the shared legacy of the region. For instance, the Kyrgyz stress their mythical hero, Manas, who illustrates their own pre-Islamic origins. The Kazaks bring their Abai, a writer and a poet, as a synthesizer of Islamic and Kazak roots; and the Turkmens are seeking to embody their roots in terms of Machtumquli. The Uzbeks have been busy trying to differentiate themselves from other Central Asiatic nations by highlighting "Amir Temur" as a state-builder and the founder of the Uzbek nation.

Turkey's Islamization Project

Turkey has been trying to use this common shared ethnoreligious culture to create a number of institutions to develop cooperation. Institutionalization in the religious domain is well advanced and still developing. Turkey has developed ties with the first two of three layers of Central Asian Islam. These layers are official, folk (Sufi brotherhoods), and the legendary (*efsanevi*) Islam.[58]

Official Islam

Establishment Islam is articulated in the form of the four Spiritual Boards of Directorate set up by Stalin in 1943 in Tashkent, Baku, Makhachkala, and Ufa. They aimed at the secularization and ultimate dissolution of Islam. These boards had administrative authority to regulate religious affairs of the state. It stressed that Islam is not opposed to communism but that the two could coexist in harmony. With newfound independence, the states formed their own national religious administration, and the government of Turkey has been more active in distribution of religious material and training of religious functionaries. In other words, the Directorate of Religious Affairs of Turkey has tried to carry out a re-Islamization of Central Asia. The Foundation of Turkish Religious Affairs, known as Türk Diyanet Vakfı (TDV), an official state-run foundation, has been at the forefront for exporting a "soft and nationalized Turkish Islam" to Central Asia. The head of the directorate, Mehmet N. Yılmaz, defines Turkish national identity in terms of Islam. Yılmaz argues that "if we take those acquired Islamic characteristics out of Turkish national identity, there will be little left behind. Islam molds Turkish national identity. Islam is both reason and guarantor of our national existence."[59]

According to the 1999 March Report of TDV, the foundation opened a Divinity Faculty (1992) in Azerbaijan; Baku Turk High School (1994) and Nahcivan Religious Education High School (1994) in Azarbaijan; Mahdumkuli Divinity Faculty (1994) and Asgabat Preacher High School (1993) in Turkmenistan; Alma Ata Divinity Faculty at the Alemdiller University (1997) and the Osh Divinity Faculty (1993) in Kyrgyzstan; and the Derbent Divinity Faculty (1996) in Dagestan. All these schools have close cooperation with one of the divinity faculties in Turkey, and their students usually spend their first or last academic year in Turkey. The TDV also developed one of the most extensive religious functionary exchange programs with most of the Central Asian states. The directorate of religious affairs has opened several training centers to educate imams (preachers). These training centers have 4,000 students (table 6.2). Between 1992 and 1995, the TDV spent 3.5 trillion TL for different mosque-building projects in Central Asia. No organization has been as active as the TDV.[60] The Turkish Directorate of Religious Affairs has 102 religious functionaries (table 6.3).

Turkey has been very active in the region. Before the February 28 "soft-coup" in Turkey, the directorate was the most powerful institution in the region. It organized the First Euroasian Islamic Congress on October 23–25, 1995, by inviting the head of twenty-one countries and autonomous regions. The Second Eurasia Congress, which included thirty-two countries and autonomous regions, took place on October 21–24, 1996, and it institutionalized itself by establishing a permanent secretariat in Ankara.[61] The Third Eurasia Islamic Congress took place on May 25–29, 1998, in Ankara. The Republic of Turkey has managed to become the main center for Islamic activism and a source of support for Turkish and Muslim communities.[62] Turkey has constructed thirty mosques in the newly independent Turkic regions.[63]

TABLE 6.2. Imam Training Centers Established by
Turkey

Country	Number of Students
Azarbaijan	897
Crimea	864
Kyrgyzstan	444
Kazakistan	687
Russian Federation	
Tatarstan	800
Turkmenistan	210
Tajikistan	140
Total	4,042

Source: Diyanet Isleri Başkanlığı Türk Cumhuriyetleri, Balkan-Kafkas
Ulkeleri, Turk ve Musluman Topluluklara Goturulen Hizmetler (Ankara:
Diyanet Yayınları, 1996).

Sufi Islam

Sufi groups in Turkey have also established close ties with old Sufi networks to
revive Sufism. This unofficial Islam is a hybrid ideology made up by combining
Sufism and local traditions. During Soviet rule, long-haired Ishans appeared in
the 1960s. They constituted the largest Sufi group in the area and resisted
atheistic propaganda.[64] People visited holy places, and mystical tombs became
centers for religious performances. Turkey-based Naksibendi and Nurcu
groups continued to be very active in the region. For instance, the Istanbul-

TABLE 6.3. TDV Religious Functionaries
in Other Countries

Country	Number of Religious Functionaries
Azerbaijan	21
Kazakistan	29
Kyrgyzstan	35
Uzbekistan	1
Russian Federation	19
Turkmenistan	23
Tajikistan	1
Crimea	19
Total	128

Source: Diyanet Isleri Baskanlığı, Dış Ilişkiler Dairesi
Başkanlığı, B.02.1.DIB.0.76.00.050-3619, June 8, 1999;
2004 [government documents].

based Iskenderpasa Naksibendi order has a number of centers in Central Asia and managed to integrate some prominent personalities into the order. The Nurcu community of Fethullah Gülen (b.1938) has carried out the most effective re-Islamization process. In spite of all the efforts of Saudi-backed Wahhabi Islam and Iranian ambitions in the region, Nurcus have been the most influential in the region for several reasons. Many people perceive the Nurcu interpretation of Islam as a "national Turkic understanding of Islam." One reason is the close connection between folk Islam and narrative-based texts of Said Nursi (1873–1960).[65] Nursi, who authored several volumes of Qur'anic exegesis, known as the *Risale-I Nur Kulliyati* (The Epistle of Light), transmitted Islamic information and knowledge through narrative stories about the family of the Prophet or other major events. There is a similar pattern of transmission between legendary/oral Islam and the print-based narrative Islam of Fethullah Gülen. Islamic knowledge and lessons are rooted in narrative stories. Second, due to the heavy-handed atheism of the Soviet period in Central Asia, Islam could only survive by reconciling reason and science.[66]

The writings of Said Nursi reflect the attempt at the reconciliation between Islam and modernity and between reason and revelation. This Sufi-oriented and "softer" Turkish Islam has been more appealing to the younger people of Central Asia to reconstruct their faith rather than the Saudi-based Wahhabism or the Iranian version of a "rigid" Islam. Knowledge in the *Risale-I Nur* is not transmitted in terms of rigid rules but through narratives. The schools of Gülen have managed to distribute the writings of Nursi and mark the geography of Central Asia with Sufi Islam. The activities of the Directorate of Turkish Religious Affairs and Nurcu networks have been reconstituting the meaning and role of Islam in Central Asia and undermining their oral and mythical Islamic practices.

Legendary Islam or Efsanevi

Efsanevi was the major carrier of Islamic tradition in the region. This mythical Islam is common among villagers and some city dwellers and derives its core beliefs from the Qur'an. It also incorporates much older religious rites and rituals, predating Islam. Mythical oral-based Islam incorporates pre-Islamic tradition and seeks to create a sacred canopy through stories, mythologies, tales, and legends. These stories indirectly dealt with the authority, community, and everyday life experiences. The oral tradition of Central Asia is very much infused with Islamic history, ethics, and theology. In the preservation and perpetuation of this oral tradition, the itinerant minstrel of Turkic culture, known as the *ashık, dzyrshy, aqyn,* and *baqsy,* played an important role.[67] Minstrels traveled from one region to another and helped to create a Turkic cognitive shared code of conduct and tastes. They embody their understanding of religion linked to geography by creating narratives around key mountains and rivers. Most of the Kyrgyz and Kazak communities are still under the influence of this oral-mythical Islam since they never achieved an Orthodox Islamic establishment. For example, several graves of Ali, the Prophet's cousin and fourth caliph, are purported to exist in the Fergana Valley. The most critical means for promoting communal ethical life are the narratives, which are used and mobilized for several purposes.[68] Finally, Turkish groups and the government institutions have been reconstructing the tombs of some prominent religious leaders. For instance, the tombs of Shah-i Zindeh in Samarkant, Bahattin Naksibend in Bukhara, and Ahmad Yesevi in Cimkent are reconstructed by this aid from Turkey.

Within the legendary Islam, there is a popular Islam that stresses funeral rites, the cult of the dead, the cult of the saints, and wedding and circumcision ceremonies.

Radical Islam or Fergana Fundamentalism

Political Islam differs from cultural and social Islam in terms of its resistance against modernity, especially cultural contradictions that are produced by modern processes. They accept modern technology and science but reject modern versions of individualism and stress instrumental rationality. Political Islamic movements reject secularism as an ideological and epistemological approach that is incompatible with Islamic worldview. And most political Islamists are anti-Western and anti-European. The colonial legacy and the continued Arab-Israeli conflict are two sources of anti-Westernism among Islamists. Many Islamists criticized the weak state structure and illegitimate state structure in the Middle East. They all stress pan-Islamic loyalty over that of the nation-state. Although many Central Asian Islamists are exposed to these ideas, they are not fully internalized. Radical Islamism is imported, either from Pakistan or some Arab countries. Since Central Asian Muslims have only a rudimentary knowledge of Islam, they are open to radical exploitation by some foreign groups. There is a great interest in Islam, especially among the youth, and when the state institutions and civil society fail to offer necessary sources, foreign sources become the only option.

Almost all writings on Islam in Central Asia focus on the Fergana Valley "fundamentalism" and link this to the Wahhabi movement, in Central Asia.

The term "Wahhabi" is shorthand for any form of religious revival. The Islamic Movement of Uzbekistan (IMU) has been seeking to overthrow the government of Kerimov. Indeed, the valley is overpopulated and suffers from land and water shortage; it has the highest unemployment rate, which is currently close to 27 percent. The Wahhabi movement is powerful in the Fergana Valley, as this region was the most difficult for the Russian and communist colonialists to control. Under Russian colonialism, local Islamic movements, known as *qadimiyyah* (Qadimists), stressed the role of the golden age of Islam and the significance of the institution of the caliphate.

Several radical Islamic groups exist in Central Asia. The most prominent is Hizb al-Tahrir al-islami, which became powerful in Namangan by resisting the state clergy. Although the movement evolved out of Jordan-based Hizb al-Tahris, under the leadership of Akram Yuldashev it localized and became an Uzbek movement. His book *Iymonga yul* (The Path to True Faith) developed twelve ways of raising one's religio-political consciousness. He believed that the only true rebirth is realized if all Muslims become conscious in the realization of the caliphate. Yuldashev argues that Muslims are in the state of *jahilliyyah* (innocence), and they could only overcome it through personal and communal Islamic consciousness. The movement later on was called "Akramiyyah" from its local characteristics. It is organized as cells (*halqa*), and its followers are urged to trade with each other and support the members with all means. These Akramiyya communities are found in the regions of Namangan, Kokand, and Osh. The leader of the movement was arrested and is still in jail.

The second most mentioned radical Islamic group is known as the Islamic Renaissance Party (IRP). It is an all-Muslim party that was created during the Soviet period in June 1990.[69] Its first goals were the introduction of Islamic law and the creation of an Islamic state. The party eventually limited its campaign with social and cultural rejuvenation of the Central Asian Islamic culture. The party became more powerful in Uzbekistan and Tajikistan. The IRP declined in the late 1990s.

The authoritarian rulers of Central Asia tend to overestimate Islamic radicalism and use it against all civic initiatives and attempts to claim Islam. The politicization of Islam and the radicalization are not real possibilities in Central Asia due to four major factors. Radicalism lacks intellectual vigor and appeal since there are no Seyyid Qutbs or Mawdudis to transform Islam (the faith and moral charter) into Islamism (the ideology). The region is not anti-Western or anti-American but, rather, anti-Russian. One would expect a more local, nativist, version of Islamism that is development oriented and seeks to rebuild civic tradition of Central Asia.

Conclusion

Islamic debates in Central Asia do not seem to be a major threat to the stability of the region. The fear of Islamism is deeply rooted in Soviet and Western scholarship, and this fear tends to exaggerate the threat of religious revivalism in Central Asia. What is taking place in Central Asia is the reclaiming of Islam from state control and turning it into a source of morality and identity.

A new framework of thinking developed in Ankara, in its ties to the region after an initial period of confident euphoria and subsequent failure and disappointment. These policies have today created a framework of cooperation between Turkey and the Turkic republics and other ethnic Turkic communities within the Russian Federation.

In the evolution of Turkey-Turkic republics relations, ethnicity and religion are the two cultural resources used by the government in Ankara. Due to the effects of Stalinist secularization in "Turkic communities," ethnicity or ethnoreligious affinity, rather than purely religious solidarity, became significant. The strategies and policies of Turkey have been more guided by societal groups such as Turkish businessman, cultural institutions, and ethnoreligious Islamic networks than the state itself.

The identity of the Turkish state is partly defined by the identity of others in the region and that of the EU. Turkey's three layers of identity have been in flux, due to the changing international system. Different identities—such as Islamic, Turkish, and European (Balkan)—have different meanings. In Central Asia and Turkey, Islam and ethnic identity are codeterminant: one becomes a Turk if he or she becomes Muslim. Different identities are likely to produce different and even competing foreign policies. Turkishness, not Islamism, shapes the perceptions of the Turkish elite. Identity is not only a tool to promote interest but also a set of views from which issues are examined and made meaningful. Turkish-Islamic identity operates at a very deep level by allowing individuals to give meanings to actions and aspirations.

In the formation of Turkey's Central Asian policy, Islam takes a subordinate role. Although the most important identity that shapes these relations is Turkism, not Islam, Islam is an essential part of Turkish identity. Islamic connections are more spread out and deeper, but not quite decisive. The ties between Turkey and Turkic-majority states and groups are articulated within the discursive tradition of Turkish nationalism. Therefore, Islamic and Turkic layers should not be seen as utterly opposing forces but mutually constitutive tendencies within Turkish nationalism. These two layers of identity imperceptibly merge and shape Turkey's orientation. In other words, the Turkish,

Uzbek, Kazak, Kyrgyz, and Tatar nations, among others, are rooted in Islamic symbolism and shaped by political conditions.

Due to the recent rise of nationalism in Turkey, new governments in Ankara have had a strong Central Asian orientation. The major foreign policy goal of the National Movement Party, for example, has been to consolidate ties with Central Asia at the expense of Turkish-EU relations. Again, in the party program, it aims to turn Turkey into a "leader of the Turkish states."[70] The election program of the party used the "Turkish world" rather than the "Turkic world" to illustrate the special role that Turkey has in the consolidation of the ties among the Turkish communities and states. Through the theme of the "Turkish world," they stress not only the ties at the state level but also, and perhaps more significantly for the future, at the communal level. The party treats cooperation within the Turkish world as "compulsory and vital," and its calls for the establishment of a "ministry of the Turkish world." It also calls for a common market binding this Turkish world together.

To ensure future stability for Central Asia, Islamic political activities should not be banned, and they should be encouraged to participate in political processes—as has been done in Tajikistan with its Islamic Renaissance Party. Central Asian Muslims are reclaiming Islam while resisting the state-centric-controlled Islam. The goal of this reclaiming is to bring in the code of ethics and to enhance civil society through religious social capital. Moreover, the containment of political Islam is not productive or successful. The long-term policy should aim to promote democracy, pluralism, and economic development rather than banning religious activism or practicing exclusionary politics. If intolerance toward democracy and Islamic participation continues in the region, and if economic development fails to benefit a significant majority of the republics' masses, the future may well be shaped by violence and constant conflict, and radical interpretations of Islam will likely act as the attractive ideology of resistance in Central Asia.

NOTES

The research and writing of this article was funded by the Middle East Center and the College of Social and Behavioral Sciences of the University of Utah.

1. Alexander Bennigsen and Marie Broup, *The Islamic Threat to the Soviet Union* (London: Croom Helm, 1983).

2. Alexander Bennigsen, "Several Nations or One People: Ethnic Consciousness among Soviet Central Asian Muslims," *Survey* 24:3 (1979), p. 53.

3. Alexander Bennigsen and S. Enders Wimbush, *Muslims of the Soviet Empire* (London: C. Hurst, 1986), p. 3.

4. M. B. Olcatt, " Soviet Islam and World Revolution," *World Politics* 34:4 (1982), p. 498.

5. Nazif Shahrani, "Islam and the Political Culture of 'Scientific Atheism' in Post-Soviet Central Asia: Future Predicament," *Islamic Studies* (Pakistan) 33:2–3 (1994), pp. 139–60.

6. S. A. Adshead, *Central Asia in World History* (New York: St. Martin's, 1993), p. 15.

7. W. Madelung, "The Early Murji'a and Transoxania and the Spread of Hanafism," *Der Islam* 59 (1982), pp. 32–39.

8. Dale F. Eickelman, "Studies of Islam in Local Context," *Contributions to Asian Studies* 17 (1983), pp. 1–16.

9. *Ziyaret* means visiting a shrine or family graves for the purpose of giving greetings. During *ziyaret*, one recites the Qur'an and also gives money to the caretakers.

10. Cliffort Geertz, *Islam Observed: Religious Development in Morocco and Indonesia* (New Haven, Conn.: Yale University Press, 1968). I do not share this sharp division between these two modes of Islam. I think in everyday practices people have both modes.

11. Adeeb Khalid, *The Politics of Muslim Cultural Reform: Jadidism in Central Asia* (Berkeley: University of California Press, 1999).

12. Nilüfer Göle, "Islami Dokunulmazlar, Laikler ve Radikal Demokratlar," *Türkiye Günlügü* 27 (March–April 1994), pp. 13–18.

13. M. Hakan Yavuz, "The Abrading of the Turkish Republican Myth," *JIME (Japanese Institute of Middle Eastern Economies) Review* 12:41 (1998), pp. 18–34.

14. According to Article 66 of the 1982 constitution, "every person who is bound with citizenship to the Turkish Republic is a Turk." In everyday life, however, being a Turk is defined in terms of being Muslim and having Turkish ethnicity.

15. *Strategic Survey 1997/1998* (London: Oxford University Press, 1998), p. 132.

16. M. Hakan Yavuz and Mujeeb R. Khan, "A Bridge between East and West Duality and the Development of Turkish Foreign Policy toward the Arab-Israeli Conflict," *Arab Studies Quarterly* 14:4 (Fall 1992), pp. 69–95.

17. A. Went, "Levels of Analysis vs. Agents and Structures: Part III," *Review of International Studies* 18 (1992), p. 183.

18. A. Went, "Anarchy Is What States Make of It: The Social Construction of Power Politics," *International Organization* 46 (1992), pp. 391–425.

19. M. Hakan Yavuz, "Turkic Identity and Foreign Policy in Flux: The Rise of Neo-Ottomanism," *Critique* 12 (1998), pp. 19–42; for more on the relationship between identity and national interests, see *Liberal Düşünce*, No. 13 (1999). Available at: http://www.liberal-dt.org.tr/*.

20. Emmanuel Adler argues that the transformation of identities and interests may be the "constructivist dependent variable" (Adler, "Seizing the Middle Ground: Constructivism in World Politics," *European Journal of International Relations* 3 [1997], p. 344).

21. This survey was conducted by the Konrad Adenauer Foundation, *Turkish Youth 98: The Silent Majority Highlighted* (Ankara: Tasarım, 1999).

22. Mujeeb R. Khan, "The 'Other' in the Balkans: Historical Construction of Serb and "Turks," *Journal of Muslim Minority Affairs* 16:1 (1996), pp. 49–64.

23. For more on the identity debate in Turkey, see Edibe Sözen, "Modernite ve Kültürel Kimlik," in *Sosyoloji Konferansları* (Istabul: Cantay Kitabevi, 1998), pp. 153–60.

24. Birol Yesilada, "The Worsening EU-Turkey Relations," *SAIS Review* 19:1 (1999), pp. 144–62.

25. Cengiz Candar, "Değismekte olan Dünyada Türkiye'nin Bağımsızlıgı Kazanan Yeni Türk Cumhuriyetleriyle Ilişkileri," by Faruk Sönmezoğlu, ed., *Yeni Dünya Düzeni ve Türkiye* (Istanbul: Bağlam, 1992), pp. 133–42.

26. For more on those "outside Turks" who had a critical role in Turkish culture and politics, see Ertugrul Yaman et al., *Türkiye'deki Türk Dünyası* (Ankara: Diyanet Işleri Başkanlıgı, Yayınları, 1998).

27. For more on ethnicity-based Turkish nationalism, see the special issue on Turkish nationalism in the twenty-first century in *Türk Yurdu* 19:139–141 (March–May 1999). This issue has 100 essays on different aspects of Turkish nationalism.

28. M. Hakan Yavuz, "Nationalism and Islam: Yusuf Akçura, Üç Tarz-i Siyaset," *Oxford Journal of Islamic Studies.* 4:2 (1993), pp. 175–207.

29. A. Suat Bilge, "Analysis of Turkish-Russian Relations," *Perceptions: Journal of International Affairs* 2:2 (June–August 1997), pp. 66–92.

30. Ahat Andican, *Degişim Sürecinde Türk Dünyası* (Istanbul: Emre Yayınları, 1996).

31. Jacob Landau, *Pan-Turkism: From Irredentism to Cooperation* (Bloomington: Indiana University Press, 1995); Hakki Öznur, *Ülkücü Hareket I–VI* (Ankara: AlternatifYayınları, 1999).

32. Ahmet Kuru, "Türkiye'nin Orta Asya'ya Yönelişi," in Mim Kemal Oke, ed., *Geçiş Surecinde Orta Asya Türk Cumhuriyetleri* (Istanbul: Alfa, 1999), pp. 128–51; Oral Sander, "Turkey and the Turkic World," *Central Asian Survey* 13:1 (1994), p. 3744.

33. Ali Faik Demir, "SSCB'nin Dagılmasından Sonra Türkiye-Azerbaycan Ilişkileri," in Faruk Sönmezoglu, ed., *Degişim Dünya ve Türkiye* (Istanbul: Baglam, 1995), pp. 221–48.

34. John Palmer, "Rule of Ottoman Empire," *Guardian*, April 3, 1992; "The Sick Man Recovers," *Times*, printed in *Newspot Turkish Digest*, February 13, 1992,.

35. Paul Kubicek, Nation, State, and Economy in Central Asia: Does Atatürk Provide a Model? Occasional Paper, No. 14 (Seattle: University of Washington, Henry M. Jackson School of International Studies, 1997).

36. Turgut Özal set the guidelines of Turkey's Central Asian policy in his opening speech at the Turkish Grand National Assembly (TBMM Tutanak Dergisi [Dönem: 19–1, Cilt 1, No. 3], p. 25). In this speech, Ozal asked Parliament to capitalize this new opportunity of establishing close ties with the Turkic states and the autonomous regions in Russia.

37. For more on Özal's statement, see *Dünya*, 6 November 1992.

38. Graham E. Fuller, "Turkey's New Eastern Orientation," in Graham E. Fuller and Ian O. Lesser, eds.,*Turkey's New Geopolitics: From the Balkans to Western China* (Boulder, Colo.: Westview, 1993), pp. 37–98.

39. Necati Utkan, "Türk Işbirligi ve Kalkınma Ajansı (TIKA) Hakkında Bir Degerlendirme," *Yeni Türkiye* 15 (May–June 1997), pp. 946–51.

40. *Milliyet*, October 31, 1992,.

41. Mustafa Öner, "Ortak Türk Alfabesi," *Yeni Türkiye* 15 (1997), pp. 207–11.

42. Mehmet Sağlam, "Türk Cumhuriyetleri ile Eğitim Ilişkilerimiz," *Yeni Türkiye* 15 (1997), p. 684; Minister of Education Statistics, 10 April 2004.

43. M. Fethullah Gülen, "Orta Asya Eğitim Hizmetleri," *Yeni Türkiye* 15 (1997), pp. 685–95. Gülen examines the reasons for his educational activism in Central Asia and other regions of the world.

44. M. Hakan Yavuz, "Osta Asya'daki Kimlik Oluşumu: Yeni Kolonizatör Dervişler-Nurcular," *Türkiye Günlüğü* 33 (1995), pp. 160–64. During my fieldwork in the Fergana Valley, I examined the impact of the Nurcu community of Fethullah Gülen.

45. Turkey shares a twelve-kilometer border with the Azeri enclave of Nakcivan.

46. Cenk Başlamış, "10 Yıl Sonra Orta Asya," *Milliyet*, July 15–22, 1998.

47. Ali Coskun, "Türk Dünyası ve Komsularımız," *Yeni Türkiye* 15 (1997), p. 764; Sükrü Elekdag, "Avrasya'nin Balkanları," *Milliyet*, April 5, 1998.

48. There are several studies about the role of Islam in Central Asia; for example: Mehrdad Haghayeghi, *Islam and Politics in Central Asia* (New York: St. Martin's, 1995); A. Bennigsen and M. Broxup, *Islamic Threat to the Soviet State* (New York: St. Martin's, 1983); Dale Eickelman, ed., *Russia's Muslim Frontiers* (Indianapolis: Indiana University Press, 1993). For a typical orientalist treatment of Islam, see Sergei Poliakov, *Everyday Islam* (London: M. E. Sharpe, 1992).

49. Osman Türer, "Türk Dünyasında Islam'in Yayılması ve Muhafazasında Tasavvuf ve Tarikatler," *Yeni Dergi* 15 (May–June 1997), pp. 174–81; Fuat Köprülü, *Türk Edebiyatında ilk Mutasavvıflar* (Ankara: Diyanet Işleri Başkanlıgı, Yayinevi, 1984), pp. 14–20.

50. M. M. Blazer, ed., *Shamanism: Soviet Studies of Traditional Religion in Siberia and Central Asia* (Armonk, N.Y.: M. E. Sharpe, 1990).

51. In recent years, the Kazak government has been seeking to nationalize his work as a "Kazak."

52. Adeeb Khalid, *The Politics of Muslim Cultural Reform: Jadidism in Central Asia* (Berkeley: University of California Press, 1998).

53. Yaacov Ro'i, "The Impact of the Islamic Fundamentalist Revival of the Late 1970s on the Soviet View of Islam," in Yaacov Ro'i, ed., *The USSR and the Muslim World* (London: George Allen and Unwin, 1984), pp. 149–77.

54. A. Bennigsen and M. Broxup, *The Islamic Threat to the Soviet State* (New York: St. Martin's, 1983), p. 114; Michael Rywkin, *Moscow's Muslim Challenge* (London: M. E. Sharpe, 1990), p. 85.

55. Bennigsen and Broxup, *Islamic Threat*, p. 117.

56. In 1989, the leadership of the Central Asian Spiritual Administration changed, and Muhammad Sadik Muhammad Yusuf took over from conformist Samsuddin-Quari Babakhanov. Sadik was educated in Libya and came from the Fergana Valley. The most religiously active cities are Andijan and Namangan. Two groups—Adalat and Tawba—were formed in 1991 and had very radical views. They captured several buildings and later were crushed by Kerimov. Things turned against Sadik in mid 1992. In February 1993, the All-Muslim Kurultai elected Muktar Abdullayev to replace Muhammad Sadik. Sadik was forced into exile, first in Saudi Arabia and currently in Turkey. Kerimov seeks to exert his power and promote depoliticization by institutionalizing the *mahalla* (neighborhood-community) as a unit of administration.

57. One of the best works on Islam in Central Asia is Yaacov Ro'i, ed., *Muslim Eurasia: Conflicting Legacies* (London: Frank Cass, 1995).

58. M. Hakan Yavuz, "Efsanevi Islam: Atatalar Dini ve Modern Baglantılar," in *Türk Dünyasının Dini Meseleleri* (Ankara: Diyanet İşleri Başkanlığı, Yayınları, 1998), pp. 11–24. This book includes the proceedings of the conference on Islamic institutions in the Turkic world. For more on Islam, see Yaacov Ro'i, "The Islamic Influence on Nationalism in Soviet Central Asia," *Problems of Communism* (July–August 1990), pp. 49–64.

59. For more on Yılmaz's speech, see I. Avrasya, *Islam Şurası* (Ankara: Diyanet İşleri Başkanlığı, 1996), p. 30. During the congress, the Turkish representatives, in particular, Bülent Ecevit, constantly stressed the virtues of Turkish Islam as Sufi Islam. Ecevit identified two major characteristics of Turkish Islam as Sufi and love-based Islam, versus fear-based Arab Islam, and saw Turkish Islam as more popular and democratic.

60. I thank Omer Turan for the information from the TDV. The figures are from the 1996 Annual Report of the TDV.

61. For more, see *Avrasya Islam Şurası* (Ankara: Diyanet Isleri Başkanlığı, 1997).

62. *II. Avrasya Islam Şurası* (Ankara: Diyanet Isleri Başkanlığı, 1998). This book includes basic information about Islamic institutions and activities in thirty-two countries and regions. It is heavily focused on Muslims in the former Soviet Union and Yugoslavia.

63. Kemal Güran, a vice president of the TDV, speech in *I. Avrasya Islam Şurası* (Ankara: Diyanet İşleri Başkanlığı, 1996), p. 156.

64. Alen Hetmanek, "Islamic Revival in the USSR," *Religion in Communist Dominated Areas* (Keston, U.K.) (Summer 1968), pp. 83–86.

65. M. Hakan Yavuz, "Efsanevi Islam: Atalar Dini ve Modern Baglantilar," in *Türk Dünyasının Dini Meseleleri* (Ankara: Turkiye Diyanet Vakfı Yayınları, 1998), pp. 11–24; M. Hakan Yavuz, "Turkistan'da halkın manevi dünyası: Efsanevi Islam," *Dergah* 62 (April 1995)

66. For more on the Soviet atheistic policies and their impact, see Nazif Shahrani, "Islam and the Political Culture of 'Scientific Atheism.'"

67. For more on oral literature in Central Asia, see Thomas Gustav Winner, *The Oral Art and Literature of the Kazakhs of Russian Central Asia* (Durham, N.C.: Duke University Press, 1958).

68. Maria Eva Subtelny, "The Cult of Holy Places: Religious Practices among Soviet Muslims," *Middle East Journal* (Autumn 1989), pp. 593–604.

69. Bess Brown, "The Islamic Renaissance Party in Central Asia," RFE/RL, *Report on the USSR*, May 10, 1991.

70. Sibel Utku, "MHP Foreign Policy: 'Turkish World' and Cyprus," *Turkish Daily News*, April 21, 1999.

7

A Provincial Islamist Victory in Pakistan: The Social Reform Agenda of the Muttahida Majlis-i-Amal

Anita M. Weiss

In October 2002, national and provincial elections were held throughout Pakistan. While little changed as a result of the national election, a decidedly Islamist political coalition, the Muttahida Majlis-i-Amal (MMA), was voted into office in the provincial election in the Northwest Frontier Province (NWFP).[1] It was also able to share power in a coalition government in the province of Baluchistan and came to head the opposition in the National Assembly. This unprecedented outcome was the first time in Pakistan's fifty-five-year history that an Islamist political party had won a significant election. The social and political implications of this event are staggering, for Pakistan is but one of many Muslim states that are grappling with balancing the demands of modernity and globalization with the often contradictory demands of their local populace. As many Muslims around the world—and particularly in Pakistan—perceive that the U.S. "war on terror" is a misnomer and is actually a "war against Muslims," the MMA's victory was perceived as a boon by those who admonished the Government of Pakistan's continuing support of the U.S. military invasion of Afghanistan. Is the outcome of the NWFP elections an isolated event, or is it setting a precedent for Islamist political groups seeking to ascend to power more and more frequently, worldwide, in the future?

The rise of this kind of Islamist political force represents one of the greatest concerns today within the Muslim world, particularly among Asian Muslim countries, where Islam is increasingly used as a rallying cry of identity politics, although little consensus exists anywhere on the priorities of an Islamist government should one come to power. Are social and cultural policies the most compelling to implement first, or should the emphasis be on legal transformations and, if so, according to which school of *fiqh* (jurisprudence)? If the former, need it prioritize the conservatism of veiling or the moderation of seeking justice? If the latter, should governments respond to constituency demands or prioritize orthodoxy as communicated increasingly through *tabliqh* groups?[2] In Malaysia, many watch guardedly as the Islamist Party (PAS) enjoys increased popularity, not only in the provinces of Kelantan and Teranganu but elsewhere, as the country has entered a new political phase in the aftermath of long-standing Prime Minister Mahathir Mohammad's retirement. While the gender-separated checkout counters in grocery stores that PAS instituted in Kota Baru, Kelantan, are universally regarded as a sham, the identity politics which PAS represents are certainly formidable. Consensus does not yet exist on the public persona of PAS, though more moderate Muslims in the country fear a Taliban-style future were PAS to come to power. In Indonesia, where consensus on political Islam is equally elusive, even mainstream *pesantran* (Islamic) schools are teaching a far more orthodox interpretation of Islam than that commonly adhered to in the country in the past. In Thailand and the Philippines, Muslim groups are rebelling against what they perceive as heavy-handed identity politics, although were these groups to come to power, what would their priorities and policies actually be?

Regardless of this lack of consensus on political Islam's priorities, many Asian Muslims now consider that a key reason why they—and Muslims worldwide—have been suffering so much is because they are veering away from "the straight path of Islam" and that the only way to respond is to recapture the faith and incorporate it into a political agenda.[3]

Myriad reasons are behind the unlikelihood of an Islamist party forming a government as a result of a national election, not the least of which is the influence of foreign powers. International forces, however, tend to have far less influence on provincial politics. The potential for provincial Islamist governments to be elected is intriguing, for such situations may place national laws and policies in direct contestation with emergent local agendas. Opponents of Islamist political parties fear that such kinds of provincial governments—as the MMA in the NWFP in Pakistan or PAS in Malaysia—may result in an abrogation of rights that are mandated at the national level to be enjoyed by a country's citizenry while cloaking their reactionary policies in the guise of implementing Islamic Sharia. But are such political entities necessarily harmful to securing human rights? Are there other rights that they may enforce that previous governments had neglected?

In this chapter, I take the above as my starting point to interrogate the policies and laws, both proposed and implemented by the Muttahida Majlis-i-Amal since it formed a government in NWFP in November 2002. Based in part on interviews I conducted with a wide range of actors in Pakistan during the fall of 2003, 2004, and 2005, I seek to understand more fully the agenda of this Islamist political coalition, what changes it has proposed, which changes it has been able to implement, and the sociopolitical implications of the major policy changes that have been proposed but not yet implemented.

Clarification needs to be made of my usage of the term "Islamist," particularly as it is not my intention to use it in the context of "othering." I use it to refer to political groups and parties which claim, at their essence, the desire to implement norms and laws consistent with those of Islam in the event they come to hold political power. I also want to clarify that the tone and actions of the MMA are not identical to those of its best-known constituent group, the Jama'at i-Islam. While this is less true of the MMA as a national entity, as a provincial entity it has certainly taken on an ethos of its own. Finally, for purposes of comparison, I point out that Islamic laws—Sharia—are positioned differently in different countries. In Pakistan, for example, Sharia laws exist at the federal level and are applicable to all Sunni Muslims (regardless of affiliation with a given school of *fiqh*). In Malaysia, however, Sharia laws are exclusively a provincial matter, a legacy of sultans past, and largely the only formidable power they hold today.

The origins behind the political success of the MMA in the NWFP lie in the history of political manipulation of Islam in Pakistan. I am not arguing that the MMA is but next in the line of political entities in Pakistan to manipulate Islam for the sake of politics, although many of its detractors will claim so. Instead, I am arguing that it is this history of manipulation that has led some, such as members of the TNSM (Tehreek-e-Nafaz-e-Shariat-e-Mohammadi) movement in Malakand,[4] to be fed up with transparent promises to implement Islam. Such promises, nevertheless, have kept the implementation of Sharia as a high, identifiable political priority.

These promises reached their apex under the regime of Zia ul-Haq after the introduction of his Islamization program in February 1979. This transformed Pakistan in many visible and subtle ways. While laws and the legal environment have certainly changed—the *Hudood* laws, the federal Shariat Bill, and the growing influence of the federal Shariat court and the federal Council on Islamic Ideology—the even more compelling transformation has been the concomitant rise in overall conservatism. In particular, it is the shift from *personal* piety to *public articulations* of piety that is of concern, as the latter continues to be susceptible to a great deal of misrepresentation and emotional manipulation. While we have seen this in the past with various statements and declarations of Islamist parties in Pakistan (most notably the Jama'at-i-Islam and the Jamiat Ulema-i-Islam), until recently they held little popular political appeal.[5] Things have changed, however, with the ascendance of the Islamist coalition, the MMA, in the elections of 2002. When members of the MMA parties vowed to fellow Pakhtuns (that if they were elected, they would implement Islam), they found a sociopolitical climate very willing to listen. In addition to having witnessed—and largely opposed—military attacks on neighboring Afghanistan a year earlier, which were supported by the federal government in Pakistan, Pakhtuns in the NWFP have been frustrated by the escalation of local onslaughts against purportedly al-Qaeda operatives but which many perceive as being indigenous freedom fighters lacking such ties to global terrorism.[6] In addition, the NWFP has not emerged from the rampant poverty that plagues the province,[7] and the Pakhtun majority has not been able to maintain its cultural hegemony. Many people pointed out to me the creeping "Punjabization" of social hierarchies that has been growing in the NWFP in the past twenty years; the Pakhtun concept of a leader being "first among equals" has been eclipsed by Punjabi practices of elites considering their constituents as inferiors who should serve *them*, which has elicited noticeable resentment against many incumbent politicians. Hence, the political landscape was ripe for change, and unprecedented numbers of voters were receptive to the message of the MMA in the fall of 2002.

Background to the Phenomenon of the MMA in Pakistan

Pakistan, founded as an Islamic republic with 97 percent of its population professed Muslims (over three-fourths of whom are Sunni Muslims), still seeks to find an appropriate role for Islam in civic and political life. What it means to be a Muslim is intrinsically tied to local cultural traditions, which, to many adherents, are inextricably intertwined. Indeed, there exists substantial confusion over where the lines are drawn between what is Islamic, what is codified tradition, and how (if at all) their separate jurisdictions should be delineated. For example, members of the Sipah-e-Sahaba, of the Jamiat-i-ulema, and of many *madaris* (residential religious schools) experience their identity as Muslims as inseparable from other component parts of their culture, and they often confuse those things that are not in accordance with cultural norms, values, or practices as being in contradiction with Islam. Alternatively, other groups (e.g., those promoting human rights, women's rights, business interests, and many political parties) question Islam's jurisdictional space in the contemporary political sphere and whether state-sanctioned Islamic injunctions should have a part to play in socioeconomic domains in Pakistan. The debate continues—and has escalated since the 1980s—over the role that Islamic law should take in the country's affairs and governance.

Pakistan was initially envisioned as a Muslim homeland, one in which Muslims would not have to live under the threat of Hindu hegemony. Allama Iqbal, considered the Father of the Country, elaborated what is known as the "Two Nations" theory: that there existed two distinct nations based on religion (Muslim and Hindu) in the Indian subcontinent. They had different historical backgrounds, traditions, cultures, and social orders. However, while Islam was envisioned as a unifying link within the country, Pakistan's founder, Muhammad Ali Jinnah, made his commitment to secularism in Pakistan clear in his inaugural address: "You will find that in course of time Hindus would cease to be Hindus and Muslims would cease to be Muslims, not in the religious sense, because that is the personal faith of each individual, but in the political sense as citizens of the State."[8]

This vision of a Muslim majority state in which religious minorities would share equally in its development came under question shortly after independence (and persists amid questions of rights of Ahmediyas, who have been declared a non-Muslim minority, and of Christians), and the debate continues over government intervention in the personal practice of Islam, whether the Hudood Ordinances should be repealed, if the federal Shariat Bill should be strengthened, and how to introduce Islamic banking practices and hence eliminate *riba* (usury).

Despite having been declared an "Islamic Republic" in its second constitution in 1965, no substantive program of Islamic reforms existed in Pakistan prior to General Zia ul-Haq's implementation of his Islamization program in February 1979. Those reforms included the establishment of a *zakat*-based welfare/taxation system, a profit-and-loss banking option in accordance with Islam's prohibitions against usury, and an Islamic penal code that had far-reaching implications for women more than men. Even though Zulfiqar Ali Bhutto's government had outlawed alcohol and changed the "day off" from Sunday to Friday in 1977, Zia's government further emphasized these features.[9]

However, the Islamization program under Zia ul-Haq was pursued in a rather complicated ideological framework. His stance contradicted popular culture in which most people were "personally" very religious but not "publicly" religious. An untoward outcome was that by relying on an Islamically based policy, the state fomented factionalism: by legislating what is Islamic and what is not, Islam itself could no longer provide unity, as it was now being defined to exclude previously included groups.[10] Shia/Sunni disputes, ethnic disturbances in Karachi between Pakhtuns and *muhajirs* (Urduspeaking Muslim immigrants from India), increased animosity toward Ahmediyas, and the revival of sectarian and intraprovincial tensions can be traced to Pakistan having lost the ability to use Islam as a common moral vocabulary. Importantly, too, the state had attempted to dictate a specific ideal image of women in Islamic society, which was largely antithetical to that existing in popular sentiments and in everyday life.

The most recent major component in the national Islamization program was passed by the government of Nawaz Sharif in April 1991, the Shariat Bill. During his tenure, Zia ul-Haq had been unable to pass this bill, which would require *all* laws in the country to be in conformity with Islam. While seemingly unpretentious, there are many ways in which such laws could be interpreted. Women's groups, in particular, were concerned that the reforms made in the Muslim Family Laws Ordinance of 1961 would be jeopardized if more conservative forces could convince the courts that it was not in conformity with religious precepts. The constitutionally. mandated council on Islamic Ideology had reviewed the ordinance in the early 1980s but obstinately refused to release its assessment until a change in its leadership in 2006. To have done otherwise would have been taking a distinct position one way or the other, possibly further polarizing Islamist and secular factions in the country.

A highly controversial law, section 295 C PPC, has drawn a lot of criticism. Introduced in 1986 by Zia ul-Haq, the Blasphemy Law—often referred to as "the blasphemy trap"—states that "whoever by words, either spoken or written, or by visible representation or by any imputation, innuendo, or insinuation, directly or indirectly, defiles the sacred name of the Holy Prophet (peace be upon him) shall be punished with death or imprisoned for life and shall be liable to fine." While the law extends to Muslims and non-Muslims alike, it has been indiscriminately used to settle personal disputes and against members of minorities. Numerous cases exist against Christians and Ahmediyahs who have been charged with blasphemy; only later has it been discovered that the case had been conveniently registered by enemies who had some sort of dispute with them.

By the late 1990s, the effects of the proliferation of *deeni madaris*, residential religious schools, began to be felt throughout the country. Pakistan had enjoyed a fairly good public education system in its first three decades, although it remained plagued by limited attendance from poor communities, especially in rural areas. In the early 1980s, Zia's government declared that the medium of instruction in all public schools would be the national language, Urdu; wealthier Pakistanis began to send their children to the English-language schools that were becoming established in urban areas. However, a crisis of confidence ensued: it was expensive to send a child to a government school as families were still required to purchase school uniforms and books and would also have to do without the benefit of the labor a child might contribute. Still, many people expected that there would be a limited return (by way of a child being able to get a well-paying job later on) by attending government school. Meanwhile, many *deeni madaris* were being established throughout the country, often with funding from Saudi Arabia or from expatriate Pakistanis now working in the Gulf region, as well as by local contributions by such workers who had returned.[11] Many of these religious schools would offer a student's family essential grains (rice, wheat, etc.), cooking oil, or even money to help toward a sister's marriage. Families considered that at the least, their son would learn to read the Qur'an and lead prayers, which has a moral benefit. They also surmised, and appropriately so, that their son could earn a living later on by being a resident mullah at a mosque and by teaching children the Qur'an and their prayers, as many families have a *maulvi saheb* visit their house daily to do so. The Zia regime indeed encouraged their proliferation by approving their syllabi for degrees being granted at government schools.

One of the largest of these *madaris* is located on the Grand Trunk (G.T.) Road, a half hour's drive east of Peshawar at Akoora Khattak in NWFP. It is run by the Jamiat ulema-e-Islam (Sami ul-Haq group) faction, which is now a constituent part of the MMA coalition. This *madari* at Akoora Khattak is a male enclave, and its most famous alumnus is said to be Mullah Omar, the leader of the fallen Taliban in Afghanistan.[12] Provincial Information Minister Asif Iqbal Daudzai of the MMA contends that *madaris* throughout the province are undergoing internal reform and are introducing new subjects, and that both English and computer science are now being taught at Akoora Khattak.

Public school curricula are teaching a less-tolerant version of Islam than that included a generation ago, in part due to the educational policies promoted by the Zia government but also from the competition of the *madari* system.[13] The result is a noticeable change in the tone of Islam practiced in Pakistan today, particularly in Punjab and Sindh, which had been historically less orthodox than the western parts of the country. It is a stricter Islam, one far removed from the *pir* and shrine-centered practices of just a generation ago. It has also contributed to the rise of numerous countless jihadi groups in Pakistan whose adherents generally blur the lines between religion, culture, and politics.[14]

The MMA Coalition

Muslim communities worldwide became politicized in the 1990s; nowhere is this truer than in the Islamic Republic of Pakistan, and especially in the Northwest Frontier Province.

The provincial MMA government in the NWFP which came to power in November 2002 is a coalition consisting of six Islamist parties: Jama'at i-Islam, Jamiat ulema-e-Islam (Fazlur Rehman group), Jamiat ulema-e-Islam (Sami ul-Haq group), Jamiat ulema-e-Pakistan,[15] Markazi Jamiat Ahle Hadith, and Tehrik Nifaz Fiqah Jaferiya (a Shia party). Only the Jama'at i-Islam had much previous experience contesting elections, and that with limited success.[16] In hindsight, one of the key factors which may have prevented electoral success in the past was that many members of the MMA's constituent parties had previously fought against each other; for the first time, they came together and formed an electoral alliance.

A decade earlier, in 1993, the more moderate part of the Jama'at i-Islam had formed the Islamic Front. It focused on social development and was led by Qazi Hussain Ahmed, now the Jama'at's national leader. Later, in the spring of 2000, Maulana Sami ul-Haq created the Pakistan-Afghanistan Defense Council, which brought together the Islamic Front and other constituent groups in response to the West's criticism of the Taliban and Osama bin Laden, in particular. After the war in Afghanistan in October 2001, the coalition transformed into the MMA.

The constituent political parties decided to make an alliance "to implement an Islamic system and to protect Islamic values" with the objective of ensuring the "supremacy of Islamic Law and enactment of legislation according to the recommendations of the Islamic Ideological Council."[17] They agreed to rotate the positions of MMA president and MMA secretary general among the heads of the component parties every six months. There were four priorities in their provincial campaign agenda: promote the Islamization process, provide greater provincial autonomy, rename the province to Pukhtunkhwa, and address social issues (e.g., lower unemployment and inflation rates).

The MMA Manifesto released for the October 2002 election went even further in stating the alliance's overall objectives:

> Establishment of an Islamic judicial system, economic prosperity, self-sufficiency, and provision of employment
> Protection of ideological and geographical boundaries and sovereignty/independence of the country—in short, checking all types of external interferences

Putting an end to the ethnic, caste and creed, regional, tribal, religious, and sectarian hatred and violence and creating an atmosphere of friendship and brotherhood

The Election Manifesto pledged to support reforms that would provide "real constitutional autonomy" to the provinces by removing "all powers resting jointly with the Federal and Provincial Governments" in Pakistan's constitution. This pledge is of particular importance to the overall agenda of the MMA, for to implement a number of its goals, it needs to ensure that it has the power to pass legislation in those domains, especially to be able to pass its own Shariat Bill and the Hisba Act.[18]

Other points made in its Election Manifesto include promising to get the federal government to duly compensate the provinces for their natural resources, to protect the rights of minorities and thus guarantee their equal rights as citizens, to promote relations with Muslim countries and support Muslim communities worldwide, and to promote equity and equality whenever possible. The latter categories include the following:

Delegation of authority and resources to the grassroots level in a judicious manner

Bold accountability without any discrimination of all the rulers, elected representatives, judiciary, armed forces, and executives

Ensuring equitable distribution of wealth, and reducing the accumulation of wealth and the wide financial gap between different classes of people to a reasonable level

Guaranteeing food, clothing, shelter, health care, and education to all citizens

Ending the cruel and unfair taxes imposed on people, employees, and the trading community

Promotion of a tax culture based on justice and implementation of an Islamic Economic System

In addition, explicit goals of an Islamic polity are identified, including provision of rights to women "according to the Qur'an and Sunnah and to enable them to play their role in society"; arranging for "healthy entertainment and mental, psychological, and moral mentoring of the youth"; and ending "unwanted restrictions on independent journalism and freedom of speech, and that journalism be made according to religious and national values." The MMA also vowed that its elected representatives would forsake living in luxurious government-owned housing and driving government-owned late model vehicles.

The MMA would hold gatherings and place the Qur'an—the holy book—on a table in the center, and tell people to cast their vote for

the book. They would say that we are not asking for the vote for
ourselves, but to vote for the Qur'an. Your sins will be forgiven if you
vote for the Qur'an. . . . At rallies, they said that if women don't vote
for the book, that would be akin to getting *talaq* (divorced).[19]

The MMA's campaign promises, importantly, laid the foundation for two of
the most important pieces of legislation that it would introduce, the provincial
Sharia Bill and the Hisba Act, in addition to various other policies.

A key component in its campaign had been the MMA's promise to institute an *effective* process of implementing Sharia laws in the province. Six
months after taking office, the MMA government passed the Sharia Law
(June 2, 2003), a creation of the Nifaz-i-Shariat Council, a watchdog body of religious clerics appointed by the MMA government to provide guidance for the
enforcement of Sharia in the province. The Sharia Law, similar to the federal
Enforcement of Shariat Act of 1991, has two key differences. First, while the
federal law states that Islam should be the supreme law in the country, the
provincial law states that all laws need to be *derived* (emphasis mine) from
Islam. Second, all issues would be decided according to Sharia which, in the
provincial Sharia Law, extends to all arenas of law. The Sharia Law declares that
Islam is based on and prospers from the philosophy to "advocate virtue and
keep away someone and something from wrongdoings," and that legal and
constitutional protection is necessary to ensure these objectives. It states that
"all local courts would interpret and execute all laws falling within the jurisdiction of the Provincial Government strictly according to Sharia" and that in
the event laws can be interpreted and implemented in more than one way, then
"the courts would adopt that interpretation which is closer to Sharia." That *local*
courts are now being given jurisdiction to interpret laws according to Islam is
revolutionary, as these tasks have thus far been shared between the constitutionally mandated Council on Islamic Ideology and the federal Shariat court.

The provincial Sharia Law provides a framework in mandating that the provincial government ensure "that all education systems that prevail must promote Islamic teachings and character building," incorporate Islamic *fiqh* into the
curricula of all law colleges within its administrative control, and promote the
Arabic language. While no distinct school of *fiqh* is mentioned in the provincial
Sharia Law, mention of *fiqh* and Sharia appears to presume a shared understanding (albeit in practice this may not be so) of what would constitute them.

The provincial law also proposed various measures—many of them fairly
detailed—for enforcement of Islam in education, culture, the economy, system of justice, and governance. It stated that mass media should be used to
promote Islamic values and teachings, and it vowed to constitute three dis-

tinct commissions to examine educational, judicial, and economic institutions in the province to ensure conformation to the requirements of Islam.

The Commission on Education, to be tasked with developing a concrete agenda on how to bring in an Islamic system of education, is still under formation. The Commission on Judicial Reforms, which is to make recommendations on how to bring in an Islamic system of jurisprudence, has also yet to be established. Of the three mandated commissions to be created within a month of the passage of the Sharia Law, only the Commission on the Economy—charged with advising how to transform the economy into one based on Islam, including the transformation of existing financial laws and laws relating to taxation, insurance, and banking so that all are "according to Sharia"—has been constituted and is functioning. The Khyber Bank was to begin Islamic banking in one of their branches on an experimental basis, using models from Malaysia and the Al-Faisal bank in Saudi Arabia, charging fees instead of interest. The MMA government also changed the Khyber Bank's managing director to steer it more effectively toward developing an Islamic banking system. In addition, the provincial government was looking into establishing an agricultural bank "on Islamic lines [at the] provincial level so that the problems of farmers are solved."[20]

The Sharia Law also delves into fairly uncharted political territory (for an official document): it vows to "put an end to corruption, embezzlement and malpractices of the provincial government" and that in order "to put an end to all social evils, the provincial government would ensure the promotion of virtue and elimination of sin according to the teachings of Qur'an-e-Pak." In addition, the provincial government is to enact "necessary legislation . . . to wipe out vulgarity and lawlessness."

Toward this end, at about the time of the passage of the Shariat Bill, the Shabab-e-Milli (the youth wing of the Jama'at Islami), protested in Peshawar against billboards depicting women. They sought to destroy these kinds of billboards (advertisements or at cinemas), as well as others that they claimed represented the United States, such as the billboard for Kentucky Fried Chicken (KFC). Although there was a police presence from the outset to ward off violence, I have heard firsthand accounts that the police did not stop the procession from becoming a riot. This angered the federal government, the World Bank, and the Asian Development Bank; the World Bank temporarily suspended support to the province, and the federal government—uncharacteristically—summarily transferred the chief secretary and the provincial inspector general of police without consultation from the provincial government. The current chief secretary, Ejaz Qureshi, suggests that he was appointed because the federal government wanted to send a message that they did not agree with such actions. One observer opined to me that since they could not remove the MMA government, they thought they would at least remove the two senior officials over whom they had jurisdiction.

The MMA government also laid out other explicit, detailed goals to promote Islamization in the NWFP. While the full rubric of recommendations on how best to Islamicize the province goes into the hundreds, I have tried to capture below the ones that underscore new ways of conceptualizing Islam and governance in various social arenas. The speaker of the Provincial Assembly, Bakht Jehan Khan, told me that they are all based on the proposition that every religion, not just Islam, says that people should have basic rights and the state should be there to help the poor and promote social justice.[21]

Importantly, it appears that there has been a distinct emphasis—critics claim an undue emphasis—on gender segregation under the MMA leadership: girls are to study in separate schools from boys, only female physicians are to treat female patients, and all new mosques are to have separate areas for women. The notion is that women's rights can best be secured in this context of gender segregation. These ideals are being conveyed in a resource-poor social context, where schools often don't have furniture, teachers, or books and female literacy rates are appallingly low; there are not enough doctors to begin with (let alone female doctors), and families are often reluctant to seek out medical care, especially for girls; and women in this area don't go to mosques for their prayers. MMA representatives, however, claim that creating an Islamic context itself will solve many prevailing social problems. Therefore, they are prioritizing the construction of more schools and colleges for girls, especially in more remote areas, and are emphasizing district colleges and postgraduate schools, saying that people are conservative and don't want to send their daughters to Peshawar. They are creating a Women's University and a girl's medical college to facilitate the training of more female teachers and physicians. The Women's University has started offering classes in the afternoons at the long-established Frontier Girls College, but the plan is to build a separate university eventually in Peshawar.[22] The long-standing Khyber Medical College, upgraded now to a university, has a new women's campus. The MMA regards the creation of this separate enclave as a way to encourage parents to educate their daughters "in a safe context." While coeducation will continue for those who prefer it, the MMA contends that separate facilities for women will be very important for those families who would only send their daughters there (and not to a coeducational school).

The impetus for a women's university apparently came from a female MMA Member of the Provincial Assembly (MPA).[23] She had not been allowed to pursue her bachelor's degree at the coeducational university in Peshawar and instead had to register as a private candidate (i.e., study through correspondence). After taking office, she told the MMA leadership that if there had been a women's university, she would have received a far better education; she found a very receptive climate.

The MMA's justification offered for such gender segregation is that this would enable women to live better lives in accordance with Islam. For example, MMA representatives told me that male doctors, ideally, should not perform electrocardiograms on females as the test requires a doctor to touch the patient's chest. MMA detractors have argued that this recommendation is being taken to the extreme and that some male doctors are refusing to treat female patients altogether. MMA representatives have countered this charge by contending that this would be an ideal scenario but that, in order to implement this recommendation, there must first be many more female physicians and, hence, the need to establish a female medical college in the province. A female MMA provincial representative, Rehana Ismail, encouraged more girls to pursue medical careers when she spoke at a reception at the Lucky Marwat Girls' School in the southern part of the province:

> There is a growing need for female doctors to treat female problems. In this way demands of modesty and purdah [the separation of males and females] during treatment can also be fulfilled. Therefore numerous women have entered this field and are providing valuable services. However, they should remember that actions are based on intentions. They should become doctors with the intention of serving females who do not want to go to *namehram* (men from whom women should observe purdah) for treatment. Also they should observe purdah so that Allah is happy with their services.[24]

Of course, it will take years for the number of practicing female physicians in NWFP to increase substantially enough to provide healthcare to the majority of women in the province. One of the dilemmas associated with educating more female doctors is that many of them never actually practice medicine. Because they have earned a higher degree, they are more appealing when their parents are arranging their marriage. So there is not only the need for more women doctors but also the need to create an atmosphere of social acceptance for them to practice medicine. As far as I am aware, the MMA has never directly addressed the latter point.

Gender segregation has also long been a contentious issue in the arena of female sports. During Zia ul-Haq's period, Pakistani female athletes were barred from participating in both domestic and international tournaments where their bodies (i.e., by wearing athletic shorts) would be seen by *namehram*.

The provincial cabinet has now decided to create a female sports directorate to "encourage girls to participate in sports." It will have a female director and will create "a more relaxed atmosphere for girls' sports, at least sports festivals in girls' schools." There is no sense here, unlike with the notion of female health care, that this will be a 'separate but equal' scenario, in that girls sports will be limited to special events held at girls' schools, but that at least "this will provide an infrastructure for more sports than we already have."[25]

The second arena to address regarding the MMA's recommendations on how best to Islamicize the province concerns education. Here, too, gender segregation is being prioritized, to the extent that there should be a complete separation of staff, by gender, in educational institutions so that purdah can be observed. This includes eliminating male officials from prize distribution ceremonies at girls' schools. In a move to encourage more girls to enroll in secondary schools (to pursue a tenth-grade degree), they have passed a law that a girl can use her fingerprints on the secondary school enrollment form if a family objects to using a girl's picture, thereby, in the words of one MMA MPA, "this way, education isn't closed for girls." She has proposed that the next step is to allow this for higher education (intermediate and college degrees).[26]

Much emphasis has been placed on reforming the content of what is taught in schools in the NWFP. The draft Islamization program emphasizes that the ultimate goal of any educational system should be to make students better Muslims:

> The goal of the education system should be to produce innovative and exemplary citizens in every field of life and to make them rich in Islamic goals and values.... Education policy goals should be to establish a fair society in which "every citizen gets his right and equal opportunity.... The purpose of education is to build Islamic character" along with nourishing educational skills.... All administrative and educational posts of educational institutions should be delegated to those people who love the Islamic ideology of Pakistan.... The entire syllabus of scientific education should be designed in such a way that it reflects core Islamic values.

I was told consistently that Islamic values should be kept in mind in the daily routines and functions of educational institutions and that education should promote equality, not class differences.

This last view can be seen in the causes behind another controversial action by the MMA government, notably the passage of a regulation that students throughout the province must wear the traditional dress, *shalwar kamize* (long shirt and baggy pants), and not trousers, to school. While critics have ridiculed the MMA for caring about what clothes schoolchildren wear, many MMA representatives told me that this was part of the overall goal to promote greater equality in the province, as poor families cannot afford other clothes.

In response to criticisms of *madari* education in Pakistan and external efforts (by both the federal government and international donors) to reform the *madari* syllabi, the MMA government has recommended combining religious and secular education, and making it compulsory for every student to acquire religious education until the intermediate (F.A.) level. Students are to pray together at school at least once daily. Mosques should be made centers of education in rural and urban areas, and Arabic should be taught as a compulsory subject from grade six to grade ten. Innovative roles are recommended for mosques, to transform them into centers to create "a system of finding solutions to public problems." (They also recommend that mosques should be exempt from paying water bills, and possibly electricity and gas bills as well.) The *madari* school system, in contrast, should "be made exemplary and broad-based with the assistance of religious scholars." Students who become Hafiz Qur'an (learn the Qur'an by heart) should be exempt from paying fees, and scholarships should be provided to them.

Another key priority of the MMA government—that of encouraging greater personal piety—can be seen in the official encouragement of people to pray more frequently. The provincial government has sent out circulars to government employees that they should say the midday prayer together, and the proposed Hisba Force (discussed below) will ensure—somehow—that this is implemented.[27] In its draft Islamization plan for the province, the MMA outlines its agenda:

It is a basic duty of the Government to ensure offering of prayers.... Students should have a pocket diary for attendance during prayer times, and spaces should be located in offices and institutions for prayers. Ministers, MNAs, and higher officials should form an example. Necessary action should be taken against people who do not offer prayers. Businessmen should be convinced to shut down their businesses voluntarily during prayer time. Peshawar City can be made as a role model for this purpose. Radio and TV should inform about prayer timings, and broadcasting should be stopped during prayer timing. Proper arrangements for offering prayer should be made at bus stops, roads, and mosques. Ladies should have proper arrangements for prayer. No building plan should be approved without the provision of prayer space in it. Construction of mosques should be given priority while using funds for construction.

The MMA government would also like to reinstate the weekly holiday on Friday, thereby making it easier for people to participate in the Juma prayers.

Along the lines of promoting personal piety in its efforts to Islamicize the NWFP, the MMA has prioritized police reform. They argue that corruption can be eliminated through a dual-pronged effort to promote religious education and moral training on the one hand and to increase the salaries of lower echelons of policing staff on the other, thereby eliminating the need to take bribes. No information exists, however, on outcomes of these efforts.

The final arena in which the MMA has been vocal is in their concerns about cultural issues and social change. These have largely fallen into two categories: disdain of Westernization and the elimination of obscenities (which it deems is a product of the West) and implementation of a reward system for honest behavior. In the former category, they have identified such things as video games as playing "a poisonous role in society" and say they should be eliminated. Music has been banned in government buildings (which, as they are often locales for wedding celebrations, also precludes music being played at such ceremonies as well) on the basis of being un-Islamic. This also includes the Nishtar Hall in Peshawar, where many concerts and plays have taken place. The MMA had announced in the fall of 2003 that anyone having a New Year's party would be arrested, regardless whether alcohol was being served, as celebrating the New Year was not Islamic. They tried to ban movies and films being played in buses on the same grounds, but their efforts were met with protests by bus owners. The provincial government had issued instructions about enforcing the ban to the police, but some zealous MPAs and ministers had felt the enforcement had been half-hearted and went themselves to a Peshawar bus stand to enforce the ban. A rowdy brawl broke out, and the bus owners went on strike, saying that the government cannot manipulate them like that. They have, similarly, had no success in eliminating vulgar film posters and vulgar Pashto films and, if anything, the situation has worsened as I heard many accounts of pornography being inserted increasingly into the middle of Pashto films in cinema halls.

A key issue here concerns women's rights: how to define them, and what to do about them. The MMA government has explicitly focused on women's rights within the family. To their credit, they have condemned the Pukhtun customary practice of *swara*,[28] deeming it as being against Islam, as well as honor killings and the trafficking of women, stating that "killing in the name of honor, trading of women, un-Islamic traditions like ransom in the form of women, and forced marriage should be totally banned."[29]

While the MMA has said it intends to ban *swara*, the Legal Reform Committee has yet to develop any concrete recommendations.[30] It has been assumed that enforcement would be left to the Hisba Force, to be created through the Hisba Act (discussed below).

The MMA has been less innovative in its stance on women's legal rights within the family. For example, in its draft Islamization agenda, it has declared that "divorce, which is also an unwanted act in Sharia and destroys many families, should be declared as a punishable act" without recognizing that there are legitimate reasons for pursuing a divorce, especially on the part of women when domestic violence occurs. Consistent with the position held by the Jama'at i-Islam, the MMA leadership criticizes the 1961 Muslim Family Laws Ordinance, claiming that it includes two un-Islamic clauses: the requirement to register divorces (registration is not required in Islam, but neglect to register often results in charges of *zina*—adultery—against women), and the require-ment for a man to acquire permission from his first wife before he can marry a second wife. One MMA leader told me that as "women cannot control their husband's sexuality, it's better that he has a legally binding second marriage than run around with ten other women."[31] Needless to say, this stance is highly controversial within Pakistan today.

I repeatedly asked different MMA representatives that, if they really wanted to redress un-Islamic practices regarding women's rights within the family, why didn't they encourage widow remarriage, as the Prophet had done in the ex-emplary act of his own marriage to a widow? I never received any substantive answer on why it has not done so, as every respondent acknowledged that widow remarriage is condoned in Islam. But to do so would require the MMA asserting a very unpopular stance in this cultural context, which deplores widow re-marriage, something that could certainly cut into their political popularity.

In the latter category of cultural issues and social change, that of insti-tuting a system of rewards for honest behavior, the MMA has asserted that in line with its efforts to promote honesty, transparency, and "justice at the doorstep," there should be "a column of honesty added in the service record of government servants, and promotion should be conditioned with honesty in their service record."[32] The provincial government encouraged its ministers and other officials to limit their expenses on foreign tours and stated they "should also refrain from attending parties given as bribes." In developing a moral code for its ministers, they have been told they are not to participate in any function where there is music or other "anti-Sharia and unethical things going on," that they should plan their prayers during visits and stop working during prayer times, and "offer Juma (Friday) prayer in a large mosque and bring government performance to the notice of the public."[33]

The MMA has also addressed prison conditions with the hope that prisoners can actually change for the better while incarcerated. Minister of

Information Asif Iqbal Daudzai told me that prisoners can now keep personal items, and that if a sentence is for more than five years the prisoner and his family can sometimes stay in one of four apartments so that children and wives need not suffer as well. If an inmate becomes Hafiz Qur'an (has memorized the whole of the Qur'an), two years is taken off the prison sentence. Those teaching the Qur'an to other prisoners also receive remission.[34]

Many of the preceding stances and recommendations can be critiqued as mere "window dressings"—as light efforts by an Islamist-oriented government to try to garner popular support for its ideology. However, they may not be as ephemeral as one might assume, for additional legislation is being promoted to ensure implementation of both the Sharia Law and various other goals to promote Islamization, termed the Hisba Act. This controversial bill would create a new ombudsman's office to "advocate virtue (*amar-bil maroof*) as it is in the Qur'an and guidance from Sunnah" and ensure that "social evils, injustices, and the misuse of powers could be checked properly." The controversy surrounding the bill is that advocates maintain it would eliminate non-Islamic practices from the province and bring "justice to people's doorsteps," whereas critics fear that it might result in an overwhelming vice squad that would compromise human rights in the process of requiring a rigid conformity to regressive practices considered to be "Islamic" by its advocates.

In explaining the goals of the Hisba Act to me, Provincial Information Minister Asif Iqbal Daudzai contends:

> We are trying to eliminate social diseases. We have banned *swara*. We have banned *talaq*.[35] Hisba will enforce this. The Shariat Bill will be completed by Hisba. It creates an ombudsman. The federal system [for an ombudsman] is here, but there is always a conflict between the federal and the provincial. We will have authority here in the province. The Hisba Force will not be a separate force, but it will be constituted from within the police. . . . We want this to be in the same system, but we want to reform it. The misperception that people have about the Hisba Act [and Hisba Force] is very unfortunate. They are taking every positive step negatively.

The Hisba Act includes an implementation force, which is the most problematic thing of everything they have proposed. Although the MMA has been criticized for its lack of implementing mechanisms, they claim that implementation will come with passage of the Hisba Act.

Critics of the Hisba Act contend that, above all, it cannot be at cross purposes with the existing laws of the Government of Pakistan. If legislation exists at the federal level, constitutionally, that must take precedence over provincial legislation, which would certainly result in a much-weakened Hisba Act. In addition, while the existing Hisba Bill states that it would ostensibly "create an administrative and judicial structure, including a special force, to enforce Islamic values and teachings," indeed its reach would be far more than this. It would ensure "compliance with Islamic moral values at public places, discouragement of lavish spending on wedding parties and other social occasions, suspension of business activities and games at prayer times, and a strict enforcement of Islam in all walks of life of the people, government institutions, and private businesses and societal activities."[36]

The implementing force, the Hisba Force (*amar-il-maroof*), was envisioned as a sort of vice and virtue patrol, similar to that which the Taliban established. The only statement explicitly about the Hisba Force included in the proposed bill is that a "police force would be provided to the provincial mohtasib and district mohtasib for dealing with the matters."[37] The vagueness of this statement opens up many possibilities, especially for the potential of the Hisba Force to overreach its mandate. The MMA initially envisioned it as a separate entity, but after being heavily criticized about creating yet another law enforcement institution, the MMA said it would be created from within the existing police force. Nothing like the Hisba Force has ever existed in Pakistan; it is difficult to imagine its potential for effectiveness.

An important dimension of the Hisba Act would be a different kind of ombudsman (*mohtasib*) than the one that already exists at the federal level and whose powers would be far more vast. The federal *mohtasib* is to intervene between citizens and government entities (e.g., the Water and Power Development Authority, Pakistan Telephone) when there is a dispute. Importantly, the *mohtasib* is to iron out differences, not make value judgments or interpretations. But the powers given to the district and provincial *mohtasibs* in the Hisba Bill are quite substantive. The *mohtasib* is to promote Islam, make people pray more, and make them better practitioners of Islam. The *mohtasib* will have powers of accountability contempt of court, as well as the ability to fine people and determine sentences (up to a month's time), somewhat like a Supreme Court justice.[38] The proposed Hisba Bill states:

> He will be responsible for investigating corruption and perjury in any agency or its office bearer; he will inspect the code of conduct throughout the province; he will control the media under the provincial government and will make it conform to the rules of Islam; persons, agencies, and other offices will be liable to work under

Shariat and will promote good governance.... [the] mohtasib or member of the Hisba force will be allowed for interrogation into any Government office and can make copies of their documents.[39]

Qualifications for the position will be a matric (tenth grade) plus a madrasa degree. This is substantially less formal schooling than that which is required for Supreme Court justices, another point that critics contend will undermine its effectiveness, wreak havoc with the system of justice, and be contradictory to federal law. A district *mohtasib* would even be able to look into every FIR (First Investigative Report) that gets filed when there is a purported crime. The bill does state, however, that the *mohtasib* would not be entitled to intervene in ongoing court trials, issues related to foreign government agreements, or laws with other agencies or related to the armed forces. To do so would clearly go beyond the boundaries of what a provincial government is allowed to legislate.

Even MMA officials acknowledge the importance of this last point. In response to a query about it, an MMA provincial minister stated to me that the MMA government is trying to Islamize those subjects who do not come under the Federal List and is seeking to implement laws in those areas where the provincial government has authority to act.[40] The question remains whether the Hisba Bill is overstepping those boundaries.

Surprisingly, the federal Council of Islamic Ideology, the constitutionally mandated institution charged with determining whether laws (and proposed laws) in Pakistan are in accordance with Islam, made a judgment on the Hisba Bill in September 2004. It deemed that, under Paragraph 23, Article 12 of Pakistan's Constitution, the proposed Hisba Bill is unconstitutionally vague. What is surprising about the judgment is that it was made at all: the Council of Islamic Ideology is notorious for not making judgments on controversial laws. For example, it has yet to publish a judgment on either the 1961 Muslim Family Laws Ordinance or on the 1979 Hudood Laws. To do so would be to take a firm position on interpreting Islam one way or another, something that the Council of Islamic Ideology has been very reluctant to do.

The judgment made on the Hisba Bill, however, did not rule on the Act's Islamic credentials per se.[41] Instead, the judgment is concerned specifically with the possibility of the Hisba Force opening the door to havoc (*mufasid*) because it raises the possibility of posing contradictions between the Qur'an and the Sunnah (laws derived from the Qur'an). An *amar-bil-maroof* (Hisba Force, as currently proposed) may create a dangerous condition of indeterminacy in the law, resulting in a situation whereby, "in the course of making laws, at any time, any government, whatsoever, can use these laws to obtain its political objectives in an unfair manner."[42]

The judgment's greatest concern seems to be with the arbitrariness that may result from both the Hisba Act and the Hisba Force. Regarding the latter, it offers that instead of creating a morals police (*amar-il-maroof*), it would be permissible instead to establish a Hisba administration for the purpose of completing the intentions of Sharia. The judgment also raises concerns about the Hisba Bill's inclusion of moral and ethical issues, about which there is no consensus or agreement. The inclusion of such controversial issues can only detract from the bill's purpose, again, of completing the intentions of Sharia.

Its greatest unease is with the goals of establishing a Hisba administration at all. It states that there is a danger of a Hisba administration being misused, especially as there is no agreement on the ethical issues it is supposedly enforcing. Implementing a uniform Islamic law and saving people from the injustices of "high-handed classes" should be the first goal of Hisba officials. Instead, this bill "has not defined what good and evil are." It cannot do this on an ad hoc basis, and "arbitrariness would bring disgrace to the institution." Importantly, the judgment recognizes that existing civil and Shariat courts have checks and balances against arbitrariness built into them, which the Hisba Bill lacks. The goals of a Hisba administration should be to implement the law, including Islamic laws, and to redress shortcomings in their implementation and especially to rectify and remove injustices. By the judgment stating that this is why a Hisba administration *should* be established, it is implying that this is not the reasoning behind the MMA government's actions.

One aspect of the Hisba Bill which has been allowed—despite its questioning of federal versus provincial powers—is that a provincial government can have its own *mohtasib*. However, the MMA government reached a compromise when it stated that the person must be qualified and eligible to become a federal Shariat court judge.

Revised Hisba Acts have been introduced two more times, most recently November 2006, just days apart from the federal government's promulgation of the Women's Protection Act that reformed the national Hudood Ordinances. The Supreme Court, on 20 February 2007, determined that they now had objections to only two clauses in the Hisba Act, though the Act could now be promulgated.[43] Indeed, this is in a much watered-down form compared to that initially envisaged by the MMA.

When queried as to what MMA leaders perceive as their greatest accomplishments since they have been in office, most point to educational and health reforms and to the passage of the Shariat Law. The provincial assembly speaker, Bakht Jehan Khan, a spokesman for the coalition, asserts that through their education audit report the MMA is addressing problems of accountability that have plagued former governments: they have allocated Rs. 50 crore for free health care for poor patients; the medical college has become a university, and they are setting up a girls' campus; and the Frontier Girls College is becoming a university, which should counter people's reluctance to send their daughters to coeducational universities. In addition, the provincial government has "forgiven" the interest that small farmers owe to the provincial cooperative society (though the principle still needs to be repaid), and that this is at least one type of relief; a special rehabilitation center opened in September for the unique needs of opium users; a burn center has been established; and they are working toward fixing sick industrial units.

Most feel they have overcome the enormous difficulties they faced when they first took office. There had been much speculation about the MMA's goals and priorities, and misperceptions were rampant. In working to rectify these misperceptions and make them positive, they say they have actively sought out bringing in reforms to benefit the people, especially from age-old traditions such as *swara* and forced marriages.

Conclusion

The MMA is trying to address traditional values, especially those associated with Islam, and bring them into a political agenda. How far will they go to ban popular practices that are not Islamic? While many MMA members may claim that they are rooting out un-Islamic elements from local culture, over four years after having taken office the ban on *swara* has not been formalized, nor have I ever heard anyone advocate something so antithetical to the culture as promoting widow remarriage. To do so would be politically very unpopular with their vote base, which sees local sociocultural mores as inextricably interwoven with Islam.

I heard fears about the kind of society envisioned by the MMA many times throughout Pakistan, and particularly in the Punjab. I heard it less *within* the NWFP. Instead, women in villages and towns told me that they were becoming disenchanted with the MMA because they *weren't* doing enough to implement true Islam. A number of women told me that they had truly believed the MMA was different from past political parties which had used Islam for its own purposes, and that it genuinely cared about Islamicizing the province. But because it had been unable to ban vulgar (i.e., those with un-Islamic themes) television programs made them question the MMA's ulterior goals.

In mid-November 2003, one of the MMA's constituent members, the Shia group Tehrik Nifaz Fiqah Jaferiya, was banned in Pakistan as a terrorist organization. The JUI–Sami ul-Haq has periodically disassociated itself from the coalition on the basis that it is not being treated equally with the other senior partners, the Jama'ati-Islami and the JUI–Fazlur Rehman group. While its leader, Sami ul-Haq, stressed that no ideological differences were separating it from the coalition, his group wants to play a greater decision-making role and hold more cabinet positions (than they already have) in the provincial government.

In searching for the fault lines between what the MMA espouses and federal laws and policies, the Hisba Bill is pivotal. The provincial government was confronted with a dilemma: how to implement its agenda to Islamicize the NWFP while also acknowledging that it is a resource-poor province. It cannot risk losing the financial support given by the federal government and by international donors such as the World Bank. The structural adjustment credit that the World Bank was to have given to the province was denied in December 2003, although the bank pledged that it would continue to review its provincial policies. (I have been told that the MMA's follow-up budget for structural adjustment credits, SAC-3, was different in the Urdu from the English versions.[44]) The extent to which World Bank personnel assess that the MMA government is moving in extremist ways will affect whether or not the funding is reinstated. That the provincial government has already encumbered a "carry forward" of six years for its budget allocations makes it very dependent on receiving this funding.[45]

The MMA's more activist-Islamist rhetoric has had an important effect on the rhetoric of the federal government of Pakistan. The latter has had a difficult time rescinding any of the laws passed under Zia ul-Haq's Islamization program out of fear of incurring charges, at the least, of not being as proactive about Islam as is the MMA. Even the most inequitable one, the Zina (Adultery) Act, which was finally amended through passage of the Protection of Women Act in November 2006, was rejected by the MMA when they threatened to quit both the Balochistan and National Assemblies entirely if it was passed. The MMA charged that the reforms "would encourage adultery in society and would further increase obscenity, vulgarity, and western culture in Pakistan."[46] Indeed, the federal government has articulated its development priorities for Pakistan within a global framework: skills training, poverty-alleviation strategies, improvement of the educational infrastructure, and promoting the empowerment of women. But it cannot leave behind the rhetoric of Islam, as this would provide the MMA with the opportunity to claim that it is the only viable Islamist alternative on the political landscape. The federal government struck back against the agenda of the MMA by cutting down the MMA's pivotal yet provocative Hisba Bill on the basis that it would introduce arbitrariness and hence disgrace Islam. To its credit, it *didn't* strike down the Hisba Bill as an intrusion into federal matters, for to do so could have brought up demands to make the Hisba Act a federal statute. As consensus does not exist at the provincial level on the ethics that Hisba is to enforce, it most certainly does not exist at the national level, where imposing such an act would definitely have resulted in heated, destabilizing conflicts.

An opposition MPA who, on the one hand, believes that the MMA has begun a process of integrating Islam into local political arenas in new ways, on the other hand assesses that the phenomenon of the MMA itself will soon fade away:

> In the beginning, the MMA had a lot of goodwill from the people because they had won a clear majority. They were considered genuine, especially the Jama'at, They refused to take official cars and houses for their ministers—but after a month, they received all the facilities again. Now it seems that many of their ministers want to make a career in politics.[47]

However, he sees an emergent Islamist phenomenon as being a permanent component of Pakistan's future, especially in the provinces:

> It's not going to die. It [the MMA] may go down a bit in NWFP as popularity for any sitting government always declines in Pakistan, but the phenomenon is here to stay. It may well increase in the Punjab; they're in a coalition now in Baluchistan ... but it is *at the level of cultural fissures* where the line will be drawn in Punjab.[48] (italics mine)

This bodes ill for Pakistan's future, as culture wars have been ripping the country asunder for some time. The MMA leadership has been actively engaged in trying to quell people's fears that it is moving in extremist directions. However, as the process is still unfolding, and a critical piece of legislation (the Hisba Act) must now be fundamentally recast, a final assessment of both the social reform agenda of the MMA and its long-term effect on the country, overall, will have to be suspended for a future date.

It is certain, however, that the ideological and substantive differences we have seen manifested in the exchanges between the provincial Islamist government of the MMA and the federal government of Pakistan are not an isolated event. We can anticipate seeing more localized Islamist political influence throughout Asia as an increasingly educated Muslim populace seeks to hold its national governments to their promises.

NOTES

I am deeply indebted to the many people who kindly met with me and shared their views in Pakistan in October–November 2003 and August–October 2004—in particular, Zulfiqar Gilani, Akbar Zeb, and Sikander Sherpao for their guidance, enthusiasm, and support, and Nilufer Javaid and Ayesha Attique for their assistance with translations. I appreciate the support of the Freeman Foundation and the Center for Asia and Pacific Studies and the Center for the Study of Women in Society at the University of Oregon, which helped make this fieldwork possible.

1. Of the 124 members of the NWFP Provincial Assembly, 70 are from the MMA, 54 are from the opposition. There are a total of twenty-three female members: only one woman, Ghazala Habib Tanoli (Sherpao Party, from Mansehra) came into the assembly on a general seat; the rest were appointed on reserve seats for women, based on proportional representation of total seats won by distinct parties. The MMA has thirteen female MPAs, and the combined opposition has ten. In Baluchistan, the MMA joined a coalition government as it did not win that provincial election outright.

2. The Tabligh Jam'at was founded in Delhi in 1920 with the goal of educating Indian Muslims about the fundamental beliefs and practices of Islam, *da'wah*. It has long since broadened its scope as its *da'wah* movement has spread worldwide. For further information, see Vahiduddin Khan, *Tabligh Movement* (New Delhi: Islamic Centre, 1986), and Muhammad Khalid Masud, *Travellers in Faith: Studies of the Tablighi Jama'at as a Transnational Islamic Movement for Faith Renewal* (Leiden: Brill, 2000).

3. John Esposito's pivotal work, *Islam: The Straight Path*, has come out in a new edition, which includes a new epilogue addressing contemporary, compelling concerns on this issue: John L. Esposito *Islam: The Straight Path*, rev. 3rd ed. (Oxford: Oxford University Press, 2005).

4. This violent local movement in the late 1990s in the Malakand division of NWFP emerged from a grassroots frustration with promises made at the national level to implement Islamic laws in the country, but which local people found lacking.

5. Clarification needs to be made of my usage of the term "Islamist," particularly as it is not my intention to use it in the context of "othering." I use it to refer to political groups and parties which claim, at their essence, the desire to implement norms and laws consistent with those of Islam in the event they come to hold political power.

6. Amnesty International has said that human rights abuses committed in the context of the Pakistani government's continued support of the U.S.-led "war on terror" resulted in the arbitrary detention of hundreds of people suspected of having links with "terrorist" organizations and their transfer to U.S. custody (Amnesty International, *Annual Report*, released May 28, 2003, available at: http://web.amnesty .org/report2003/Pak-summary-eng. Accessed June 2007). Nowhere are people more acutely aware of this than in the NWFP, where the majority of raids have occurred.

7. In fiscal 2001–2002, the Pakistan government committed Rs. 7,986 million to the NWFP; this figure was dramatically increased to Rs. 12,420 million in

2002–2003. By comparison, development funds allocated to Baluchistan, equally poor but not considered as politically volatile at this time, were Rs. 7,952 million and Rs. 8,511 million, respectively, for an increase of just 7 percent (Government of Pakistan, Statistics Division, Federal Bureau of Statistics, *Pakistan 2003: Statistical Pocket Book* [Federal Bureau of Statistics, Planning and Development Division, 2003], p. 158).

8. As quoted in C. M. Naim, ed., *Iqbal, Jinnah, and Pakistan: The Vision and the Reality* (Syracuse: Syracuse University Press, 1979), p. 213.

9. In an effort to promote economic growth, the "day off" in the country reverted to Sundays in the late 1990s, so that the business week in Pakistan would be the same as in much of the world.

10. I have elaborated on this crisis of the loss of a moral vocabulary in Pakistan previously. See, for example, the discussion in Anita M. Weiss and S. Zulfiqar Gilani, eds., *Power and Civil Society in Pakistan* (New York: Oxford University Press, 2001).

11. Philanthropy in Pakistan has grown to surprising proportions. According to the National Survey of Individual Giving conducted by the Pakistan Centre for Philanthropy, individuals gave an estimated Rs. 41 billion in cash and goods in 1998. Of the total share going to organizations (35 percent), 94 percent went to religious institutions and causes (Pakistan Centre for Philanthropy, *Philanthropy in Pakistan: A Profile* [Islamabad: Pakistan Centre for Philanthropy, 2002]).

12. This is the "urban legend" about the *madari* at Akoora Khattak. However, a number of people in NWFP have said to me that this is inaccurate and that Mullah Omar never attended the *madari* there. I have not been able to confirm or repute either allegation.

13. An excellent assessment of these changes, including the intolerance being taught in public schools, is in A. H. Nayyer, "Pakistan: Islamisation of Curricula," *South Asian Journal* (Lahore) 2 (October–December 2003), pp. 71–87.

14. For an extensive discussion of the countless jihadi organizations that have emerged in Pakistan, see Muhammad Amir Rana, *A to Z of Jehadi Organizations in Pakistan*, trans. Saba Ansari (Lahore: Mashal, 2004).

15. The Jamiat ulema-e-Pakistan in 2002 was headed by Noorani, who was also the official head of the MMA coalition. He died in December 2003, resulting in a much-weakened party.

16. For a fuller discussion of the history of the Jama'at Islami and its history with electoral politics in Pakistan, refer to Seyyed Vali Reza Nasr, *The Vanguard of the Islamic Revolution: The Jama'at-i Islami of Pakistan* (Berkeley: University of California Press, 1994); for a further discussion of its role in influencing state power in Pakistan, see Seyyed Vali Reza Nasr, *Islamic Leviathan: Islam and the Making of State Power* (New York: Oxford University Press, 2001), and, more recently, Seyyed Vali Reza Nasr, "Islam, the State and the Rise of Sectarian Militancy in Pakistan," in Christophe Jaffrelot, ed., *Pakistan: Nationalism without a Nation?* (London: Zed Books, 2002), pp. 85–114. The Jamiat Ulema-i-Islam (JUI) had only contested the 1973 elections. For further elaboration on the JUI, see Sayyid A. S. Pirzada, *The Politics of the Jamiat Ulema-i-Islam Pakistan, 1971–77* (Karachi: Oxford University Press, 2000), and Ahmad

Husain Kamal, *Tarikh-i Jam'iyyat-i 'Ulama'-i Islam* (Lahore: Makki Darulkutub, 1997). Two good synopses of the role of Islamist groups and the state are in Mumtaz Ahmad, "The Crescent and the Sword: Islam, the Military, and Political Legitimacy in Pakistan," *Middle East Journal* 50:3 (1996), pp. 372–87, and in Saeed Shafqat, "From Official Islam to Islamism: The Rise of Dawat-ul-Irshad and Lashkar-e-Taiba," in Christophe Jaffrelot, ed., *Pakistan: Nationalism without a Nation?* (London: Zed Books, 2002), pp. 131–47.

17. Constitution of the MMA (in Urdu; author's translation).

18. The issue of the Federal and the Concurrent Lists of laws is an ongoing tussle between the provinces and the federal government deriving from the 1973 constitution. Laws on the Federal List could be made only in the National Assembly, and laws on the Concurrent List could be made jointly by the National Assembly and a Provincial Assembly. However, this arrangement was to last only ten years (i.e., until 1983), after which time responsibility for laws on the Concurrent List would devolve to the provincial governments.

19. Personal interview, Islamabad, October 27, 2003.

20. MMA, "Islamization in NWFP Draft Document," fall 2003 [exact date uncertain].

21. Personal interview, Peshawar, October 29, 2003.

22. NWFP Chief Minister Akram Khan Durrani performed the opening ceremony on September 1, 2004.

23. Personal interview, Peshawar, October 30, 2003.

24. Speech by Rehana Ismail, MMA MPA, at a reception at the Lucky Marwat School, NWFP (undated).

25. Personal interview, Peshawar, October 29, 2003.

26. Personal interview, Peshawar, October 30, 2003.

27. "Order for Zohr prayer goes unheeded," in *Dawn* (October 28, 2003, available at: http://www.dawn.com/2003/10/28/local39.htm; accessed June 2007) quoted NWFP Chief Minister Mohammad Akram Khan Durrani as expressing, in a letter circulated on October 16, his "deep concern over the lack of punctuality in the saying of Zohr prayers by government employees and has asked the heads of all the departments to ensure that they did so during the office timings." The MMA government has issued directives to the heads of all line departments, "asking them to make elaborate arrangements for the zohr prayers (noontime) at their respective departments in line with the provincial cabinet's decision with regard to the Islamization of the province." It said that the directives be implemented "in letter and in spirit within 15 days positively." Departments have also been instructed to have a thirty-minute break between 1:00 and 1:30 for prayers, to provide space for prayers and arrange for water and bathrooms for ablution. The October letter said that in the wake of the Shariat Bill passed by the provincial assembly and recommendations of the Shariat Council, the departments concerned were required to implement the decision.

28. The customary practice of *swara* is used as a final conclusion in dispute resolution generally involving a murder. A female from the family of the murderer is given to marry someone from the family of the victim, on the assumption that the

former belligerent won't harm them if one of their own women is in that household, and that long-term peace is assured once there are children from that marriage. However, in practice, the life of a girl given in *swara* becomes a living hell, for the strong, lingering animosity toward the murder is taken out on the girl. Even very young girls have been given in *swara*.

29. MMA, "Islamization in NWFP Draft Document."

30. Information Minister Asif Iqbal Daudzai, personal interview, Peshawar, September 2004.

31. Personal interview, Islamabad, November 4, 2003.

32. MMA, "Islamization in NWFP Draft Document."

33. Ibid.

34. Personal interview, Peshawar, September 2004.

35. By stating *talaq* three times, a husband divorces his wife. This simple act has already been banned by the 1961 federal Muslim Family Laws Ordinance (MFLO), and the Jama'at Islami has long advocated that the MFLO should be repealed as it includes many aspects (noted earlier in the case of registration of divorce and permission from a first wife before marrying a second) that have nothing to do with Islam. The MMA has singled out this issue and banned it, stating that now, a month must be inserted each time *talaq* is pronounced, and only then is a divorce finalized. There is no provision in the provincial law that such divorces need to be registered.

36. Pakistan Institute of Legislative Development and Transparency (PILDAT), "State of Democracy: Revival of Democracy in Pakistan Report, 3rd Quarter of Democracy, May 16, 2003 to August 15, 2003," Lahore, September 2003, p. 16.

37. Section 22, "Hisba Force," of the Amended Version of the proposed Hisba Act.

38. The bill includes twenty-seven additional "Special Powers" that the *mohtasib* will hold, too numerous to list here, but which includes such powers as to ensure moral ethics in public places; to discourage beggary; to stop indecent behavior in public places; to stop loitering; to eliminate professional jugglery, palmistry, and selling of amulets; to safeguard women's rights—specifically, to outlaw honor killings and ensure their due share in inheritance and eliminate the abusive tradition of *swara*; and to check artificially created inflation.

39. Section 9, "Mohtasib's Powers and Responsibilities," of the Amended Version of the proposed Hisba Act.

40. Personal interview, Peshawar, October 29, 2003. The ongoing issue concerns federal and provincial authority surrounding the Concurrent and Federal Lists, and when distinct items should be removed from the Concurrent List and authority for them be allowed to devolve to the provinces.

41. I am grateful to Juan Cole for helping me translate the judgment on the Hisba Act.

42. Hisba Judgment by Council of Islamic Ideology, September 2004; translation by Juan Cole.

43. Iftikhar A. Khan, "SC upholds most parts of Hasba," *Dawn* (available at: http://www.dawn.com/2007/02/21/top1.htm; accessed February 21, 2007).

44. This charge was leveled by an opposition member of the provincial assembly in an interview in Peshawar, September 2004.

45. A non-MMA federal official in Peshawar told me this in fall 2003.

46. This quote by MMA MNA Razia Aziz captures the tone of rhetoric used by MMA members once the Hudood reforms were tabled in the National Assembly. "Amendment to Hudood laws will encourage adultery: JI," *Dawn* (27 August 2006, available at: http://www.dawn.com/2006/08/27/local20.htm; accessed on 28 August 2006).

47. Personal interview, Islamabad, October 27, 2003.

48. Ibid.

PART II

Religion and Politics in Muslim Minority Societies

8

Muslims in
Post-Independence India

Steven I. Wilkinson

Many observers think that the outlook for India's 13 percent Muslim
minority is bleak. The Congress Party, the post-independence guarantor of secularism and minority rights, has been losing power
in India's state assemblies since the 1960s, to a host of different
ethnic and regional parties. In the late 1980s and 1990s, the party's
grip on power at the national level was shaken by two different political movements: one based around middle-caste and lower-caste
interests, and the other around an aggressively anti-minority
Hindu nationalism. In the 1999 parliamentary (Lok Sabha) elections,
one of these movements, in the shape of the Hindu nationalist
Bharatiya Janata Party (BJP), finally won enough seats to form a stable
coalition in New Delhi. After 1999, the BJP-led government of
the National Democratic Alliance (NDA) took steps to Hinduize the
education system (the leading hawk, Murli Manohar Joshi, headed
the Ministry of Human Resources Development) and various
cultural bodies, and it raised the sensitive issue of whether to abolish
Muslims' right to separate personal laws. Although the Congress
Party unexpectedly won just enough seats in the 2004 elections to
enable it to form a national coalition, this victory was a long way from
restoring the party to national dominance. Congress's 2007 state
election losses have thrown into question the party's prospects
of retaining power at the national level.[1]

In economic terms, Muslims still remain one of the poorest communities in India, backward on almost every measure, with

minimal representation in the national civil service and armed forces, and poor health outcomes, levels of educational attainment, and levels of income and employment. The recommendations of the new Congress Party government's Sachar Commission on the Status of Muslims, appointed in 2004 to examine steps to improve the community's welfare, are likely to have little effect on improving these outcomes, given that much of the constitutional power on minority issues rests with the states. Finally, since the late 1980s, the Hindu right has precipitated several major episodes of Hindu-Muslim violence, throughout the whole country during the Ayodhya campaign of 1989–1992 and the violence that followed the destruction of the Babri Masjid in December 1992, and more recently from February to April 2002 in the important western state of Gujarat. In the December 1992–January 1993 violence, more than a thousand people were killed, many thousands injured, and over a hundred thousand were forced to flee their homes. In the 2002 violence in Gujarat, more than a thousand people were killed, including, symbolically, retired Muslim Member of Parliament Ehsan Jaffrey, murdered after his many phone calls for help were ignored by the local police.

In this chapter, while trying not to minimize the level of discrimination and violence that Muslims still face in India, I take a more optimistic view of the community's future. In the first section, I point out that things were never quite as good for Muslims during the golden era of Congress Party secularism as many believed. The "Congress system" may have had the impeccably secular Nehru at the top from 1947 to 1964, but many of the Congress Party state leaders, who had the constitutional authority to implement minority protections, viewed Muslims as either a disloyal and nondeserving minority or at least as less deserving of state patronage than their own (Hindu) political supporters. It is true, however, that there have been many negative developments since the late 1980s, and I lay these out in the second section: several waves of anti-Muslim political mobilization and violence, the communalization of some parts of the administration and police, and terrorist attacks both inside and outside India, which have been used as the pretext for state repression that has primarily been directed against Muslims. Finally, as some Muslims in Kashmir and elsewhere have despaired of their opportunities within India, they have been attracted to militant or terrorist organizations, whose violent attacks on Hindu targets further intensify a cycle of violence and repression.

Despite these problems, however, the general prospects for Muslims in contemporary India are much less bleak than is often portrayed. In particular, as I show in the third section, the increase in political competition and electoral volatility in many states in the 1980s and 1990s has given Muslims an increasingly important role as a pivotal swing vote. Middle-caste and lower-caste parties and several important regional parties (such as the Telegu Desam Party (TDP) in Andhra Pradesh) have offered Muslims state protection from riots, increased development spending, and access to job and education reservations in order to win their electoral support. There are certainly problems, but the overall picture is one in which we can expect increasing electoral competition in the states and New Delhi to reduce conflict and tensions over the long run, as well as improve Muslims' economic opportunities.

Why the Congress Era Wasn't a Golden Age

The conventional view is that under Prime Minister Jawaharlal Nehru, post-independence India provided a secure and welcoming home for all India's minorities, especially the Muslims. Muslims were proportionately represented in the dominant Congress Party, and a variety of constitutional provisions ensured their freedom from employment discrimination, as well as freedom of religion, freedom of speech, the right to educate their children in religious schools, and separate personal laws.[2]

This portrayal of the post-partition reality, however, is much too rosy, largely because it focuses on formal constitutional and legal protections rather than how they were implemented (poorly) and because it focuses on the national Congress leadership (mostly secular) rather than on those state level leaders who, under the 1950 constitution, actually had responsibility for most issues that affected Muslims: education, language policy, agriculture, police, and state employment.[3] In reality, Muslims suffered significant discrimination in education, employment, housing politics, and access to capital, as well as their dealings with state officials.[4] This discrimination was due partly to the fact that Muslims were seen as the disloyal minority that had caused partition and partly to the fact that Muslims, most of whom had supported the Muslim League before independence, had little influence with the Congress Party politicians who now controlled all the levers of state patronage.[5] In consequence, Muslims found it difficult to get jobs or promotions in the state civil services and police forces, along with government contracts and bank loans.[6] Muslim *zamindars* (landlords), because of their post-1947 lack of influence in politics and the administration, also found it more difficult than their Hindu peers to avoid the full force of the land reforms that were introduced into many states in the early 1950s.

Iqbal Masud, who entered the Indian Revenue Service in 1947, describes vividly in his memoirs how most of the officials he encountered took the attitude that "[Muslims]... asked for Pakistan. Now let them go there and leave the jobs to Hindus."[7] Muslims in northern and western India found that their command of the Urdu language and Perso-Arabic script, which had once given them an edge in recruitment for the police and civil service, was now a distinct disadvantage, as state and local governments now insisted that their employees be able to write in a highly Sanskritized form of Hindi. In October 1947, for instance, the town of Bareilly threatened its employees who used Urdu with the loss of their jobs unless they conducted all business in Hindi within six months.[8] In the autumn of 1947, the provincial United Provinces and Central Provinces governments followed suit, over Gandhi's objections, and forced their employees to conduct government business only in Hindi and the Nagari script.[9] Muslim legislators who complained that these measures broke Congress's promises to the minorities were told that the Muslims, by causing partition, had canceled these pledges.[10] When the Muslim League members in Uttar Pradesh lost the vote on the introduction of a Hindi-only policy in the province, they walked out in protest, to the sounds of Congress Party legislators calling out, "Don't come back; go to Pakistan."[11]

The post-independence discrimination against the Muslim middle and upper classes and the lack of Muslim access to government patronage had several practical effects. For one thing, it meant that the flow of Muslims out of India to Pakistan continued well into the 1950s, as much of what was left of the Muslim middle class and upper middle class decided that the opportunities in Bombay or Lucknow were very poor compared with those that awaited them in Karachi or Lahore.[12] Fully half a million Muslims, for instance, left India for West Pakistan between January 1950 and February 1952.[13] For another, Muslim influence in politics and government administration declined rapidly. At the center, the few token Muslims were kept away from the major ministerial positions such as Home, Defence, and Foreign Affairs and were appointed to less important areas such as Education (a state subject) or Science and Cultural Affairs.[14] In the states, the same general rule applied: Muslims were kept away from important state ministries such as Education and Home Affairs. The Muslim home minister of India's most populous state, Uttar Pradesh, for instance, was kicked upstairs to an unimportant central government ministry in 1947 because some Hindu politicians protested that it was dangerous to have a Muslim in such a sensitive law and order position.[15] Muslim ministers at the center were also warned by the Congress High Command not to "interfere" in Muslim issues in the states.

In government administration, Muslim employment declined precipitously in the late 1940s and 1950s. Muslims had been 24 percent of the officer corps and 32 percent of the troops in the pre-partition army, but the transfer of Muslim regiments and most Muslim officers to Pakistan and the nonrecruitment of

Muslims to new positions reduced these percentages to less than 1 percent by the 1950s.[16] The vast majority of Muslim officers from the elite Indian Civil Service (ca. 25 percent Muslim in 1947) also either transferred to Pakistan or had retired by the 1950s. Data collected in the 1960s, 1970s, and 1980s showed that Muslim representation in central government employment was rarely more than 2 or 3 percent.[17] In central services that were regarded as "sensitive," there was a tacit ban on Muslims: even as late as the mid 1990s, there was no Muslim serving in India's equivalent of the FBI and CIA, the Research and Analysis Wing (RAW).[18]

In most states, it was a similar story, with the partial exception of the south. Muslims already employed were kept away from positions that were regarded as "sensitive" and were generally not recruited for new jobs.[19] When the Hindu police minister of India's most populous state expressed reservations about his mixed police force's loyalty in 1947 and announced that he was going to recruit a new, "absolutely loyal," paramilitary force, everyone understood that this meant the force would recruit only Hindus.[20] Discrimination within India, the decline in Muslims' economic fortunes after partition (which reduced the supply of educated youth who could pass the service exams), and the positive attraction of job opportunities in Pakistan all served to sharply reduce Muslim influence in administration.[21] Muslims had been 50 percent of the police force in Uttar Pradesh in 1947, but emigration and the fact that few Muslims were hired after independence reduced this to fewer than 10 percent a decade later; in Bihar, where Muslim representation in government service had been 25–33 percent prior to 1947, it was less than 6 percent by 1960.[22]

Economically, too, the situation for Muslims in post-independence India was far from good. National sample survey data consistently showed that Muslims were more likely than Hindus to be poor and have intermittent and unpredictable earnings, and that almost half of Muslims live below the (low) Indian poverty line, compared with around a third of the overall population.[23] Their lack of access to state patronage was the most critical factor, preventing them from improving their economic prospects in the same way as the more politically powerful Hindu middle and lower castes. Data collected in the early 1980s suggest that Muslims were consistently at the back of the queue when state jobs, grants, and development programs were being handed out: for example, Muslims had only 2–3 percent of senior positions in state corporations (a real problem when most of the growth from the 1950s to the 1980s had been in state employment), and Muslims received less than 3 percent of the subsidized housing and loans provided by Indian states.[24] Contributing to these poor outcomes, of course, was the poor quality of the education Muslims received in the state sector (most Muslims cannot afford the better-quality private schools) or in the madrasas, where the curricula have not adapted to needs of changing labor markets. This poor educational preparation means that only a minority of Muslims is qualified to sit the exams for public employment: only 2.59 percent of those who took the elite Indian Administrative Service exams in the 1980s were Muslim.[25] And outside the highly transparent examination process for the central civil service cadres (where, according to the Sachar Committee, Muslims actually do a little better than average in securing employment), there are continuing concerns that Muslims are discriminated against in recruitment procedures where individual officers have a wide degree of discretion in whom to hire.

Recent Problems

Even if we acknowledge that the period from independence to the mid 1970s hardly constituted a golden age, it is nonetheless true that there have been several major threats to majority-minority relations since the early 1980s: a major dispute over the status of Muslim personal laws; the massive Hindu nationalist mobilizations that led to BJP state governments coming to power in the early 1990s and then, in 1999, to a Hindu nationalist-led coalition in New Delhi; a sharp rise in Hindu-Muslim violence, often facilitated by these Hindu nationalist state governments; and partly in response to these other three factors, a rise in Muslim militancy, with a very small minority of alienated Muslims now participating in terrorist activity within India.

First, in 1984, the Indian Supreme Court opened up the issue of Muslim personal laws in a controversial manner, when it ruled that a divorced Muslim woman then in her seventies, Shah Bano, was entitled to financial support from her ex-husband under section 125 of the Indian legal code, even though he claimed he had fulfilled his obligations to her under Islamic law. The judgment—in which the Hindu justices alienated many Muslims by interpreting the *Shariat* and also expressed their hope that the anomalous survival of a separate Muslim personal law would be ended—opened up the whole question of whether a separate Muslim civil code should even exist. Shah Bano herself was a highly sympathetic plaintiff, and the overwhelming majority of Hindu opinion, as well as many liberal Muslims, supported her case.[26] Leading political and religious figures from the Muslim community, however, were overwhelmingly opposed to the Supreme Court's judgment, and they mobilized in protest against the ruling Congress Party. After losing several key by-elections in seats in which Muslims were a large share of the electorate, Congress Prime Minister

Rajiv Gandhi decided to satisfy Muslim conservatives and allow passage of a bill—the "Muslim Women (Protection of Rights on Divorce) Act, 1986"—which largely entrenched the legal position of Muslim personal law and made clear that, on matters such as divorce, Muslim law took precedence over the Indian civil code.

Having infuriated many Hindus with this action, which was widely interpreted as "minority vote bank politics," Rajiv Gandhi then tried to recover his standing with Hindus by throwing the Hindu right what would prove to be a very dangerous bone: he allowed the question of the "disputed" religious site at Ayodhya in Uttar Pradesh, which had been closed since Hindus had installed a religious statue in the Babri Masjid in 1949, to be reopened. Over the next eight years, the Hindu nationalist BJP and its allied organizations in the Hindu nationalist "family" masterfully exploited the Babri Masjid issue, solidifying Hindu opinion behind the party by claiming that the mosque stood on the site of the Ram Janmbhoomi (Lord Ram's birthplace) and that the Muslims were being unreasonable by not giving up the "disused" mosque. From 1989 to 1991, Hindu nationalists carried out a succession of semireligious processions throughout India to try to mobilize support for the building of a temple to Lord Ram on the site of the mosque. In 1992, several years of violent mobilization culminated in the destruction of the mosque by tens of thousands of militants. The Indian state was highly complicit in this destruction, which sparked off a month of rioting throughout India in which perhaps 2,000 people were killed. The BJP government in Uttar Pradesh allegedly ordered its police forces surrounding the Babri Masjid to stand back while the Hindu militant *kar sevaks* (volunteers) demolished the mosque. But in a larger sense, the responsibility for the destruction was the Congress Party central government's, because it had accepted the BJP leadership's highly questionable promises to protect the site and refused to order the federal troops and paramilitary forces located near the mosque to prevent its destruction if the state forces failed to do their duty. This Congress procrastination was the direct outcome of two factors. First, the Congress Party leadership recognized that many Hindus were broadly sympathetic to the Hindu right's position on Ayodhya (see below). Second, the party headed a weak coalition government, which was reluctant to do anything that might lead to a shift in Hindu voters' support away from the party. Throughout the 1990s and early 2000s, these two factors led to the Congress Party's treading a shaky and increasingly problematic line: on the one hand, trying to prevent anti-Muslim mobilization and violence, while, on the other hand, trying not to position itself in the Hindu electorate's mind as "pro-Muslim" on issues such as whether a temple should be built at Ayodhya or whether there should be a unified civil code.[27]

Successive anti-Muslim mobilizations were clearly a highly effective short-term electoral tactic for the Hindu right, helping the party win control of four state governments in the early 1990s, then other major states (such as Gujarat and Maharashtra later in the decade). In 1999, the BJP won sufficient votes in parliamentary elections to let it form a coalition government in New Delhi. Although it initially appeared as if the price the BJP would have to pay to form this coalition would be to moderate its stance on divisive majority-minority issues, it had a greater flexibility to pursue a pro-Hindu line than many anticipated. In particular, hard-line Hindu nationalist Murli Manohar Joshi was put in charge of the Ministry of Human Resources, where he pursued an aggressive campaign to Hinduize schools and higher educational and research institutions—for example, by emphasizing in new versions of secondary and junior school textbooks the facts of India's Hindu heritage and the dangers posed to India over the years from Muslim "invaders."

In the states, Hindu nationalist governments have also tried to Hinduize their administrations—for example, by allowing police officers to display religious imagery on their vehicles or in their offices, and (in Gujarat) by removing the ban on state officials joining Hindu nationalist organizations. Most dangerously, the government in Gujarat, in an effort to solidify the Hindu vote in advance of state elections, facilitated a massive anti-Muslim pogrom in February–April 2002, in which perhaps a thousand people were murdered and tens of thousands had their property destroyed and were forced to flee.

The disputes over Hindu personal law, the growing role of Hindutva (Hinduness) in administration and politics, and several anti-Muslim pogroms together have created a deep sense of despair among some Muslims, at least before the 2004 victory of the Congress coalition in New Delhi, and they have pushed a very small minority of alienated Muslims to violence. (Of course, this is not the only reason for Muslim militancy in India.) In the aftermath of the anti-Muslim pogrom in Bombay in 1992–1993, Muslims in the Bombay underworld organized several major bomb blasts targeted at the Hindu-controlled financial sector, including a major explosion at the Bombay Stock Exchange. Since then, a very small minority of young and often well educated Muslims have been drawn to an assortment of militant organizations that claim to defend Muslim interests in the absence of state protection. The largest is the Students Islamic Movement of India (SIMI), a wing of the Jamaat-e-Islami, with around 400 active members and 20,000 *ikhwans* (students). This group was banned after several bomb blasts in Bombay in 2002, and its leaders are either under arrest or in hiding. Another group, the Gujarat Revenge Group, was formed specifically to extract revenge after the 2002 violence. Several of the major Kashmiri separatist organizations such as Lashkar-e-Toiba and

Jaish-e-Mohammad are also reported to have links with Muslim militants in cities such as Mumbai and Delhi, and to have assisted them in bomb attacks.[28]

The several major terrorist attacks launched by these movements beginning in 2000—including attacks on major railway and bus stations, symbolic sites such as the Red Fort in Delhi and the Gateway of India in Bombay, and a major attack on the Indian Parliament itself in December 2001—have killed more than a hundred people in all and have increased the perception among many ordinary Hindus that they are under threat from Muslims. The Hindu nationalist government in Delhi used the September 11 terrorist attacks in the United States, as well as the heightened violence in India, to push through some draconian anti-terrorist legislation in March 2002, the Prevention of Terrorism Act (POTA), which allowed—until its repeal by Congress in late 2004—extended detention without trial on the basis of often flimsy evidence. This act was directed almost exclusively against Muslims, despite the fact that Hindus were also involved in attacks on Muslims. After several years of having to defend its anti-minority policies against international criticism, the BJP government now took the public position that the West was now waking up to a problem that it had long recognized. The United States, in particular, seemed to regard India as a key ally in its global "war on terror," and there was no public criticism from the United States of the Indian government's mass roundups of Muslims between 2001 and 2004 under POTA.

Many secular academics place all the blame for the Hindu nationalist mobilizations and violence since the late 1980s on Hindu nationalists who have deliberately stirred up conflicts. My own work has explored the ways in which violence against Muslims has often deliberately been fomented for electoral purposes, so I am certainly not going to dispute the fact that much of the anti-Muslim campaign has been engineered by politicians. But despite this, academics often downplay the fact that these political campaigns would not succeed were it not for the fact that, at some level, many Hindus still regard Muslims with some suspicion: as a coddled, potentially disloyal, and militant minority that should be "nationalized" for its own good and the good of the nation. This is notwithstanding the recognition given by all Indians to a few exemplary and high-achieving Muslims: for instance, nuclear scientist (and president of India from 2002 to 2007) A. J. Kalam; Bollywood film stars Shahrukh Khan and Aamir Khan; information technology and outsourcing tycoon Azim Premji; and sportsmen such as cricket stars Mohammad Azharuddin and Wasim Jaffer. These negative perceptions of Muslims have their roots, of course, in the partition period, but they have been strengthened in recent decades by the conflict with Pakistan, international coverage of Islamist movements, and conflicts over such issues as the survival of Muslim personal laws (Hindu personal laws were integrated into the general civil code in the 1950s) or the Ayodhya issue.

A 1993 poll (table 8.1) revealed many of these dangerous fault lines. Although it was conducted in the aftermath of the destruction of the Babri Masjid (and therefore probably exaggerates the extent of negative Hindu views about Muslims), the basic findings are generally consistent with other surveys: a solid majority of Hindus believe that separate Muslim personal laws are divisive and contrary to national integration (78 percent opposed in 1993), that Muslim leaders are generally fundamentalist extremists, and that Muslims are somehow less committed to India as a nation than Hindus.

In the 1990s and 2000s, this general mistrust has been entrenched by the long insurgency in Kashmir, the actions of Islamists in nearby Afghanistan and Pakistan, the international discourse since 2001 of the "war on terror," and the more recent terrorist attacks and arrests of Muslim in India. All these developments have helped the BJP central government make its case that the Muslim minority is a "problem" and that the community needs to be integrated, forcibly if necessary, into the Indian mainstream. As Acharya Giriraj Kishore, a prominent Hindu nationalist leader, puts it: "If Muslims want to buy peace and social harmony, they have to respect the sentiments of the Hindus."[29]

TABLE 8.1. Opinion Poll of Hindus' Views on Muslims, 1993

Statement	% in Agreement
Until a uniform civil code is established, there will never be national integration.	78
Violence is not the way to settle matters between Hindus and Muslims.	74
Indian Muslims consider themselves Muslims first and Indians later.	64
The Muslim population is growing at a much faster rate than the Hindu population.	58
Muslims must reject their fundamentalist leaders.	58
Muslims believe that all non-Muslims are their enemies.	53
Muslims are fine craftsmen and skilled artisans, without whom our arts and crafts would suffer.	51
The underworld is controlled by Muslims.	49
The Muslims were justified in reacting angrily to the demolition of the Ayodhya mosque.	44
Hindu and Muslim cultures are so different that they cannot really live together.	28
Muslims should not be allowed in the armed forces.	20
Hindus should not employ Muslims in their businesses or homes.	13

Source: MARG opinion poll of 481 Hindus, conducted February 1993 in Bombay. Reported in "India's Muslims Fear New Physical Threat: Militant Hindu Nationalism, Discrimination Solidify Group's Sense of Alienation," *Washington Post*, March 12, 1994.

Good News

Despite the many negative developments since the late 1980s, there are at least three reasons for optimism about the position of Muslims in India. First, despite their deep reservations about the status of Muslim personal law and their occasional worries about Muslims' loyalty to the state, most of the Indian population is firmly opposed to highly discriminatory policies toward Muslims. Second, India has relatively strong judicial institutions and a thriving civil society that checks the actions of Hindu nationalist politicians and will eventually prevent the widespread misuse of acts such as POTA. Third, trends in state-level political competition since 1980 are likely to increase the pivotal value of Muslim votes in state politics, which will increase politicians' attempts to offer Muslims security, as well as better economic opportunities.

Public Opinion Does Not Support Aggressive Anti-Minority Actions

One reason for optimism about the future of India's Muslims is that the electoral success of the BJP in recent decades does not represent any great rise in popularity in India of the idea of a Hindu state, which has never gained the support of more than 30 percent of the population in opinion polls. In fact, the BJP has only been able to do as well as it has electorally by (a) paying more attention to caste and distributive issues, which most voters consistently rank in opinion polls as more important to their voting choice than religious issues, and (b) allying with regional parties, some of which (like the Trinamool Congress in West Bengal and the TDP in Andhra Pradesh) themselves rely on minority votes.[30] Consistently throughout the 1990s, opinion polls found that around two-thirds of the Indian population rejected aggressively pursuing an anti-minority agenda by demolishing mosques on "disputed" sites or legally banning Muslim participation in the army or security forces. For example, a March 1993 poll of 1,300 voters in seven major cities found 73 percent opposed to the demolition of "disputed" mosques in Mathura and Varanasi. Some 62 percent of voters were opposed to a Hindu state: the highest level of support for a Hindu Rashtra was in Bombay (not Mumbai) (45 percent), and the highest level of opposition to it was in the south, with 80 percent of voters in Madras (now Chennai) opposed.[31] A 1996 Gallup poll found that there was "relatively little support for Hindu nationalists who wish to recast the country's legal and political institutions along less secular lines." When asked their opinion of "people who say this country's laws should give preference to the Hindu religion over other religions," only 26 percent said they tended to approve of such persons, while 45 percent—the fourth highest for any item—expressed disapproval."[32] Finally, as we can see in table 8.1, only a minority of Hindus (13–20 percent) support widespread employment discrimination against Muslims in private or state employment.

Strength of India's Institutions and Civil Society

A second reason why we should be optimistic about the future of Muslims in India is the relative strength of two important checks—the judiciary and civil society—on Hindu nationalists' tendency to use their control of the national and state administrations to increase communal tensions and discriminate against Muslims. India's supreme court and high courts have regularly taken actions against state and national governments found to be abusing the legal process to take action against minorities. In 2003, for example, the supreme court essentially blocked the Hindu right's campaign to build a major religious site next to the destroyed Babri Masjid at Ayodhya. The court prevented the national BJP government from giving sixty-seven acres next to the site of the destroyed mosque to the Hindu nationalist Ram Janmbhoomi Nyas so that organization could carry out religious ceremonies and (possibly) build a temple on the site.[33] Other government institutions, such as the National Human Rights Commission, have also restrained the executive branch; for instance, in 2003, the commission came out strongly against the lack of safeguards in the POTA legislation.[34]

India is also blessed with a very active civil society. It has a robust free press, and many major newspapers sharply criticize governments for their actions against minorities. There are also a large number of NGOs with both the will and the capacity to uncover the facts about anti-minority actions and, on occasion, to launch public-interest litigation against measures that are used to discriminate against Muslims.[35] For example, in April 2003, the People's Union for Civil Liberties sought a judgment from the supreme court quashing POTA on the grounds that many of its provisions (particularly those on the admissibility of evidence obtained by policemen while the accused were in custody) were unconstitutional infringements to legal due process.[36]

Political Incentives for Moderation

India's twenty-eight state governments control all local law enforcement and local administration, and they have day-to-day responsibility for most of the major issues that affect minorities, such as education and minority language rights. So, ultimately, the security of Muslims in India is determined largely by the actions of these state governments. What, then, determines whether state governments will take measures to help or hurt their Muslim minorities? In my book *Votes and Violence*, I make the argument that state governments will protect minorities—and may also take measures to improve their economic position—where either of two conditions applies: (1) there is a high number of political parties competing for power, which makes Muslim votes increasingly important (because even if a party does not rely on Muslim votes today, it may have to form an alliance with a party that does tomorrow); or (2) the party in power relies directly on significant minority support (figure 8.1).

Empirically, I demonstrate in my book—using statistical analysis of thirty years of data on elections and violence, as well as case studies and interviews—that these two factors explain most of the variation in state levels of Hindu-Muslim violence. For one example here, consider what happened during the 2002 violence in Gujarat and elsewhere in India. Figure 8.2 shows data that I collected from Indian press reports during the Gujarat violence (March 27 to April 30, 2002). Reported "precipitating events" of the kind that normally spark off mass violence, such as Hindu nationalist processions, organized attacks on individual members of the other community, demonstrations, forcible attempts

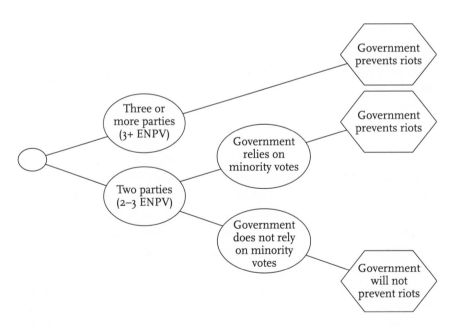

FIGURE 8.1. Link between electoral competition and minority protection. ENPV, effective number of parties (votes). *Source:* Wilkinson, *Votes and Violence: Electoral Competition and Ethnic Riots in India* (New York: Cambridge University Press, 2004). Reproduced by permission of Cambridge University Press.

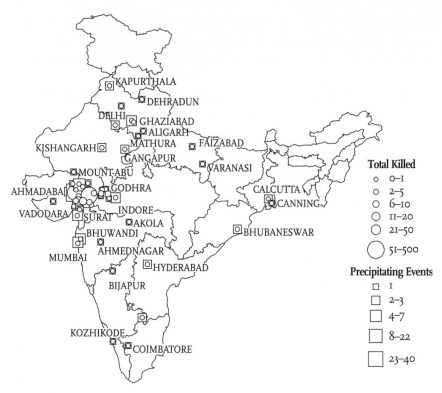

FIGURE 8.2. Number of persons killed and injured and number of precipitating events during the Gujarat violence (March 27 to April 30, 2002). Data collected from Indian press reports. *Source:* Wilkinson, *Votes and Violence: Electoral Competition and Ethnic Riots in India* (New York: Cambridge University Press, 2004). Reproduced by permission of Cambridge University Press.

to get Muslim shopkeepers to close their shops as part of a Hindu nationalist "strike," or attacks on property belonging to the other community, are shown along with the number of total casualties (deaths and injuries) reported in each town from February to April 2002 as a result of these precipitating events. It is striking that large-scale attempts to heighten tensions and cause violence occurred throughout India in 2002, not just in Gujarat, many of them in "riot-prone" cities that had a long history of violence, such as Indore, Hyderabad, Aligarh, Bhopal, and Calcutta. Despite these attempts to foment trouble through-out India, however, only one state—Gujarat—actually experienced large num-bers of casualties.

The immediate reasons for the differences between Gujarat and other states are not hard to uncover. The short answer is that, as Human Rights Watch and others have conclusively demonstrated, the Hindu nationalist state

BJP government in Gujarat facilitated the violence against Muslims through sins of omission and commission—for example, by refusing to fire on rioters and transferring officers who took strong actions against Hindu nationalists involved in rioting—while governments in other states took many steps to prevent violence from breaking out in their major cities.[37] The West Bengal government, for instance, ordered police to fire on Hindu nationalist demonstrators near Calcutta when they refused to disperse. In Madhya Pradesh and Rajasthan, two states right next to Gujarat, the state governments carried out thousands of preventive arrests and enforced curfews in sensitive towns and districts; in Rajasthan, the police were prepared to use deadly force against rioters when these measures were not enough. Similar stories could be told about Andhra Pradesh, Karnataka, and elsewhere.

My research shows that the underlying causes of these different patterns of state action are electoral. Where states were either very competitive (with what political scientists refer to as a high number of "effective parties") or in which the main party in power relied on minority support, then the states prevented violence.[38] Where these conditions were absent, as in Gujarat (and no other state), the state acted in a highly biased manner. Figure 8.3 shows the levels of party competition that I calculated for each state in 2002, as well as the violence that actually took place, indicating localities where there were no reported casualties and where there were varying numbers of dead and injured. At low levels of party competition with only around three effective parties in a state, things depend on which party is in power: the one with a multiethnic coalition that relies on Muslim support, or the one that has no minority support and that stands to gain from Hindu-Muslim polarization.

There were four low-competition states in 2002 (Gujarat with 2.97 effective parties, Andhra Pradesh with 2.78, Madhya Pradesh with 3.09, and Rajasthan with 3.19). In Gujarat, the BJP state government is basically in a two-party system with the Congress Party (the effective number of parties is 2.97 because close to 20 percent of the vote is shared among many small parties), and, according to exit polls, it has zero percent of the Muslim vote in the state. As the general electoral argument would have predicted, it acted in a very biased way: officers who prevented anti-Muslim attacks, suspended negligent officials, or tried to register criminal cases against BJP, Rashtriya Swayamsevak Sangh, or Vishwa Hindu Parishad members who were inciting riots were transferred from their posts almost immediately. For example, the deputy commissioner of police in Ahmedabad city, P. B. Godhia, was transferred for registering a case against a local BJP member of the state assembly (Jaydeep Patel), while the superintendent of police in the town of Bhavnagar was transferred after he ordered his men to fire on a Hindu nationalist mob attacking

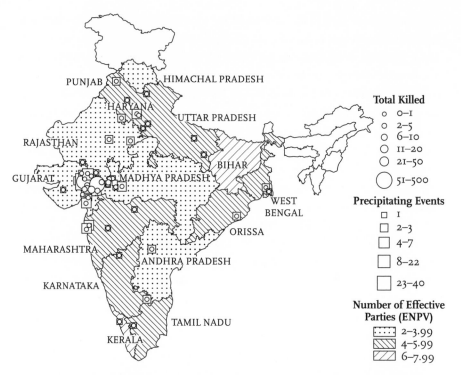

FIGURE 8.3. Levels of party competition and violence in Gujarat, indicating areas where there were no reported casualties and where there were varying numbers of dead and injured. Data collected from Indian press reports and recalculated. *Source:* Wilkinson, *Votes and Violence: Electoral Competition and Ethnic Riots in India* (New York: Cambridge University Press, 2004). Reproduced by permission of Cambridge University Press.

a madrasa, an action that resulted in four rioters being killed and the rescue of 400 people from inside the madrasa.

In the remaining low-competition states, however, the parties in power all relied heavily on Muslim votes. (Opinion polls show that in Andhra Pradesh, the ruling TDP had 30–50 percent of Muslim support, and the main opposition party also sought Muslim votes; in Rajasthan, the ruling Congress Party had 92 percent of the Muslim vote, and in Madhya Pradesh, the Congress Party had 97 percent of Muslim support.)[39] These state governments acted as we would expect: with determination to prevent anti-Muslim violence that might break up the multiethnic coalitions that keep them in power. They used arrests and curfews to try to prevent violence from breaking out in the first place, and then they were prepared to use deadly force if necessary to stop riots if they did break out.

At higher levels of party competition, as my general electoral explanation predicts, governments also did very well in preventing violence, not just in states where middle-caste and lower-caste parties with substantial Muslim support were in power (such as Bihar), but even in the state of Orissa, where the ruling coalition included the BJP. Orissa had 4.26 effective parties, with Biju Janata Dal and BJP in a coalition supported by only 16 percent of Muslims, if we believe polls, but this coalition government still did well in preventing violence, using force to break up an attack in Cuttack.[40]

Conclusion

The good news for India, and for India's 130 million Muslims, is that there are several factors likely to restrain any Hindu nationalist attempts to establish a Hindu Rashtra that will turn permanently turn Muslims into second-class citizens. First, opinion polls consistently show that over two-thirds of Indians reject this option, and that Indians are committed to religious pluralism. Second, India's strong legal institutions and civil society impose real restraints on politicians' ability to target minorities in order to stay in power. Third, a broad increase in electoral volatility and competitiveness since the early 1980s is working in Muslims' favor, because a higher level of party competition leads to more competition for Muslims' votes. The increase in political competition in Indian states has had good effects— not just on the country's level of violence, as Hindu politicians offer security to Muslims in exchange for political support, but also on Muslims' economic prospects. In the south, which has historically been much more politically competitive than the north, Muslims have long benefited from reserved places in public employment, as well as educational institutions. In recent years, as politics in the north of India has also become more competitive, we are beginning to see politicians there also offer Muslims not just physical protection but reserved places in government employment and educational institutions as well. In the long term, it is these improvements in Muslims' educational and economic outcomes that may prove to be the most significant developments in the next twenty years.

NOTES

1. For an analysis of this 2004 election result, see Steven I. Wilkinson, *Votes and Violence: Electoral Competition and Ethnic Riots in India* (Cambridge: Cambridge University Press, 2004).

2. Arend Lijphart "The Puzzle of Indian Democracy: A Consociational Interpretation," *American Political Science Review* 90:2 (1996), pp. 258–68.

3. For extensive documentation, see Steven I. Wilkinson, "India, Consociational Theory and Ethnic Violence," *Asian Survey* (2000), pp. 767–91.

4. Mushirul Hasan, *Legacy of a Divided Nation: India's Muslims since Independence* (Boulder, Colo.: Westview, 1997); and A. R. Saiyed, "Changing Urban Ethos: Some Reflections on Hindu-Muslim riots," in K. S. Shukla, ed., *Collective Violence: Genesis and Response* (New Delhi: Indian Institute of Public Administration, 1988), pp. 97–119. For extensive documentation on the community's economic and educational backwardness, and their low levels of representation in government service, see Syed Shahabuddin's journal *Muslim India*, which provides invaluable data culled from state and central reports and debates from 1983 to 2004.

5. Although Muslims supported a diverse range of political parties when genuine provincial elections were first introduced in India in 1936, by the 1946 elections about 14 percent of Muslims who could vote overwhelmingly supported the Muslim League. In 1946, the league won all thirty Muslim seats for the Central Assembly and 428 of the 492 seats reserved for Muslims at the provincial level (Ian Stephens, *Pakistan*, 3rd ed. [London: Ernest Benn, 1967], p. 138).

6. The best exploration of the dilemma of the post-independence Muslim minority is in M. S. Sathya's 1973 film, *Garam Hava* (Hot Wind), which examines the economic and emotional breakdown of a once-prosperous Muslim family in post-1947 north India.

7. Iqbal Masud, *Dream Merchants, Politicians and Partition: Memoirs of an Indian Muslim* (New Delhi: HarperCollins, 1997), p. 48.

8. *Pioneer*, October 6, 1947, and November 5, 1947.

9. *Pioneer*, October 15, 16, 1947.

10. Wilkinson, *Votes and Violence*, p. 119.

11. *Pioneer*, November 5, 1947.

12. In Uttar Pradesh, half a million Muslims, 7 percent of the state's Muslim population, emigrated to Pakistan between 1947 and 1951. These Muslims were overwhelmingly from urban areas (*Census of Pakistan 1951*, Vol. 1: *Reports and Tables* (Karachi: Government Press, no date), p. 31, sections 19/1–19/2.

13. *Pakistan Constituency Assembly Debates*, 1952, Session 10, 2:1, November 12, 1952, p. 67.

14. For figures on this exclusion, see Wilkinson, *Votes and Violence*, pp. 108–23.

15. Wilkinson, *Votes and Violence*, pp. 122–23.

16. *India, Legislative Assembly Debates*, March 12, 1947, pp. 174–250.

17. Hasan, *Legacies of a Divided Nation*, table 8.6, gives data showing Muslim representation at 2.99 percent in the elite Indian Administrative Service, 2.85 percent in the Income Tax Department, and 3.06 percent in the Railway Service (p. 282).

18. The same applies to the Indian Foreign Service: according to a knowledgeable Washington insider, there was no Muslim listed among the directory of the large staff of the Indian embassy in Washington, D.C., in 2003.

19. Interviews with police officials in charge of post-partition recruitment, Uttar Pradesh, August 1995.

20. Wilkinson, *Votes and Violence*, p. 111. The police minister concerned, Lal Bahadur Shastri, later became prime minister after Nehru's death in 1964.

21. Wilkinson, *Votes and Violence*, p. 112.

22. Uttar Pradesh State Archives (Lucknow), Box 957, GAD File 49H/1958. Inquiry made by the Government of India about the employment of members of the minority communities. Bihar data from Sharif al-Mujahid, *Indian Secularism: A Case Study of the Muslim Minority* (Karachi: University of Karachi Press, 1970), pp. 153–59.

23. Hasan, *Legacies of a Divided Nation*, p. 281.

24. Ibid., pp. 282–84.

25. Ibid., pp. 293–94.

26. Ashgar Ali Engineer, ed., *The Shah Bano Controversy* (London: Sangam, 1987), is a collection of most of the relevant court, press, and political documents.

27. Current Congress Party President Sonia Gandhi's usual stance on Ayodhya is to avoid taking a stance. She typically argues that she respects whatever judgment the courts will hand down "They said Demolish the Babri Mosque," *Outlook India*, June 23, 2003, pp. 25–28).

28. *Outlook India*, September 8, 2003, pp. 32–40.

29. "What Lies Beneath," *Outlook India*, April 14, 2003, pp. 18–19.

30. A massive India-Marg poll in 1996 found that most Indians ranked the need to address poverty (42 percent), unemployment (22 percent), and corruption (16 percent) as the most important issues influencing their votes (*India Today*, June 30, 1996, pp. 28–31.

31. "The Week-MODE Opinion Poll," *Muslim India* 123, March 1993, pp. 106–107.

32. Gallup 1996 Poll Announcement.

33. "What Lies Beneath," *Outlook India*, April 14, 2003, pp. 18–19.

34. "National Convention on POTA," *People's Union for Civil Liberties Bulletin* (June 2003), available at http://www.pucl.org/Topics/Law/2003/poto-convention.htm (accessed June 6th 2007).

35. For example, reports of the People's Union for Civil Liberties agitation against POTA, at ibid.

36. Ibid.

37. " 'We Have No Orders to Save You': State Participation and Complicity in Communal Violence in Gujarat," *Human Rights Watch* 14:3(C) (April 2002). For details of state actions to prevent violence elsewhere, see Wilkinson "Putting Gujarat in Perspective," *Economic and Political Weekly* (April 27 2002), pp. 1579–83.

38. In many Indian states, there are literally dozens of parties that compete in elections, though usually only a handful of these are serious competitors. The "effective number of parties" measure gives a greater weight to more successful parties, in order to provide a better indication of the real level of electoral competition than if we were to simply count the total number of parties standing in a state in an election. The formula for the effective number of parties (votes) is: $ENPV = 1/(vi2$ (where vi is the *vote share* of the ith party).

39. Source for data on Madhya Pradesh, Andhra Pradesh and Rajasthan is a survey by the Center for Studies in Developing Societies, reported in *Frontline* 16:23 (November 6–19, 1999). Available at: http://www.lokniti.org/publications _chronologicallybyyear.htm (accessed June 7, 2007).

40. Orissa polling data from Oliver Heath "an Unequal Alliance in Orissa,", *Frontline*17:7 (April 1–14, 2000). Available at: http://www.lokniti.org/publications _chronologicallybyyear.htm (accessed June 7, 2007).

9

Islam in China

Jacqueline Armijo

Although there have been Muslims in China since the time of the Prophet Mohammad, few people today are aware of China's large Muslim population and their complex history of survival living among a people and culture renowned for their ability to absorb and assimilate outsiders. Over the centuries, the Muslim population evolved from a small settlement of Persian and Arab traders along the southeast coast of China to a large and diverse population scattered throughout the country. Muslims in China today represent China's most geographically dispersed minority groups, as well as the most urbanized and the most integrated into all walks of life.

Despite intermittent periods of religious and ethnic persecution, the Muslim population has managed to survive, and often thrive. At present, China's Muslim population is conservatively estimated at 20 million, although Muslim scholars put the total at closer to 50 million. The Muslims are identified by the state not through their religion but by their ethnicity. Of China's fifty-five officially recognized minority peoples, ten are primarily Muslim: the Hui, Uighur, Kazak, Dongxiang, Kirghiz, Salar, Tajik, Uzbek, Bonan, and Tatar. The largest group, the Hui, is spread throughout the entire country, while the other nine live primarily in the northwest provinces of Xinjiang, Gansu, Tibet, and Ningxia.[1] As the most dispersed group, the Hui are also the ones whose lives have been most closely tied to the communities in which they live, be they Han Chinese or other minority peoples. They also enjoy a broader degree of religious freedom than other Muslim groups. The second largest group, the Uighur, live primarily in Xinjiang Province in northwest China (officially known as Xinjiang Uighur Autonomous Region). The Uighur are a Turkic people whose ancestors have lived in China from pre-Islamic times. Their culture is distinctively Central Asian, and their mother tongue is Uighur. Unlike the Hui, they are concentrated in one region, and their lives, including their political, cultural, and religious activities are closely monitored and restricted by the Chinese government. (Their situation is discussed more fully in the section on human rights concerns.)

Given the diversity of China's Muslim populations, their wide distribution throughout the country, and their varying histories, cultures, and languages, it is difficult to make generalizations about their practice of Islam. However, one can say that Muslims living in rural areas and the northwest are more likely to follow the basic tenets of Islam. Muslims living in relative isolation from other Muslim communities and those living in cities are the ones most likely to have lived through extended periods of pressure to abandon religious practices and ignore prohibitions against pork and alcohol. The vast majority of Muslims in China are Sunni and follow the Hanafi school of law. Unlike Muslim minorities in other countries, Muslims in China are not allowed to use Islamic laws for any official legal proceedings, even those only concerning family law.

The mosques, like the communities they serve, are equally diverse. In some regions, there are mosques set aside for women only,[2] whereas in other areas, women are forbidden from praying in congregational mosques. In the southwest, however, the women pray beside the men, separated only by a partial curtain. Of the tens of thousands of mosques spread throughout the country, many date back centuries. There are mosques in northwest China that are Central Asian in style and design; in southwest China, one finds mosques that look as though they came from communities in southeast Asia. However, the older mosques in most regions of China resemble Buddhist temples, with sloping tiled roofs, carved pillars, and entryways decorated with brightly colored images of nature scenes painted on wooden panels. In some areas, the nature scenes are combined with equally colorful depictions of Mecca; and although the subject is Islamic, the style is decidedly Chinese. Within the mosques, one will also see an extraordinary range of Arabic calligraphy styles, reflecting each region's own history and the evolution of its own styles.[3]

Beginning in the mid 1980s, funding began to flow into China to rebuild mosques destroyed or damaged during the Cultural Revolution (1966–1976). Unfortunately, in many instances, the funding came with certain strings attached: the rebuilt mosque would no longer reflect their non-Islamic cultural history. Buddhist architectural style together with its florid decorations would not be allowed. The result was mosques that were touted as "authentic" but, in fact, reflected nothing. Many were made entirely of concrete and white tile.[4]

Although the Hui Muslims in different regions of China have their own histories of varying degrees of persecution by the state, their position in China today is fundamentally different from that of the Uighurs, the second-largest Muslim group in China. The Uighurs, like other primarily Turkic Muslim minorities, are concentrated in China's strategic border regions and in regions noted for their important natural resources. Moreover, the Uighurs, who are viewed as the most threatening by the Chinese government, live lives under increasingly severe political, cultural, and religious state control.[5]

This chapter on Islam in China provides a historical background to the arrival and development of Muslim communities, followed by a discussion of some of the most important challenges facing Muslims in China today as they seek to maintain their religious and cultural identity during this present period of rapid economic development and growing social unrest. As disparities in wealth and development opportunities increasingly divide Chinese society, communities have found themselves facing unprecedented threats to social cohesion and traditional values.

Muslim communities, like most minority communities who find themselves under threat, have sought to protect themselves by supporting their traditions. For the Muslims, this has taken the form of developing Islamic education programs, together with the creation of informal civil society projects. However, in Xinjiang, these types of community development projects are now impossible. While in the past, Uighurs may have been able to take part in a limited number of community projects, in the present post-9/11 world, the Chinese government has used the U.S.-sponsored "war on terror" to restrict almost all activities related to religious, cultural, and ethnic identity.

Others issues addressed include pluralism, minorities, and human rights. The final section deals with the position of women within Chinese Muslim communities and the increasingly important role of Islamic and secular education in improving their status.

Historical Background

Shortly after the advent of Islam in the seventh century, there were Muslims in China, for sea trade networks between China and Southwest Asia had existed since Roman times when traders from Western Asia learned to harness the monsoon winds to traverse the Indian Ocean.[6] Small communities of Muslim traders and merchants survived for centuries in coastal cities, but there was limited intermixing between them and the local Chinese population. It was not until the thirteenth century, with the establishment of the Mongolian Yuan dynasty (1274–1368), that tens of thousands of Muslims from Central and Western Asia were both forcibly moved to China and also recruited by the Mongols to assist in the governance and development of their rapidly expanding empire. Although some of the higher-ranking Muslim officials may have been able to arrange marriages with women from their places of origin, it is generally assumed that most of the soldiers, officials, engineers, architects, craftsmen, astronomers, scientists, physicians, and farmers who settled in China during this early period married local women.[7] Despite centuries of intermarriage and relative isolation from the rest of the Islamic world, the Muslims who arrived at this time were able to establish communities that have survived down to this day, with many of their cultural and religious traditions intact.[8]

The Mongol Yuan dynasty, which witnessed this huge influx of hundreds of thousands of Muslim and other foreigners into China, was followed by the Ming dynasty (1368–1644), during which power reverted to the Han Chinese. The Han lost no time in reasserting their political and cultural dominance of the Middle Kingdom. During this period, numerous laws were passed requiring "foreigners" to dress like Chinese, adopt Chinese surnames, speak Chinese, and essentially, in appearance, become Chinese.

Despite the focus on restoring traditional Chinese culture, one of the earliest Ming emperors, Yongle, launched a series of massive naval expeditions to explore the known world. In all, between 1405 and 1432, seven major expeditions were launched, involving hundreds of Chinese vessels and thousands of tons of goods and valuables to be traded throughout the Southeast Asian archipelago, the Indian Ocean, and as far as the east coast of Africa.[9] The success of these trading expeditions was no doubt in part due to the fact it was led by Zheng He, a Muslim from southwest China. A man known for his intelligence and formidable presence, his religion and ability to interact with many of the Muslim rulers and merchants encountered along the way, would have greatly facilitated this series of complex diplomatic and trading missions.[10]

However, shortly after the death of the Yongle emperor, China's cosmopolitan and international initiatives gave way to a period of conservatism and the redirection of imperial resources toward domestic issues and projects. It was also during this time that officials within the Ming government changed the character used to denote the Muslims (hui), by adding the dog radical. Although historically the dog and insect radicals had been used when developing names for the non-Han or "barbarian" people the Chinese encountered either within China or along its borders, this is the only known case in which a derogatory radical was added to an ethnonym.[11]

Despite these restrictions and requirements, the Muslims of China continued to actively practice their faith and pass it on to their descendants. By the end of the Ming dynasty, there were enough Chinese Muslim intellectuals who were thoroughly educated in the classical Confucian tradition that they developed a new Islamic literary genre: religious works on Islam written in Chinese that incorporated the vocabulary of Neo-Confucian, Buddhist, and Daoist thought.[12]

In 1644, the Manchu Qing dynasty (1644–1911) was established, marking the beginning of a period of tremendous growth and expansion, in terms of both territory and population.[13] The Manchu Qing dynasty, like that of the Mongols, represented another period of non-Han Chinese rule of China. Travel restrictions were lifted, and the Muslims of China were once again allowed to make the pilgrimage to Mecca and study in the major centers of learning in the Islamic world. During this period, several Hui scholars studied abroad and, upon their return, started a movement to revitalize Islamic studies by translating the most important Islamic texts into Chinese and thus making them more accessible.

Despite the opportunities for travel and study that arose during this period, the Manchu Qing dynasty also represented a period of unparalleled violence against the Muslims in China. In northwest China, a series of conflicts arose within Muslim communities, when Chinese Muslims who had returned from years of study overseas sought to introduce what were seen as new and unorthodox Islamic practices. In several instances, the government intervened, supporting one group against another, leading to an exacerbation of the conflict and outbreaks of mass violence and rebellion, eventually resulting in the massacre of hundreds of thousands of Muslims. A rebellion involving Muslims also broke out in southwest China, but although the consequences were equally devastating for the Muslim population, the initial catalyst was quite different. This uprising resulted in the establishment of an independent Islamic State, known as the Dali Sultanate, which lasted for sixteen years. A careful review of its origins allows us to examine the most common, pernicious, and damaging stereotypes about Muslims in China: that they are inherently violent.

This stereotype of Muslims in China was first developed by Chinese officials who were seeking to justify the massacre of entire Muslim communities, including women and children.[14] A close examination of one historical event in the history of Islam in China—which culminated in the 1870s with the state-sponsored slaughter of as many as 750,000 Muslim men, women, and children—will help explain how such prejudices have evolved over time.

During the seventeenth and eighteenth centuries, China experienced a massive population explosion, resulting in millions of Han Chinese moving into frontier regions. As more immigrants moved into Yunnan province along the southwest frontier, there were increasing clashes with the indigenous peoples and the Hui (who had settled there in the thirteenth century and whose population is estimated to have been 1 million). The Han settlers, not unlike European settlers throughout much of colonial history, did not view the local peoples as full humans or citizens with equal rights under the law. Land and forests were taken from local peoples, who were left destitute and forced to move either further up into mountainous regions or further south. In one instance, several different ethnic groups rose up in a violent protest against settlers who had destroyed an entire forest to grow cash crops. However, armed with both weapons and the direct support of the state, the settlers easily subdued the local tribes.[15]

Later, the settlers turned to the land and businesses owned by Muslims, most of whom had been living in the region for over half a millennium. Many of the Hui lived in cities and towns, were well educated, and were very much a part of established communities. When conflicts arose with the newly arrived settlers, the Hui turned to local officials to uphold the law. However, in a series of legal disputes between these immigrants and the Hui, local Han Chinese officials (who were themselves recent immigrants) repeatedly ruled in favor of their fellow Han Chinese against the local residents. The Muslims then sent envoys to Beijing seeking justice, but to no avail. Fighting escalated, and after a government-led massacre of the Muslim population of Kunming, the provincial capital, in desperation, a Chinese Muslim scholar led a movement to establish an independent state based on Islamic ideals. His followers included other indigenous peoples, as well as many of the Han Chinese who had also settled there centuries earlier.

Established in 1856 and centered in Dali, in northwest Yunnan, the Dali Sultanate survived for almost sixteen years.[16] But after he quelled other major rebellions, the Chinese emperor ordered his troops to concentrate their efforts on Yunnan. The massacres that ensued wiped out the majority of Muslims in the region. Estimates of the percentage killed range from 60 to 85 percent, and more than a century later, their population still has not recovered its original number. Another consequence of the rebellion was a series of government regulations that severely restricted the lives of Muslims. Muslims were no longer allowed to live within city walls, were restricted to certain occupations, and, in most cases, lost all their personal property, businesses, farm land, and communal property, such as schools and mosques.[17]

From a Han Chinese perspective, the insistence on the part of the Muslims to fight for their rights, against the most overwhelming odds, was seen as a sign of violent tendencies rather than as evidence of a determination for justice, regardless of the consequences. During the twentieth century, at different points in time when Chinese Muslims have faced persecution from the state, they have continued to stand up for their rights, refusing to back down.

For the remaining years of the Qing dynasty, Muslims in regions that had suffered mass violence sought to rebuild their communities, and Muslims in other regions sought to avoid conflicts with the state. It was not until the rise of the Communist Party in the 1930s and 1940s that Muslims were once again brought into the forefront of political affairs. In an effort to gain as broad a base of support as possible in their ongoing struggle against the Japanese and the Nationalists (Guomindang) led by Chiang Kai-shek, the Communists had promised relative independence and freedom of religion to the Muslims, in exchange for their support. Although these promises were respected in the early years of the People's Republic of China, during subsequent political campaigns, culminating with the Cultural Revolution (1966–1976), the Muslims of China found their religion outlawed and their religious leaders persecuted, imprisoned, and even killed. During this period, all worship and religious education were forbidden, and even simple common utterances, such as *insha'llah* (God willing) and *al-hamdulillah* (thanks be to God), could cause Muslims to be harassed, imprisoned, tortured, and, in extreme cases, killed.[18] Despite the danger, Muslims in many parts of China continued their religious studies in secret.[19]

Mosques, as the centers of communities, were targeted by the state.[20] Local officials throughout the country took control of mosques, appropriating their buildings and land and turning them into factories, storage areas, barns, and schools. Many were simply destroyed. In addition, deliberate efforts were made by local officials to defile the mosques and their adjacent land. For example, mosques were used to raise pigs, and pig bones or carcasses were thrown down the drinking wells in mosque courtyards to permanently pollute them.[21]

The most extreme example of state-sponsored violence against Muslims during the Cultural Revolution took place in July 1975, when Shadian, a Muslim village in Yunnan province, was completely destroyed by a group of Red Guards.[22] The Red Guards had occupied the village and set about harassing the villagers as part of a political education campaign. In a scene reminiscent of the actions leading up to the massacres of Muslims in this region over a century earlier, the villagers, after repeatedly failing to get the outsiders to desist in their harassment, organized a delegation of local leaders to go to Beijing to seek justice. Once again, assistance was not forthcoming. Instead, the Red Guards called in the army and, over the course of one week, destroyed the entire village, even going so far as to call in MIG jet fighters to bomb the village. In all, some 1,600 Muslim men, women, and children were killed, and over

5,000 were wounded. Although people throughout China, especially intellectuals, minorities, and members of religious groups suffered tremendously
during this period, the government never really owned up to what was done.
However, the utter depravity of what happened in Shadian was so extreme that
in 1979 the government officially apologized and provided compensation to the
surviving residents.[23]

Recent Revival of Religious Identity

In the years immediately after the Cultural Revolution, the Muslims of China
lost no time in rebuilding their devastated communities. Throughout China,
Muslims slowly began to restore their religious institutions and revive their
religious activities. Their first priority was to rebuild their damaged mosques.
Once communities were able to pray together again, the next priority was to
organize Islamic studies classes. As early as the 1980s, some mosques began
to organize classes for girls, boys, and young adults, as well as for the older men
and women of their communities who had not had the opportunity to study
their religion. Beginning in the early 1990s, independent Islamic colleges were
also established throughout most of China, except for Xinjiang.

These schools offer a full curriculum, including classes on the Qur'an,
hadith, *tafsir, fiqh*, Islamic history, the history of Islam in China, Arabic gram-
mar, and Chinese language. At present, most of the textbooks of the traditional
Islamic sciences are from Saudi Arabia, the Arabic-language textbooks are from
the Foreign Language Institute in Beijing, the Islamic history texts are translated from the Arabic, and the texts on the history of Islam in China are just
being published. Many of the graduates from these colleges go on to teach in
smaller schools and establish new schools in different regions. A growing number have chosen to continue their Islamic studies overseas.

Within China, when asked how to explain the recent resurgence in
Islamic education, community members cite two main reasons: a desire to
rebuild what was taken from them, and the hope that a strong religious faith
will help protect Muslim communities from the myriad of social problems
presently besetting China in this day and age of rapid economic development.
Chinese Muslims are adamant about the importance of religion in preparing themselves and their communities for their future in a state that seems to
be ideologically adrift.

That Muslim communities should place so much emphasis on education,
both secular and religious, should not be a surprise. As other minority groups
who have survived the vicissitudes of state persecution over time, they have

learned that the only thing that cannot be taken away from them is their education. Consequently, Muslims in several regions of China are overrepresented among teachers, professors, and college graduates.

Expanding Networks and Developing Identity

In addition to promoting religious knowledge, Islamic schools have also taken important roles in strengthening networks between Muslim communities, both within China and abroad, and in promoting different degrees of religious identity. In the different regions in China, even in the most remote and impoverished areas, Muslim villagers are informed and aware of the situation of Muslims living in the region and in other parts of China, as well as the latest issues concerning Muslim communities throughout the world. These networks were originally based on the trade routes plied by Muslims throughout the country, as they have for centuries dominated the transport trade (originally through horse carts, and now through trucks). Muslims traveling to study under different religious scholars has also been a constant source of flows of information. Muslim communities have established journals and newsletters and, most recently, websites. The range of this network of information has xpanded dramatically recently, with increasing numbers of students going overseas to further their Islamic studies. Although there are no official records kept, it is estimated that there is a total of between 1,000 and 1,500 Chinese Muslims presently studying in Egypt, Syria, Pakistan, Iran, Saudi Arabia, Turkey, and Malaysia.[24] Al Azhar has the largest number, with approximately 300 students. Most of the students are sponsored by their family and community, and they receive a small stipend at whichever Islamic university they attend.[25]

In conversations with Chinese Muslims who were studying, or had graduated from Islamic universities in Damascus, Cairo, Malaysia, Pakistan, Saudi Arabia, and Iran, it became clear that these young people had learned a tremendous amount about the rest of the world and the challenges faced by Muslims elsewhere. Most students stay abroad for between five and eight years. Some go on for postgraduate degrees, while others choose to settle, at least temporarily, in the cities where they studied. I met graduates in Damascus and Cairo who had set up small businesses or were working as translators for Middle Eastern companies doing business with China. There are also students who decide to study overseas for more practical reasons. As the Chinese government has abandoned its long-standing policy of fully funding college education, and passed the bulk of the expense onto students and their parents, some families have chosen to use the money they would have spent educating their child at home to send them abroad. Islamic universities overseas are often a popular option, as the expense is reasonable and it would be relatively easy to make contacts with other Chinese Muslims studying there, thus facilitating the process.[26]

Those who return to China bring back an awareness of the world and a strong foundation in Islamic studies. Although many hope to immediately take up positions as imams (or *ahong*, from the Persian *akhund*, as they are known in China) in their home towns and villages, it is often the case that the religious leaders of the community, although impressed with their foreign training, want to make sure the future imams have also acquired an understanding of their own communities and their needs.

One final indication of the growing awareness of multiple degrees and facets of religious identity is the recent trend among religious educated Muslims in China to distinguish between ethnic and religious identity. In the past, if you wanted to ask if someone were Muslim, you would say, are they "Hui." Technically, Hui refers to ethnicity only, but that has been conflated with religious identity. Now, Chinese Muslims very self-consciously will distinguish between someone being "Hui" and their being Muslim. For example, the response could now be, "yes, they're Hui, and they are also Muslim," or "they are Hui, but they are not Muslim."

Human Rights Concerns: From the Cultural
Revolution to the Post-9/11 War on Terror

In the immediate aftermath of 9/11 and the United States' subsequent "war on terror," the Chinese government lost no time in further restricting the lives of Muslims in Xinjiang.[27] Claiming extensive ties existed between separatist groups in Xinjiang and international terrorist networks, China used their "support" of the "war on terror" as justification for a widespread attack on all forms of popular resistance to state policies in Xinjiang. As the Uighurs in Xinjiang (the largest Muslim ethnic group in northwest China) had always faced severe political, religious, and cultural restraints by the state, concern was immediately raised that the "war on terror" could have a serious effect on them. In a November 2001 visit to China, United Nations High Commissioner for Human Rights Mary Robinson, "warned China not to use the American-led campaign against terrorism as a pretext to suppress ethnic minority groups."[28] Unfortunately, China did not heed such warnings. Moreover, China's increasingly severe policies in Xinjiang appeared to gain international support in August 2002, when American Deputy Secretary of State Richard Armitage announced during an official visit to Beijing that the Bush administration had decided to acquiesce to Beijing's request that an obscure Uighur group, the ETIM (Eastern Turkestan Islamic Movement) be listed as a "terrorist organization."[29] This group was so small and so obscure that even experts in the field had never heard of it. Nevertheless, its placement on an international list of terrorist organizations implied that China was also a victim of international terror networks and would thus be an important and active participant in the "war on terror."[30]

Initial reports in the Chinese press claimed hundreds of Muslim extremists had been caught in Afghanistan. And although these reports did prove to be greatly exaggerated, twenty-two Uighurs did end up in Guantanamo. At least half of them are ready to be released, but the United States is reluctant to return them to China for fear of their being executed. As of February 2005, the United States had not been able to persuade any third-party countries to accept the Uighurs; in part, this may be because the United States is refusing to accept any themselves. So far, Germany, Switzerland, Finland, and Norway have all rejected U.S. requests.[31]

Closely linked to the impact of 9/11 on Muslims in China is the issue of human rights, specifically those of the Uighurs in Xinjiang. Although Muslims throughout China face a variety of challenges and are the subject of a wide range of discriminatory actions, the situation for the indigenous peoples of Xinjiang is unprecedented in its severity, surpassing even the repressive policies facing the Tibetans. Muslims who hold official positions, including faculty at the universities, are forbidden to carry out any religious activity in public. They are not allowed to attend mosque, fast during Ramadan, or in any other way respect their religious traditions in public. There are signs on mosques refusing entry to anyone under eighteen years of age.[32] Islamic education outside the one officially controlled school is forbidden.

Once the overwhelming majority in Xinjiang, Uighur and other Muslim peoples will soon be outnumbered by Han Chinese immigrants. In the early years of the Communist rule, millions of Han Chinese were forcibly relocated to Xinjiang to work on state farms and in the mining and oil industries. When government laws controlling migration were eased, some of the early settlers decided to return to their birthplaces. More recently, once again millions of Han are moving to Xinjiang, but this time on their own in search of jobs. The government is encouraging this trend, often offering subsidies to Han settlers.[33] And although the government is committed to spending millions of dollars on development projects there, the primary beneficiaries in virtually every major industrial and development project have been the immigrant Han Chinese population, and often with tremendous negative environmental impact on the region.

In addition to being the most natural resource-rich region of China (with major sources of oil and natural gas), Xinjiang is also a strategic border region with its neighbors, Pakistan, India, Tajikistan, Kyrgyzstan, Kazakstan, Mongolia, and Russia. Furthermore, it is the site of China's nuclear weapon development and testing site. Consequently, it is highly unlikely that the Chinese government will accede to any of the demands of the indigenous Muslim population to grant them greater political autonomy and greater freedom of religious practice.

The state has conflated the practice of Islam with separatist activity and completely overreacted in illegally prohibiting almost all forms of Islamic education and public religious practice. Thousands of Uighurs in Xinjiang have been thrown in jail and sentenced without public trial. An untold number have been executed upon being accused of political crimes.[34]

In one of the most well documented cases of government harassment, a prominent Uighur businesswoman, Rebiya Kadeer, was arrested in August 1999, as she was on her way to a scheduled meeting with a member of a U.S. Congressional Research delegation. In March 2000, in a secret trial, during which neither she nor her lawyer was allowed to speak in her defense, she was sentenced to eight years in prison. Accused of spying, her actual crime was reported to have been sending her husband, who was living in the United States, clippings from local newspapers.[35] Kadeer's case is especially troubling because for years she had been held up as an example by the government as an ideal citizen. A successful businesswomen (and mother of eleven), she had used her wealth and resources to establish the "Thousand Mothers' Movement," a project that provided job training and employment for Uighur women.[36] She also established evening schools to combat illiteracy among adult Uighurs. In 2004, she was awarded the Thorolf Rafto Human Rights Award, Norway's prestigious annual humanitarian award (and a frequent precursor to the Nobel Peace Prize winner). After years of demands for her release from a range of governments and international human rights organizations (including the U.S. government, the British Foreign Office, and Amnesty International),[37] it was only in March 2005, just days before an official visit by Secretary of State Condoleezza Rice, that Kadeer was finally released.[38]

Another controversial case is that of Tohti Tunyaz, a Uighur historian who had been working on his Ph.D. at Tokyo University in Japan. He was arrested in February 1998, while he was visiting Xinjiang to collect material for his dissertation on the history of China's policies toward ethnic minority groups. He was sentenced to eleven years in prison for "illegally acquiring state secrets."[39]

This attack on a historian with no known ties to any extremist groups, or history of political activity, is an example of the government's increasing attempts to control culture as much as religion and political ideas. Even language has recently come under attack. In 2002, the government issued a proclamation ending the use of Uighur language in colleges and universities in Xinjiang.[40] In addition, there was also a public book-burning campaign that resulted in hundreds, if not thousands, of books written in Uighur being destroyed.[41] These attacks on cultural identity have had a chilling effect on the Uighurs in Xinjiang, as well as on those in exile, for it seems that the state is seeking to undermine the survival of a culture. In the past, it was during times of persecution and hardship that Muslims found renewed faith. By seeking to undermine the religion and culture of the Uighurs, the state may, in fact, be strengthening them. What is most troubling is the prospect of creating a self-fulfilling prophecy of widespread violent unrest, for as one scholar has argued, "the Chinese are sowing seeds of an ethnic resentment so profound as to jeopardize the very stability they claim to defend."[42]

Current repressive tactics not only undermine the Muslims' rights to practice their faith and pass on their religious, moral, and cultural values to their children, they also undermine the Muslims' trust in the Chinese government. And although there are numerous reports made by the Chinese state, and often repeated in the Western press, that radical separatism is a common desire in Xinjiang, in fact, the overwhelming majority of Uighurs in Xinjiang, while not uncritical of China's policies, are resigned to the reality of Chinese rule. The small number of violent protests are resented by most and seen as adding to the state's further justification of political crackdowns and control. Uighurs speak with increasing despair of their desire simply to be allowed to practice their religion, continue to use their language in their studies, and uphold their traditional cultural practices, as citizens of China.

Democratization, Civil Society, and Islamic Education

Although limited village elections have been held in different regions of China, in point of fact China has made little progress toward real democratization. Even if village elections continue, it is unlikely that minorities in China, including the Muslim nationalities, will experience any significant democratic reform, as most of these populations tend to live in politically strategic border regions or in regions with major natural resources of which the state seeks to maintain control. As Chairman Mao is reported to have said, "China is rich in people, land, and natural resources; but in fact it is the Han who are rich in people, and the minorities who are rich in land and natural resources."

Since the early 1990s, a wide range of civil society programs have been established in China. Some focus on rural development and public health issues, while others focus on urban social problems. However, the degree to which these organizations are truly nongovernmental is debatable, as the government still maintains a high level of control over most levels of society. Nevertheless, many of these organizations have proven to be extremely effective in their efforts to develop projects to address a range of development issues in China today, some with the support of the state, and others independently.

Muslim groups in China face a particularly daunting challenge in establishing civil society organizations, for technically any organization involving Muslims must be established through the auspices of either the Religious Affairs Bureau or the Islamic Association of China. These organizations, staffed by Communist Party cadres, are able to control almost all aspects of public religious activity. Although one of its responsibilities is to protect religious practices, as Communist Party members are required to be atheists, many religious leaders in China believe that the Religious Affairs Bureau is more interested in controlling religion than in supporting it. With regard to the Muslim populations, the Religious Affairs Bureau has the final say in the appointment of imams to every mosque in the country, and it decides which ones will be allowed to lead Friday prayers. They decide whether to approve the repair or construction of new mosques and Islamic schools. The bureau is also in charge of the several government Islamic colleges spread out around the country, and it selects the curriculum, teachers, and students admitted. Muslim students hoping to travel abroad to continue their studies must first receive permission from the bureau,[43] as must those planning to go on hajj.

The issue of the hajj continues to be one of the most serious grievances of Muslims in China against the contraints placed on them by the Chinese state. Beginning in the 1980s, Muslims in China were once again allowed to go on the annual hajj pilgrimage. According to the China Islamic Association, every year approximately 2,000 Muslims take part in the government-sponsored pilgrimage. However, the state has instituted severe restrictions: for example, pilgrims must be at least sixty years old and not traveling with their spouse. Also, the official quota of 2,000 per year is much lower than the usual Saudi calculation of 1,000 pilgrims for every 1 million of a country's Muslim population. In China's case, that should result in a quota of at least 20,000. Some Muslims who already have passports are able to make the pilgrimage independently, or travel via a third country, but for the vast majority of Muslims in China, the possibility of making the hajj remains distant. In 2004, reports surfaced that China has loosened some of the restrictions regarding age, and although the official quota remained 2,000, according to Chinese government reports in January 2006, an estimated 7,000 Chinese Muslims took part in the hajj.[44] It appears that many, if not most, of these pilgrims obtained their visas from neighboring countries such as Pakistan and Thailand.

In response to this strict government control, Muslim communities throughout China have established informal civil society projects that seek to support those communities most in need. The long-standing informal networks that connect Muslim communities throughout China, in addition to acting as conduits for a continual flow of information, have acted to ensure that there is a constant redistribution of resources among different communities. Large mosques and Islamic schools are the most common sources of funding for both individuals and communities in need. But, in addition, beginning in the 1990s, more and more individual Muslims who have become very wealthy have developed their own methods of contributing to the welfare of the Muslim community as a whole. Most of these projects focus on education, from preschool to university programs, but there are also projects to develop Muslim orphanages and nursing homes. The lack of nursing homes for elderly Muslims has recently become a pressing issue, as more and more older Muslims find themselves in government-operated nursing homes where it becomes difficult, if not impossible, for Muslims to adhere to dietary restrictions.

Once again, it is through Islamic education that most of the activism of the Muslim communities is organized. Every year, hundreds of young people who have just graduated from Islamic colleges throughout China volunteer to teach for several years in whichever communities are most in need of access to Islamic studies classes. Although it might mean years away from family and friends, often living in the most impoverished regions of China, these young people are determined to share their knowledge, teaching Arabic and a basic knowledge of Islam to Muslims of all ages. They also serve as yet one more tie between the different Muslim communities. Those from wealthier communities often organize drives for food, clothing, and school supplies, to benefit those living in poorer communities. These young people are also a tremendous source of information about Muslim communities in other parts of China, as well as the world Muslim *ummah*. Moreover, in many poor villages, these volunteer teachers also provide the only source of education children might receive. Since the mid 1990s, as the state has dramatically reduced its funding of all levels of education, increasing numbers of poor village children are not being educated. Although technically, public schools are not allowed to charge tuition, they are allowed to charge a wide range of fees, which although individually are almost negligible, quickly add up to make education unaffordable for a rapidly growing segment of the rural population. Consequently, in some particularly poor villages, Islamic schools may be the only means for children to learn to read and write in Chinese.

Beginning in 2000, Muslim college students have taken an increasingly active role in supporting both civil society and Islamic projects. For example, through donations from a wealthy businessman, a group of Muslim college students was able to take part in an intensive medical care training program at a major medical school. In addition, in one city in southwest China, Muslim students from several different universities pooled their resources in order to facilitate the students fasting during Ramadan. As none of the university cafeterias would adjust their schedule to allow for students to have an early morning meal or dinner at the appropriate time, students took it upon themselves to rent an apartment near the universities and organize the cooking of meals at appropriate times. Activities like these further strengthen the practice of Islam among Muslim college students and facilitate the ties among them.

Although in the past there is evidence that Muslim communities actively supported *waqf* foundations, in the present period this has not been possible. At the beginning of Communist rule in China, land, and later all businesses were nationalized, and although recently there has been a land reform process by which individuals have been given limited ownership over property and business, to what extent this ownership can be passed on is not clear. Furthermore, although most mosques were eventually returned to their communities in the aftermath of the chaos of the Cultural Revolution, throughout China, mosques (and their surrounding neighborhood) that have been deemed to be in the way of urban development projects have been systematically torn down.

The loss of Muslim neighborhoods in urban areas has been devastating to Muslim communities. Although historical neighborhoods in cities throughout China have fallen victim to the wreckers' ball, the effect on Muslim communities, already tiny minorities in an ocean of Han Chinese, have proved disastrous. In addition, unlike all other minority groups, who tend to live in relative proximity to one another in rural areas, the Hui are the one minority most likely to live in cities in every region of China. When government city planners decide to tear down old neighborhoods, residents who can prove ownership of their homes are usually assigned public housing in developments on the edge of the city. In the case of Muslim neighborhoods, residents have been promised that their communities will remain intact as they will receive adjacent public housing assignments. However, in numerous cases, once neighborhoods were destroyed, when public housing project assignments were subsequently issued, these promises had not been kept.

For example, in Kunming, of the five traditional Muslim neighborhoods that had existed for centuries, only two remain, and in both cases they are a small fraction of their original size and growing smaller every year. The residents of the neighborhoods destroyed since 1990 found themselves indiscriminately scattered throughout the public housing projects; not only were they now living far away from their mosques and markets, they were also living widely separated, with no Muslim neighbors and no means of community support. In one particularly poignant case, an elderly woman I knew ended up living alone in a large apartment block with no Muslim neighbors or friends nearby. When she died, less than two years after moving to her assigned government apartment, it was days before her body was found. For many older Muslims living in cities, forced to abandon the neighborhoods they grew up in, these policies have proved devastating, and in some cases a nightmare.

According to some reports, a handful of cities in China have turned over historic Muslim districts to the Muslim population in perpetuity. But the majority of Muslim districts in the country do not have complete control of the future of their community. To the best of my knowledge, independent Islamic nongovernmental organizations (NGOs) that focus on public health,[45] development projects, or micro-credit initiatives (i.e., along the Grameen model) have yet to be established. However, with increasing contacts between Muslims in China and those outside, as well as Chinese Muslims being exposed to a range of civil society projects in the countries in which they study overseas, it is only a matter of time before such organizations begin to flourish.

Economic Growth, Social Unrest, and Ethnic Tensions

As minorities in a nation state controlled by a communist party and one dominant ethnic group, Muslims in China are extremely vulnerable to state policies, and they are not readily in a position to actively promote pluralism. For the most part, Muslims in China have not been activists, regularly demonstrating or demanding certain rights. On occasion, however, they have organized demonstrations in response to specific actions that they felt represented an attack on Islam. The most famous example became known as the Chinese Salman Rushdie case, as it involved the publication of a book that included statements extremely insulting to Islam. Muslims throughout China demonstrated, demanding that the government (which controls all publishing houses in China) immediately stop publication and recall all copies of the offending text.[46]

Since the early 1990s, China has experienced an extraordinary level of economic development and made huge improvements in quality of life. However, these advances have been concentrated in urban coastal regions and for the most part have left the rural population behind, in the proverbial dust. As 80 percent of China's population remain peasants tied to the land, this means that there are more than 900 million people who have not been able to fully benefit from the development taking place along the coast and in larger cities. Income inequalities are now among the worst in the world, and still growing.[47] As urban residents enjoyed significant increases in income, improvement in quality of housing, access to an ever-growing range of quality consumer goods, and a general improvement in quality of life, peasants found their lives under increasing strain. Every year, millions leave their villages in search for jobs in cities, and those left behind struggle under the increasing burden of low prices for their crops and increasing taxes. Greatly exacerbating their precarious position is the increasing problem of local officials preying on peasants by illegally instituting literally hundreds of fees. Although the state has repeatedly promised to crack down on this form of corruption, it appears to be making little headway.

As a result, a rapidly increasing number of protests have broken out throughout China, with more and more becoming violent. According to *Outlook*, an official publication of the Chinese Communist Party, in 2003, there were more than 58,000 reported incidents of social unrest in different regions of China.[48] These protests are concentrated in rural areas and are rarely covered by local or international media, as the government usually issues a news blackout immediately. It is only recently, with the growing use of the Internet and cell phones, that news of protests has leaked out before a clampdown can be instituted. Some of the protests are by peasants who have lost their land to development projects or dams, but most are related to accusations of corruption against local officials.

It in within this context of increasing rural protests and violence that ethnic unrest has broken out in different regions of China between Han Chinese and Hui. Although the Han Chinese greatly outnumber the Hui, they often claim to feel threatened by the Hui. The Hui, meanwhile, due to their small numbers and minority status, are vulnerable to harassment by Han and local officials. Many of these incidents are sparked by minor accidents that set off a series of reactions, eventually leading to violence. Although Han and Hui have lived side by side for centuries, it seems that recent hardships faced by most rural Chinese have begun to be expressed in ethnic violence. The Han view the Hui as clannish and prone to violence; the Hui claim that when attacked by Han, they have no choice but to call on other Hui in the village or their brethren from neighboring areas for support. As Hui stream in to support their beleaguered comrades, Han often panic.

Two recent incidents have been fairly well documented and are no doubt representative of other outbreaks that have occurred. The first incident took place in Shandong province in 2000, and the second in Henan province in central China, in 2004. The first incident took place over several months and was initially triggered when Muslim villagers organized protests against a Han butcher who had insisted on setting up a "Muslim Pork" stand. After repeated efforts to persuade the butcher to take down the offensive sign failed, the Hui organized a march to the local county government office to petition for their assistance. Not only did the local officials refuse to address their complaint, they arrested three of the petitioners. When word spread of the arrests, Hui from neighboring villages descended on the town and demonstrations continued. The incident might have just ended then, but in December, in the middle of Ramadan, a Han villager hung a pig's head outside the local mosque.[49] Demonstrations ensued, with thousands of Hui streaming in from an even larger area. As they approached the city, members of China's People's Armed Police opened fire, killing six and injuring more than forty.[50] At that point, Beijing had to intervene; several local officials were fired, and compensation was promised to the families of those killed.[51]

In the fall of 2004, in Henan province, there was another major case of unrest involving Hui and Han Chinese. In this incident, a car accident triggered a series of events that led to martial law being declared. Although the exact nature of the accident is unknown, violence broke out between Han and Hui and then quickly escalated. Homes and businesses of both groups were looted or burned down; untold numbers were injured. As Hui from neighboring regions began to arrive to support their greatly outnumbered brethren, panic rose among the Han as rumors spread of "a planeload of Huis flying in from the northwest region of Ningxia." Local authorities called in as many as 10,000 anti-riot and military police to restore order. Martial law was declared, and checkpoints were set up all around the village; no one was allowed in, including reporters. Local religious leaders helped the security forces convince Hui who came to support those under siege that order had been restored and there was no need for their assistance.[52] According to some reports, 148 people were killed; however, the government claims a much smaller number.[53]

Although there are some Muslim communities that prefer to have as little contact as possible with neighboring villages (be they Han Chinese or another minority community) there are others who actively cultivate good relations with non-Muslim neighboring villages. One example of a Muslim community that has maintained close relations with their Han Chinese neighbors for over

700 years, and continues to do so down to this day, are the villages of Najiaying and Gucheng, in south central Yunnan. First settled by Muslims at the beginning of the fourteenth century, this fertile plain also became the home of early Han Chinese settlers from central China. Over the centuries, these communities formed close relations, to the extent that when a rebellion broke out in Yunnan in the 1850s, the two communities formed a mutual protection pact. During this rebellion, hundreds of thousands of people were massacred, but in these villages no lives were lost. When government soldiers approached the village, the Han Chinese villagers would come out to meet them and assure them that no Muslims lived there. And when rebel soldiers arrived, Muslim villagers would come out and assure them that they were all Muslim and supported the rebellion. As a result of this close cooperation, this area was spared the bloodshed and destruction that prevailed elsewhere in the province, and to this day this area is one of the most prosperous in the region.

Since the mid 1980s, residents have established a wide range of small factories and businesses that attract workers from all over southwest China. Although extremely successful, local village leaders continue to be aware of the importance of close relations with neighboring Han Chinese and local officials, and as a result they regularly invite them as guests to all their major celebrations and religious activities. They also invite representatives of the major government bureaucracies to give presentations on the responsibilities of their offices. And finally, when community resources are needed for public development projects such as road building or installing electrical systems, the wealthier Muslim communities make a point to subsidize neighboring communities who lack the resources.

As mentioned earlier, Muslims in China are all identified through their government-assigned ethnicity and not through any means of personally stated religious belief. There are several consequences of this policy. One is that many Muslims now conflate ethnicity with religion and will, for example, ask if someone is Hui when they actually mean to ask if they are Muslim. In addition, there is a growing number of converts to Islam, but there is no way to identify them as such in the national census.

Despite their large population, in China, Muslims still (officially) only make up less than 2 percent of the total population of more than 1.3 billion. As a result, they continue to be a relatively vulnerable minority group. Unlike other minority groups, the Muslims have for the most part escaped state efforts to exoticize and commodify them. For example, in the several ethnic minority theme parks located in different parts of China, where tourists come to watch different minority groups sing and dance in colorful indigenous clothing, the Muslim minorities have not been included. This is partly because they have no wish to be included and partly because the Han Chinese have yet to figure out a way to make the Muslims sufficiently exotic and entertaining.

Relations between China's ten major ethnic groups identified as Muslim, as well as relations between Chinese Muslims and other minority groups, is a complex and dynamic phenomenon. In Xinjiang there is a long history of intermittent conflict between the sedentary Uighur, who live primarily in the oasis towns, and the Kazak, who are nomadic and live in the surrounding mountains. Within the towns, there have also been occasional conflicts between the Uighurs and the Hui. Although there are historical reasons for tensions between these communities, more recently Uighurs have expressed resentment over the fact that the Hui, who are the most assimilated of China's Muslim groups, are able to pass as Han and therefore are not subject to the widespread harassment suffered by the Uighur. As one Uighur explained, "if we are all demonstrating in the streets together, when the police come, all the Hui have to do is take off their skull caps, and they can blend right in with the crowd, whereas we can't, and we end up getting beaten up."[54] Today, however, as Muslims throughout China have been subjected to additional constraints by the state, and as a result of growing strength of an international Muslim identity, relations between China's different Muslim communities are strengthening.

One final note regarding minorities in China: One of the most extraordinary characteristics of the Hui in China is the degree to which they have assimilated to whichever large ethnic group they live among. Over the centuries, as Muslims settled in virtually every region of China, many found themselves living among different minority peoples. For example, in western China, there are Tibetan-Hui, Bai-Hui, Dai-Hui, Wa-Hui, and Yi-Hui, to name just some. They are indistinguishable from the minority group among whom they live, but they also happen to be Muslim. For example, Tibetan-Hui live in Tibet, speak Tibetan, wear Tibetan clothing, live in traditional Tibetan style homes, and eat a traditional Tibetan diet. And although their identity is further complicated by yet one more layer, Dai-Hui, Bai-Hui, and other mixed Hui people with whom I have spoken are equally adamant and proud of each of their three identities: ethnic, religious, and national.

Challenges Facing Women and Girls in China and the Role of Islam as a Mitigating Factor

Although Mao once proclaimed, "Women hold up half the sky," recent economic reforms have had negative if not disastrous effects on the lives of many women and girls in China. Since the late 1980s, the status of women, particularly in rural areas, has declined. The slow dismantling of the state's social welfare benefits and guarantees, combined with the growing dependence on a market-driven economy, and the continued enforcement of China's policy of only one child in a family, have resulted in the undermining of the status of women. Trafficking in women has become a serious problem in virtually every region of the country. Every year, millions of women migrate from rural areas to coastal cities in search of factory jobs. Away from their families and networks of support, growing numbers of these women are vulnerable to being either lured or forced into prostitution, or they are sold as wives to men from areas that have severe shortages of women.

One of the reasons for the shortage of women is the untold millions of baby girls who have been killed or aborted since the implementation of the one-child policy in 1979. As rural couples are completely dependent on the support of their sons when they grow old, many families are adamant that their one child be a boy. It is now estimated that by 2015, there will be between 40 and 60 million missing women in China, resulting in an equal number of young men who will never be able to find wives.[55] Throughout Chinese history, emperors have known of the serious social unrest caused by having large numbers of unmarried men. Known as "bare sticks" in Chinese, as they resembled branches that would never bear fruit, they were held responsible for causing excessive violence and crime. Today in China the shortage of women has resulted in a huge increase in prostitution, in addition to the forcible trafficking in women.

Other evidence of the extreme difficulties facing women in China today can be seen in the rise in female suicides, especially in rural areas. China is now one of the very few countries in the world where more women kill themselves than men.[56]

Although Muslim women in rural areas of China face many of these same challenges, in some respects their religion has protected them from some of the worst dangers facing others. To begin with, Chinese Muslims do not practice female infanticide. Although some scholars have argued it is because of the less strict enforcement of family planning laws for minorities living in most areas, the more likely explanation is the extremely negative affiliation of female infanticide with the *jahaliyya* period. One of the defining characteristics of bedouin living in the days before Islam was their practice of carrying out female infanticide by burying baby girls in the desert. One of the most dramatic descriptions of the day of judgment is found in Surah 81, and it refers to all those infant girls:

When the sun is overthrown,
And when the stars fall,
And when the hills are moved,
And when the camels big with young are abandoned,
And when the wild beasts are herded together,
And when the seas rise,
And when souls are reunited,
And when the girl-child that was buried alive is asked,
For what sin she was slain,
And when the pages are laid open,
And when the sky is torn away,
And when hell is lighted,
And when the Garden is brought nigh,
(Then) every soul will know what it hath made ready.[57]

As a consequence, Muslim communities are not suffering the serious shortage of women experienced by Han Chinese communities. Prostitution, while common in most areas of China, is relatively uncommon in Muslim communities. Also, as Muslim women appear to be less likely to travel to distant cities in search of jobs, they are less vulnerable to being kidnapped and trafficked or forced into prostitution. Finally, in some regions of China, Muslims take special pride in their daughters, and one of the ways they define themselves vis-à-vis the Han Chinese is that they seem themselves as a community which respects women, whereas Han are characterized as having a "zhong nan, qing nu" attitude, or one that favors men and belittles women.

Throughout China, Muslim women are playing an active role in the revival of Islamic education, as both teachers and students. Young women attend the coeducational Islamic schools and colleges, as well as the schools designated for women only. The female graduates of these schools have taken an active role in promoting the study of Islam among other Muslims. Most become teachers themselves upon graduation, either working in Islamic schools that are already established or helping to establish new schools in poor and remote regions. Several recent graduates have also established Islamic before-school and after-school programs for Muslim children.

In China, the state maintains complete control over the curriculum of all primary and secondary schools. Although in the past, Muslim communities established their own schools in which they were able to combine both secular and religious studies, after 1949 the state took over control of these schools and their curriculum. As these schools were often among of the finest in the area, their loss was a significant blow to Muslim communities in different regions of China. Today, because state law prohibits children from attending any school other than a government school during regular school hours, all Islamic education classes are offered in before-school and after-school programs and intensive sessions organized during school vacations. These efforts represent some of the most important ways in which Muslim communities are reviving their religious identity.

These women speak clearly and confidently about the importance of Islam in their lives, their commitment to Islamic education, and their determination to educate others. Many of these young women volunteer upon graduation from Islamic colleges to teach in remote impoverished villages, isolated from friends and family. Others have established independent Islamic girl's schools. One spoke of the fundamental role women played in society and the importance of the role of education, for as she put it, "educate a man, educate an individual; educate a woman, educate a nation." Sitting in a small village in a remote part of China, she listed the various ways in which a young girl's education could have a major effect on the health and social well-being of her future children and grandchildren and the community at large. She seemed to know intuitively what it had taken several international NGOs years of research and millions of dollars to realize.

Chinese Muslims' commitment to girl's education has also allowed for an important alliance between religious leaders and government officials determined to stem the tide of rural households forgoing education for their daughters. Since the 1990s, government fiscal reforms have resulted in the burden of support for public education being passed from the central government to local governments. As a result, due to lack of funds, local governments have often introduced school fees that have multiplied over the years. These fees have now reached crippling proportions, and as a result, an increasing number of rural farmers are choosing to forgo educating their children, especially their daughters. In response, the All-China Women's Federation has begun a rural campaign to encourage the education of daughters. In Muslim regions, imams have worked together with this government group to remind peasants in rural areas of their religious obligation within Islam to educate all their children.

Conclusion

At present, despite the fact that their Islamic identity makes them significantly more vulnerable to government surveillance and potential harassment, for the Muslims of China, Islam is a major source of conviction and pride. Their faith engenders a strength of identity and self-confidence that enables them to more readily meet the challenges caused by the myriad of contemporary social problems presently besetting China. While so many in China today desperately seek an ideology in which they can believe and place their faith, the Muslims of China are able to look to their religion as one that may have been attacked and persecuted in the past but has never been discredited. Moreover, the social problems in China today are serious, and they directly or indirectly affect virtually everyone in every region. HIV/AIDS and drug addiction are now problems in every province of China, prostitution is rampant, violent crime has increased exponentially, women are kidnapped and bought and sold throughout the country, and unemployment is a growing concern everywhere. Exacerbating the feelings of social malaise accompanying these problems is the government's systematic dismantling of the socialist welfare state. Free housing, education, and medical care are now things of the past. Emergency patients are literally left to die on the doorsteps of hospital emergency rooms because they are now not allowed in unless they have cash on hand to pay for their medical care. As mentioned earlier, education fees are now prohibitively expensive in many rural areas. Although Muslims face these same challenges, and in many regions of China they are significantly poorer than the Han Chinese, Muslim communities have tried to band together to give each other as much support as possible. But, perhaps most importantly, at a time when so much seems to be changing so fast in China, and almost always for the worse in rural China, the Muslims are at least able to find some solace and hope in their faith.

In conclusion, although maintaining their religious beliefs and practices over the centuries has been a continual challenge, Muslims in China have always been confident of their identities as both Muslims and Chinese. Although many scholars have presumed that these identities were somehow inherently antagonistic, the survival of Islam in China for over a millennium belies these assumptions. Islamic and Chinese values have both proven to be sufficiently complementary, dynamic, and fluid to allow for the flourishing of Islam in China, and for the Muslims of China there is no doubt that their traditions are authentically Islamic, their faith is strong, and they are true Muslims.

NOTES

1. According to the 2000 China national census, the Hui population of China is approximately 9.2 million and the Uighur population is 8.6 million. The other Muslim populations are Kazak, 1.3 million; Dongxiang, 400,000; Kirghiz, 171,000; Salar, 90,000; Tajik, 41,000; Uzbek, 14,000; Baonan, 13,000; and Tatar, 5,000. Muslim scholars estimate the population total to be at least 50 million.

2. Women's mosques in China date back centuries. Led by woman imams, they act as a center for women's Islamic studies and community development projects. For more on women's mosques in central China, see Maria Jaschok and Shui Jingjun, *The History of Women's Mosques in Chinese Islam: A Mosque of Their Own* (Richmond, Surrey: Curzon Press, 2000).

3. Ironcially, after surviving in relative isolation for centuries, Islamic calligraphy in China has come under the greatest threat since the mid 1990s. As increasing numbers of Chinese Muslim students study overseas, they learn the more traditional Arabic calligraphy styles and then introduce them to communities in China. Often viewed as more "authentic" than local styles, they are often quickly adopted. In addition, many of the Muslims who in the past would have decorated their homes with Islamic calligraphy made by local artists are now buying the readily available Islamic-themed posters imported from Pakistan and the Middle East. For an excellent account of Arabic calligraphy in China, see Wasma'a K. Chorbachi et al., "Arabic Calligraphy in Twentieth-Century China," paper presented at a conference, "The Legacy of Islam in China: An International Symposium in Memory of Joseph F. Fletcher, Harvard University, April 14–16, 1999.

4. Traditional mosques in China were not the only ones to suffer this fate. Outside funding from the Middle East, primarily Saudi Arabia, has resulted in mosques throughout South and Southeast Asia being built in styles that reflect neither the indigenous cultures nor their natural physical environments. For a survey of this phenomenon, see Barbara Crossette, "The World: (Mid) East Meets (Far) East; A Challenge to Asia's Own Style of Islam," *New York Times*, December 30, 2001, p 3, Week in Review section.

5. In 2005, Human Rights Watch issued a comprehensive report on the deteriorating conditions facing the Uighurs in Xinjiang: "Devastating Blows: Religious Repression of Uighurs in Xinjiang," at http://hrw.org/reports/2005/china0405/ (accessed October 16, 2006).

6. Kuwabara Jitsuzo, "On P'u Shou-geng," *Memoirs of the Research Department of the Toyo Bunko* 2 (1928), p. 72, n. 32.

7. Muslims from Central and West Asia served the Mongols in China in a wide range of capacities: it was Muslim architects and engineers who helped design and build the Mongols' new imperial capital, Dadu, later known as Beijing; Muslim hydraulic engineers introduced irrigation techniques from Central Asia; Muslim physicians introduced new medicinal plants and techniques; and Muslim astronomers assisted in the establishment of the Astronomical Bureau. Under the patronage of the Mongols, Muslims were able to settle in different regions of China and enter into a myriad of different fields.

8. Although somewhat outdated, the most comprehensive overview of the history of Islam in China remains Donald Leslie's *Islam in Traditional China: A Short History to 1800* (Canberra: Canberra College of Advanced Education, 1986).

9. The six-hundredth anniversary of the first of these voyages in 2005. Scientists, explorers, and academics in Taiwan and China have worked together on a project to re-create the voyages as accurately as possible. A replica of the Ming-era boat was

built, though on a smaller scale and equipped with modern navigational instruments, and was expected to set sail in July 2005 on a three-year expedition to Southeast Asia, India, the Middle East, and East Africa ("Odyssey Modeled on Ancient Oceanic Trip," *China Daily*, January 9, 2004, at http://www.china.org.cn/english/China/ 84369.htm [accessed June 2, 2007]).

10. Originally from a prominent Muslim family in Yunnan, southwest China, Zheng He had been captured by government soldiers as a boy, castrated, and forced to work for the Ming army. For more on the life of Zheng He, see Louise Levathes, *When China Ruled the Seas: The Treasure Fleet of the Dragon Throne 1405–1433* (New York: Simon and Shuster, 1994).

11. Chinese characters are almost all made up of several components, the most important being the radical, which usually denotes the general category of the character's meaning. The insect radical is used in the characters for a range of insects, and the dog radical is used for dogs, as well as other small dog-like animals. For centuries, the character used for the Hui, or Muslims, of China had been "hui," which means "to return," and has no negative connotations.

12. These philosophical and religious texts, collectively known as "Han Kitab," adopted the highly complex language of Neo-Confucian thought, not in an effort to make Islam more accessible to non-Muslim Chinese but as a reflection of their own intellectual immersion in and understanding of traditional Chinese philosophy and thought. For a further understanding of this intellectual and religious phe-nomenon, see Sachiko Murata, *Chinese Gleams of Sufi Light* (Albany: SUNY Press, 2000), and Zvi Ben-Dor Benite, *The Dao of Muhammad: A Cultural History of Muslims in Late Imperial China* (Cambridge, Mass.: Harvard University Press, 2005).

13. In 1685, the population of China was estimated to be 100 million; less than 200 years later, the number had risen to 430 million. For more detailed informa-tion on the influx of migrants into Yunnan, see James Lee, "Food Supply and Population Growth in Southwest China, 1250–1850," *Journal of Asian Studies* 41.4 (August 1982), pp. 711–46.

14. Interestingly enough, several Western scholars have perpetuated this essen-tialist view of Muslims in China. One of the most well known examples is the work of Raphael Israeli; see his *Muslims in China: A Study in Cultural Confrontation* (London: Curzon Press, 1978). A related unexamined but often-perpetuated as-sumption about Muslims in China is that they lead lives in a constant state of tension between their Chinese and Muslim identities. However, as the vast majority of Muslims in the world are not Arab, and Islam has flourished for centuries throughout much of the world, why would Muslims in China alone have been unable to develop an identity that incorporated both their religious and cultural/national identities?

15. The local peoples involved were the Lisu, Dai, and Yi. An excellent account of this conflict can be found in Christian Daniel's "Environmental Degradation, Forest Protection and Ethno-History in Yunnan: The Uprising by Swidden Agriculturalists in 1821," *Chinese Environmental History Newsletter*, November 1994, pp. 7–14.

16. David Atwill has documented the events leading up to the establishment of an independent state in his book, *The Chinese Sultanate: Islam, Ethnicity and the*

Panthay Rebellion in Southwest China, 1856–1873 (Stanford, Calif.: Stanford University Press, 2005).

17. For an account of the role played by Muslim women in ensuring the survival of the Muslim community in the aftermath of the massacres, see Jacqueline Armijo "Narratives Engendering Survival: How the Muslims of Southwest China Remember the Massacres of 1873," in Meaghan Morris and Brett de Bary, eds., *"Race" Panic and the Memory of Migration*, vol. 2 of *Traces: A Multilingual Series of Cultural Theory and Translation* (Hong Kong: Hong Kong University Press, 2001), pp. 293–329.

18. Although Muslims in China today will speak in private about the persecution faced by their communities during the Cultural Revolution, it is extremely difficult to find published accounts written by Muslims of this time period. Although more than thirty years have now passed since the height of the Cultural Revolution, certain aspects, particularly the treatment of Muslim and other minorities, remains politically highly sensitive.

19. In the aftermath of the Cultural Revolution, many of these teachers became the most respected members of their community and are credited with helping to ensure the survival of Islam in China. In addition, many of the young people willing to risk their future by taking these illegal classes went on to become the vanguard of Muslim religious leaders in China. They led the efforts to establish independent Islamic schools throughout China and were also among the first Chinese Muslims allowed to continue their studies overseas at Islamic universities.

20. The only mosque allowed to function as a place of worship during this time was the one used by foreign diplomats in Beijing.

21. On a visit to Lanzhou in northwest China in 1982, I happened upon a mosque that was still being used as a glue factory. Piles of horse, cattle, and pig bones lay stacked up in the courtyard. A local Muslim explained how the mosque was still being defiled by local officials, even after the end of the Cultural Revolution.

22. The Red Guards were radical youth groups Mao used to carry out political campaigns throughout China during the Cultural Revolution. Millions of Chinese suffered at the hands of these groups.

23. In travels throughout this region, I have heard dozens of accounts of this event, known locally simply as the "Shadian incident." To many Muslims, it represents just another example of the folly of putting one's complete trust in the state. Although well known among Muslims, a full account of the incident has never been published in China. However, two brief accounts can be found; see Dru Gladney, *Muslim Chinese: Ethnic Nationalism in the People's Republic of China* (Cambridge: Harvard University Press, 1991), pp. 137–40; and Wang Jianping, *Concord and Conflict: The Hui Communities of Yunnan Society in a Historical Perspective* (Lund: Studentlitteratur, 1996), p. 15.

24. In the past, there have also been students in Indonesia, Libya, and the Sudan, but it is not clear if there are students in these countries at present.

25. For more on the development of Islamic education among Chinese Muslims, see Jacqueline Armijo-Hussain, "Resurgence of Islamic Education in China," *Inter-*

national Institute of the Study of Islam in the Modern World Newsletter 4 (1999), p. 12, and Elisabeth Alles, "Muslim Religious Education in China," Chinese Perspectives 45, January–February 2003, at http://www.cefc.com.hk/uk/pc/articles/art_ligne .php?num_art_ligne=4502 (accessed 2 June 2007). Also, there are several chapters related to Islamic education in China in the recent work edited by Stephane Dudoignon, Devout Societies vs. Impious States? Transmitting Islamic Learning in Russia, Central Asia and China, through the Twentieth Century (Berlin: Klaus Schwarz Verlag, 2004).

26. Recently, however, both the Chinese and the U.S. governments have made studying overseas significantly more difficult for Chinese Muslim students. In March 2002, under U.S. pressure, Pakistan agreed to expel all foreign students and bar future enrollment of foreign students in religious schools in Pakistan ("Pakistan Prepares to Expel Foreign Religious Students," New York Times, March 9, 2002, p. 8A). According to students in Damascus, in the summer of 2003, the Syrian government also agreed, under U.S. pressure, to stop allowing foreign students to study in religious schools in Syria.

27. The Chinese government has always tightly monitored the Uighur population of Xinjiang and reacted to any signs of discontent immediately and often with excessive force. In February 1997, a peaceful demonstration in Gulja, Xinjiang province, came under attack by Chinese security forces. A news blackout was immediately imposed, but according to some estimates, dozens were killed. The original cause of the demonstration was growing discomfort with recent attempts by the state to control almost all forms of religious and cultural public activity. For more on this case, see Amnesty International Public Statement, "China: Remembering the Victims of Police Brutality in Gulja, Xinjiang on 5–6 February 1997," February 4, 2005, at http://web.amnesty.org/library/index/engasa170052005 (accessed June 2007).

28. "Robinson Warns China on Repression," BBC News, November 8, 2001.

29. "American Gives Beijing Good News: Rebels on Terror List," New York Times, August 27, 2002, p. 3A. This action, seen by many as an opportunistic move by both countries to further different political agendas, did much to undermine any faith Chinese Muslims may have had that the United States would play a part as an international protector of human rights.

30. While the government was quick to use 9/11 as a pretext to further certain policies against the Muslims on Xinjiang, in other parts of China, 9/11 caused a very different response among the general population toward Muslims in China. To begin with, the reaction to 9/11 by the general public in China was complicated by the fact that, although many Chinese have very positive views about certain aspects of the United States and American life and culture, there is also a tremendous resentment of what is perceived as American arrogance and international bullying. The U.S. bombing of the Chinese Embassy in Yugoslavia in 1998, together with the downing of a Chinese fighter jet after a midair collision with a U.S. intelligence-gathering aircraft in 2001, resulted in violent public protests critical of U.S. actions. Consequently, in the immediate aftermath of 9/11, there was a commonly shared

sentiment among many that, while the loss of innocent lives was regrettable, the illusion of U.S. invincibility had been burst, and that in and of itself was a positive thing. In a rather unusual incident related to me by a Chinese Muslim woman in Kunming, shortly after the attack, upon entering a store wearing hijab, the woman was approached by the owner who walked up to her and said, "You people are our heroes now. You are the only ones who have had the courage to stand up to the Americans and put them in their place." This particular exchange is surprising because, in general, the Muslims in China are often looked down on. Although they are often seen as not quite fully Chinese, they are usually not so closely identified with Muslims from the Middle East.

31. Demetri Sevastopulo, "US Fails to Find Home for Uighur Detainees," *Financial Times*, October 28, 2004, p. 8. In addition, although the United States has been reluctant to return this initial group of Uighurs to China, they did allow an official Chinese delegation to go to Guantanamo in September 2002 to carry out interrogations of the Uighur detainees. According to an Amnesty International Report, the interrogations included excessive tactics (Amnesty International, "People's Republic of China: Uighurs Fleeing Persecution as China Wages Its 'War on Terror,'" July 7, 2004, http://web.amnesty.org/library/index/engasa170212004 [Accessed June 2007]).

32. The rationale behind this law is that there should be no compulsion in religion. And as children are too young to make their own decisions, they should not have to follow their parents' decision regarding religion but, instead, should be allowed to make up their own minds once they become adults. It is significant that this policy has only recently begun to be enforced and is only being enforced with Muslims in Xinjiang; not with Muslims in the rest of China or people of other religions—that is, Christians or Buddhists—in any region of China.

33. John Pomfret, "Go West, Young Han," *Washington Post*, September 15, 2000, p. 1. This mass influx, and the resentments it is engendering, is reminiscent of the effect of the Han Chinese mass migration in Yunnan in the nineteenth century.

34. According to an Amnesty International report, Xinjiang remains the only place in China where people are still commonly executed for political crimes (People's Republic of China: Uighurs fleeing persecution as China wages its "war on terror," at http://web.amnesty.org/library/index/engasa170212004 [Accessed June 2007]).

35. Erik Eckholm, "Beijing Jails Muslim Woman for Sending Newspapers Abroad," *New York Times*, April 20, 2000, p. 12A.

36. Nora Boustany, "A Pioneering Woman as Political Prisoner," *Washington Post*, February 22, 2002, p. 20; Isabel Hilton, "A Remarkable Woman Is Suppressed," *Guardian*, March 15, 2000, at http://www.guardian.co.uk/comment/story/0,3604,181795,00.html (accessed June 2007).

37. Erik Eckholm, "Fight over a Chinese Prisoner Goes Public," *New York Times*, February 10, 2000, p. 18A; "British FCO to Raise Uighur Case," *BBC News*, March 15, 2000. http://news.bbc.co.uk/2/hi/asia-pacific/678698.stm (accessed June 2007). Amnesty International has several reports related to her case, including the following

call for her release: "China: Amnesty International Calls for Release of Business-woman Rebiya Kadeer and Other Uighur Prisoners of Conscience," August 9, 2002, at http://web.amnesty.org/library/index/ENGASA170352002 (accessed June 2007).

38. Although Kadeer is presently settled and living in the United States, her family in China is still vulnerable to Chinese government harassment. In 2006, in response to government actions, Kadeer wrote an op-ed piece for the *Wall Street Journal*, "The Price of Speaking Out: Why Beijing Beat and Jailed My Sons," June 27, 2006, http://www.opinionjournal.com/extra/?id=110008572 (accessed June 2007).

39. "Worldwide Appeal, China: Uighur Historian behind Bars," Amnesty International Worldwide Appeal, August 1, 2002, at http://web.amnesty.org/library/index/ENGNWS220022002 (accessed June 2007).

40. Rupert Wingfield-Hayes, "Language Blow for China's Muslims," *BBC News*, June 1, 2002, http://news.bbc.co.uk/2/hi/asia-pacific/2020009.stm (accessed June 2007).

41. Nicholas Becquelin, "Criminalizing Ethnicity: Political Repression in Xin-jiang," *China Rights Forum* 1 (2004), pp. 39–45.

42. Ibid., p. 45.

43. According to religious teachers in China, after 9/11 it became significantly more difficult for Muslim students to receive permission to study abroad. Because religion is linked to ethnicity, and ethnicity is included in every citizen's identification card and passport, it is not difficult for the state to restrict Muslims ability to travel.

44. Sun Shangwu, "Chinese Pilgrims to Haj Hit Record," *China Daily*, January 19, 2006, at http://english.people.com.cn/200601/19/eng20060119_236646.html (accessed June 2007).

45. One of the most potentially devastating problems facing China today is HIV/AIDS. In Xinjiang, where rates are particularly high due to intravenous drug use, some NGOs are working together with local religious leaders to develop education and prevention programs that incorporate Islamic values and precepts.

46. Dru Gladney has covered this event extensively; see his "Salman Rushdie in China: Religion, Ethnicity, and State Definition in the People's Republic," in Helen Hardacre, Laurel Kendall, and Charles F. Keyes eds., *Asian Visions of Authority* (Honolulu: University of Hawaii Press, 1994), pp. 255–78.

47. "Rich Man, Poor Man," *Economist*, September 27, 2003, p. 39–40.

48. Philip Pan, "Civil Unrest Challenges China's Party Leadership: Protests Growing Larger, More Frequent, Violent," *Washington Post*, November 4, 2004, p. 18.

49. Han Chinese are well aware of Islamic prohibitions against eating pork and the general repugnance in which Muslims hold pigs. Thus, during the Cultural Revolution, Muslims were often forced not only to eat pork but also to raise pigs in their homes. In the years immediately after the Cultural Revolution, Muslims who were traveling, and thus dependent on the small number of government-run restaurants for a meal, often met with hostility if not absolute refusal when trying to get a meal without pork. One major advantage of the market economy today is that Muslims throughout China have opened up restaurants that cater to both

Muslims and Han Chinese; the latter may have some negative prejudices against Muslims but think that, generally, Muslim restaurants are better and cleaner than non-Muslim restaurants. A related form of harassment by Han Chinese, written claims that the Muslims avoid eating pork out of respect for their common ancestor, a pig, has occurred intermittently for centuries.

50. Ironically, the People's Armed Police was initially established as an alternative to the People's Liberation Army to deal with social unrest. One explanation for the large number of deaths during the protests in Tiananmen Square in 1989 was that the army simply did not know how to deal with civilian protests ("China Tries to Dampen Simmering Muslim Unrest," *Agence France Presse*, December 18, 2000, http://web.lexis-nexis.com/universe/document?_m= 6dddaf7067a34c335edbd806f1754915&_docnum=11&wchp=dGLbVtb-zSkVA&_md5 =61ac5d4863969f03d81cf4bc5198a768.

51. "Officials Removed over Deadly Religious Strife," *Agence France Presse*, December 31, 2000, http://web.lexis-nexis.com/universe/document?_m= 7c967adaa35eb4aa3ed2a4bd36e54300&_docnum=2&wchp=dGLbVtb-zSkVA&_ md5=cebd843f75ebffa85089dca6d22aeb2f.

52. Jehangir S. Pocha, "Violent Ethnic Clashes Plague China," *Boston Globe*, December 19, 2004, pp. 14.

53. Damien McElroy, "Muslim Conflict Now Hits China as 148 Die in Ethnic Violence," *Sunday Telegraph*, November 14, 2004, p. 32.

54. Personal communication with Uighur academic currently living in the United States, Mountain View, California, June 2003.

55. "China Grapples with Legacy of its 'Missing Girls'" by Eric Baculinao, NBC News, at http://www.msnbc.msn.com/id/5953508 (accessed June 2007).

56. Michael Phillips, Xianyan Li, and Yanping Zhang, "Suicide Rates in China, 1995–99," *Lancet* 359, March 9, 2002, pp. 835–40.

57. Surah 81:1–14, Marmaduke Pickthal translation.

10

The Effect of 9/11 on Mindanao Muslims and the Mindanao Peace Process

Eliseo R. Mercado

> Creeping murmur and the pouring dark
> Fill the wide vessel of the universe:
> From camp to camp, through the foul womb of night
> The hum of either army stilly sounds
> That the fixed sentinels almost receive
> The secret whispers of each other's watch. . . .
> Each battle sees the other's umber'd face.
> —William Shakespeare, *King Henry V*, act 4

So Shakespeare's chorus described the eve of Agincourt. The words might well have been written also of Mindanao, more particularly of Muslim-Christian relations. When faiths and religious traditions confront each other, it is, for the most part, with "fixed sentinels" and even with the "whispers of the other's watch."

It is said that Christianity and Islam are physically adjacent. Yet, for all their nearness, the relations between these two faiths and their respective adherents are largely shrouded in mutual suspicion and darkness. There are few exceptions on either side to rise above the general ignorance and suspicion that obscure one from the other. But these are rare, for when faiths and religious traditions confront each other, it is, for the most part, with "fixed sentinels."

In the Philippines, particularly in the south, Christianity and Islam have always been presented as two competing faiths for the same geographical area. Wittingly or unwittingly, the recent spate of lawlessness—kidnappings, terrorism, and plain and simple banditry—is read along the understood "separateness" between Christianity and Islam.

This tragic and sad reality is further exacerbated by the recent surge of the so-called Islamic fundamentalist movements. The likes of the Abu Sayyaf and the Pentagon kidnapper groups are often associated with terrorism and fanaticism that send jitters to the people in the area.

In the post–September 11, 2001 era, there is a general tendency to lump together groups and movements opposing the present global and regional status quo under one label: that is, "fundamentalists" at best or "terrorists" at worst. This generalization is a result of an "emotional revulsion" to horrific attacks "near at home." The subsequent "war on terror" after 9/11, under U.S. leadership, exacerbates the journalistic reading and analysis of the complex and varied realities that give rise to groups and movements that oppose the prevailing systems or, in particular, the U.S. policies, in both the Middle East and Southeast Asia. Recent bombings in Bali and Jakarta in Indonesia and Manila and in Zamboanga in the Philippines are often seen as activities or operations of both indigenous and international terrorist groups, and those elements of the two have been closely interlinked.

Southeast Asia (before and after 9/11) has frequently been the scene of political violence that has either been explicitly or closely linked to terrorism -for example, Indonesia, Malaysia, and the Philippines. This has included activities by separatist groups and Islamist groups. But terrorism has also, at times, been state-sponsored or condoned, as in the case of Christian anti-separatist groups in the southern Philippines (opposing Muslim secessionists) and Muslim militias in Maluku Province, Indonesia, and in East Timor.

Cultural Processes

Three cultural processes are at work in the southern Philippines, and they contribute to the dynamism, complexity, and dilemmas of peace and development. First is the Lumad (indigenous people) cultural process that emanates in differing intensities and ways from over twenty ethnolinguistic traditions that are literally scattered in the hinterlands of the region and that have remained vibrant, despite the effect of urbanization and modernization. Cultural values distinct to each tribe have been preserved through the observance of customs and practices, especially those rituals associated with the rites of passage and with indigenous (native) religion. They are also enshrined in the varieties of oral literature (like epics, proverbs, and poetry), as well as in music,

dances, and the arts. Each ethnic group tends toward isolation and independence but maintains reciprocal relations with other groups through trade.[1]

The second cultural process ensues from the Bangsamoro people, who are
represented by thirteen Muslim ethnolinguistic groups. While they maintain
their distinct ethnic traditions, they are also bound together by a common ad-
herence to the Islamic faith. They constitute what Islam refers to as distinct
ummah (community) united to the Islamic world. It is this spiritual bond of
Islam that distinguishes them from the Lumad groups that have no unifying
ideology other than their love for the "ancient liberties" or "freedoms." When
not threatened by external forces, the Bangsamoro tend to give importance and
preference to their ethnicity; when their Islamic life is imperiled, however, they
transcend ethnic considerations. Like the Lumads, they have distinct and colorful ethnic traditions blended with Islamic flavor and features.

The third cultural process comes from the migrant Christians settlers who
brought into Mindanao's "cul-de-sac" their ethnic folk Christian traditions from
the Visayas and Luzon. They are bound by a common Christian faith that has
been nurtured through the centuries until contemporary times by conscious
missionary efforts of the church. While ethnicity has remained important,
devotion to the Christian faith tends to be given preference by the Christians of
Mindanao. But because of the pioneering character of the Christian faith, relations with the Muslims and Lumads have been often marred by irritations
and conflict, largely because of politics and issues of governance and land use
ownership.

Rise of Bangsamoro Nationalism

The Bangsamoro people take the Jabidah Massacre in March 1968 as the
"new" turning point in their "separatist" struggle. It was the single event that
set the fuse of the Bangsamoro rebellion under the leadership of the Moro
National Liberation Front MNLF). Although, by itself, the Jabidah Massacre
was simply a flashpoint that ignited the conflict, it became a powerful symbol
of the Manila government's discrimination against Muslims.[2]

As an aftermath of the Jabidah Massacre, the Muslim population (under
the leadership of young intellectuals) launched massive protest actions and
demonstrations in Manila. The occasion also provided a good backdrop for the
public declaration of the Muslim Independence Movement (MIM) by Datu
Udtog Matalam, former governor of the Empire Province of Cotabato, on May
1, 1968. The organization of the MNLF in 1972 (under the leadership of Nur
Misuari) followed, and it became the sole front until 1978 to carry on the
Muslim struggle for secession from the Republic of the Philippines.

Moro Rebellion and Peace Process in the Southern Philippines

Poverty, injustice (real or perceived), and political exclusion are concrete issues that fueled the separatist war from its inception. But attributing to these issues the popular sentiment of politics of separatism under the banner of Islam does not lead to the whole truth. Religion and ethnicity matter, especially in terms of the accent on their Islamic identity and their desire to determine and shape their future according to their own set of beliefs.

The Mindanao Peace Process is not a new invention of our era. In fact, the present realities in Mindanao are the fruit of various peace processes with differing foci and emphases, depending on the mood and temper of the Manila-based central government.[3]

Historically, the establishments of Fort del Pilar in the present Zamboanga City, the naval station at Polloc in the present province of Maguindanao, the "intramuros" in the town of Jolo, and the military stations along the Rio Grande de Mindanao from Taviran to Reina Regente are a few examples of containment programs to build peace in the southern Philippines. The so-called Moro problem haunted the Spanish government in Manila for more than three and a half centuries. Northern Mindanao and some parts of western Mindanao were successfully brought into mainstream politics by way of settlements beginning in the second half of the nineteenth century. But in southern Mindanao, including the islands of Sulu, Tawi Tawi, and Basilan, the Spanish presence was limited to military stations and garrisons, except for pockets of civilian settlements in today's Zamboanga and Cotabato.

The political and economic configurations in the southern Philippines were radically altered during the American occupation. The U.S. colonial government, with its far superior army, brought to an end practically all Moro resistance to the American rule.

To put the peace in southern Mindanao on a more solid footing, several peace programs were unfolded. First was the economic development of Mindanao's fertile land: plantations were opened, and businesses were established in major trading posts, including Zamboanga, Cotabato, Jolo, and Iligan. Second, Mindanao was opened to settlement from Luzon and the Visayas. It began with the establishment of the agricultural colonies in the fertile plains of the then empire province of Cotabato. This was followed by massive and well-planned settlement programs during the Commonwealth period and continued unabated in the postwar era during the subsequent administrations of Presidents Manuel Roxas, Elipido Quirino, and Ramon Magsaysay after World War II.

The southern Philippines has also seen several administrative structures from 1899 to the present. Military rule—from General Leonard Wood to

General John J. Pershing— was followed by the establishment of Moro Province under a civilian governor. Then the Departments of Mindanao and Sulu were created, followed by the Bureau for the Non-Christian Tribes and, finally, regular provinces. Civilian governors were first appointed by the president; subsequently, they were elected under the 1935 constitution. This system remained in place until the eruption of the Muslim Separatist War in the early 1970s.

During the twentieth century, a dramatic shift in population and land ownership in Mindanao contributed to the beginning of the modern conflict. In 1900, the Muslim population in Mindanao made up more than 90 percent of the island's inhabitants, but by 1970, the Muslims constituted barely 20 percent. The population shift came about through policies that gave the Christian population from Luzon and the Visayas incentives to migrate to Mindanao. The new immigrants, with legal titles issued by the government, claimed and tilled large tracts of land that the Moro and other indigenous peoples considered to be their homeland.

The Muslim secessionist war in Mindanao attracted the attention of the Organization of the Islamic Conference (OIC). Attempts at reconciliation between the MNLF and the Government of the Republic of the Philippines (GRP) were initiated through mediation by the OIC. On December 23, 1976, the Marcos government and the MNLF signed the Tripoli Peace Agreement as a concrete response to the Moro people's demand for local self-rule in what was recognized as the "Bangsamoro homeland" within the sovereignty and territorial integrity of the Republic of the Philippines.

Political Structures Adopted by GRP vis-à-vis Muslim Autonomy

The Philippine government, from President Ferdinand Marcos to President Gloria Arroyo, has developed a number of political arrangements to address the autonomy issue in the southern Philippines.

On July 7, 1975, prior to the historic Tripoli Agreement, then-President Marcos issued Presidential Decree 742 and Letter of Instruction 290 establishing the Office of the Regional Commissioner for Region IX and Region XII. The government believed that by creating special regional commissions in that area of Mindanao, both the social and the economic causes of conflict could be better addressed. Then, on December 23, 1976, the GRP and the MNLF, under the auspices of the Organization of Islamic Countries through its Quadripartite Commission, signed a peace agreement in Tripoli, Libya, thereafter called the Tripoli Agreement (TA). They also signed an agreement for immediate cessation of hostilities. The environment of war was transformed into a hope-filled expectation for an enduring peace settlement in the the the southern Philippines.

On March 26, 1977, President Marcos established a provisional government in the thirteen provinces, as stipulated in the Tripoli Agreement. In the first plebiscite, conducted on April 17, 1977, in the thirteen provinces, the people overwhelmingly rejected the merger of all the provinces into one autonomous region. They opted for two separate regional autonomous governments, one for Region IX and one for Region XII, with the provinces of Davao del Sur, South Cotabato, and Palawan opting for exclusion from the autonomous regions. As a result of the referendum, President Marcos issued Proclamation 1628A, defining the composition of the two autonomous regions. After that, the Batasan Pambangsa (National Parliament) passed Batas Blg. 20, which provided for the organization of a Sanguniang Pampook (Regional Legislative Council) and a Lupong Tagapagpaganap (Executive Council) in each autonomous region. Then, on July 25, 1979, President Marcos issued Presidential Decree 1618, implementing the organization of the Sanguniang Pampook and Lupong Tagapagpaganap in Autonomous Regions IX and XII, thus providing the final political structure and framework of autonomous governance in Regions IX and XII.

The Aquino Presidency and the Moro Fronts

On February 2, 1987, the new 1987 Aquino Constitution was unanimously ratified. This constitution provides for the creation of autonomous regions in Muslim Mindanao and the Cordilleras by an Act of Congress with the assistance of a Regional Consultative Commission. President Corazon Aquino convened the RCC in Cotabato City on March 11, 1988. The RCC was mandated to come up with a draft Organic Act to be submitted to Congress for enactment. In 1989, the Philippine Congress passed Republic Act 6734 or the Organic Act for the Autonomous Region in Muslim Mindanao (ARMM), and on August 1, 1989, President Aquino signed it into law.

On November 19, 1989, Republic Act 6734 was submitted to the people of the thirteen provinces and nine cities for a second plebiscite, as stipulated in the Tripoli Agreement. Only four out of thirteen provinces and nine cities ratified the Organic Act. These were the provinces of Lanao del Sur, Maguindanao, Sulu, and Tawi Tawi. On July 9, 1990, ARMM elections for all elected offices were held. Zacaria Candao and Benjamin Loong were elected regional governor and vice governor, respectively. The ARMM elections regularized and completed the 1987 constitutional steps in creating the autonomous region in Muslim Mindanao.

Under the Ramos Government

President Fidel Ramos established the National Unification Commission (NUC) and appointed Attorney Heidi Yorac as chair. Ramos also tapped the personnel and infrastructures of the two well-established institutions, the Catholic Bishops Conference of the Philippines and the National Council of Churches of the Philippines, in the work of the commission. The stated goal of the commission was to conduct a nationwide people's consultation to find out the root causes of rebellion and unrest in the country.

After the results of the national consultation were published, Ramos issued Executive Order 125 on August 25, 1996, articulating the vision and the framework of the peace process that his administration would pursue to address the three internal armed conflicts: the National Democratic Front (NDF), the Muslim Separatist Movements in Southern Philippines, and the Military Rebellion.

Then followed the formulation of the famous six paths to peace that became, more or less, the "Magna Carta" that guided the government in responding to the issue of armed conflict in the country. They are the following:

1. Government must initiate and implement social, economic, and political reforms to address the root causes of rebellion and social unrest.
2. Government shall pursue consensus-building and people empowerment through mobilization and facilitation of people's participation and support for community peace initiatives.
3. Government shall seek peaceful and negotiated settlements with rebel groups with no surrender or shame but with dignity for all concerned.
4. Government shall initiate reconciliation with and reintegration of former combatants and indemnify civilian victims of the armed conflict.
5. Government shall ensure the continued protection of civilians caught in the midst of armed conflict, reduction of violence in conflict areas, and prevention and management of conflict.
6. Government shall build and nurture a climate of peace that includes peace advocacy and peace education.

On September 2, 1996, the 1996 Peace Agreement was signed, which, in the words of President Ramos, "[brought] to a close almost 30 years of conflict, at the cost of more than 120,000 Filipino lives." He hailed the Peace Agreement as the beginning of "a new era of peace and development for the southern Philippines, and for Philippines as a whole." Truly, a new era has begun, the era of rebuilding, of forging partnership between and among diverse peoples of the land, and establishing one community and one future for all.

The Peace Accord established a Zone of Peace and Development out of the contested provinces and cities in the southern Philippines. The approach was innovative and followed the trodden path in resolving conflicts involving territories, borders, and frontiers. The establishment of the Special Zone of Peace and Development consisting of the fourteen provinces and nine cities provided for a new framework of identity and consolidation on the basis of intense peace and development initiatives.

The Philippine government had the mandate to legislate an amendment to Republic Act (RA) 6734 that would incorporate in toto the 1996 Final Peace Agreement. In many ways, this sovereignty was compromised a bit when the government entered into the Tripoli and Jakarta Agreements, inasmuch as MNLF also compromised its position by accepting the constitutional processes of plebiscite in drawing the geography and coverage of autonomy in the southern Philippines.

After the new law, RA 9054, had been ratified in five provinces (Basilan, Lanao Sur, Maguindanao, Sulu, and Tawi Tawi) and in one city (Marawi), the Philippine government pursued the creation of the New Expanded Autonomous Region in Muslim Mindanao (ARMM) and conducted an election for the purpose of filling up the officials of both the Executive and Legislative departments of the New ARMM. With the new officials installed on the 7th of January 2002, the Philippine government declared that it has fulfilled the final obligation and requirement of the 1996 Final Peace Accord between the GRP and the MNLF.

The Nur-led MNLF rejected the law, RA 9054, and rejected, in turn, the results of the plebiscite in 2001. This faction does not recognize either the law or the result of the plebiscite on the premise that both are part of the 1996 Final Peace Agreement. But the other faction of the MNLF under the leadership of the so-called top-thirteen leadership of the MNLF Central Committee recognized the new law and the results of the plebiscite. These leaders served as government partners in the new expanded ARMM.

"On and Often Off" Peace Talks between the GRP and the MILF

The Moro Islamic Liberation Front (MILF) is a breakaway faction of the Moro National Liberation Front. The birth of this faction occurred in 1978 when Chairman Nur Misuari expelled Salamat Hashim from the MNLF Central Leadership. Salamat and his group named this breakaway group the Moro

Islamic Liberation Front. The word "Islamic" replaced the word "National" to indicate the ideological shift that this group would like to adopt.

Hashim, the MILF chair and its ideological brain, defined the ideology of the MILF as "la ilaha illa-llah wa Muhammadul-rasullallah." This ideology is actually the Islamic confession of faith that states, "there is no deity but Allah and Muhummad is the Messenger of Allah." The return to Islamic rule is key to the reorganization of the Muslim community.

To understand this radical Islamic movement, there is a need to situate it within the historical matrix that gave it birth. Two prominent Muslim theologians gave the theoretical principles to this radical Islamic movement. First was Abul A'la al-Mawdudi (1903–79), founder of the Jami'atul-al-Islamiyya, and second was Sayyid al Qutb (1906–1966) of the Ikwan al Muslimun (Muslim brotherhood). Both advocated strongly the exclusive sovereignty of Allah and jihad (holy struggle) against the so-called conspiracy of the West to destroy Islam. Modern civilization is labeled as a new era of *jahiliyya* (ignorance). The three principles that govern today's society are secularism, nationalism, and democracy. These are against the very beliefs and principles of Islam. For al-Mawdudi and al-Qutb, secularism is an idea that excludes God, while democracy arrogates unto itself the sovereignty that is exclusive to God. Secular democracy is a deliberate violation of divine law and a reversion to the era of pagan ignorance.

Both al-Mawdudi and al-Qutb are the major influences in shaping this ideology and aspiration of the MILF. The Islamic ideology of the oneness of God and Muhammad as the messenger of God points to the desire and objective to reinstate Islam as a political system. The assertion of the absolute sovereignty of God negates the concept of the legal and political sovereignty of human beings and nations.

By its chosen name, the MILF puts an emphasis on religion. It explicitly espouses the establishment of an Islamic community (*ummah*) and Islamic rule in areas under its control or influence. This has been the beginning of its articulated goal of "creating a Separate and Independent Islamic State" in the southern Philippines. How this Islamic state shall take shape is a continuing debate among the Muslim scholars and the MILF constituency. After the GRP and the MNLF Final Peace Accord in 1996, the MILF now claims to be the "Sole and Legitimate Representative" of the Bangsamoro people, who are still in rebellion.

In 1997, the Agreement on the General Cessation of Hostilities was inked between the Government of the Republic of the Philippines (GRP) and the Moro Islamic Liberation Front. After a series of high-level consultations, both groups agreed to constitute their respective peace panels to begin the formal peace talks. The peace talks between the GRP and the MILF were progressing well, albeit beset by some problems, particularly in the implementation of the ceasefire agreement.

The Estrada Presidency

In July 1998, Joseph Estrada became the president of the Philippines. Initially, he followed the Ramos peace initiative. But upset by a series of lawlessness in the south, specifically the wanton kidnapping of foreigners by the Abu Sayyaf group and their reported cruelties, his government, upon the advice of his chief of staff, General Angelo Reyes, adopted a military solution that led to the"total war" policy against the MILF. The Defense Department painted the MILF "terrorist front" in the same league as the Abu Sayyaf groups following September 11 and the subsequent U.S. "war against terror."

From the second week of March 2000, the National Defense and the Armed Forces of the Philippines (AFP) got into the "flag-raising ritual" in all MILF camps. These military operations concluded with the take over and military occupation of the MILF Main Camp Abubakar with the president himself leading the flag raising and the feasting of roasted pigs and beer for the "victorious" AFP.[4]

On the Abu Sayyaf Groups

Since 1992, the group that has become notorious in the south is the Abu Sayyaf group under the joint leadership of Abdulrajak Janjalani and Gerry Angeles (a convert to Islam). Terrorism by this group reached a new peak during the famous burning of the town center of Ipil, Zamboanga del Sur, in 1995. It waned during the rest of the term of President Ramos, especially after the death of Janjalani and Angeles. Its ugly face resurfaced in 2000 under the leadership of the young Qaddafi Janjalani in Basilan and the erstwhile MNLF Commander Robot in the province of Sulu. The kidnapping of schoolchildren and Father Rhoel Gallardo in Basilan and the hostage taking of foreign tourists in Sipadan, Sabah, Malaysia, have made the Abu Sayyaf an international terrorist group. But even before these two internationally covered acts of terrorism, by all calculations the Abu Sayyaf had become notorious for kidnapping and other lawless activities in the island provinces of Basilan and Sulu and in the Zamboanga Peninsula.

There has always been a suspicion that the Abu Sayyaf and the MILF are somewhat "connected," especially when Abu Sayyaf has begun espousing some major aspirations of the MILF. The MILF officially denies any connection to the Abu Sayyaf and the leadership of the MILF, particularly the religious, openly condemned the lawless and kidnapping activities of the group as "Un-Islamic." But even with the denial and open condemnation, there are people who still believe that these two groups are somewhat connected. There is no proof to support this suspicion. But the continued use of Islamic slogans by the Abu Sayyaf group simply confirms, to many, the suspicion.

The very complex issue of the Bangsamoro people is now hostage to three dangerous currents in Philippine society. First is the trend of an overly simplistic view and the pursuit of an "instant" solution to the centuries-old problem. The prevailing culture of "instant" coffee makes people look for an easy fix to the problem in the south. What makes this trend very dangerous is the perception that this easy fix and instant solution is the military option to the Bangsamoro issue. Second is the natural and dangerous proclivity of many in the military and in the civil government to lump all Muslims together into one basket. Third are the strong anti–Abu Sayyaf sentiments following the brutal murder of Gallardo and the continued agonies over what seem to be endless cases of criminalities and lawlessness. The lawless activities of the Abu Sayyaf group are the major obstacles in the understanding, today, of the Bangsamoro issue.

The Estrada-Reyes–led Mindanao War in 2000 was presented as a prelude to a "war against terror" that would, in time, reinforce the U.S.-led "war against terror" following September 11. No doubt, the war with its massive displacement of Bangsamoro civilians, especially women and children, further complicated the peace process between the GRP and the MILF. The trauma of that war runs deep, especially with the civilians who suffered massive displacement, destruction of homes, and the "pulverization" of the MILF camps, particularly Camps Abubakar, Bushrah, and Rajah Muda. The AFP continues its massive presence in all the former MILF camps; to be sure, their presence guarantees continued "armed skirmishes" between the AFP and the MILF in and around the camp areas.

The AFP has become a force of occupation. This fact, in a way, has made the AFP's claim of liberating the areas and highways hollow. The displaced will not return to their villages and homes while the AFP continues to occupy those villages. This is a dangerous twist in the previous peace process that recognizes that the true war to win is not the one over areas and territories but the one over the hearts and minds of the Bangsamoro people.

The only way for the government to avoid this natural pitfall is to transform the role of the AFP in these occupied territories. Can the AFP become "builders" and development workers? If the AFP continues to be perceived as "occupation forces," the entire military operation would be in vain and would only fuel the hatred and animosity of the Muslim population against the government and the AFP.

Peace and War under President Arroyo

In January 2001, the people revolted, once again, against the perceived corruption and immorality of President Joseph Estrada that led to his downfall. This revolt backed by the Armed Forces of the Philippines installed the Vice President Gloria Arroyo in the presidency. Under her new administration, the government launched the peace process with all the rebel fronts. President Arroyo reconstituted the peace panels to begin the peace talks, both with the National Democratic Front and the Moro Islamic Liberation Front. She coined the word "all-out peace" (contrasting it to Estrada-Reyes's all-out war policy) to define her administration's peace impetus. The new Arroyo government and the rebel fronts (NDF and the MILF) once again "reaffirmed" all the agreements that had been negotiated and signed during the Ramos and Estrada administrations.

With the MILF, the peace process was on track and very promising, with Malaysia acting as the broker. Both parties agreed to pursue, jointly, the relief, rehabilitation, and reconstruction of the livelihood of the displaced, as well as the communities in conflict areas, even before the final peace accord was signed. The creation of the Bangsamoro Development Agency and its interface and coordination with all government development and service agencies looked bright for a new era dawning on the victims of war (both individuals and communities). It was also heart warming to behold the enthusiasm of the MILF to bring development and reconstruction to the ravaged communities.

The formal peace talks were scheduled for early March 2003 when the AFP, again under the leadership of the same General Angelo Reyes (the secretary of national defense under the Arroyo government) attacked and assaulted the "headquarters" of the MILF chairman, Ustadz Hashim Salamat, on February 11, 2003—the day of Islam's holiest Feast of the Sacrifice (Idul Adha).

Again, as during the administration of Estrada, but more specifically following 9/11, the MILF is being tagged as a terrorist front connected to Jama'at Islam (JI) and al-Qaeda. Formal peace talks are one of the casualties of the "war against terror." The powerful symbol of the continuance of the all-out war policy from Estrada to Arroyo is no less than Reyes himself, who served as chief of staff of the AFP during the Estrada administration and as secretary of national defense under President Arroyo.[5]

Recent developments, particularly the accession of more pragmatic leadership in the MILF after the demise of Hashim Salamat, paved the resumption of the peace talks, though informal, in the southern Philippines. During these informal talks between the GRP and some representatives of the MILF in Kuala Lumpur, both parties reaffirmed their commitment to pursue the peace process. However, they, too, acknowledged the difficulties and the hurdles to put the peace process on track once again. This "intent," hopefully, would lead to more formal peace talks between the GRP and the MILF in order to continue the discussion over the issues that had already been raised before the all-out war policy of the year 2000.

At this stage, the formal peace talks increasingly became hostage to cease-fire violations and the alleged "anti-terror" policy of the government. The informal peace talks would continue to prepare the groundwork through mutual confidence building measures for the eventual resumption of the formal peace talks. But this prospect would depend on the political will and courage of the Arroyo government. No doubt, there is a need for an increase in confidence-building measures, because the policy of war continues to destroy the remaining trust and confidence built in the initial months of the Arroyo presidency.

The years 2002 and 2003 did not make any progress in the peace talks. The alleged attacks against civilian communities and the bombing of civilian targets, particularly the Davao International Airport a week after the unprovoked military attack against "Buliok," Pikit (though officially denied by the MILF) are believed by the AFP and the PNP to be the work of the MILF. However, the young military officers' brief revolt in July 2003 exposed the top military leadership as the perpetrator of the series of bombings in Mindanao in order to convince the U.S. Defense Department that the MILF is, indeed, a "terrorist front," thereby winning U.S. support for the AFP's own "war against terror."

The civilian casualties once again revealed the brutal and ugly visage of a resumption of an all-out war between the GRP and the MILF. Several sectors in Mindanao, particularly the religious and business, appealed to the GRP and the MILF to go back to the negotiating table or to limit the fights between and among combatants. At no time should civilians and their communities be targets of military actions, neither offensive nor defensive.

In the second half of 2003, interesting developments favored a political settlement with the MILF. First was the entry of more pragmatic people into the top leadership of the MILF since late July 2003, following the death of Chairman Hashim Salamat. Second was the seeming "retreat" and defensive stance of the military hawks, resulting from the military rebels' direct accusations that top brass in the AFP instigated the series of bombing in Mindanao to project the "terrorist" image of the MILF. Third was the sympathetic push of the OIC, particularly of Malaysia, toward an earlier settlement of the GRP and MILF peace talks, although conditions for a successful settlement remained unfavorable.

The assumption to the MILF top leadership of Hajj Ibrahim Murad as the new chair of the MILF Central Committee is viewed as a "swing" to a more pragmatic and "lay" style of Moro leadership within the Bangsamoro. Similarly, the choice of Mohagher Iqbal as the new chair of the MILF Peace Panel reinforces the pragmatic and lay leadership, since Iqbal has always been associated with Chairman Murad. The triumvirate leadership of Murad, Ghazzali (vice chair for political affairs), and Iqbal results in what I refer to as the pragmatic perspective in the present MILF leadership, contrasted to what seemed to be the previous "religious" slant within the MILF leadership.

This development points to a greater focus on three important issues on the pragmatic agenda in the peace talks and possible settlement. These are the following:

1. Down-to-earth issues like ancestral domain, rehabilitation, and reconstruction of war-affected Moro communities
2. Representation of the Moro people in national and regional governance, coupled with their self-governance in local affairs in places and areas where Muslims are the majority population
3. The issue of MILF "demobilization and disarmament" tied to the economic package and development for former combatants

Conclusion

At this stage, it is good to observe that the electoral victory of President Arroyo in 2004 is not associated with the policy of the peace process in Mindanao. The opposition, as in 2001 elections, has once again won in Mindanao—a fact that points to the continued popularity of the all-out war policy of former President Estrada beginning in 2000. Thus, the new electoral mandate in the May 2004 national elections has really not changed the ambiguity or ambivalence in peace making, neither in Mindanao with the MILF nor in the national level with the National Democratic Front (NDF).

With the deepening economic and leadership crisis, what appears as the paramount agenda of the top leadership in the country is survival amid the mounting dissatisfactions of the present dispensation. It is noteworthy to point out that all the polls taken before Christmas 2004 gave the president the lowest popularity image in years. Both of these situations greatly influence the pursuit of peace, particularly in Mindanao where peace making policy is not popular.

There is no doubt that the GRP–MILF peace talks and the possible peace settlement would be bound to be controversial. The mood and the prejudice of the Christian majority against the talks and any political settlement with MILF would be seriously weighed in the equation of "poll popularity" for President Arroyo.

With the increasing crisis in the country and the "incapacity" of the government to pursue a bold peace policy, I believe that peace will not be a priority in the political agenda of Arroyo, notwithstanding the lip service that is often given to the issue. Once again, the peace agenda is subsumed to the larger and more pressing national political agenda.

There are two imperatives for peacemaking: courage and political will. These two are terribly lacking in the present leadership of President Arroyo. What we see in the present trend is a continuance of ambiguity and lack of leadership and direction in the current peace talks. The talks would go "on and off" without a political settlement in sight.

This is, indeed, tragic, because the favorable changed conditions within the MILF may not last, as, increasingly, the young people within the ranks of the MILF will be disillusioned—not only by the conduct of the present talks but also by the pragmatic leadership that has gripped the MILF since the demise of Chairman Salamat. The religious members within the central leadership and from the rank and file continue to long for a leader akin to the late Chairman Salamat, who was both an imam and a commander.

In the end, the people of Mindanao—not the government—should be the major stakeholders in peace. Until the Mindanao people and leaders from all sectors take counsel from each other and take responsibility for the process, no peace settlement can work. Meanwhile, we as peace advocates must not rest. We need to pursue peace with greater fervor and immense hope, praying and working ceaselessly for peace . . . and believing in miracles!

NOTES

1. E. Mercado and M. Floirendo, eds., *Mindanao on the Mend* (Manila: Anvil Publishing, 2003), pp. 13–19.

2. Thomas M. McKenna, *Muslim Rulers and Rebels: Everyday Politics and Armed Separatism in the Southern Philippines* (Berkeley: University of California Press, 1998).

3. Eliseo Mercado, *The Southern Philippines Question* (Cotabato City: Notre Dame University Press, 1997).

4. DND (Department of National Defense), "Briefing on the War against Terrorism in Mindanao," Paper presented in Malacanang Palace, Manila, March 2000.

5. OPAPP (Office of the Presidential Adviser on the Peace Process), "Peace and Development in Mindanao," Briefing Papers (Manila: OPAPP, 2001).

II

Thai and Cambodian Muslims and the War on Terrorism

Imtiyaz Yusuf

The state of relationship between the world of Islam and the West since the event of 9/11 and the subsequent wars in Afghanistan and Iraq has been topic of many discussions with which we are familiar—for example, "Unholy Terror,"[1] "A Fury for God,"[2] "The Crisis of Islam,"[3] and "Clash of Ignorance."[4] All these discussions have focused on the Middle Eastern political scenario. But in view of the world-wide presence of Islam, it is necessary that we also look at and understand the Asian Muslim interpretations and responses to the same events, including those of Muslim minorities in Thailand and Cambodia.

Some commentators are of the opinion that Asian Islam is now taking center stage.[5] This is largely due to the emergence of fissures between the dominant trend of moderate "cultural Islam" and emergent "political Islam" in Southeast Asia.[6]

In this chapter, I discuss how the Thai and Cambodian Muslim minorities have been affected by and how they have responded to recent global events such as the bombing of the World Trade Center and the war in Afghanistan. This is illustrated not only in light of the effect of external events on the local front but also in how the internal evolution of politics of democracy has enabled local Islam to express itself in relation to global events. First, I outline the evolution of democratic politics in Thailand and Cambodia; second, I look at the Thai Muslim responses to the events of 9/11 and the

Afghan war. I also consider the ramifications of alleged charges of engaging in terrorism for Muslim organizations operating in Cambodia.

Political Evolution of Democratic Politics in Thailand and Cambodia

Thailand: A Political Profile

Contemporary Southeast Asian states are evolving on the path of democratic politics in their own patterns. Thailand is a religiously pluralistic country with a Buddhist majority of 94 percent, Muslims constituting about 5 percent, and Christians and others 1 percent of the population. Even with this majority, the Thai constitution does not declare Buddhism to be the official religion of Thailand. Thailand is a constitutional monarchy in the form of a "secularized Buddhist polity" with a "stable semi-democractic" political system.[7]

The history of democratic political evolution in Thailand has to be understood in light of the history of Thai politics. The relationship between Thai state and society follows a three-dimensional pattern, where the interaction is directed by concerns for security (S), development (D), and participation (P), "where development takes precedence over participation,"[8] with security being the foremost objective of the concerned government.[9] It follows the communitarian democracy model, "a ... process ... that is characterized by stability, peace, and order, the upholding of shared moral and cultural values, and the priority of communitarian interests."[10] This is evident from the history of the role of ethnic and religious communities in the development of Thai democracy.

Since the adoption of the model of constitutional monarchy in 1932, the Thai political system has undergone major shifts, advances, and setbacks along the democratic path. These were factors in the role of the military, bureaucracy, ethnic groups like the emergent Chinese middle class, and the sub-religiocultural groups such as that of Thai Muslims. Along the way, Thailand was also launched on the process of statism by then-strongmen such as Major General Luang Pibulsonggram, who ruled during 1938–1944 and 1948–1957, and Field Marshal Sarit Thanarat, who held power between 1958 and 1963, and other military generals. This situation lasted until the 1973 students' revolt, which began a democratic process marked by party politics and constitutionalism.

The 1992 political uprising ended military rule, and since then Thailand has embarked on "a political system in which the military and bureaucratic forces largely determine the role as well as the mode of participation of the nonbureaucratic forces."[11] It is a system in which the parliament is not the center of power but "is only now becoming a new source of power, struggling to institutionalize its legitimacy."[12]

Amid all these political developments, the Thai Muslims have developed their own political space, which, over the years, has allowed them to express their cultural and pan-Islamic concerns on the Thai political stage.

HISTORY OF ISLAM IN THAILAND. Islam spread to Thailand from different directions: The Malay-Indonesian archipelago, Yemen (Hadhramawt), Persia, India, Burma, China, and Cambodia. Just as other Southeast Asian Muslim communities, the Thai Muslim community is made up of two groups: native/local Muslims and immigrant Muslims. Hence, there is ethnic, linguistic, cultural, and political variety within the Thai Muslim community.

In southern Thailand, the Malay form of Islamic religiosity reached as far as the town of Chana on the way to Hatyai, marking the culturo-language border between the Thai-speaking and Malay-speaking cultures. One reason that Malay Islam has not spread far beyond Chana is the consolidation of the "orthodoxy of Singhalese (Theravada) Buddhism, which had been introduced on the Indochinese Peninsula by the Mons of Burma and was disseminated further by the Thai."[13] The encounter between Malay Islam and Thai Buddhism was one between two religious orthodoxies of native types founded on ethnolinguistic distinctions. Both agreed to coexist.[14] Today, the majority of Thai Muslims reside in the five southern provinces of the country: Songkla, Satun, Pattani, Yala, and Narathiwat. The southern Muslims make up about 44 percent of the total Thai Muslim population.

The second arrival of Islam into Thailand was made up mostly of immigrant Muslims of different sectarian and ethnic backgrounds. Persian Muslims belonging to the Shia sect served at the court of the Ayudhaya Kingdom in different official capacities.[15] Thai Muslims in the central plains of Thailand are of Persian, Pakistani, Indonesian, and Cham descent.[16] In contrast, those in the northern provinces of Lampang, Chiangmai, and Chiang Rai are of Bengali, Burmese, and Yunnanese origins who migrated from Bangladesh, Burma, and southwestern China.[17] These migrant Muslims from neighboring countries came to settle in Thailand for economic and political reasons. They fled religious persecution at the hands of the communists in China and the nationalists in Burma. There are also Thai converts to Islam, either through marriage or religious conversions.

Apart from the ethnic differences, there is also linguistic diversity within the Thai Muslim community. Most Thai Muslims who reside in the south speak Malay language, whereas those residing in other parts of Thailand converse in Thai, both at home and in the public. They are not familiar with the languages of their ancestors.

Most Thai Muslims belong to the Sunni sect, but there is also a small Shia community belonging to the Imami and Bohras/Mustali Ismailis subgroups within the Shia sect.[18] Thai Muslims make up the largest minority religious group in the country and are generally considered to be "a national minority rather than a border minority."[19]

THAI MUSLIMS AND POLITICS. Thai Muslim politicians have represented Thai political parties such as the Democrat Party and the New Aspiration Party (NAP), which is now merged with the Thai Rak Thai Party (TRT) in the various parliamentary elections that have taken place in the country. Thailand has also witnessed the Malay-Muslim struggle against the policy of Thaiization in the form of a separatist movement.[20]

The relations between the Muslims and the government consist of continuous negotiations. In 1988, the first Thai Muslim political faction of the Wahdah (Unity) group was established, made up of Muslim politicians who withdrew from the Democrat Party. The Wahdah has been described as an ethnic movement seeking to achieve the interests of Thai Muslims from within the political system. The Wahdah saw itself as an independent political group ready to offer its support to any political party that promised to pay special attention to developmental issues and problems facing Thai Muslims.

Collectively, the Thai Muslim members of Parliament and the Senate agree on the need to address specific developmental issues facing Thai Muslims. They have succeeded in achieving improvements in the infrastructure and economic development of the Muslim majority provinces, in easing travel arrangements for Thai pilgrims going to the Hajj, in obtaining legal permission for Thai Muslim females to wear the *hijab* in public places of work, and in the establishment of an Islamic bank as an alternative financial institution.

In the previous Thai government led by the TRT, Wan Muhammad Nor Matta of the Wahdah faction served as the minister of agriculture. Surin Pitsuwan of the Democrat Party has previously served as the foreign minister of Thailand.

The political expressions by Thai Muslims in relation to their religious, cultural, and group concerns—at both the national and international levels—have been expanding over the decades. These Muslim political expressions have been taken by the Thai state in the spirit of "globalized communitarianism" rather than that of a "clash of civilizations":

> The future world is more likely to witness dynamic interactions over
> and under the state propelled by the coexistence of opposing and

complementary forces. The combined forces of globalization, the historical *longue dur* of distinct civilizations and ethnic pluralism across the world will, I believe, give birth to "globalized communitarianism" and not the "clash of civilizations."[21]

Cambodia

Cambodia has a total population of approximately 12 million.[22] The main cities of the country are Phnom Penh (the capital), Battambang, and Kampong Cham. Buddhists make up the majority of the population at 93 percent, Muslims at 5 percent (700,000), and others at 2 percent. Buddhism is the state religion, with the Ministry of Cults and Religious Affairs in charge of religious matters.

Cambodia became a French protectorate in 1863 and was occupied by the Japanese between 1940 and 1945; it gained independence in 1953. Cambodia became member of the ASEAN grouping in 1999.

The local Cham ethnic group adopted Islam around 1000 c.e. Cham Muslims took a significant role in the Kingdom of Champa until its end in 1470. Persecuted under the Marxist/Maoist ideology of the Khmer Rouge regime, many Muslims fled to Malaysia, Thailand, Saudi Arabia, France, and the United States. Cambodian Muslim refugees from Thailand and Malaysia have now returned to the country.

The political change effected through the 1993, 1998, and 2003 elections has brought about political and religious freedom, including the freedom to practice Islam. Several Muslims serve as members of the parliament, armed forces, and the civil service. Of the 700,000 Muslims in the country, most are ethnic Chams; of these, about 40 percent reside in Kampong Cham, 20 percent in Kampong Chenang, 15 percent in Kompot Province, and about 30,000 in the Phnom Penh area. There are three types of Muslim groups in Cambodia: the Malay-influenced Shafi'i branch constitutes 90 percent of the total Muslim population; the Saudi-Kuwaiti-influenced Wahhabi branch represents 6 percent; and the traditional Iman-San branch, who practice a syncretic form of Islam that assimilates ancient Cham culture with mystical Sufi teachings, make up 4 percent.

Since 1994, several Muslim organizations have been established, including the Cambodian Islamic Association, the Cambodian Khmer Islamic Association, the Cambodian Cham Islamic Association, the Islamic Students and Teachers Association, and the Jamiyah Ansar as-Sunnah Muhayid

A total of 220 mosques exist in Cambodia. In October 2001, the Ministry of Cults and Religious Affairs released a circular on "maintaining order in the

Islamic religion in the Kingdom of Cambodia" with the intention to impose new restrictions on mosques, which would require the ministry's approval for certain activities, especially those involving contact with Muslim foreigners. However, Prime Minister Hun Sen cancelled the circular three days later, citing it as contrary to the policy on freedom of religion.

Muslim affairs at the national level are managed through the Islamic Affairs section of the Department of Minority Religious Affairs in the Ministry of Cults and Religious Affairs. In 1994, the state sponsored the formation of a national Muslim representative body called Majlis Sheikul Islam Cambodia.

The War on Terror and Its Implications for Thai and Cambodian Muslims

Radicalization of Thai Muslims

The emergence of democracy in Thailand has made available opportunities for Thai Muslims to take an independent stand on global events affecting the Muslims.

Immediately after the events of 9/11, Surin Pitsuwan, a Muslim and the former Thai foreign minister, remarked in an article that the barbaric act of 9/11 needed condemnation, but it also offered an opportunity for a renewal of mankind as it could allow the prophesied theory of "clash of civilizations" to be checked against reality:

> We are facing one of the most serious threats to international order and security in the history of mankind. The search for a common strategy to deal with the new form of terrorism must be pursued on a multilateral basis. The resources of the entire international community must be garnered. It cannot be accomplished in a unilateral manner. It must be comprehensive, inclusive, and with nobility of purpose for the entire world community.[23]

Surin called for promotion of the United Nations project of a "dialogue of civilizations," saying it was time to address the fact that terrorism is a symptom of a deeper malaise that afflicts us all. He called for prevailing of wisdom, rationality, and compassion in addressing human acts such as the destruction of the Twin Towers, for it represented "the final moment of darkness brought about by the clashes of civilizations."[24]

In contrast, a Thai Muslim senator, Imron Maluleem, was of different opinion:

I believe that the U.S. fears the establishment of an Islamic state
in any part of the world because it believes an Islamic state will
destroy American civilisation and interests. First, we (Muslims)
certainly feel very sad that many innocent people died. By the same
token, there is also satisfaction that, at least, America's dignity
and reputation as the world's most powerful country has been den-
ted. I believe that the terrorists did not want to kill many innocent
people. Otherwise, they would have done it later in the morning
when more people would have been in the buildings.[25]

Imron commented that if America targets Afghanistan, it will ignite a pro-
longed jihad in which the Muslims will side with the Afghans: "Muslims
believe that Muslims are brothers. Whenever and wherever a Muslim is hurt,
Muslims all around the world are hurt too."[26] This became the populist view
among the Thai Muslims concerning the U.S. attack against the Taliban. Thai
Muslims took the stand that the United States had no evidence to justify an
attack against Afghanistan, and they called on the Thai government to adopt a
neutral stance by refusing the use of Thai airbases to the United States.[27]

Meanwhile, the Thai government had decided that it would side with the
United States in its campaign against terror. The Shaikh al-Islam, or the Chularajmontri, the official head of Thai Muslims, expressed support for the government's policy of joining in the campaign against terror. He remarked that
"if war breaks out, it is not jihad because the action is aimed against terrorists,
who are the destroyers of religion and lands."[28] Nevertheless, he asked the Thai
government not to commit troops or allow the use of Thai military bases for
U.S. attacks against Afghanistan.[29]

Initially, Thai Muslims did not believe that Muslims were behind the 9/11
attacks. They concluded that it was an act by the adversaries of Islam. And they
made appeals for the support of Afghan people in the face of impending attacks by the United States.[30] These Thai Muslims saw the war against terror as
a means of spreading suspicions about the good intentions of Muslims, brand-
ing them as potential terrorists and a way to sideline the resolution of the core
issue of the Israeli-Palestine conflict in the Middle East. Meanwhile, many
seminars, discussions, prayer meetings, and protests were held during the U.S.
attack on Afghanistan, leading to the boycott of American products as an act of
protest.[31]

After 9/11 and the war in Afghanistan, Thai Muslims still believed that
Muslims were made scapegoats by the United States, and they expressed
distress over such an American stand. They held that the post-9/11 U.S. action
created disunity among countries in the world, resulting only in the killing

of thousands of Afghan civilians and children. They also believed that the U.S. administration was out to threaten Muslim countries because they do not comply with U.S. policies and thus classify them as terrorists.[32] The Thai Muslims' disappointment with the American administration's campaign— what is seen as being directed against Muslims—continues.

In Thai Muslim opinion of today, America has become a foe of Islam. Islam is under siege by America, guided by the thesis of the clash of civilizations, as exhibited by the American interventions in Afghanistan and now Iraq. Thai Muslims are calling for a change in the stance of American policy as it relates to the Muslim world at large.

Thai Jemaah Islamiyah?

Over the decades, Thai Islam has been influenced by the Islamic resurgence movements such as the 1979 Islamic revolution in Iran and the Wahhabi Puritanism. One can easily say that the contemporary state of the majority Islamic trend in Thailand is oriented more toward resurgence than traditional. In the Sunni context, the situation has been influenced by the Islamic movements of the Indian subcontinent, including those in Malaysia, Egypt, and Saudi Arabia. Hence, the term "Jemaah Islamiyah" in the Thai context has acquired a local socioreligious meaning of "religious community."

Thai governments (being sensitive to the religious and cultural needs of Thai Muslims) have allowed Thai Muslims to pursue their own theological development. They allowed thousands of Thai Muslim youth to attend Muslim universities such as the al-Azhar in Cairo, Egypt; the Islamic University in Madina and Ibn Saud University in Riyadh, Saudi Arabia; the Nadwatul Ulama of Lucknow and the Aligarh Muslim University in India; the Karachi, Abu Bakr, and Islamic universities in Pakistan; and the universities and religious schools in Malaysia, Indonesia, and Qum, Iran—all for acquiring bachelor's, master's, and doctoral degrees in theology. Influenced by the religio-theological trends of reformist and revivalist Islam during their educational stay, the returnee Thai students have engaged in promoting Islamic resurgence in Thailand along the revivalist and resurgent patterns encountered in the Middle East and in South and Southeast Asia. This contributes to the religious reform of Thai Muslim society along puritan lines, but the authorities do not consider such promotion to be a threat.[33]

Hence, Thai Islam today—in both the city and the country, the south and the north—is more puritanical in its orientation and stands for the support of Islamic resurgence. This is based on two grounds: (a) the influences of global

Islamic resurgent movements, and (b) the availability of democratic space in the Thai political forum, allowing for the freedom of religion and expression.

But this does not mean that Thai Islam is pro-action-oriented in the local context; rather, it is pro-vocalist in expression of its concerns with the events taking place in and affecting the Muslim world. The U.S. military actions in Afghanistan and Iraq radicalized Thai Muslims to oppose the United States. Thailand witnessed large protest rallies, both in the south and in Bangkok, but these rallies were not linked directly to violence in the streets. Rather, these were peaceful rallies in the spirit of pan-Islamism. Thailand's initial low-key support for the U.S. war against terror had won the confidence of the Thai Muslims, but the recent passing of the executive decrees against potential terrorists—which many fear may scapegoat the Muslims and the American designation of Thailand as a key non-Nato ally at the recently held APEC summit—has disappointed many.[34]

Islamic Terrorists in Cambodia?

Cambodia's embarking on the path of democracy opened up a freer religious environment in the country, whereby the religious communities started paying attention to their own developmental needs.

The Cambodian Muslims are basically rural people, the majority of whom are primarily engaged in fishing and farming activities. Since 1995, Muslim organizations from Saudi Arabia, Kuwait, Malaysia, and Indonesia—representing different Islamic trends and objectives—have engaged in the reconstruction of the Cambodian Muslim community. One form of assistance was sending personnel and aid to relieve the economic and educational needs of the Cambodian Muslims who were the victims of many of years of war and ravage. Such religious schools do not offer multicultural education, but religious only, and they are staffed by foreign teachers who are unaware of local Islamic customs and culture in a multireligious country.[35] In 2002, an American diplomat remarked, "There do seem to be growing links with the Middle East. It actually does make us a little nervous that this is happening that these links are being formed."[36]

On May 30, 2003, the Cambodian authorities arrested two Thais and an Egyptian on suspicion of having links with the Jemaah Islamiyah (JI). These persons were teachers at the Saudi-financed Islamic religious school named Umm al-Qura. The two Thais were sentenced to life imprisonment in December 2004.[37] The CIA could not find any evidence to link the two persons to JI.[38] The Thais were arrested after an alleged Singaporean JI operative, Arifin bin Ali, who was arrested in Bangkok in May 2003, alleged that they were members of the terror group and had helped plan an attack. The same allegation from Arifin led to the arrest of four Thai Muslims in Thailand, including the well-known physician Waemahadi Wae-dao, but the four were later acquitted of charges of plotting attacks on Bangkok embassies. After his release, in the 2006 senatorial elections, Waemahadi was elected to the Thai senate from the southern Thai province of Narathiwat.

On May 31, 2003, the Cambodian authorities ordered the expulsion of twenty-eight foreign teachers from the same school, along with their families, on the charges of links with JI; they had come from Nigeria, Pakistan, Sudan, Thailand, Yemen, and Egypt. The media reported that this action was taken on the basis of U.S. intelligence reports about associations between the Umm al-Qura and JI.[39] The most likely reason for this action, however, was the upcoming meetings of the foreign ministers of the ASEAN and ASEAN Regional Forum (ARF) member-countries in Phnom Penh during June 16–21, which were attended by General Colin Powell, the U.S. secretary of state.[40] Earlier the International Religious Freedom Report 2002, released by the Bureau of Democracy, Human Rights and Labor in the U.S. Department of State, had mentioned tensions between the various Muslim groups that receive foreign financial support and the types of Islam that each of them promote. It also reported that the Buddhists had expressed concerns about the foreign financial assistance coming to the Cham Muslim community.

Several foreign Muslim groups ranging from the Tabligh Jamaat, the Islamic Relief Organization, al-Rabitah, RISEAP, and the Kuwait Society have engaged in the reconstruction of Islam in Cambodia in affiliation with the locals.[41] Since each of them represents a certain religious stance within the purview of Islamic religious thought, this resulted in a proxy war between different groups and may be the reason behind the arrests and the closing down of the Umm al-Qura school in the name of the war against terrorism. It was alleged that many Saudi organizations, including Umm al-Qura, were engaged in promoting the Wahhabi type of Islamic resurgence, leading to internal tensions and divisions within the local Muslim community.

Furthermore, the activities of Islamic movements such as the Tabligh Jamaat and Umm al-Qura in Cambodia were directed toward removing the influences of communism, Buddhism, and Hinduism from the minds of the Cambodian Muslims with the aim to spread orthodox Islam or Wahhabism. This was interpreted concisely by Ahmad Yahya, a member of the Cambodian Parliament, who, in response to an interview in the *New York Times* (December 23, 2002) about Cambodian Muslim involvement in terrorism said, "I told the (U.S.) Ambassador, don't worry about our people. Our people I can guarantee.

But the Bangladeshis, Afghans, Pakistanis, Saudis and people like that who come here, I cannot guarantee."[42]

The Cambodian case is somewhat similar to that in Central Asia where "religious ideology has found fertile soil in societies where economic development is poor and moral and political decay are rampant."[43] Such a situation in a Muslim minority country attracts donations from various Muslim sources of different ideological backgrounds, leading to Muslim infighting and resulting in the government taking action against the foreign groups. Hence, the combined effect of 9/11, the Afghan war, and the activities of Umm al-Qura provided grounds for the Cambodian government to take against the Saudi-related institution. The comments by an Islam expert of the International Crisis Group stationed in Jakarta are interesting; he remarked that there have been speculations about JI members seeking refuge in Cambodia, but it was unlikely that there were direct links between the school and the terrorists.[44]

The above-mentioned event in Cambodia has to be understood in the aftermath of Khmer Rouge persecution, reconstruction of democracy, economic poverty, theological challenges to local Islam, and the demands of development. Cambodian Muslims feel that they became the victims of a global venture and targets of discrimination in their own country. Furthermore, the aid received to meet their developmental needs was severed and may not come back for some time,[45] as the foreign Muslim aid organizations are now weary of engaging in social construction projects in Cambodia.

Conclusion

The security concerns on the part of Thai and Cambodian governments have shaped the action of the states vis-à-vis Islamic groups in these countries. The state and management of concerned affairs were more democratic in orientation in Thailand than in Cambodia.

Since the event of 9/11 and its aftermath, Asian Muslims have faced many questions about the state of Islam in the region. There has emerged a growing tension between the customary mode of "cultural Islam" and the rise of "neo pan-Islamism" in Southeast Asia. In some instances, the combination of local factors and the aggressive nature of international relations has made local Muslims accidental victims of the global war against terrorism.

It is hoped that the accommodative and moderate nature of Southeast Asian Islam functioning within the state of religious diversity will still continue to be play a representative role in the promotion of the Islamic way of life and thought across the region. And that it will be in the interest of America and

Europe that they repair their relations with Southeast Asian Islam, both in its majority and minority situations, by convincing the locals that they are not engaged in a blind war against Islam and Muslims, neither in the region nor elsewhere.

Southeast Asian Muslims having developed within a democratic environment, generally possess a moderate outlook toward religion and society, and are always in favor of friendly and dialogical relations with other traditions and cultures. They cannot afford to be hijacked by both internal and external forces. Thus the war against terrorism should not serve as a metaphor for creating tensions and wrecking relations between the world of Islam and the West.

The trail of post-9/11-related events in Cambodia and Thailand illustrates that contemporary Islam in these countries faces new types of challenges in managing itself, at both the local and global levels. The events in Cambodia showed how local issues within a Muslim community got intertwined with global matters affecting the state of Islam in a not yet politically stabilized country. The Thai Muslim responses to the events of 9/11 and the Afghan war showed how far the Thai Muslims have come in publicly expressing their concerns on pan-Islamic matters in a democratic country.

This purpose of this chapter has been to present both the Thai and Cambodian Muslim responses to contemporary global events so that information about self and other can become a means for building an understanding and enhancing coexistence and dialogue to the mutual benefit of all. Until now, the Cambodian and Thai Muslims have maintained a moderate and traditional form of Islam, but the turn of events in the globalized era and the "war on terror" has seen the growth of anti-Western Muslim attitudes in these countries.

As the United States continues to be engaged with affairs in the Muslim world, it should tread the path with an understanding of how the societies and communities of the *ummah* perceive its role as the superpower. Only then can there be reduction of conflicts and hostile imagining about self and other on both sides.

NOTES

1. John Esposito, *Unholy War Terror in the Name of Islam* (New York: Oxford University Press, 2002).

2. Malise Ruthven, *A Fury for God* (London: Granta Books, 2002).

3. Bernard Lewis, *The Crisis of Islam Holy War and Unholy Terror* (London: Weidenfeld and Nicholson, 2003).

4. Edward Said, "The Clash of Ignorance," available at: www.thenation.com/doc.mhtml?i=20011022&s=said.

5. "Asians Take Centre Stage at Muslim Summit," *Bangkok Post*, October 11, 2003, p. 12.

6. Azyumardi Azra, "The Challenge of Political Islam," *Panorama* 1 (2002), pp. 14–35; "Islamic State Has No Appeal to Ordinary Indonesian," *Bangkok Post*, October 11, 2003, p. 13.

7. Chai-Anan Samudavanija, "Thailand: A Stable Semi-Democracy," in eds. Larry Diamond, Juan Linz, and Seymour Lipset, eds., *Democracy in Developing Countries: ASIA* (Boulder, Colo.: Lynne Rienne, 1989), p. 340. The term "secularized Buddhist polity" is borrowed from Somboon Suksamarn, "Buddhism, Political Authority, and Legitimacy in Thailand and Cambodia," in Trevor Ling, ed., *Buddhist Trends in Southeast Asia* (Singapore: Institute of Southeast Asian Studies, 1993), p. 127.

8. Chai-Anan Samudavanija, *Thailand: State-Building, Democracy and Globalization* (Bangkok: Institute of Public Policy Studies, 2002), p. 8.

9. Ibid., p. 12.

10. Ibid., p. 36.

11. Ibid., p. 136.

12. Ibid.

13. G. Coedès, *The Indianized States of Southeast Asia* (Honolulu: University Press of Hawaii, 1971), p. 218.

14. I use the term "orthodoxies" in the sense that both religious traditions view themselves as the only correct beliefs, as determined by their own standards.

15. Raymond Scupin, "Islam in Thailand before the Bangkok Period," *Journal of Siam Society* 68 (1980), pp. 55–71.

16. Raymond Scupin, "Cham Muslims of Thailand: A Haven of Security in Southeast Asia," *Journal of the Institute of Muslim Minority Affairs* 10 (1989), pp. 486–91. See also Seddik Taouti, "The Forgotten Muslims of Kampuchea and Vietnam," *Journal of the Institute of Muslim Minority Affairs* 4 (1982), pp. 3–13.

17. Suthep Soonthornpasuch, "Islamic Identity in Chiengmai City: A Historical and Structural Comparison of Two Communities," Ph.D. dissertation, University of California–Berkeley, 1977. See also David Wilson and David Henley, "Northern Comfort: The Contented Muslims of Chiang Mai," *Bangkok Post Outlook*, January 1995, sec. 4, pp. 33, 40.

18. "Ismailiya" and "Shi'a," *Shorter Encyclopedia of Islam*; see also Moojan Momen, *An Introduction to Shi'i Islam* (New Haven, Conn.: Yale University Press, 1987).

19. Omar Farouk, "The Muslims of Thailand," in Lutfi Ibrahim, ed., *Islamika* (Kuala Lampur: Sarjana Enterprise, 1981), pp. 97–121.

20. W. K. Che Man, *Muslim Separatism: The Moros of Southern Philippines and the Malays of Southern Thailand* (Singapore: Oxford University Press, 1990); M. Ladd Thomas, "Thai Muslim Separatism in South Thailand," in Andrew Forbes and Sachchidanand Sahai, eds., *The Muslims of Thailand* (Gaya, India: Center for Southeast Asian Studies, 1989), vol 2, p. 21.

21. Samudavanija, *Thailand: State-Building, Democracy and Globalization*, p. 185.

22. Some information sources on the Muslims in Cambodia are the following: Directorate of Islamic Affairs, the Central Islamic Association of the Khmer Republic,

and the Association of Islamic Youth, *The Martyrdom of Khmers Muslims* (microform; Phnom Penh, Khmer Republic: Central Islamic Association of the Khmer Republic, 1974); Imanaga Seiji, "Kanbojia no Chamjin Israam shakai no chosa gaiyo" (A summary of the survey on the Cham Muslim Community in Cambodia), in Seiji Imanaga, ed., *Tohoku Tai, Laos, Kanbojia no Musrim Kyodotai no gakujutsu chosa* (An empirical survey of the Muslim network in Northeastern Thailand, Laos, and Cambodia) (Hiroshima: Monbusho, 1998), pp. 81–144; Omar Farouk Bajunid, "The Reconstruction of Islam in Cambodia," in Imanaga, pp. 1–80; Raymond Scupin, "Historical, Ethnographic and Contemporary Political Analyses of the Muslims of Kampuchea and Vietnam," *Sojourn* 10:2 (1995), pp. 301–28; Seddik Taouti, "The Forgotten Muslims of Kampuchea and Vietnam," *Journal of the Institute of Muslim Minority Affairs* 4 (1982), pp. 3–13. Population figures and other pertinent country information were gathered from *CIA World Fact Book 1998*, Internet edition, available at http://www.odci.gov/cia/publications/factbook/cb.html; *Muslim Almanac Asia-Pacific*, compiled by Regional Islamic Da'wah Council of Southeast Asia and the Pacific (RISEAP), Dato' Ahmad Nordin Md. Zain, Project General Editor (Kuala Lumpur: Berita Publishing, 1996); and U.S. Department of State report on International Religious Freedom Report 2002, released by the Bureau of Democracy, Human Rights and Labor, available at www.state.gov/g/drl/rls/irf/2002/13869.htm.

23. "Let's Look beyond Revenge," *Bangkok Post* September 16, 2001, perspective sec., p. 1.

24. Ibid.

25. "Sorry but Afraid," *Bangkok Post,* September 23, 2001, perspective sec., p. 1.

26. Ibid.

27. "Muslims Say US Has No Evidence to Justify Attack," *Bangkok Post,* September 24, 2001, p. 3.

28. "Wan Nor to Explain to People in South," *Bangkok Post,* September 24, 2001, p. 3.

29. "Top Muslim Urges Neutral Stance," *Bangkok Post,* September 21, 2001, p. 4.

30. "Thai Muslims Show Displeasure," *Bangkok Post,* September 22, 2001, p. 4.

31. "No Boycott Please, We Love Beckham," *Bangkok Post,* November 4, 2001, perspective sec., p. 6.

32. "Thai Muslims Doubt Bin Laden the Culprit," *Nation,* September 11, 2002, p. 1A.

33. "The Thai Jemaah Islamiyah Is Unlike Others," *Nation,* January 6, 2003, p. 6A.

34. "No Logic, No Reason," *Bangkok Post,* August 14, 2003, p. 1; "Non-Nato Ally Status Invites Terror Attacks-Democrats," *Bangkok Post,* October 24, 2003, p. 4.

35. Bjorn Blengsli, "Religious Globalization and the Potential for Terrorism among Cambodia's Muslims: Trends in the Islamic Community," *Phnom Penh Post,* June 6–19, 2003, available at: http://www.phnompenhpost.com/full/papers/is1212/is1212/trends.htm (accessed June 1, 2007).

36. "US Fears Islamic Militancy in Cambodia," *Bangkok Post,* December 23, 2002, p. 10.

37. "Case against Thai Teachers Flimsy," *Bangkok Post*, June 23, 2003, p. 3; "JI Suspects' Spouses Seek Freedom for Detained Duo," *Nation*, July 16, 2005, available at http://www.nationmultimedia.com/2005/07/16/regional/index.php?news= regional_18051718.html (accessed June 1 2007).

38. "CIA Grills Thais in Cambodia Jail," *Nation*, July 24, 2003, available at http:// www.nationmultimedia.com/2005/07/16/regional/index.php?news=regional_ 18051718.html (accessed June 1, 2007).

39. "Cambodia Busts Terror Suspects," available at http://www.casperstar-tribune.net/articles/2003/05/29/news/world/46564f304973bb641acf8a9f08c59bed .txt (accessed June 1, 2007).

40. B. Raman, "Cambodia Meets Islam Head On," available at www.atimes.com 3 June 2003 available at http://www.atimes.com/atimes/Southeast_Asia/ EF03Ae02.html (accessed June 1, 2007).

41. Omar Farouk Bajunid, "The Muslim Minority in Contemporary Politics: The Case of Cambodia and Mynmar," *Hiroshima Journal of International Studies* 8 (July 2002), p. 6.

42. Ibid., p. 11.

43. Esposito, *Unholy War Terror in the Name of Islam*, p.115.

44. Ibid.

45. "Cambodia's Chams Are Latest Target in War on Terror," *Bangkok Post*, June 27, 2003, p. 12.

I2

Conclusion: Asian Islam at a Crossroads

John O. Voll

Contexts: Global Transformations

Every society and human tradition is experiencing major transformations at the beginning of the twenty-first century. An examination of Islam in Asia must place itself firmly in this context of global transformations.[1] Asian Islam is at a major and significant crossroads, and this is an experience shared by virtually every other society around the world. Old and long-established patterns of politics and society are rapidly disappearing and being replaced by new ways of thinking and doing things. Yet, the underlying historical and cultural foundations continue to shape events in significant ways. In this present time of turmoil and rapid change, it is clear that conscious and unconscious decisions of leaders and the general public are determining which paths are being taken in this crossroads era of history.

There are important global developments that have an effect on Asian societies, but this involvement does not create a homogeneous or standardized result, neither globally nor within the region. Instead, the result is the emergence of distinctive local expressions of the global, as global elements are incorporated into long-standing particular cultures and modes of life. Some analysts have used the awkward but helpfully descriptive term of "glocalization" for this process of the mutually interactive globalization of local life and the localization of the global processes as they operate in specific and particular societal conditions.[2]

The consequences of the interaction of contemporary global and local developments are contrary to the expectations of many scholars. Modernization of societies around the world did not create a homogeneous global "modern" society. Instead, what has emerged is a complex array of multiple forms of modernity. In fact, in the words of S. N. Eisenstadt, "the best way to understand the contemporary world, including the upsurge and reconstruction of the religious dimension on the contemporary scene—indeed the history of modernity—is to see it as a story of continual development and formation, constitution and reconstitution of a multiplicity of cultural programs of modernity and of distinctively modern patterns, of *multiple modernities*."[3] In the development and definition of these multiple forms of modernity, religion takes an important role.

The continuing significance of "religion" in the main dynamics of contemporary life is itself also a surprise to many. Many people had assumed that secularization of society was an inherent part of the processes of modernization. Increasingly there is agreement that the old assumptions of secularization theory are wrong, and while there is disagreement over the future role of religion in society, there is little disagreement about its continuing significance.[4]

For Muslims in Asia, as in other parts of the world, this changing understanding of the relationship between "secular" and "modern" is transforming the nature of discussions about the relationships between Islam and contemporary social order. Among the reformers of the late nineteenth and early twentieth century in the Muslim world, the debate about "secularization" of state and society was at the heart of many of the issues involving reform programs. The Kemalist transformation of the Ottoman Empire into the Turkish Republic had at its core the implementation of an activist program of secularization. Nationalist programs advocating revolutionary socialist transformations of societies were implicitly and sometimes explicitly secular in orientation, and these dominated the ideological scene in the middle of the century. However, by late in the twentieth century, many of the basically secular visions of state and society were seen as ineffective and even as failed. This combined with a growing conviction among both scholars and believers that secularization was not an inherent part of modernization. As a result, the debates involving issues of secularism have now shifted with the secularist position frequently being viewed as one among a number of competing ideological positions within the context of multiple modernities rather than as an inevitable part of a homogeneous modernity.

In Muslim communities and societies in Asia, these broad and long-term processes are clearly visible, and they help shape the nature of Asian Islam in this crucial era. The involvement of these societies in economic globalization is matched by a participation in broader social and cultural globalizations as well. The continued significance of religion in global terms is reflected in the regional developments that are often spoken of as the "resurgence of Islam." The dynamics of global and local interaction—of glocalization—in the Muslim communities and societies of Asia and the region as a whole, along with the "local" implications of the global religious resurgence set the broad context for examining "Islam at the crossroads" in Asia. These broad themes help define a framework for understanding more specific issues and developments in the region, especially in terms of the Islamic dimensions of life. They are a necessary part of any study of Asian Islam at the beginning of the twenty-first century.

Mainstream Islam at the Crossroads: Struggle for the Soul of Islam

Many people speak of the "struggle for the soul of Islam" that is taking place throughout the Muslim world. This struggle involves much more than problems in the war on terror or issues of political repression. The struggle is the competition to define the nature of the religious experience and life of the majority of Muslims in the world. In many ways, the core issue is not controlling marginal—and often violent—extremists; it is shaping and maintaining the mainstream consensus on issues of social and political morality and religious piety. In Muslim Asia, among the many developments shaping the future of mainstream Islam are those that involve education, the mass media and the new means of electronic communication, and the changing nature of pop culture. While these aspects are not often as "headline grabbing" as terrorist activities or dramatic—but usually of short-term impact—political events and crises, these three dimensions of Muslim life shape the basic nature of mainstream Islam.

Education

One of the most important arenas in the battle to define Islam for the future is in education. The success of the Taliban and the relatively high visibility of the militant madrasa culture in the developing Afghan crisis of the 1990s did cause some attention to be given to issues of education. It is regularly emphasized that the madrasas were crucial in shaping the mentality of the warriors engaged in the Afghan jihad and the subsequent establishment of the Taliban state. However, little attention is given to the educational alternatives.

The madrasa reform program announced by President Pervez Musharraf early in 2002, for example, received little notice or support.

The struggle to define the content of madrasa education in Pakistan reflects the broader contest among the different Islamic visions competing for followers in the contemporary Muslim world. At one extreme is the Taliban style of Islamic interpretation, which emphasizes the struggle against non-Muslims and advocates militant jihad as the necessary mode of operation for "true" Muslims in the contemporary world. The content of such a vision is framed within the theologically conservative tradition of the South Asian Deobandi tradition of strict and narrow interpretation of the faith. At the other extreme are secularist modernizers, who believe that secular, Western-style education is necessary for modernization and development in Muslim societies. The broad mainstream of Muslim opinion runs between these two extremes, seeing an Islamic dimension in education as being essential but an extreme conservative fanaticism as destructive. The competition becomes the struggle to define the degree to which the mainstream will reflect more "fundamentalist" or more "secularist" visions of the needs of Muslims in the contemporary world. The largest Muslim organizations in Asia, like Muhammadiyya and Nahdatul Ulama in Indonesia, work consciously and actively to create a dynamic mainstream Islam in their educational institutions, while schools of the smaller, militant organizations like the Jemmah Islamiyya are the core institutions of hardline "jihadism" in the area.

In the history of the Islamic community—the *ummah*—education and scholarship has been central to the identity of the believing community. In a pre-modern manifestation of interregional relations (an early form of globalization), scholars moved freely across the Afro-Eurasian Islamic *ummah* from Morocco and West Africa to China and the islands of Southeast Asia. Teachers and the school communities in which they taught shaped the nature of Muslim life in profound ways. The madrasas of the Saljuqs and the great schools of the Ayatollahs in Safavid Iran are important examples of how the educational institutions shaped the nature of mainstream Islam in major historic societies.

If one hopes to understand what will be the nature of Islamic life in Asia in the twenty-first century, it will be essential to know what the coming generations of Muslims are being taught and where that learning is taking place. Many actively believing Muslims have had little contact with formally structured "religious" education, while others have studied within the framework of a more formally organized curriculum of Islamic studies, either in more secular schools or in schools that are identified as Islamic. The ways that Islam is presented within the educational experiences of the majority defines the foundation for what will be the mainstream Islam of the twenty-first century.

It is very important to determine, in each of the countries of the region and in the broader region as a whole, where people have received their instruction in Islam and what the nature of the instruction has been. This must involve some awareness of the influence of "secular" education on religious sensibilities, as well as information about developments in the more "traditional" educational institutions. At the level of higher education, for example, it is important to have information about the impact of institutions like the International Islamic Universities in Kuala Lumpur and Islamabad and the Syarif Hidayatullah State Islamic University in Jakarta, and how that impact might compare with the influence of more secular institutions in shaping the Islamic consciousness of the mainstream majority. Similarly, it is important to know about the continuing influence of pre-university education as organized within the schools established by organizations like Nahdatul Ulama in Indonesia. In societies where Muslims are a minority, it is also crucial to know what role religious schools have in maintaining a sense of Muslim identity.

In the context of globalization and the Islamic resurgence, the old networks of scholars extending across regions take new forms. Growing numbers of students from countries in South and Southeast Asia study in many different countries. Where they study and what they learn becomes an important component in shaping the nature of mainstream Islam. Scholars studying militant Muslim groups have given more attention to the importance of this international circulation of students, noting how many have been trained in camps in Afghanistan or those students who studied in Cairo and returned to their homeland with the perspectives of the Muslim Brotherhood. Where the students study shapes the ideas that they bring back with them. A report of the impact of international Islamic education in China, for example, notes that Chinese Muslims studying in the University of Medina had a more narrow and rigid definition of Islamic practice than those who had studied with the Grand Mufti of Syria in Damascus.[5] Information about the international dimension of Islamic education in all of the countries in the regions, and the possible regional impact, is of great importance.

In general terms, *education* is the key to the future of mainstream Islam in Asia in the twenty-first century. The many different visions of Islam, ranging from the militant conservative to more pluralist visions, compete to define the Islamic future, and the schools are the places where the battles are most frequently won and lost. An agenda for understanding Islam in Asia must include the examination of all levels and types of education.

Media: Mass and Electronic

Mainstream Islam is also strongly influenced by the nature of the sources of information, public and private. During the second half of the twentieth century, newspapers, radio, and television gained great importance in shaping public opinion in the countries of Asia. Initially, these media were not major sources for religious information or instruction. However, Islam has become an increasingly important part of the content of these media, and it is important to gain a better understanding of the interaction that takes place: How does Islam influence what is presented in the mass media, and how does presentation in these media shape the religious material that is being presented? Is the message of a tele-preacher, for example, going to have a character different from that of the traditional *khutbah*, because television shapes how one can present the message?

Periodicals and newspapers have greatly influenced mainstream Islam. The modernist Salafi journal published in Egypt, *al-Manar*, for example, helped shape the development of modernist thought in Indonesia early in the twentieth century. Throughout the regions, newspapers have been significant in presenting a variety of Muslim views, and they remain important. Radio and television also have important roles in presentation of ideas and in shaping the views of the people, however. By the late twentieth century, it was recognized that

> television serves as an effective vehicle for the transmission of
> Islamic doctrine and for the holding of discussion forums on Isla-
> mic matters in both Malaysia and Indonesia.... [In government-
> controlled television,] it is important to see television program-
> ming as demonstrating part of the Malaysian and Indonesian gov-
> ernments' efforts to Islamise their respective countries in a
> modernist way during the 1990s, rather than taking the more radi-
> cal approach of Islamist governments in some other parts of the
> Muslim world.[6]

It is important to know more about how much the media reflect mainstream Muslim beliefs and experiences, and how much influence they have on the actual definition of those beliefs.

By the end of the twentieth century, new modes of communication relying on new technologies have had increasing importance. The development of cassette technology transformed major aspects of popular culture. A study of the impact of cassette technology on the music industry in India notes the wider impact as well: "Cassettes and tape players constitute a two-way, potentially interactive micro-medium whose low expense makes it conducive to localized grassroots control and corresponding diversity of content."[7] The "small media" open the way for important grassroots activity:

> The basic mass-media model of vertical message transference sees the audience as a group of message consumers.... Yet the proliferation of new media, the lowering of costs, the differentiation of the audience into taste cultures, and new models of the active audience offer opportunities for communications participation so that the erstwhile "passive" audience can actively produce not only meaning but messages.[8]

The importance of the small media technology in the Iranian Revolution has been noted by many scholars.[9]

The ways in which the small media communications revolution affects mainstream Islam in Asia are a vital part of the picture of Islamic life in the region in the twenty-first century. How effectively the advocates of different visions of Islam and its future make use of the small media will play an important part in shaping the nature of the mainstream Islam of the next generation. Early in the twentieth century, modernist advocates were clearly effective, but at the beginning of the twenty-first century, some of the most effective use of small media communication is by the advocates of violence, as seen in the videos and cassettes produced by supporters of Osama bin Laden.

Similarly, the global electronic communications network represented by the Internet also needs to be understood. The globalizing impact of Islamic sites providing fatwas and other information is an aspect of this. Again, it becomes important to ask how the medium used shapes the content, as well as noting the dissemination of content. In general terms, development of Internet capacity is an important aspect of creating institutions and structures that will be effective in the contexts of the world of the twenty-first century. Muslim societies in Southeast Asia, especially Malaysia, have been leaders in this development, while Muslim majority societies in the Middle East and North Africa have lagged behind.[10] While Malaysian leaders are willing to assume the risks of economic and political transparency that are involved in connecting effectively with the global communications network, leaders in the Middle East were not: "All of this suggests that the big political issues of freedom of expression and democracy in the Muslim world (as elsewhere) in the 21st century will be fought out within the context of the radically new medium of exchange that we call the Internet."[11]

Understanding the influence of the media on the articulation and presentation of Islam in the twenty-first century and the influence of Islam on the modes of media present becomes a significant element in the agenda of understanding mainstream Asian Islam at its current crossroads.

Pop Culture

The study of "popular Islam" is well established in the standard scholarship on Islam in Asia, as it is in the study of Islam in other parts of the world. In this established scholarly tradition, "popular" Islam is identified with the practices of the less-educated believers and is frequently placed in contrast to "orthodox" Islam.[12] In this definition, local religious traditions and practices are included in what is identified as Islam, but terminology, especially in the older literature, often talks about "saint worship" and "superstitions" that are in sharp contrast to the expectations of Muslim scholars. A key concept in this standard discussion of "popular" religion is syncretism, in which cultural patterns existing when Islam comes to a society are incorporated into what becomes considered "Islamic."[13] Movements of renewal and revival are often seen as "Islamizing" such syncretistic mixtures of Muslim and local elements (i.e., "popular Islam").

While this conceptualization of popular Islam is useful for understanding historical developments, the context is changing dramatically. As societies demographically shift from having rural majorities to urban ones and have increasing proportions of the population under the age of twenty, and as the economies are transformed, the popular culture of the bulk of the population is also changing. At the beginning of the twenty-first century, the old popular culture is disappearing and is being replaced by what many people might think of as "pop culture." This is still the culture of the less educated and poorer classes, but it has been transformed by new media resources and the new contexts of glocalized societies.

The nature of the relationships between the old popular culture, the popular Islam of pre-modern village life, and the cosmopolitan Islam of the scholars was relatively clear. However, the relationship between the new pop culture and the Islam of the scholars is still in the process of being defined. The evolution of this relationship is an important component of the future mainstream Islam of the region, and it is a hotly contested arena that needs to be thoroughly examined.

The issues involved in the relationship between the emerging pop culture and mainstream Muslim sensibilities are illustrated in two controversial pop culture icons. In Indonesia, there has been some dispute over current developments in what was a traditional popular culture dance style, *dangdut*. A singer-performer, Inul Daratista, has added a vigorous hip movement to the more traditional mode of presentation and has been strongly condemned by some hard-line scholars, "who branded her dancing as 'devilish' and 'lustful.'"[14] However, her popularity has expanded the audience for *dangdut* from its traditional rural and lower-class constituency to the urban middle-class and professional audience. Inul identifies herself as a Muslim who prays regularly and appears to have the support of mainstream urban Muslim society.[15] Abdurrahman Wahid, former president of Indonesia and head of Nahdutul Ulama, defended Inul, saying that "no cleric has the right to decide what people can and cannot do in a democratic society."[16]

Similarly, the popularity of a Pakistani rock band, Junoon, and its leader, Salman Ahmad, has aroused the strong opposition of militant, theologically conservative teachers, who argue that the Qur'an forbids music. However, Junoon has a very large audience and has had support from important Sufi teachers. Ahmad also prays regularly and considers himself a faithful Muslim. His faith, he says, gives him "the confidence to try to form a modern Pakistani identity."[17] Here the issue becomes the definition of the faith of the mainstream majority, and it is not automatically the militant teachers who define what that faith is.

The relationship between pop culture and mainstream Islam needs to be more clearly understood. It is a relationship that shapes the nature of mainstream Islam in the coming century.

In the "struggle for the soul of Islam," the real issue is the evolving nature of mainstream Islam, the Islamic faith of the majority of the population. Radicals and extremists may be highly visible but in the long run will have a major effect only if they can convince the majority. In understanding the dynamics of this "struggle," it is essential to know what is happening in the areas of education, the media, and pop culture.

Islam and Politics

Islam's political role is often the most visible and frequently discussed aspect of Islam's role in contemporary societies. The emergence of what became labeled "political Islam" was seen as a key development of the late twentieth century. Debates revolved around whether there was a "failure of political Islam,"[18] whether Islam and democracy are compatible, and similar issues. However, the political dimensions of contemporary Islamic life are shaped fundamentally by the broader developments of mainstream majority faith and piety. In Muslim Asia, two issues have high visibility and great importance: the nature of an Islamic State and the nature of the Sharia and what it means to implement the Sharia in contemporary societies. A third area of major importance is the issue of the relationship between Islam and violence: What is the appeal of the call for violent action in the cause of Islam?

The Islamic State

In South and Southeast Asia, the question of whether or not the state should be formally (possibly constitutionally) identified as an "Islamic State" has been debated since at least the middle of the twentieth century. Independence gave special urgency to the issue, as new leaders engaged in the process of postcolonial state formation. Pakistan was identified as an "Islamic state" by the very process of its achievement of independence with the partition of British India in 1947. What that actually meant, however, was the subject of much debate in the following decades, with no clear consensus emerging, even at the beginning of the twenty-first century.

In every Muslim majority society in South and Southeast Asia, the issue of formally identifying the state as an "Islamic State" has been hotly debated. In Indonesia, the subject was raised almost immediately after World War II and independence, and it was resolved by an inclusive definition of the role of religion and Islam in state definition. Advocates of a more exclusivist definition of the Islamic State remained relatively marginal, and the largest Islamic organizations, like Nahdutul Ulama and Muhammadiyya, argued that Islam is important as a moral foundation for society but they were not active in supporting a more standard Middle Eastern conceptualization of an Islamic State. In Malaysia, advocacy of a formally declared Islamic State was an important part of the political program of the major opposition party, PAS, but the PAS definition of what an Islamic State is differed significantly from what was meant by Mahathir Muhammad when, as prime minister, he proclaimed Malaysia to be an Islamic State in 2001. Even in the context of Muslim minority communities, the nature of an Islamic State sometimes becomes a divisive factor, as can be seen in the competing definition of goals and the conflicts between the Moro National Liberation Front (MNLF) and the Moro Islamic Liberation Front (MILF) in the Philippines, especially during the 1990s.

An examination of the different visions and definitions of the "Islamic State" articulated by Muslim groups in Asia becomes an important part of the agenda for examining the possible paths that might be followed in the coming century. In this analysis, it is extremely important to be aware of the diversity of definitions, even among those who advocate the formal proclamation of an Islamic State. There is no single vision of a restored caliphate that is advocated by all, and an Islamic State is not simply conceived of as a theocracy. Some

advocates of an Islamic State conceive of such a state as democratic or repre-
sentational, while others define the state more in terms of the guided republic
model of Iran or a more authoritarian hierarchy.

These debates have been changed by the changing understanding of
"secularism" by the end of the twentieth century. In many of the earlier discussions, "secularism" was defined broadly as the separation of "religion" from
"politics." In the new historical contexts of the 1990s, an older and more
narrow understanding of secularism—considering it as an institutional program of separation of religious institutions from those of the state—has come
to be a more important part of the discussions to define an Islamic State. In the
Islamic Republic of Iran, for example, some people have been identified as
secularist because they advocate the withdrawal of the mullahs from politics,
even though they remain committed to having a state based on Islamic principles.

The relationship between Islam and democracy is an issue of special importance in these debates. In this context, both "Islam" and "democracy" are
highly contested terms, and much of the disagreement revolves around the
fundamental definitions that are being used. For those who insist that Islam
can only be understood in the terms articulated by medieval thinkers and
experience and for those who insist that the only valid definition of democracy
is Western-style liberal democracy with institutions identical to those found in
the United States and Western Europe, Islam and democracy appear to be incompatible. Others argue that Islam provides conceptual resources and traditions that make it possible to articulate "Islamic democracy."[19] However, there
is a broad spectrum of views on this issue, and understanding the full breadth
of that spectrum and its relationship to mainstream Islam is a necessary part of
any analysis of Islam's role in politics and what a state based on Islamic faith
and principles should be.

These issues involve the definition of the foundation of authority of the
political regime. For Muslims, Islam provides at least a part of the basis for the
normative order of society. In this context, the state must in some way reflect
and affirm the Islamic normative order. Legitimacy of the state and political
regime depends on a minimum recognition that the regime is not counter to
Islam and in some way is in accord with the Islamic normative order. This
legitimacy becomes the basis for a state to be "Islamic" in the broadest definition.[20]

Understanding this diversity of visions of the nature of an Islamic State
requires a careful understanding of the specifics of local movements. It must
also be aware of the impact of globalization on the interactive awareness of
Muslims in the region and the importance of Middle Eastern and other models

in shaping new iterations of the Islamic State visions in Muslim Asia in the twenty-first century.

Implementation of Sharia

Although many people see the implementation of the Sharia as the primary reason for the establishment of an Islamic State, these are two related but different issues. The specific structure of an Islamic State can vary, and the modes of implementation of Sharia can also be different, depending on time and circumstance. The issues involved in the debates over implementation of Sharia go to the very heart of how Muslims in the contemporary world define Islam.

One of the long-standing issues in Islamic legal thought is the tension between the approach that primarily accepts precedent and the following of the judgments of major scholars of the past (*taqlid*) and the approach that argues for the necessity of continued informed analysis for deciding how Islamic principles are to be applied in particular and changing conditions (*ijtihad*). In terms of the issue of implementation of the Sharia, these two approaches are reflected in two different views of what constitutes the Sharia. One approach views the Sharia as an established body of rulings and laws that already exists and simply needs to be applied. The second approach understands the Sharia to be a set of basic principles and standards that establishes a framework for rules and regulations, but this is a dynamic and not a static legal structure. These two approaches involve very different understandings of the nature of the scholarly discipline for the study of Sharia, which is *fiqh*, and the relationship between *fiqh* and Sharia. Some argue that the static vision of Sharia in fact confuses *fiqh* with Sharia and that what some people are in reality advocating is the implementation of a particular and outmoded *fiqh* rather than implementing Sharia.

Throughout South and Southeast Asia, scholars debate about the need for changing the methodology of *fiqh* in order to get an understanding of Sharia that is effective (and implementable) in the contemporary world. It is important to describe the political battles that take place over whether or not a static vision of Sharia should be implemented. This is an important part, for example, of understanding the programs of PAS in Malaysia. However, it is essential to understand that these battles are taking place in the context of broader conceptual debates about the nature of *fiqh* and Sharia. It is not simply a matter of deciding whether or not to implement an existing corpus of legal rules; it is also a matter of defining the foundations of those rules and how they should be applied. When the two largest Muslim organizations in Indonesia, Nahdatul Ulama and Muhammadiyya, opposed a constitutional amendment to implement Sharia, they were opposing the implementation of the static conceptualization of Sharia. They were not in opposition to having Islamic principles be foundations for state and society.

In ways similar to the issues involved in establishing an Islamic State, the issues of implementation of Sharia begin with the fact that Muslims in Asia approach the subject in many different ways. These approaches involve defining new methods of analysis in the discipline of *fiqh*, as well as a conflict between dynamic and static understandings of Sharia itself. Again, it is essential to be aware of this diversity of perspectives and approaches if one is to understand the nature of the choices being made by Muslims in South and Southeast Asia that are shaping their future.

Islam and Violence

Although the majority of Muslims in Asia do not engage in acts of violence as a result of their religious and political commitments, the call for violent jihad has a growing appeal. In virtually every country where there is a Muslim community, there are reports of growing numbers of people being attracted to previously marginal, militant organizations. Some of these reports are a reflection of the increased attention given to terrorism since the destruction of the World Trade Center in September 2001 and of the tendency among some journalists and policy makers to label every active Muslim organization as a terrorist, or potentially terrorist, group. However, it is clear that this dimension of Muslim life, in Asia as elsewhere, has growing importance and needs to be better understood.

One important aspect of this rapidly changing situation is the transformation of old-style Muslim associations and networks into new modes of organization and operation. An example of this is the evolution of the group associated with Abubakar Baasyir. This group began in an old-fashioned way. Baasyir established a small religious school with a conservative curriculum in the 1970s. Over the years, some of his associates also established schools, and a small network of teachers emerged. Baasyir advocated the adoption of Sharia (conceived in the static version) as the law of Indonesia and was arrested and jailed in 1978 on charges of opposition to the state. After his release from prison, he moved to Malaysia in 1985, where he became a part of the broader networks of Islamic activists that were emerging on a global scale, especially in the context of the anti-Soviet jihad in Afghanistan. He traveled widely, and his "religious philosophy became more global in ambition and scope, according to interviews with associates who knew him before, during, and after his exile."[21] Baasyir's group gradually became better organized and emerged as the Jemaah

Islamiyah (JI), and by the beginning of the twenty-first century the JI is described by many as one of the significant new-style terrorist organizations in Southeast Asia. The JI was identified with the terrorist bombing of a nightclub in Bali in October 2002, and the United States formally declared the group to be a "terrorist organization."[22]

The example of the evolution of the JI shows the importance of the observation made by the rector of the Indonesian National Islamic University, Azyumardi Azra: "We should not hesitate to recognize the potential for the radicalization of Indonesian Islam."[23] This potential exists throughout Muslim Asia, and it is actualized in many different ways. It is not a sufficient explanation simply to note that a militant Middle Eastern style Islam—often called "Wahhabism"—is being exported to Southeast Asia. Analysts need to deal with the question of why growing numbers of Muslims in countries like Indonesia are open to adopting such a style of Islam at the beginning of the twenty-first century, even though it clashes with the mode of Islamic faith that has historically been more characteristic of religious belief and practice in the region. The emergence of new types of Muslim associations and the evolution of old types needs to be better understood.

The analysis of the relationship between Islam and violence in Asia must be done within as inclusive a perspective as possible. As the example of the evolution of JI illustrates, simply viewing developments within the framework of separate countries is no longer a viable framework for analysis. Remaining confined to the geographic boundaries of individual states opens the way for a misleading exceptionalism. It also misses the impact of globalization and the direct involvement of globalization in historical developments. Baasyir traveled widely, and the emergence of JI cannot be understood without seeing it in the context of the globalization of activist organizations. Similarly, such developments must be viewed within the framework of global religious resurgence. This is not a phenomenon that is restricted to Muslim organizations in South and Southeast Asia. The issue of the relationship between religion and violence involves examination of Hindu, Jewish, Christian, and other traditions, as well as Islam. The role of violence in religion is an important part of the challenges facing Asian Islam at the crossroads of history in the beginning of the twenty-first century.

Islam's political role has many important dimensions. The very nature of an "Islamic State" provides an important arena for political debate and activism, and this is joined with the issues of defining the significance of Sharia for societies in the twenty-first century. Islamic politics is always the arena of mainstream Muslim activity, but it is also increasingly shaped by the violence of extremists, whose appeal appears to be growing. These many dimensions of Islam's political role need to be better understood.

Islam and the Social Order

The whole structure of society is being transformed in the modern era. Issues involving the definition of the nature of the social order are an important part of the crossroads situation of Muslim communities and societies in Asia at the beginning of the twenty-first century. Concern about the changing nature of the social order is, in many ways, a continuation of long-standing Islamic perspectives. The real center of the Islamic concepts of how human life should be organized is not "the state"—it is the community, or *ummah*. The concentration on the issue of the "Islamic State" is, in important ways, a "modern" concern, reflecting the general tendency of modernity to be state-centered rather than community-centered. However, the often-repeated statement that "Islam is not solely 'a religion,' it is a total way of life" reflects a concern for the whole of society, including the political order, but goes beyond the state.

The views of Muslims, both mainstream and extremist, regarding the relationship between Islam (both their own personal faith and the historic tradition) and the nature and structure of their community are of great significance. Debates defining the developing nature of the whole social order are a major part of the dynamics that determine what the nature of Muslim societies in Asia will be in the twenty-first century. In the broadest terms, this involves defining the role of Islam in civil society (and organizations in civil society), the nature of the public sphere for human activity, and the complex issues of interactions between religion and politics, morality and social order, that arise in defining "secular" relationships in contemporary glocalization and the global religious resurgence. Concrete issues in the contemporary transformations involve the redefinition of both male and female roles in society in the context of increasing global and local sensitivity to gender issues. This also involves recognizing dimensions of societal diversity in ways that can avoid social instability and violence. Recognition of distinctive ethnic or regional identities and supporting the rights of religious minorities are part of the necessary responses to the diversity present in all of the societies of Asia.

Islam in Secular and Civil Society

The whole of the social order and its constituent parts are being transformed in many ways. This is true for societies in Muslim Asia, as it is true for all societies around the world in this current transformative era. Much has been written describing the changes that are taking place, and important conceptual frameworks have been developed for the analysis of these changes. However, many of the basic analytical concepts have been defined almost entirely in terms of Western European and North American experiences. Three such concepts, which are very important in contemporary analyses, are "civil society," the "public sphere," and "secular."

One of the first challenges for analysis of Islam and the social order in Asia is to redefine and adapt these Western-based conceptualizations in an effort to create a more globally oriented framework for study. One cannot do this by creating a new set of terms that apply specifically to Muslim experiences. Simply creating separate terms that apply only to the Islamic experience results in an exceptionalism that denies the relevance of the Muslim experience for the rest of the world and gives a false impression of the "Islamic world" as an exotic, mysterious place that is difficult, if not impossible, to deal with or understand. The real challenge is to redefine the concepts in ways that make them relevant to the Muslim experience. A number of scholars have already been working on this for a number of years and have made significant contributions. One might note as an example the work of the "Civil Society in the Middle East Project" at New York University.[24]

The concepts of "civil society," the "public sphere," and "secular" are all related to efforts to understand the relationships among different parts of society, especially as they relate to issues of political authority. Each draws attention to particular aspects of social organization and how they relate to the broader operation of the social order.

Civil Society

Civil society distinguishes between the state and the general population that is primarily concerned with matters of local and domestic life. "Civil society" is identified as those organizations and institutions that provide nongovernmental links between the state and nonstate society. Most scholars use definitions that are similar to that of Edward Shils: "The idea of civil society is the idea of a part of society which has a life of its own, which is distinctly different from the state, and which is largely in autonomy from it. Civil society lies beyond the boundaries of the family and clan and beyond the locality; it lies short of the state."[25] The development of the concept of civil society was a part of the evolving understanding of the modern social order as it emerged in Western Europe. In this conceptualization, "civil society came into existence as the corollary of a depersonalized state authority" in the seventeenth and eighteenth centuries.[26] As a "category of bourgeois society," it was tied to modern Western social orders.

By the 1990s, however, significant work was done to broaden the definitions, recognizing the existence of institutions and structures in many societies that were and are between the individual-clan-locality and the state. This new and broader conceptualization is especially important in the context of analysis of processes of democratization, since civil society came increasingly to be viewed as having an important role in democracy. By the beginning of the twenty-first century, the term has become an important part of political and social discourses around the world. As John Keane observes, "So striking is the popularization of the term that it could even be said that the language of civil society is currently undergoing a vertical and horizontal 'globalization.' Individuals, groups, organizations in every corner of the earth now speak its language. Some even speak of an emergent 'global civil society.' "[27]

This global expansion of the concept and its use can be seen in South and Southeast Asia. Malaysian Prime Minister Mahathir Muhammad, in defining the basic goal of his long-term vision for the country, said: "We want to become a developed nation in our own mould ... [and the content of the mould is] the creation of a civil society. By civil society we mean a community which is self-regulating and empowered through the use of knowledge, skills, and values inculcated within the people."[28] In Afghanistan, it is being used as a self-identification of groups who are not part of the government but seek an active role in shaping constitutional development. For example, a group of academics, students, NGO representatives and others met on July 26, 2003 in the Foundation for Culture and Civil Society and drafted recommendations for the formation of the Constitutional Loya Jirga. In this action, they saw themselves as "representatives of civil society" in Afghanistan.[29]

However, there continues to be a tendency to identify civil society with Western liberal values and modern modes of social association. In some analyses, so-called traditional social organizations are not considered part of civil society. This raises an important issue for understanding the development of the social order in the twenty-first century in all parts of the world. In an analysis of state and civil society in Malaysia, Vidhu Verma states the issue clearly: "The question is: if civil society is closely connected with liberal politics of the West, should it be modified to account for a different set of associations in the intermediate realm between family and state, or should we discard it as a weak concept? I argue for the need to broaden the concept in order to analyze the associational life characteristic of a variety of civil societies."[30]

The nature of civil society has become a subject of great interest in South and Southeast Asia, and the broader debates are reflected in discussions in Indonesia during the 1990s and to the present. Traditionalist and modernist intellectuals in Indonesia have emphasized different definitions:

Traditionalist Muslims, as demonstrated in the thoughts of Moh. A. S. Hikam for instance, understand civil society as a discourse in defense against the domination of the state, while modernist Muslims observe the importance of the state in the development of civil society. The former stresses the importance of the self-governing and self-supporting society, an idea promoted by Alexis de Tocqueville amongst others. The latter, through its proponents such as Nurcholish Madjid, looks for the legitimacy of civil society in Islamic history and civilization, their point being that the idea of civil society is already embedded in the body of Islam.[31]

An important part of the research agenda for understanding Islam in South and Southeast Asia at the beginning of the twenty-first century is the examination of the nature of social institutions that are in the part of society that is neither state nor personal and local, that is, the "civil society." There are many associations that are identified in some way with Islam that have roots in pre-modern society and others that are products of modern colonial and independence experiences. It is important to discuss the degree to which civil society in the region is Islamic or is at least partially defined by Islam.

The Public Sphere

The public sphere is defined as "that arena of collective opinion and activity that, together with the state and the individual, makes up contemporary civil society."[32] The emergence of the "public sphere" has been discussed in terms of the development of the modern nation-state in Western Europe. The analysis was developed by Jürgen Habermas, who "argued that the bourgeois public sphere that emerged in Western Europe had at its heart a public opinion that was shaped by open access to information circulated through the print media and that functioned by exercising surveillance over the state."[33] Although specifics of Habermas's views have been debated, and there have been significant revisions in the conceptualization, both the concept and the reality to which it refers continue to have great significance: "The public sphere is likely to concern social historians for some time, as it historically has performed a critical function in the legitimation of power in the emerging nation-state, while also serving as the locus of resistance and contestation to the state."[34]

As is the case with the study of civil society, the concept of the public sphere was initially defined by scholars in terms of the development of modern society in Western Europe. However, the concept has been increasingly applied in analysis of societies outside of the West and in pre-modern eras. Some important scholarship in this area has been done in the area of Islamic history and Muslim societies. Nimrod Hurvitz, for example, shows the existence of a religious public sphere in the ninth century Abbasid Empire, within which the ulama had "discursive autonomy" in shaping Islamic doctrine and public opinion at the center of the empire.[35] In the world of multiple modernities, such study provides an important insight into the distinctively Islamic dimensions of what might be conceived of as the Islamic modernities of the twentieth and twenty-first centuries. Analysis of "the characteristics and dynamics of public spheres in Islamic societies illustrates how one might account for the internal dynamics of these non-European modern civilizations at least to some extent in their own terms; how one might analyze the ways in which power and culture are interwoven in different societies and shape also the distinct dynamics of these societies."[36]

The public sphere is where the contest for the "soul of Islam" is taking place. It is the arena of debate in which the nature of mainstream Islam is being defined. It is essential to understand the nature of the public sphere and Islam's place in that public sphere if one is to understand the present and future of Islam in Asia.

Secular

"Secular" is a term that is at the heart of many of the debates about contemporary political legitimacy and authority and the nature of modern and contemporary society. It is also a term whose current definitions come from a base that involves description of modern Western history and experience. However, it has a much longer history as a descriptive and analytical term than either "civil society" or "public sphere." "Secular" referred to matters pertaining to the world in the sense of the "material world," in contrast to the spiritual world or in the sense of "this world" in the contrast with "the next." As a result, in medieval usage, priests who served in parishes were "secular priests," in contrast to monks who lived separate from "the world." Increasingly, the contrast became the difference between the church and the secular world.[37]

Two related terms are also important in discussions of the nature and development of modern society: "secularization" and "secularism." In recent years, the term "secularization" has been associated with theories of modernization that asserted that the separation of religion from other major arenas of society, especially the political, was an inherent part of the processes of modernization. In the context of the emergence of a modern public sphere, it was thought that religion would increasingly be confined to the private sphere and lose its importance in the dynamics of the public sphere. However, the term secularization was first used to describe a process by which the church in Western Europe was divested of control of properties: "The term *secularization* came into use in European languages at the Peace of Westphalia in 1648, where it was used to describe the transfer of territories previously under ecclesiastical control to the domination of lay political authorities."[38] In this early usage, the emphasis was on defining relationships between the social institutions of church and state, and there was no thought, in the context of Westphalia, of being able to separate politics from religion.

It was not until the self-conscious programs of Westernization and modernization undertaken by reformers like Mustafa Kemal Ataturk in the twentieth century that an ideological dimension was added, advocating the separation of religion from politics. This position is called "secularism," which is "an ideology; its proponents consciously denounce all forms of supernaturalism and the agencies devoted to it, advocating nonreligious or antireligious principles as the basis for personal morality and social organization."[39]

In Muslim Asia in the twenty-first century, issues related to secular dimensions of societal transformation are of great significance. They are part of the debates about establishing an Islamic State and the nature of democracy in Muslim societies. However, the terms "secularization" and "secularism" reflect two significant dimensions of the debates about the nature of the state and political authority.

In Muslim societies historically, the nature of institutions and their relationships has been different from the situation in Western Europe. It has often been noted that there is no formal institution that can be identified as "church" in Islam. In the early community of believers under the leadership of Muhammad and his immediate successors, there was no distinction between the religious and political dimensions of community life. However, relatively rapidly, there was a transition

> from an early identification of politics and religion to a differentiation of political and religious life into organized and partly autonomous entities. . . . This initial differentiation of religious and communal institutions from the political institution of the Caliphate grew more profound and more clearly defined. In later centuries . . . the Caliph lost his *de facto* political power to secular military and administrative regimes, albeit to regimes nominally loyal to Islam. At the same time, the several religious communities, Sunni and Shi'ite, developed religiously organized forms of socioreligious life independent from that of states and empires.[40]

This set of processes can be viewed as the "secularization" of the state in Muslim societies, which followed a different path from that of political development in Western Europe. In the West, this involved the development of two independent institutions, the Church and the State. However, since political and religious institutions did not develop in the same way in the Muslim world, Seyyed Hossein Nasr suggests that "instead of applying the terms Church and State to Islam, it is perhaps wiser to use spiritual and temporal authorities which are free from the implications characteristic in the Christian tradition."[41] Within this conceptual framework, the secular "implies ideas and institutions of purely human origin, not derived from an inspired source, no matter what the origin," while "religion means all the teachings and institutions of Divine origin."[42]

Within this type of framework for analysis, it is possible to identify the differentiation of political and religious institutions—that is, a form of secularization of the polity—in historic and current Muslim societies. This does not mean that the temporal authorities departed from Islam. Instead, historic Islamic societies inherited

> a repertoire of cultural and religious ideas [from early Muslim society] which remain operative in Islamic lands to the present day.... This period [up to 1200 CE] also gave rise to the basic elements of Islamic social organization: states, schools of law, and Sufi tariqat. Finally, this era set the precedent for a separation between state institutions and Muslim religious communities. All the while the persistence of non-Islamic modes of social and economic organization, and non-Islamic cultures, generated an endlessly rich variety of social and communal possibilities, and an abiding ambiguity as to what constituted an Islamic society. Wherever Islam was established, these institutions and cultural concepts would be combined and recombined and merged with local traditions to form new types of Islamic societies.[43]

The different forms of institutional differentiation are an important aspect of diversity among Muslim societies, but in historical terms, such differentiation is an important part of Muslim tradition and heritage.

Heritage and Modernity

In Muslim Asia at the beginning of the twenty-first century, the issues of how this heritage is to be structured in the context of modernity, the modern nation-state, and the new contexts of globalization and religious resurgence are hotly debated. It is possible to identify two general approaches. One that is a minority view among intellectuals in South and Southeast Asia insists "that anything short of a total Muslim state regulated by divine law (Sharia) is a betrayal of Islam's promise."[44] The second perspective insists that "Islam does distinguish between the religious and the secular...[and allows] great latitude for human reasoning in the organization of the latter—including in this instance, the organization of modern government. According to this liberal interpretation of *tauhidic* truth, then, it is imperative not to confuse the urgent reality of God's oneness with any particular state structure, political establishment, or, least of all, powerholder."[45] However, this position rejects the Western secularist position that advocates a sharp separation of religion from the state and the public sphere. Instead, "these civic Muslims insist that to restrict religion to the private domain is to deprive it of its vital ethical role in public discourse and activity.... Hence, as a source of moral guidance, religion is never just a matter of personal belief, but the most vital of public concerns."[46]

In the era of the transformation of the social order in Muslim societies of South and Southeast Asia, it is essential to understand the nature of civil society, the public sphere, and the relationships between the temporal and spiritual dimensions of human life in those societies. This understanding requires analysis that does not impose categories that apply simply to modern Western experience while avoiding as well an essentialism that makes comparison impossible.

Islam, Social Order, and Gender

One significant dimension of the contemporary transformations of the social order involves the redefinition of both male and female roles in society in the context of increasing global and local sensitivity to gender issues. The transformations do not simply involve changes in the status and roles of women in society. Speaking of "gender" rather than "women" recognizes that "information about women is necessarily information about men, that one implies the study of the other."[47] The modern transformations in Asia reflect broader transformations elsewhere, in the changing roles of both men and women in society. Economic globalization has created new opportunities and new challenges for men and women in terms of employment in multinational industrial enterprises. The evolution of the public sphere, with its necessary complement of the private or domestic sphere, involved significant changes as well. The identification of women's activities with the domestic sphere, in both modern Western and Muslim societies, has been changing significantly.

Women in modernizing Muslim societies have been increasingly active in the public sphere, and more traditional expectations for behavior have been changing. At the beginning of the twenty-first century, a number of competing developments are taking place. In some areas, the resurgence of religion has involved "a return to the veil, with increased emphasis on the separation of sexes, and the restriction of women's role in public."[48] In contrast, "some Islamic activists and intellectuals have in recent years engaged in a reassessment of women's status and role in society, emphasizing not only greater gender equality in worship and piety but also in education and employment."[49] In many parts of the Muslim world, women have been increasingly active in the public sphere. Notably in South and Southeast Asia, women have served as heads of government in the three largest Muslim majority countries, Indonesia, Bangladesh, and Pakistan. In addition, "Muslim women empower themselves not just as defenders of women's rights but as interpreters of the tradition."[50] This function of women as scholars is illustrated by the careers of "female ulama" in Indonesia, like Lutfiah Sungkar, who "is a popular preacher who appears to have succeeded in using technology as a media [sic] to provide religious teachings for her audiences," and Zakiyah Darajat, who became a professor at the State Institute for Islamic Studies (IAIN) in Jakarta and Yogyakarta.[51]

In the major political developments of recent years in South and Southeast Asia, women have had increasingly important roles. In the transition to democracy, this was visible, for example, in Indonesia: "The year 1998 saw an undeniable upsurge in the dynamics of women's struggle in Indonesia. Generally invisible, not regarded as important enough for major roles in development projects, women became an irresistible force when the monetary and financial crisis, with its ensuing political confusion, hit the country."[52] There are growing numbers of activist associations in the region dealing with gender issues. Although still relatively small in number, "they may well, as has occurred in other religions, prove to be a vanguard in a long-term process of reassessment, reform, and transformation."[53]

An understanding of Islam in the twenty-first century in South and Southeast Asia must include an examination of gender issues in these societies. This cannot be limited to more traditional "women's studies" concerns but must have an inclusive perspective that sees the transformations of the status and roles of males as well as females in society.

Islam, Diversity, and Societal Pluralism

Issues of diversity and pluralism are central to many aspects of social trans-formation and political development. In Asia, this has two very important and different dimensions for Muslims. Muslim communities are both ma-jority and major minority communities in the region, with one of the four largest Muslim communities in the world being the Muslim minority in India.

The wide spectrum of positions held by Muslims that is visible in other major social and political issues shapes policies and attitudes regarding diver-sity as well. At one extreme is the position of the militants, who insist on a rigid and limiting definition of membership in religious or ethnic groups or national citizenship. At the other end of the spectrum is an open pluralism that accepts diversity of identities. The mainstream perspectives range between these two poles, accepting the reality of diversity in society but also insisting on the importance of distinctive identities.

In Muslim majority societies, the Islamic resurgence has had an effect on non-Muslim minorities within those societies. The traditional protections within Islam for religious minorities are sometimes ignored as militant move-ments emerge: "Reactionary religious leaders have found it easy to mobilize or incite their followers against minorities."[54] This has raised serious concerns, both within the societies and globally, about the basic human rights issues as they relate to religious and ethnic minorities. Attacks on Chinese Indonesians since the late 1990s illustrate the tensions involved, and the conflict in East Timor showed how destructive conflicts resulting from these tensions can be. Muslim-Christian communal conflicts continue in places like Ambon. Attacks on Shi'i groups in Pakistan raise similar issues regarding the treatment of religious minorities who are viewed as apostate or heretic by militant groups within the majority. Movements of ethnic or regional identity, like the sepa-ratist movement in Aceh and the Parbatta Chattagram Jana Sanghati Samity (PCJSS) in the Chittagong Hill Tracts in Bangladesh, also raise issues of the degree to which the majority is willing to give recognition to elements of diver-sity within society.

In addition to the rigid revivalism of militant extremists, many highly visible Muslim intellectuals and activists "have marshaled scripture and his-tory to argue that Islam supports the equality and pluralism of the human community."[55] Muslim thinkers from Southeast Asia play an especially im-portant part in this development of faith and practice: "The multireligious and multiethnic societies of Malaysia and Indonesia provide a substantial example of pluralism—the issues, problems, and possibilities for change, accommo-dation, and coexistence."[56]

In societies where the majority is non-Muslim, Muslim minority com-munities face the same issues, but in a symmetrically opposite way. Pressures to assimilate into the majority culture are strong and create tensions within all of the minority communities. Movements of religious and cultural affirmation are part of the response to those pressures, and there is always the choice between militant opposition to the majority society and political system or accommodation and assimilation. The experiences of Muslims in China, Thai-land, and the Philippines are of special significance. They raise the funda-mental question of whether or not a community can be authentically Islamic if it is a minority in a non-Muslim state and society. This dimension is also an important part of Asian Islam at the beginning of the twenty-first century.

In the struggle for control of mainstream Islam, issues of pluralism and diversity are of major significance. The crossroads at which Asian Muslims stand at the beginning of the twenty-first century opens two very different paths. One is a path of activist exclusivism that insists on a standardized conformity in belief and practice, and the other path emphasizes the importance of a pluralist response to the diversity of the societies that are being increasingly shaped by the processes of glocalization. Understanding the nature of this struggle is essential for any examination of Islam in South and Southeast Asia at the beginning of the twenty-first century.

Conclusion

The world of the twenty-first century is one of dynamic change and transfor-mation. No society escapes these processes, and old ways of life are disappear-ing. The purely nomadic lifestyles of Bedouin or the gathering-hunting peoples of the Kalahari are disappearing, and more complex traditional social orders are being changed almost beyond recognition. In this context, the emergence of multiple modes of modernity that are shaped by processes of glocalization and religious resurgence is a key element in the historic situation in which all human societies find themselves.

Muslims in Asia are at a crucial crossroads in their historic experiences. To understand the dynamics of Islam in Asia in the twenty-first century, it is necessary to take into account the full range of human institutions and expe-riences. There is a struggle for defining what the mainstream of Islam will be in the coming century. There are many different positions being advocated, with varying degrees of success. These positions range from the militant exclusivism of groups like the Taliban to old-style secularist positions, with the largest groups in the middle, open to more pluralist views but affirming the viability of Islam in the contemporary world. The competition among groups and visions involves the education of the coming generations, the media for transmitting and shaping information and knowledge, and the changing nature of the popular culture of the general population. In terms of specific institutions, the issues of political authority are of great importance as debates rage over the nature of a truly Islamic political system, the implementation of Sharia, and whether or not violence is necessary for defending and enforcing Islam. All of this takes place in a framework of the transformation of the whole social order, with the evolution of civil society and the public sphere and the definition of those arenas of activity in terms of the meaning of secularization in contemporary contexts. Specific issues of particular importance in this transformation are the ways that Muslims define and redefine gender and the significance of diversity in the social order.

These complex issues set an important agenda for research and examination in the effort to understand what will be the nature of Muslim faith and experience in South and Southeast Asia in the twenty-first century.

NOTES

1. For purposes of the analysis in this paper, "Asia" refers to the countries and societies in Asia but outside of the region called the "Middle East."

2. For example, Roland Robertson, "Glocalization: Time–Space and Homogeneity–Heterogeneity," in Mike Featherstone, Scott Lash, and Roland Robertson, eds., *Global Modernities* (London: Sage, 1995), pp. 25–44. Other related analyses of the global-local interaction are the essays in Rob Wilson and Wimal Dissanayake, eds., *Global/Local: Cultural Production and the Transnational Imaginary* (Durham, N.C.: Duke University Press, 1996).

3. S. N. Eisenstadt, "The Reconstruction of Religious Arenas in the Framework of 'Multiple Modernities,'" *Millennium: Journal of International Studies* 29:3 (2000), p. 592; emphasis added.

4. For example, the essays in Peter L. Berger, ed., *The Desecularization of the World: Resurgent Religion and World Politics* (Grand Rapids, Mich.: William B. Eerdmans, 1999). A discussion of the failure of secularization theory is in Rodney Stark, "Secularization, R. I. P.," *Sociology of Religion* 60:3 (Fall 1999), pp. 249–74.

5. I am grateful to Jacqueline Armijo for this information, provided both in private communication and in a paper, "The Impact of International Islamic Education on Muslims in China," presented at the Twentieth Annual Conference of the American Council for the Study of Islamic Societies at the University of Victoria, Victoria, BC, May 3, 2003.

6. Peter G. T. Riddell, *Islam and the Malay-Indonesian World: Transmission and Responses* (London: Hurst, 2001), p. 290.

7. Peter Manuel, *Cassette Culture: Popular Music and Technology in North India* (Chicago: University of Chicago Press, 1993), p. 2.

8. Annabelle Sreberny-Mohammadi and Ali Mohammadi, *Small Media, Big Revolution: Communication, Culture, and the Iranian Revolution* (Minneapolis: University of Minnesota Press, 1994), p. 31.

9. For example, the relatively comprehensive analysis in Sreberny-Mohammadi and Mohammadi, 1994.

10. For example, the analysis in Toby E. Hoff, "Globalization and the Internet: Comparing the Middle Eastern and Malaysian Experiences," *Middle East Journal* 55:3 (Summer 2001), pp. 439–58.

11. Ibid., 458.

12. For example, the discussion in James Grehan, "Middle Eastern Popular Religion," in Peter N. Stearns, ed., *Encyclopedia of Social History* (New York: Garland, 1994), pp. 385–86.

13. A helpful discussion of this process of incorporation can be found in Olaf Schumann, Alfred Willms, and Lode Frank Brakel, "Der Islam und locale Traditionen: synkretistische Ideen und Praktiken," in Werner Ende and Udo Steinbach, eds., *Der Islam in der Gegenwart* (Munich: C. H. Beck, 1984), pp. 560–81.

14. Dan Murphy, "Indonesian Singer Wags Hips, Bumps Heads with Clerics," *Christian Science Monitor*, May 9, 2003, p. 1.

15. Ellen Nakashima, "Muslim Clerics in a Twist over 'Dangdut' Dancer," *Washington Post*, May 31, 2003, pp. C1, C3.

16. Murphy, "Indonesian Singer." P. 8

17. Jon Pareles, "A Rock Star's Struggle Where Militant Islam Rules," *New York Times*, July 17, 2003, p. E7. This is quoting from "Junoon: The Rock Star and the Mullahs," first shown on "Wide Angle," PBS, July 17, 2003.

18. For example, the analysis presented in Olivier Roy, *The Failure of Political Islam*, trans. Carol Volk (Cambridge: Harvard University Press, 1994).

19. For example, John L. Esposito and John O. Voll's analysis in *Islam and Democracy* (New York: Oxford University Press, 1996).

20. An important discussion of the issues of state legitimacy in Southeast Asia can be found in the essays in Muthiah Alagappa, *Political Legitimacy in Southeast Asia: The Quest for Moral Authority* (Stanford, Calif.: Stanford University Press, 1995).

21. Alan Sipress and Ellen Nakashima, "A Quiet Voice Echoes among Islamic Radicals," *Washington Post*, January 3, 2003, p. A12.

22. Jane Perlez, "U.S. Labels Indonesian Faction as Terrorist," *New York Times*, October 24, 2002, p. A15.

23. Quoted in Dan Murphy, "A Village in Java Tells Story of Militant Islam's Growth," *Christian Science Monitor*, January 23, 2003, p. 1.

24. There is a useful summary of some of the results of this project in Jillian Schwedler, ed., *Toward Civil Society in the Middle East? A Primer* (Boulder, Colo.: Lynne Rienner, 1995).

25. Quoted in Jillian Schwedler, "Introduction: Civil Society and the Study of Middle East Politics," in Schwedler, *Toward a Civil Society*, p. 5.

26. Jurgen Habermas, *The Structural Transformation of the Public Sphere: An Inquiry into a Category of Boureois Society*, trans. Thomas Burger (Cambridge: MIT Press, 1991), p. 19.

27. John Keane, *Civil Society: Old Images, New Visions* (Stanford, Calif.: Stanford University Press, 1998), p. 32.

28. Quoted in ibid., p. 3.

29. "Press Release: Recommendations on the Constitutional Loya Jirga Decree Made by Representatives of Civil Society on July 30, 2003," *APA [Afghanistan Peace Association] News Monitor* 1:15 (August 3, 2003).

30. Vidhu Verma, *Malaysia: State and Civil Society in Transition* (Boulder, Colo.: Lynne Rienner, 2002), p. 4.

31. A synopsis distributed by the publisher of Hendro Prasetyo and Ali Munhanif, eds., *Islam dan Civil Society: Pandangan Muslim Indonesia* (Jakarta: Gramedia Pustaka Utama–PPIM IAIN Jakarta, 2002).

32. Sandria B. Freitag, "Public Sphere," in Stearns, ed., *Encyclopedia of Social History*, p. 601.

33. .Ibid.

34. Ibid., pp. 602–3.

35. Nimrod Hurvitz, "The *Mihna* (Inquisition) and the Public Sphere," in Miriam Hoexter, Shmuel N. Eisenstadt, and Nehemia Levtzion, eds., *The Public Sphere in Muslim Societies* (Albany: State University of New York Press, 2002), pp. 17–29.

36. Shmuel N. Eisenstadt, "Concluding Remarks: Public Sphere, Civil Society, and Political Dynamics in Islamic Societies," in Hoexter et al, *Public Sphere*, p. 159.

37. For example, "Secular," in *The Compact Edition of the Oxford English Dictionary* (New York: Oxford University Press, 1971), vol. 2, pp. 365–66.

38. Bryan R. Wilson, "Secularization," in Mircea Eliade, ed., *The Encyclopedia of Religion* (New York: Macmillan, 1987), vol. 13, p. 159.

39. Ibid.

40. Ira M. Lapidus, "The Separation of State and Religion in the Development of Early Islamic Society," *International Journal of Middle East Studies* 6:4 (October 1975), p. 384.

41. Seyyed Hossein Nasr, *Islamic Studies: Essays on Law and Society, the Sciences, and Philosophy and Sufism* (Beirut: Librairie du Liban, 1967), p. 6.

42. Ibid., p. 16.

43. Ira M. Lapidus, *A History of Islamic Societies*, 2nd ed. (Cambridge: Cambridge University Press, 2002), p. 193.

44. Robert W. Hefner, "Islam in an Era of Nation-States: Politics and Religious Renewal in Muslim Southeast Asia," in Robert W. Hefner and Patricia Horvatich, eds., *Islam in an Era of Nation-States: Politics and Religious Renewal in Muslim Southeast Asia* (Honolulu: University of Hawai'i Press, 1997), p. 27.

45. Ibid., p. 28.

46. Ibid.

47. Joan W. Scott, "Gender: A Useful Category of Historical Analysis," *American Historical Review* 91:5 (December 1986), p. 1056.

48. John L. Esposito, *Islam and Politics*, 4th ed. (Syracuse, N.Y.: Syracuse University Press, 1998), p. 332.

49. Ibid., p. 333.

50. Ibid.

51. Synopsis distributed by the publisher of Jajat Burhanudin, ed., *Ulama Perempuan di Indonesia* [Female Ulama in Indonesia] (Jakarta: Gramedia Pustaka Utama–PPIM IAIN Jakarta, 2002).

52. Rita Serena Kolibonso, "The Gender Perspective: A Key to Democracy in Indonesia," in Arief Budiman, Barbara Hartley, and Damien Kingsbury, eds., *Reformasi: Crisis and Change in Indonesia* (Clayton, Australia: Monash Asia Institute, 1999), p. 335.

53. Esposito, *Islam and Politics*, p. 334.

54. Ibid.

55. Ibid., p. 337.

56. Ibid., p. 338. See also Robert W. Hefner, *Politics of Multiculturalism: Pluralism and Citizenship in Malaysia, Singapore, and Indonesia* (Honolulu, HI: University of Hawai'i Press, 2001), passim.

Index

Abdülhamid II, 119
Abdullah Ahmad Badawi, 83, 84, 85, 94,
    95, 98, 100–102, 103–4, 105*n*14,
    108*n*34. *See also* Malaysia
Abdurrahman Rasulaev, 113
ABIM. *See* Muslim Youth Movement
    of Malaysia
Abu Sayyaf, 4, 230, 238–40
activists, Islamic, 4, 7. *See also individual
    countries*
Advani, K. L., 50
Afghanistan
    civil war in, 35
    colonialism in, 38
    constitution for, 45
    Islamic government in, 3–4
    mujahideen in, 4
    Pakistan and, 32
    al-Qaeda in, 38
    Soviet occupation of, 4, 23–24, 35
    Taliban in, 3, 4, 35, 38, 39, 41, 251
    training camps in, 34–35
    U.S. attack on, 17, 38, 65, 245,
        251–53, 255
AFP. *See* Armed Forces of the Philippines
Ağaoğlu, Ahmet, 122–23
Agreement on the General Cessation
    of Hostilities, 237
AHAB. *See* Ahl-e-Hadith Andolan
    Bangladesh
Ahl-e-Hadith, 50, 54, 67–72, 73–74
Ahl-e-Hadith Andolan Bangladesh
    (AHAB), 68–72

Ahl-e-Hadith Mohila Sangstha, 70
Ahmadiyah sect, 20
Akayev, Askar, 125
Akçura, Yusuf, 122–23
AL. *See* Awami League
Al Azhar, 13, 252
Al-Harmain Foundation, 70
bin Ali, Arifin, 253–54
Ali, Maulana Karamat, 64
ALIRAN. *See* National Awareness Current
Ali, Sayyid Ameer, 63–64
Al-Jamiyat-ul-Ahya-assunnah (Society for
    the Revival of the Sunnah of the
    Prophet), 70
Al-Jamiyat-ul-Ahyah-assurah al-Islami
    (Revival of Islamic Heritage
    Society), 70
All-China Women's Federation, 220
Alternative Front (BA), 103. *See also*
    Anwar Ibrahim
Angeles, Gerry, 238
animism, 11, 28
Ankara Declaration, 125
Anwar Ibrahim, 88, 89, 96–97, 99,
    103, 107*nn*30–31. *See also* Peoples
    Justice Party
APEC summit, 253
apostasy, 20–21, 90, 91, 97, 147,
    149, 164
Aquino Constitution, 234
Aquino, Maria Corazon, 234
ARF. *See* ASEAN Regional Forum
Arkoun, Muhammad, 67

Armed Forces of the Philippines (AFP),
    238–40
Armitage, Richard, 206–7
ARMM. *See* New Expanded Autonomous
    Region in Muslim Mindanao; Organic Act
    for the Autonomous Region in Muslim
    Mindanao
Arroyo, Gloria, 233, 240, 242
ASEAN grouping, 249
ASEAN Regional Forum (ARF), 254
Ash'arite school of Sunni theology, 82
Ashraf, Seyyed Ali, 61, 66, 67
Asian Development Bank, 155
Asian Strategy and Leadership Institute
    (ASLI), 83
ASLI. *See* Asian Strategy and Leadership
    Institute
Association of Indonesian Muslim Intellectuals
    (ICMI), 14–15
Ataturk, Mustafa Kemal, 37, 117, 121. *See also*
    Turkey, Republic of
atheism, of USSR, 111, 112, 135
Atkin, Muriel, 110
Awami League (AL), 50, 51, 56–57, 60, 62,
    68, 69, 74, 75n11
ayatollahs, 4
Ayodhya. *See* India
Ayudhaya Kingdom, 247
A'zam, Tariq, 40
Azerbaijan, 113, 124, 125, 126t, 127, 133, 134t,
    142n45. *See also* Central Asia
Azeri-Armenian conflict, 127
Azharuddin, Mohammad, 185
Aziz, Shaukat, 43, 44

BA. *See* Alternative Front
Ba'asyir, Abu Bakar, 23, 26
Babri Masjid. *See* India
Bali and Java, bombings in, 4, 23, 26, 27, 230
Bangla Bhai. *See* Islam, Siddiqul
Bangladesh
    AHAB in, 68–72
    Ahl-e-Hadith in, 50, 54, 67–72
    AL in, 50, 51, 56–57, 60, 62, 68, 69, 74, 75n11
    Arab philanthropy for, 54
    BJP in, 50
    BNP in, 57, 60, 61, 62, 69, 70, 74
    bombing in, 49, 68, 71, 75n2
    constitution for, 51, 52, 53
    democracy in, 51
    education in, 49, 52, 55–59, 77n29, 77n31,
        77n39
    Indian relations with, 49–50, 53, 75n6, 75n9
    intellectualism in, 66–67
    IOJ in, 62
    Islamic militancy in, 67–72, 73–74
    Islam in, 3–4, 52, 53
    JAHB in, 68–69
    JMB in, 50, 68, 70–72, 79n60
    JMJB in, 50, 67–68, 71–72, 79n60
    language in, 51, 53
    madrasas in, 55–57, 57t, 68, 74,
        77n31, 77n36
    media in, 52, 65–66, 78n53
    military in, 49, 50
    mosques in, 55
    nationalism in, 51, 52, 64–65, 72, 73
    NGOs in, 54, 68, 70
    Pakistan and, 37, 51, 68, 72–73
    pir in, 60, 69–70
    politics versus Islam in, 5, 50, 53,
        74, 76n11
    religious extremism in, 49–50, 75n1, 76n6
    secession of, 37
    secularism in, 51, 52, 72
    Sharia in, 54–55, 62
    Sufism in, 54, 59–61
    terrorism in, 49–50, 68, 71, 75n2, 76n9
Bangladesh Nationalist Party (BNP), 57, 60,
    61, 62, 69, 70, 74
the Bangsamoro, 7, 231, 233, 237, 239, 242
Bangsamoro Development Agency, 240
banking, Islamic, 14, 28, 149, 155, 248
Bari, Abdul, 68–69
Barisan Nasional (BN), 83, 94. *See also*
    Abdullah Ahmad Badawi
Bartlett, Frederic C., 115
Bennabi, Malek, 67
Bennigsen, Alexandre, 110, 131
Bey, Hüseyinzade Ali, 122–23
Bharatiya Janata Party (BJP-India), 50, 177, 182,
    183, 184, 185, 186, 187, 191, 193
Bhartia Janata Party (BJP-Bangladesh), 50
Bhutto, Benazir, 33, 34, 44. *See also* Pakistan
    Peoples Party
Bhutto, Zulfiqar Ali, 32, 149
bin Laden, Osama, 17, 24, 27, 50
Biswa Ijtema, 62
BJP. *See* Bharatiya Janata Party; Bhartia
    Janata Party
Blasphemy Law, 150. *See also* Pakistan
BN. *See* Barisan Nasional
BNP. *See* Bangladesh Nationalist Party
bombing
    in Bangladesh, 49, 68, 71, 75n2
    in Indonesia, 4, 23, 26, 27, 230
    in Philippines, 230
    of World Trade Center, 245
Broxup, Marie, 110
van Bruinessen, Martin, 18–19

Buddhism, 247, 249, 257n14
Bush, George H. W., 124
Bush, George W., 26

Cambodia
    Buddhism in, 249
    democracy in, 255
    economic development in, 255
    JI in, 23, 27, 30n32, 252, 253, 254
    Khmer Rouge in, 249, 255
    Majlis Sheikul Islam Cambodia in, 250
    Ministry of Cults and Religious Affairs in,
        249–50
    mosques in, 249–50
    9/11 and, 245, 255
    refugees from, 249
    religious freedom in, 249–50
    security concerns in, 255
    terrorism in, 253–55
Cambodian Cham Islamic Association, 249
Cambodian Islamic Association, 249
Cambodian Khmer Islamic Association, 249
Campus Association of Muslim Students, 23
Candao, Zacaria, 234
capitalism, 19
CAS. See Central Asian states
Catherine II, 113
Catholic Bishops Conference of the
        Philippines, 235
cell phones, 214. See also media
Center for Public Policy Study (CPPS), 83
Central Asia. See also individual countries
    Ankara Declaration and, 125
    as anti-Russian, 137
    CAS and, 128
    Central Spiritual Directorate for, 113
    Cold War and, 109–10, 131
    cultural roots in, 132
    education in, 113, 116, 125–27, 126t
    Efsanevi in, 135–36
    ethnicity versus religion in, 114, 132, 143n56
    expressivist versus scripturalist Islam in,
        115, 140n10
    Fergana fundamentalism in, 136–37
    IMU in, 137
    Iran in, 124
    IRP in, 137
    Islamic conversion in, 130
    Islamic factor in, 109–10, 111, 116, 130,
        143n62
    Islamic missionaries to, 117
    Islamic opposition in, 3–4, 116–17, 131
    Islamic oral tradition in, 135–36
    Jadidism in, 116, 122, 130–31
    mosques in, 112, 115

nation building in, 132
nomadism versus settler peoples of, 111, 112
religiosity in, 112, 115–16
Russian colonialism in, 112, 113, 131, 137
SADUM in, 113
Sharia in, 113
Silk Road in, 112
Spiritual Boards of Directorate in, 113, 132–33
Sufism in, 114, 130
TIKA and, 125
traditional versus enlightened Islam in, 112
Turkish policy for, 124–28, 126t, 138,
        141n36, 142n45
Central Asian states (CAS), 128
Central Spiritual Directorate, 113
Chandra Muzaffar, 88, 101
Chatterje, Partha, 113
Chechnya, 128–29
Chiang Kai-shek, 203
China
    assimilation in, 197, 200
    civil society programs in, 210
    Communist Party in, 203, 207, 210, 214
    community development in, 199, 211, 213,
        216, 221n2
    corruption in, 214, 220
    cultural identity in, 209
    Cultural Revolution in, 198, 203, 224n18,
        227n49
    Dali Sultanate in, 201, 202
    democratization in, 209–10
    drug addiction in, 221
    economic development in, 199, 204, 214,
        227n49
    education in, 199, 201, 203, 204–5, 208, 210,
        211, 219–20, 221, 223n12, 224n19,
        224n24, 225n26
    environment in, 207
    ethnic identity in, 197, 199, 202, 206, 208,
        209, 214, 216–17, 221
    ETIM in, 206–7, 225n29
    executions in, 7, 208, 226n34
    female infanticide in, 218
    female trafficking in, 218, 219, 221
    forced resettlement/migration in, 200, 207,
        222n7, 226n33
    Hanafi school of law in, 198
    Han Chinese in, 197, 200, 201–2, 207,
        214–17, 221, 226n33, 227n49
    HIV/AIDS in, 221
    housing in, 214, 221
    Hui in, 7, 197, 199, 200, 201, 202, 212,
        214–15, 217, 221n1, 223n11
    human rights in, 199, 206–9
    income in, 214

China (*continued*)
Islamic calligraphy in, 198, 221*n*3
Islamic networking in, 205, 211, 217
language in, 209
Manchu Qing dynasty in, 201
Ming dynasty in, 200, 201
Mongol Yuan dynasty in, 200
mosques in, 198–99, 203, 204, 207, 210, 211, 212, 222*n*2, 222*n*4, 224*nn*20–21, 226*n*32
Muslim employment in, 199–200, 205
Muslim minorities in, 7, 197–98, 199, 221*n*1
Muslim persecution in, 7, 199, 201, 202–4, 206–7, 209, 220–21, 224*n*18, 224*nnn*21–23
Muslim rebuilding in, 204
Muslim stereotypes in, 201, 223*n*14
NGOs in, 210, 213, 220
9/11 and, 199, 206, 227*n*43
nuclear weapons and, 208
one-child policy in, 218
People's Armed Police in, 215, 228*n*50
pluralism in, 199, 213
population of, 201–2
prostitution in, 218, 219, 221
Qing dynasty in, 203
Red Guards in, 203, 224*n*22
Salman Rushdie case in, 213
Shadian incident in, 203–4, 224*n*23
social unrest in, 199, 210, 214
Sufism in, 7
suicide in, 218
Thousand Mothers' Movement in, 208
trading expeditions by, 200, 222*n*9
Uighurs in, 6, 7, 197–98, 199, 207, 208, 209, 217, 221*n*1, 222*n*5, 225*n*27, 226*n*31
U.S. and, 206–7, 225*nn*29–30
violence in, 201, 202–3, 209, 214–15, 218, 221, 223*n*15
women in, 217–21
China Islamic Association, 210
Chinese Salman Rushdie case, 213
Christianity, 5, 7, 12, 18–20, 21, 22, 25, 26, 28, 86, 229, 231
Chularajmontri. *See* Shaikh al-Islam
CIA. *See* U.S. Central Intelligence Agency
civilizational Islam. *See* Abdullah Ahmad Badawi; Islam hadhari
Cold War, 109–10, 121–22, 131
colonialism
in Afghanistan, 38
in Central Asia, 112, 113, 131, 137
in India, 112
in Malaysia, 91, 93
resistance to, 112, 131

Commander Robot, 238
communism, 6, 19, 109, 115, 118, 124, 132, 203
Confucianism, 89
Congress of Mujahidin, 24
cosmopolitanism, 19
Council of Islamic Ulemas, 17, 25
Council on Islamic Ideology, 147, 154, 164
CPPS. *See* Asian Strategy and Leadership Institute; Center for Public Policy Study
Cultural Revolution, 198, 203, 212, 224*n*18, 227*n*49. *See also* China
Cyprus, 122

Dakwah Council. *See* Dewan Dakwah Islamiyah Indonesia
Dali Sultanate, 201, 202
DAP. *See* Democratic Action Party
Darul Arqam, 20
Darul Islam, 18, 23
Daudzai, Asif Iqbal, 161–62
Demirel, Süleyman, 127
democracy
acceptance of, versus application, 25
in Bangladesh, 51
in Cambodia, 255
in Indonesia, 11, 12, 15, 22, 24–26, 28
in Malaysia, 4, 6, 84, 103–4
in Pakistan, 33, 35, 39, 44
in Philippines, 237
process for, 6
in Thailand, 250
Democratic Action Party (DAP), 96, 99–100, 102
Democratic Party of Struggle, 13. *See also* Indonesia
Deobandi JUI, 40, 41, 42
Department of Islamic Development (JAKIM), 101
Dewan Dakwah Islamiyah Indonesia (Dakwah Council), 18, 21
Dewan Perwakilan Rakyat (DPR), 15, 16
discrimination
in India, 178–81, 186*t*, 187, 188, 195*n*20
in Indonesia, 4, 18, 19, 22, 26, 28
in Pakistan, 150
in Philippines, 231
Divan-I Hikmet (Yesevi), 130
divorce, 21–22
DPR. *See* Dewan Perwakilan Rakyat

Eastern Turkestan Islamic Movement (ETIM), 206–7, 225*n*29
ECO. *See* Economic Cooperation Organization (ECO)

Economic Cooperation Organization (ECO), 124–25
Economic Planning Unit (EPU), 82–83, 105n6
education
  in Bangladesh, 49, 52, 55–59, 77n29, 77n31, 77n39
  in Central Asia, 113, 116, 125–27, 126t
  in China, 199, 201, 203, 204–5, 208, 210, 211, 219–20, 221, 223n12, 224n19, 224n24, 225n26
  content for, 158
  gender separation for, 156–58
  in India, 177, 179, 181–82, 184, 188, 193
  in Indonesia, 8, 13–14, 21, 24, 28, 146
  Islam and, 8, 13–14, 21, 24, 28, 38, 49, 52, 55–59, 77n29, 77n31, 77n39, 89, 111, 113, 116, 125–27, 126t, 146, 150–51, 154–55, 156–59, 177, 179, 181–82, 184, 188, 193, 199, 201, 203, 204–5, 208, 210, 211, 219–20, 221, 223n12, 224n19, 224n24, 225n26
  madrasas for, 14, 24, 28, 38, 55–59, 57t, 68, 74, 77n31, 77n36
  in Malaysia, 89
  in Pakistan, 38, 150–51, 154–55, 156–59
  in Turkey, 111
  for women, 156–58
EEC. See European Economic Community
Efsanevi (legendary Islam), 135–36. See also Islam
Egyptian Muslim Brotherhood, 14
Elchibey, Ebulfez, 125
Elcibey, Ebulfeyz, 127
Emre, Yunus, 130
Deobandi JUI, 40, 41, 42
EPU. See Economic Planning Unit; Malaysia
Ershad, Hussain Muhammad, 52–53
Estrada, Joseph, 238, 240, 242
ETIM. See Eastern Turkestan Islamic Movement
EU. See European Union (EU)
European Council, 121
European Economic Community (EEC), 121
European Union (EU), 119, 121, 138
executions, in China, 7, 208, 226n34
extremism
  al-Qaeda as, 4
  in Bangladesh, 49–50, 75n1, 76n6
  in Indonesia, 4, 18, 19
  as minority, 4, 28
  in Pakistan, 35, 36
  as religious, 4
  trends in, 4

Fadzil Nor, 99
Far Eastern Economic Review, 49–50
fatwas, 20, 43
Fergana Fundamentalism, 109, 136–37, 143n56
Fethulah Gülen, 126, 135
Feyizhani, Huseyin, 122
Final Peace Agreement (1996), 236, 237
First Euroasian Islamic Congress, 133
Foundation of Turkish Religious Affairs. See Türk Diyanet Vakfi
fundamentalism. See also activists, Islamic
  in Central Asia, 136–37
  Fergana Fundamentalism as, 109, 136–37, 143n56
  in Indonesia, 12, 18–20, 21, 22, 25, 26, 28
  in Philippines, 230
funding, Islamic, 13, 54, 70, 74, 151, 170n11

Gallardo, Rhoel, 238, 239
Gandhi, Mahatma, 180
Gandhi, Rajiv, 182–83
Gandhi, Sonia, 183, 195n27
Gaspirah, Ismail, 122–23
Gatra (magazine), 27
genocide, 65
Ghalib, Asadulah, 68, 69–72
al-Ghazzali, Abu Hamid, 60–61, 82
Gibb, Hamilton, 64
globalization
  effects of, on Muslims, 4
  Pakistan and, 145
  politics and, 8
  threat of, 19
  U.S. domination of, 85
Godhia, P. B., 191–92
Government of the Republic of the Philippines (GRP), 233, 236–38, 239, 241, 243
GRP. See Government of the Republic of the Philippines
Guantanamo, 207. See also war on terror
Guenon, Rene, 61
Gujarat Revenge Group, 184
Gulf War, 65

Hadi Awang, 99
Haghayeghi, Mehrdad, 110
hajj (pilgrimage), 62, 210–11, 248
Halbwachs, Maurice, 115
Hambali. See Isamuddin, Riduan
Hanafi teachings. See al-Maturidiyya
ul-Haq, Maulana Sami, 152, 167
ul-Haq, Mawlana Sami', 43
Hashim, Salamat, 236–37
Haz, Hamzah, 16, 17, 20
Hikmatyar, Gulbidin, 35

Hinduism, 11, 28, 177, 178, 182–85, 186t, 187,
    188, 191, 193
Hisba Act, 153, 154, 162–65, 167–68, 171n18,
    172n38. See also Pakistan
Hisba Force, 163–65
Hizb al-Tahrir al-islami, 137
Hizb al-Tahris, 137
Hizbullah Front, 23
honor killings, 160
hudood law. See apostasy
Hui nationality, 7, 197, 199, 200, 201, 202, 212,
    214–15, 217, 221n1, 223n11
human rights
    abuse of, in NWFP, 148, 169n6
    in China, 199, 206–9
    Human Rights Watch for, 190–91
    neo-modernists for, 12, 29n1
    Thorolf Rafto Human Rights Award for, 208
    in Turkey, 128
    U.S. Bureau of Democracy, Human Rights
        and Labor for, 254
Human Rights Watch, 190–91
Hun Sen, 250
Husain, Mushahid, 36

Ibrahim, Abdürreşid, 122–23
ICMI. See Association of Indonesian Muslim
    Intellectuals
ICS. See Islami Chhatra Shibbir
IJI. See Islami Jumhoori Ittihad
Ikwan al Muslimun (Muslim brotherhood), 237
Ilyas, Maulana Muhammad, 62
Imron, Maluleem, 250–51
IMU. See Islamic Movement of Uzbekistan
India
    armed/security forces in, 178, 179, 180–81,
        186t, 187, 195n20
    Ayodhya/Babri Masjid in, 183, 185–86,
        188, 195n27
    Bangladesh relations with, 49–50, 53,
        75n6, 76n9
    Biju Janata Dal in, 193
    BJP in, 50, 177, 182, 183, 184, 185, 186, 187,
        191, 193
    civil service in, 178, 179, 180, 181, 194n17
    colonialism in, 112
    Congress Party in, 177, 191
    corruption in, 195n30
    discrimination in, 178–81, 186t, 187, 188,
        195n20
    economic development in, 178–79,
        187, 193
    education in, 177, 179, 181–82, 184, 188, 193
    electoral competition in, 191, 192f, 193,
        196n38

Gujarat in, 178, 184, 189, 190–91, 190f,
    191, 192f
Gujarat Revenge Group in, 184
health issues in, 178, 179
Hindu nationalism in, 177, 185, 187, 188
Hindu opinion of Muslims in, 186t
Hindu Rashtra in, 187, 193
Human Rights Watch in, 190–91
income/employment in, 178, 179, 188, 193,
    195n30
Indian Civil Service in, 181
Indian Foreign Service for, 181, 194n18
Jaish-e-Mohammad in, 184–85
judiciary in, 187, 188, 193
Kashmir and, 36, 178
land reform in, 179
language in, 180, 188
Lashkar-e-Toiba in, 184–85
media in, 188, 193
militancy in, 178, 182, 184
minority rights in, 177, 178, 180, 189,
    189f, 191
Muslim community in, 3, 6–7, 177, 178
Muslim integration in, 186, 186t
Muslim League in, 179, 194n5
Muslim legal system in, 177, 178, 182–83,
    184, 185–86
Muslim Women Act, 1986 for, 182–83
National Human Right Commission for, 188
NDA in, 177
NGOs in, 188
Pakistan and, 36, 179–80, 181, 185, 194n12
partition of, 179–80, 185
People's Union for Civil Liberties in, 188
POTA for, 185, 187, 188
poverty in, 177–78, 181, 195n30
Ram Janmbhoomi Nyas in, 188
Rashtriya Swayamsevak Sangh in, 191
RAW in, 181
religious pluralism in, 193
Sachar Commission on the Status of
    Muslims, 178
secularism in, 177, 178
Shariat in, 182
SIMI in, 184
state patronage in, 178, 179, 180, 181
states' rights in, 178, 179
violence/terrorism in, 178, 182, 183, 184–85,
    186t, 189–90, 190f, 191, 192–93
Vishwa Hindu Parishad in, 191
Indonesia
    animism in, 11, 28
    Bali/Java bombings in, 4, 23, 26, 27, 230
    Christians versus Muslims in, 12, 18–20, 21,
        22, 25, 26, 28

Council of Islamic Ulemas in, 17
Dakwah Council in, 18
democracy in, 11, 12, 15, 22, 24–26, 28
Democratic Party of Struggle in, 13
discrimination in, 4, 18, 19, 22, 26, 28
DPR in, 15, 16
education in, 8, 13–14, 21, 24, 28, 146
extremism violence in, 4, 18, 19
fundamentalism in, 12, 18–20, 21, 22,
    25, 26, 28
government in, 25
Hinduism in, 11, 28
Islamic banking in, 14, 28
Islamic United Front in, 17
Islam in, 3, 4–5, 11, 16
Islam Jawa in, 13
Java in, 11
KISDI in, 18
Kommando Jihad in, 18
marriage laws in, 21
military in, 15, 16, 18, 20, 23, 26
modernists in, 12, 29n1
MPR in, 16
Muslim identity in, 3, 16
Muslim literature in, 13
Muslim Students Association in, 19
Nahdatul Ulama in, 11–12, 15–16, 19, 29n1
Nasution in, 19
National Awakening Party in, 12
nationalism in, 12
National Ulemas Council in, 20
neo-modernists in, 12, 29n1
9/11 and, 11, 15
the Pancasila for, 14
paternalism in, 21
pluralism in, 11, 18–22
PPP in, 16
al-Qaeda in, 23, 24
religious funding in, 13
religious laws in, 20
religious pluralism in, 20
religious radicalism in, 11, 22–24
religious resurgence in, 14
Sarekat Islam in, 11–12, 29n1
SBY in, 16
secularism in, 12, 13, 19, 24
separatism in, 19
Sharia in, 12, 16, 21, 24, 26
Sufism in, 13
Sukarno in, 14, 15
Sunni in, 13
terrorism and, 25–27
Thalib in, 20
traditionalists versus modernists in, 12,
    15, 29n1

U.S. and, 17
Wirayuda in, 17
women in, 12, 19, 20, 21–22
Indonesian Committee for Solidarity with the
    Islamic World (KISDI), 18
International Crisis Group, 255
International Islamic University, 89
International Religious Freedom Report
    2002, 254
Internet, 214. See also media
IOJ. See Islami Oiyko Jote
Iqbal, Allama, 149
Iqbal, Mohagher, 242
Iqbal, Muhammad, 3, 63–64
Iqba, Masud, 179–80
Iran
    in Central Asia, 124
    ECO and, 124–25
    Islamic government in, 4
    religious revolution in, 13, 74, 100, 252
    Shia in, 13
Iraq
    Pakistani fatwa for, 43
    sanctions against, 65
    U.S. attack on, 16, 17, 245, 253
IRP. See Islamic Renaissance Party
Isamuddin, Riduan, 23
Islam
    apostasy and, 20–21, 90, 91
    Christianity and, 229
    as code of conduct, 117
    as colonialism resistance, 112, 131
    conversion to, 86, 88, 89, 90–91, 91–92, 130
    culture of, 3, 4
    destruction of, 237
    education and, 8, 13–14, 21, 24, 28, 38, 49, 52,
        55–59, 77n29, 77n31, 77n39, 89, 111, 113,
        116, 125–27, 126t, 146, 150–51, 154–55,
        156–59, 177, 179, 181–82, 184, 188, 193,
        199, 201, 203, 204–5, 208, 210, 211,
        219–20, 221, 223n12, 224n19, 224n24,
        225n26
    Efsanevi as, 135–36
    ethnic tolerance by, 4
    as expressivist versus scripturalist, 115,
        140n10
    five zones of, 129
    government use of, 116
    identity through, 6, 64, 66
    intellectualism and, 66–67
    as law versus socioeconomic domain, 149
    legitimization through, 3–4
    literature of, 13, 66–67
    madrasas for, 14, 24, 28, 38, 55–57, 57t, 68,
        74, 77n31, 77n36

Islam (continued)
al-Maturidiyya interpretation of, 112
military versus, 5
morality of, 4
nation building by, 6, 132
neo pan-Islamism for, 255
patriotism through, 64–66
as political, 4, 94–95, 96, 97–98, 99–101,
102, 147, 152, 169n5, 237, 245
Qur'an for, 52, 62, 71, 86, 95, 115, 140n9,
151, 153–54, 162, 164, 204
as reformist, 63–64, 78n50
religious tolerance by, 4
secularism versus, 5, 24
size of, 3
social structure of, 114
tabligh groups for, 146, 169n2
terrorism and, 27
in Thailand, 247–49, 252–53, 257n14
in Turkey, 118
in Turkic world, 130
types of, 249
ummah of, 15–16, 28, 52, 54, 81, 89, 211,
231, 237, 256
Islam hadhari, 85, 95, 97, 101, 103, 108n33
Islamic Academy. See Islamic Foundation
Islamic Association of China, 210
Islamic Defenders Front, 23
Islamic Foundation, 52, 76n17
Islamic Front, 152
Islami Chhatra Shibbir (ICS), 62, 78n45
Islamic Ideological Council, 152
Islamic law. See Sharia
Islamic Movement of Uzbekistan (IMU), 137
Islamic Party (PAS), 83, 90, 95–96, 97, 98–99,
100, 102, 146
Islamic Renaissance Party (IRP), 137, 139
Islamic Students and Teachers
Association, 249
Islamic United Front, 17
Islamic Youth Movement, 23
Islami Jumhoori Ittihad (IJI), 33–34
Islami Oiyko Jote (IOJ), 62
Islam Jawa, 13
Islam, Siddiqul, 50, 67–68, 69, 71
Ismail, Rehana, 157
Israel
in Lebanon, 17, 65
radicalization and, 16–17, 24
Turkey and, 122
U.S. support of, 17
Iymonga yul (Yuldashev), 137

Jabidah Massacre, 231
Jadidism, 116, 122, 130–31

Jaffer, Wasim, 185
Jaffrey, Ehsan, 178
Jagarta Muslim Janata Bangladesh (JMJB), 50,
67–68, 71–72, 79n60
JAHB, 68–69
Jaish-e-Mohammad, 184–85
Jakarta Agreement, 236
Jakarta Charter, 21
Jakarta State Institute of Islamic Studies, 19
JAKIM. See Department of Islamic
Development
Jamaah Salamullah, 20
Jamaat-e-Islami, 51, 69–70, 74, 184
Jama'at-i Islami, 32, 33, 34–35, 40, 61, 147, 152
Jamaat-i-Islami, 61–62
Jama'at Islam (JI), 240
Jamaat-ul-Mujahidin Bangladesh (JMB), 50,
68, 70–72, 79n60
Jamhari, 25, 28
Jami'at-i Ulama-i Islam (JUI), 33, 35, 41, 151
Jami'at-i Ulama-i Pakistan (JUP), 33
Jami'atul-al-Islamiyya, 237
Jamiyah Ansar as-Sunnah Muhayid, 249
Jamiyat-e-Ulama-e-Islam, 51
Janjalani, Abdulrajak, 238
Janjalani, Qaddafi, 238
Java. See Indonesia
Jehovah's Witnesses, 20
Jemaah Islamiyah (JI), 23, 27, 30n32, 252,
253, 254
JI. See Jama'at Islam; Jemaah Islamiyah
Jididism, 116
jihad (armed struggle), 17, 69, 71, 237, 251
Jinnah, Muhammad Ali, 149
JMB. See Jamaat-ul-Mujahidin Bangladesh
JMJB. See Jagarta Muslim Janata Bangladesh
Joshi, Murli Manohar, 184
JUI. See Jami'at-i Ulama-i Islam
JUP. See Jami'at-i Ulama-i Pakistan

Kadeer, Rebiya, 208, 227n38
Kalam, AJ., 185
Karimov, Islam, 125
Karpal Singh, 103
Kashmir
India and, 36, 178
militant activism in, 36, 178, 186
Pakistan and, 5, 32
training camps in, 34–35
Kazakistan, 114, 115, 126t, 134t. See also
Central Asia
Kemal, Mustafa. See Ataturk, Mustafa Kemal;
Turkey, Republic of
Khan, Aamir, 185
Khan, Abdul-Qadeer, 43, 45

Khan, Bakht Jehan, 156, 165–66
Khan, Sayyid Ahmad, 63
Khan, Shahrukh, 185
Khmer Rouge, 249, 255
King Henry V (Shakespeare), 229
KISDI. *See* Indonesian Committee for
    Solidarity with the Islamic World
Kishore, Acharya Giriraj, 186
Koh, Kamal, 90
Kommando Jihad, 18
Kursavi, Abdunnasir, 122
Kuwait, 54, 70
Kyrgyzstan, 109, 111, 114, 124, 126t, 133, 134t.
    See also Central Asia

Lashkar-e-Toiba, 184–85
Laskar Jihad, 19–20, 22, 23–24, 25, 26
Laskar Jundullah, 23
Laskar Mujahidin, 23
Latif, Nawab Abdul, 64
Lebanon, Israel in, 17, 65
Legal Framework Order, 42–43
Libya, 13
Lim Kit Siang, 99–100, 103
Lings, Martin, 61
Lintner, Bertil, 49–50
Loong, Benjamin, 234
the Lumad, 7

Ma'arif, Syafi, 25
Madjid, Nurcholish, 3, 19, 25
madrasas (Islamic schools), 14, 24, 28, 38,
    55–57, 57t, 68, 74, 77n31, 77n36
Magsaysay, Ramon, 232
Mahathir, Mirzan, 83. *See also* Malaysia
Mahathir, Mohamed, 81, 94, 95, 99, 100,
    105n10, 105n14, 146. *See also* Malaysia
Majelis Mujahidin Indonesia (MMI), 23–24, 26
Majlis Sheikul Islam Cambodia, 250
Malaysia
    ABIM in, 88, 90
    ALIRAN in, 88
    apostasy in, 90, 91, 92
    BA in, 103
    birth rate in, 86
    BN in, 83, 94
    Christianity in, 86
    colonialism in, 91, 93
    Confucianism in, 89
    constitution for, 91, 92, 93, 98, 103,
        107nn25–26
    DAP in, 96, 99–100, 102
    democracy in, 4, 6, 84, 103–4
    economic development in, 4, 82–84, 104
    education in, 89

Election Commission for, 102
EPU of, 82–83, 105n6
ethnic pluralism in, 6, 82, 84, 86–87, 89,
    91, 92, 106nn20–21
Islam hadhari for, 85, 95, 97, 101, 103, 108n33
Islamic conversion in, 86, 88, 89, 90–92
Islam in, 4–5, 81–82, 84, 85, 87, 88, 92–93,
    105n14
JAKIM in, 101
justice system for, 93, 107n26
kidnappings in, 238
labor recruitment for, 86
Malay identity in, 82–83, 85, 90–91, 97–98
marriage in, 86
media in, 89, 95, 101–2
modernization of, 81, 84, 87, 104
MSC in, 84
Muslims in, 3
NGOs in, 88, 97–98, 101, 107n32
PAS in, 83, 90, 95–96, 97, 98–99, 100,
    102, 146
as peace broker, 240
People's Justice Party in, 83
PERKIM in, 90
PKR in, 96–97, 98, 102
political Islam in, 4, 94–95, 96, 97–98,
    99–101, 102, 103
religious pluralism in, 86–87
Sharia in, 93, 147
SIS in, 101, 107n32
UMNO in, 36, 83, 90, 94, 95, 96, 97–99, 102
Wawasan 2020 for, 84
Malaysian Islamic Welfare Association
    (PERKIM), 90
Maniruzzaman, Talukdar, 72
Mao Zedong, 209–10, 217–18. *See also* China
Marcos, Ferdinand, 233, 234
marriage, in Indonesia, 21
Masjumi, 11–12
Matalam, Datu Udtog, 231
Matta, Wan Muhammad Nor, 248
al-Maturidiyya, 69, 112, 130–31, 198
Maududi, Maulana Abul Aa, 61
al-Mawdudi, A'la, 3, 237
media
    in Bangladesh, 52, 65–66, 78n53
    cell phones for, 214
    effect of, on Muslims, 4
    in India, 188, 193
    Internet as, 214
    in Malaysia, 89, 95, 101–2
    for Muslims, 14, 28, 52
    in Pakistan, 154–55
    in Singapore, 95–96
    TRT Avrasya as, 125

Mercani, Sehabettin, 122
MILF. *See* Moro Islamic Liberation Front
military
  in Bangladesh, 49, 50
  in Indonesia, 15, 16, 18, 20, 23, 26
  Islam versus, 5, 38, 39, 44, 46
  in Pakistan, 31–32, 35, 37–38, 42, 43–44
  in Philippines, 232–33, 235
  as secular, 45–46
  terrorism and, 26
  in Thailand, 246
  in Turkey, 37
Military-Mullah Alliance. *See* Mutahhidah
  Majlis Amal
Military Rebellion, 235
MIM. *See* Muslim Independence Movement
Mindanao. *See* Philippines, Mindanao
Mindanao Peace Process, 232
Mindanao War, 239
Ministry of Cults and Religious Affairs, 249–50
minorities
  advocacy for, 7
  extremists as, 4, 28
  in India, 177, 178
  Islamic intolerance towards, 4, 18, 19, 26,
    28, 150
  movements by, 6
  Muslims as, 6, 7, 197–98, 199, 221*n*1, 246
  in Pakistan, 153
Mir-i Arab Medrese, 113
MMA. *See* Mutahhidah Majlis Amal
MMI. *See* Majelis Mujahidin Indonesia
MNLF. *See* Moro National Liberation Front
modernists, 12, 15, 29*n*1
Moro Islamic Liberation Front (MILF), 236–38,
  240–43
Moro National Liberation Front (MNLF),
  231, 236–37
mosques
  attacks on, 19
  in Bangladesh, 55
  in Cambodia, 249–50
  in Central Asia, 112, 115
  in China, 198–99, 203, 204, 207, 210,
    211, 212, 222*n*2, 222*n*4, 224*nn*20–21,
    226*n*32
  closing/destruction of, 7, 112, 212
MPR. *See* Peoples Consultative Assembly
MSC. *See* Multi-Media Super Corridor
Muhammadiyah, 12, 15–16, 17, 19, 25,
  26, 29*n*1
mujahideen, Afghan, 4
Mujahidin Manifesto, 25
Mullah Omar, 151, 170*n*12
Multi-Media Super Corridor (MSC), 84

Murad, Hajj Ibrahim, 242
Musharraf, Pervez, 35–46
Muslim Family Laws Ordinance (1961), 150,
  161, 164. *See also* Pakistan
Muslim Independence Movement (MIM), 231
Muslim League, 51, 179, 194*n*5
Muslims
  autonomy for, 6
  Christians versus, 12, 18–20, 21, 22, 25,
    26, 28
  clerics for, 12
  conversion of, 20
  dietary restrictions of, 211, 227*n*49
  ethnic/religious tolerance by, 4
  identity of, 6
  intellectuals as, 3, 14–15, 66–67
  leaders of, 186
  local versus national agendas for, 146
  location of, 3
  marketing for, 14
  media for, 14, 28, 52
  as minorities, 6, 7, 197–98, 199, 221*n*1, 246
  persecution of, 7
  political agenda of, 146
  rituals for, 14
  Sharia for, 12, 16, 21, 24, 26, 146–47
  women as, 4, 20
Muslim Separatist Movements in Southern
  Philippines, 235
Muslim Separatist War, 233
Muslim Students Association, 19
Muslim Women Act, 1986, 182–83
Muslim Youth Movement of Malaysia (ABIM),
  88, 90
Mutahhidah Majlis Amal (MMA). *See also*
  Pakistan
  Election Manifesto for, 152–53
  as Islamist political coalition, 39–45, 152
  as opposition in National Assembly, 145
Muzadi, Hasyim, 27

Nahdatul Ulama (NU), 11–12, 15–16, 19, 26,
  27, 29*n*1
Naksibend, Bahattin, 129–30, 136
Nasiri, Kayyum, 122
Nasrin, Taslima, 64
Nasr, Seyyed Hossein, 61, 67
Nasution, Harun, 19
National Awakening Party, 12
National Awareness Current (ALIRAN), 88
National Council of Churches of the
  Philippines, 235
National Democratic Alliance (NDA), 177
National Democratic Front (NDF), 235,
  240, 242

nationalism
    in Bangladesh, 51, 52, 64–65, 72, 73
    by Hindu India, 177, 185, 187, 188
    in Indonesia, 12
    in Philippines, 237
    in Turkey, 118, 123, 139
Nationalist Thought and the Colonial World:
    Derivative Discourse (Chatterje), 113
National Movement Party (MHP), 118, 123, 139
National Ulemas Council, 20
National Unification Commission (NUC), 235
NATO. *See* North Atlantic Treaty Organization
Nazarbayev, Nursultan, 125
NDA. *See* National Democratic Alliance
NDF. *See* National Democratic Front
Nehru, Jawaharlal, 178, 179
neo-modernists, 12, 29n1
neo pan-Islamism, 255
New Expanded Autonomous Region in Muslim
    Mindanao (ARMM), 236
New Order, 5, 15, 22. *See also* Suharto, Raden
New York Times, 254–55
NGOs. *See* nongovernmental organizations
Nifaz-i-Shariat Council, 154
9/11. *See* September 11, 2001
Niyazov, Safarmurad, 125
Nizam-e-Islam Party, 51
Noer, Deliar, 23
nongovernmental organizations (NGOs), 54,
    68, 70, 88, 97–98, 101, 107n32, 188, 210,
    213, 220
Noorani, Mawlana Shah Ahmad, 41, 152,
    170n15
North Atlantic Treaty Organization (NATO),
    121
Northwest Frontier Province (NWFP), 40,
    41, 42, 45, 145, 148, 167, 169n1,
    169nn6–7, 195n30
NU. *See* Nahdatul Ulama
NUC. *See* National Unification Commission
nuclear technology, 43, 45
Nurcu movement, 126
Nur, Misuari, 231, 236
Nursi, Said, 135
NWFP. *See* Northwest Frontier Province

occupation, Soviet, of Afghanistan, 4, 23–24, 35
OIC. *See* Organization of the Islamic
    Conference
oil, funding through, 13
Olcott, Martha Brill, 110
Organic Act for the Autonomous Region in
    Muslim Mindanao (ARMM), 234
Organization of the Islamic Conference (OIC),
    121, 233, 242

Ottoman Empire, 117, 119, 120, 121, 122.
    See also Turkey, Republic of
Outlook (publication), 214
Özal, Turgut, 118, 124, 127, 141n36

Pakistan
    Afghanistan and, 32
    apostasy in, 91, 97, 147
    Ayub Khan regime in, 32, 37
    Bangladesh and, 68, 72–73
    Blasphemy Law for, 150
    conservatism in, 147–48
    constitution for, 149
    Council on Islamic Ideology for, 147, 154, 164
    culture wars in, 168
    democracy in, 33, 35, 39, 44
    Deobandi JUI in, 40, 41, 42
    development/modernization in, 31, 33, 36,
        37, 145
    discrimination in, 150
    ECO and, 124–25
    education in, 38, 150–51, 154–55, 156–59
    extremism in, 35, 36
    foreign policy of, 33
    gender separation in, 156
    globalization and, 145
    Hisba Act for, 153, 154, 162–65, 167–68,
        171n18, 172n38
    Hisba Force in, 163–65
    Hudood Ordinances for, 149, 164
    Indian Muslim immigration to, 180, 194n12
    Iraqi fatwa in, 43
    Islamic banking in, 149, 155
    Islamic law versus socioeconomic domains
        in, 149, 170n9
    Islamic politics in, 3–4, 32–33, 44, 46, 145–47
    Islamic prayer in, 159–60, 171n27
    Islam versus military in, 5, 38, 39, 44, 46
    jihadi groups in, 151
    Kashmir and, 5, 32
    Legal Framework Order for, 42–43
    media in, 154–55
    military in, 31–32, 35, 37–38, 42, 43–44
    minorities in, 153
    MMA in, 39–45
    Musharraf in, 35, 37, 39, 42
    Muslim Family Laws Ordinance for, 150,
        161, 164
    nuclear technology sale from, 43, 45
    partition of India and, 179–80, 185
    Pathans in, 40, 41, 42, 43
    Pathans versus Punjabis in, 41
    philanthropy in, 151, 170n11
    PML in, 33, 34, 35–36, 39
    PML(Q) in, 41, 43

Pakistan (*continued*)
  PPP in, 33–34, 39
  Protection of Women Act, 167, 173*n*46
  provincial versus federal government in, 153, 162, 164, 171*n*18, 172*n*40
  secularism in, 31, 32, 38, 40, 149
  Sharia laws in, 147, 154
  Shariat Bill for, 147, 149, 150, 153, 154–55, 165
  socialism in, 32
  SSP in, 40
  Taliban and, 41
  TNSM in, 147, 169*n*4
  U.S. ties with, 38, 42, 145
  Westernization of, 155, 160
Pakistan-Afghanistan Defense Council, 152
Pakistan Muslim League (PML), 33, 34, 35–36, 39, 43
Pakistan Peoples Party (PPP), 33–34, 39, 43
Palestine, solidarity with, 18–19, 65
the Pancasila, 14
Partai Persatuan Pembangunan (PPP), 16
PAS. *See* Islamic Party
paternalism, 21
Pathans, 40, 41, 42, 43
Peoples Consultative Assembly (MPR), 16
Peoples Justice Party (PKR), 83, 96–97, 98, 102
PERKIM. *See* Malaysian Islamic Welfare Association
Pershing, John J., 232–33
Pew Research, 25
philanthropy. *See* funding, Islamic
Philippines, Mindanao
  Abu Sayyaf in, 4, 230, 238–40
  activism in, 7
  AFP for, 238–40
  American occupation of, 232
  Aquino Constitution for, 234
  ARMM for, 234
  autonomous regions in, 234
  Bangsamoro Development Agency in, 240
  Bangsamoro in, 231, 233, 237, 239
  bombing in, 230
  Christian missionaries in, 231
  Christians in, 7, 231
  democracy in, 237
  discrimination in, 231
  economic development in, 232
  Final Peace Agreement (1996) for, 236
  fundamentalism in, 230
  GRP in, 233, 236–38, 239, 241, 243
  identity politics in, 146
  Islamic fundamentalists in, 230
  Islamic opposition in, 3–4
  Jabidah Massacre in, 231

  land reform in, 233
  lawlessness in, 230, 238–39
  Lumad in, 230–31
  Malaysia as peace broker for, 240
  MILF in, 236–38, 240–43
  Military Rebellion in, 235
  military rule in, 232–33
  MIM in, 231
  Mindanao War in, 239
  MNLF in, 231
  modernization in, 230
  Moro people in, 233
  Moro Province in, 232–33
  Muslims as minority in, 6
  Muslim Separatist Movements in, 235
  Muslim Separatist War in, 231–32, 233
  National Defense for, 238
  nationalism in, 237
  NDF in, 235, 240, 242
  9/11 and, 230, 238
  NUC in, 235
  OIC and, 233
  Peace Agreement for, 235–36
  population of, 233
  al-Qaeda in, 240
  RCC in, 234
  regulations for, 234–36
  secularism in, 237
  TA for, 233, 236
  trade within, 231
  urbanization in, 230
  Zone of Peace and Development for, 236
Pibulsonggram, Luang, 246
pir (guide), 60, 69–70
Pitsuwan, Surin, 248, 250
PKR. *See* Peoples Justice Party
pluralism
  as ethnic, 6, 82, 84, 86–87, 89, 91, 92, 106*nn*20–21, 199, 213
  as political, 4, 11, 18–22
  as religious, 4, 20, 193, 246, 252–53
PML. *See* Pakistan Muslim League
PML(Q). *See* Pakistan
polygamy, 21–22
POTA. *See* India; Prevention of Terrorism Act
poverty
  in India, 177–78, 181, 195*n*30
  in NWFP, 148, 167, 169*n*7, 195*n*30
Powell, Colin, 254
PPP. *See* Pakistan Peoples Party; Partai Persatuan Pembangunan
Premji, Azim, 185
Prevention of Terrorism Act (POTA), 185, 187, 188

Prince Alwaleed Bin Talal Center for
    Muslim-Christian Understanding, 5
prostitution, 218, 219, 221
Protection of Women Act, 167, 173n46.
    See also Pakistan; women

al-Qaeda
    in Afghanistan, 38
    as anti-American, 45
    as extremism, 4
    in Indonesia, 23, 24
    in Philippines, 240
al-Qardhawi, Yusuf, 67
Qazi Hussain Ahmed, 34, 39, 40,
    42–43, 152
Qudrat-i-Khuda, Muhammad, 58
Quirino, Elipido, 232
Qur'an, 52, 62, 71, 86, 95, 115, 140n9, 151,
    153–54, 162, 164, 204. *See also* Islam
Qureshi, Ejaz, 155–56
al Qutb, Sayyid, 237

Rabita-al-'Alam al-Islami (World Muslim
    League), 70
radicalization, Islamic
    in Bangladesh, 49–50, 75n1
    in Indonesia, 11, 22–24
    Israel and, 16–17, 24
    in Thailand, 250–53
    U.S. and, 16–17
Rahim, Muhammad Abdur, 60, 71
Rahman Mawlana Fazlur, 40
Rahman, Mujibur, 51–52, 53, 58, 68
Rahman, Shamsur, 64
Rahman, Sheikh Abdur, 50, 68, 69, 70
Rahman, Tunku Abdul, 99
Rahman, Ziaur (Zia), 52, 53, 57, 70, 74
Rais, Amein, 16, 17, 24–25
Rakowska-Harstone, Teresa, 110
Ramadan, observance of, 14, 23, 114, 207,
    212, 215
Ram Janmbhoomi Nyas, 188
Ramos, Fidel, 235, 240
Rashiduzzaman, M., 73
RAW. *See* Research and Analysis Wing
RCC. *See* Regional Consultative Commission
refugees, 249
Regional Consultative Commission
    (RCC), 234
Religious Affairs Bureau, 210
Republic Act (RA) 6734, 236
Research and Analysis Wing (RAW), 181
Reyes, Angelo, 238, 240
Riaz, Ali, 50–51
Rice, Condoleezza, 208

Risale-I Nur Kulliyati (Nursi), 135
Robinson, Mary, 206
Rome Treaty, 121
Roxas, Manuel, 232
Roy, Asim, 60
Rushdie, Salman, 213
Russia. *See also* Soviet Union
    Central Asia in opposition to, 137
    Turkish ties with, 128–29
Rywkin, Michael, 132

Sachar Commission on the Status of Muslims,
    178. *See also* India
SADUM. *See* Spiritual Board of Central Asian
    and Kazak Muslims
Said, Edward, 67
Salamat, Hashim, 240, 241, 243
Saltuk, Sari, 129–30
sanctions, 65. *See also* Iraq
Sarekat Dagang Islam, 18
Sarekat Islam, 11–12, 29n1
Saudi Arabia
    funding by, 13, 54, 70, 74
    missionaries from, 117
SBY. *See* Susilo Bambang Yudhoyono
Schuon, Frithjof, 61
Second Eurasia Congress, 133
secularism
    in Bangladesh, 51, 52, 72
    in India, 177, 178
    in Indonesia, 12, 13, 19, 24
    Islam versus, 5, 24
    of military, 45–46
    National Awakening Party versus, 12
    in Pakistan, 31, 32, 38, 40, 149
    in Philippines, 237
    in Turkey, 117
separatism
    in Indonesia, 19
    by Uighurs, 7
September 11, 2001 (9/11). *See also* terrorism
    Cambodia and, 245, 255
    China and, 199, 206, 227n43
    Indonesia and, 11, 15
    Philippines and, 230, 238
    terrorist attack of, 5, 11, 15, 37–38, 40, 85,
        185, 199, 206, 227n43, 230, 238, 245,
        250–52, 255
    Thailand and, 245, 250–52
Shah, Bano, 182
Shah-i Zindeh, 136
Shahrani, Nazif, 111, 113
Shaikh al-Islam, 251
Shakespeare, William, 229
shamans, 28

Sharia
    in Bangladesh, 54–55, 62
    in Central Asia, 113
    implementation of, 12, 82, 146–47
    in India, 182
    in Indonesia, 12, 16, 21, 24, 26
    in Malaysia, 93, 147
    for Muslims, 12, 16, 21, 24, 26, 146–47
    in Pakistan, 147, 149, 150, 153, 154–55, 165
Shariat (India), 182
Shariat Bill, 147, 149, 150, 153, 154–55, 165.
    See also Pakistan
Shariati, Ali, 67
Sharif, Nawaz, 31, 33, 34, 35–36, 37, 44, 150.
    See also Pakistan Muslim League
Silk Road, 112. See also Central Asia
SIMI. See Students Islamic Movement of India
Singapore, 95–96
Sinha, Yashwant, 50
Sipah Sahabah Pakistan (SSP), 40
SIS. See Sisters in Islam
Sisters in Islam (SIS), 101, 107n32
socialism, 32
Sonamoni, 70
Soviet Union (USSR)
    in Afghanistan, 4, 23–24, 35
    collapse of, 6, 109, 115, 118, 124, 132
    colonialism of, 112, 113, 131, 137
    Islamophobia in, 110
    scientific atheism of, 111, 112, 135
    Spiritual Boards of Directorate in, 113,
        132–33
    Turkish ties with, 123
Spiritual Board of Central Asian and Kazak
    Muslims (SADUM), 113
Spiritual Boards of Directorate, 113, 132–33
SSP. See Sipah Sahabah Pakistan
Stalin, Joseph, 112, 132–33
Students Islamic Movement of India
    (SIMI), 184
Sudan, 4
Sufism
    in Bangladesh, 54, 59–61
    in Central Asia, 114, 130
    in China, 7
    in Indonesia, 13
    in Turkey, 129, 130, 134–35, 143n59
Suharto, Raden, 13, 14–15, 18, 19
Sukarno, Ahmed, 14, 15
Sukarnoputri, Megawati, 13, 16, 22.
    See also Indonesia
Sunnah, 62, 164
Surakarta Islamic Youth Forum, 23
Susilo Bambang Yudhoyono (SBY), 16
swara, practice of, 160, 166

TA. See Tripoli Peace Agreement
tabligh groups, 146, 169n2
Tablighi Jamaat, 52, 61, 62–63, 254
Tajikistan, civil war in, 109
talaq (divorce), 162, 172n35
Taliban
    in Afghanistan, 3, 4, 35, 38, 39, 41, 251
    Pakistani ties with, 41
    U.S. attack on, 17, 38, 65, 252–53, 255
Talibanization, 41, 42
Tan, Anuar, 90
TDV. See Türk Diyanet Vakfi
Tehreek-e-Nafaz-e-Shariat-e-Mohammadi
    (TNSM), 147, 169n4
Tehrik Nifaz Fiqah Jaferiya, 152, 166–67
Tempo poll, 27
terrorism
    by Abu Sayyaf, 4, 230, 238–40
    in Bangladesh, 49–50, 68, 71, 75n2, 76n9
    in Cambodia, 253–55
    in India, 178, 182, 183, 184–85, 186t, 189–90,
        190f, 191, 192–93
    in Indonesia, 25–27
    Islam and, 27
    military and, 26
    9/11 as, 5, 11, 15, 37–38, 40, 85, 185, 199, 206,
        227n43, 230, 238, 245, 250–52, 255
    POTA for, 185, 187, 188
    as state-sponsored, 230
Thailand
    activism in, 7
    Ayudhaya Kingdom in, 247
    boycott by, of American products, 251
    Buddhism in, 247, 257n14
    constitutional monarchy in, 246
    democracy in, 250
    identity politics in, 146
    Islamic banking in, 248
    Islam in, 247–49, 252–53, 257n14
    language in, 247–48
    military rule in, 246
    Muslim improvement in, 248
    Muslim radicalization in, 250–53
    Muslims as minority in, 6, 246
    9/11 and, 245, 250–52
    religious pluralism in, 246, 252–53
    security concerns in, 255
    TRT in, 248
    Wahdah (unity) group in, 248
Thai Rak Thai Party (TRT), 248
Thalib, Ja'far Umar, 20
Thanarat, Sarit, 246
Third Eurasia Islamic Congress, 133
Thorolf Rafto Human Rights Award, 208
Thousand Mothers' Movement, 208

TIKA. *See* Turkish International Co-operation Agency

TNSM. *See* Tehreek-e-Nafaz-e-Shariat-e-Mohammadi

Topcubaşi, Ali Merdan, 122–23

traditionalists, 12, 29*n*1

trafficking, in women, 160, 218, 219, 221

training camps, 34–35

Tripoli Peace Agreement (TA), 233, 236

TRT. *See* Thai Rak Thai Party

TRT Avrasya (television station), 125. *See also* media

tsunami, U.S. aid for, 17

Tunyaz, Tohti, 208

Türk Diyanet Vakfi (TDV), 133, 143*n*60

Turkey, Republic of

Ankara Declaration and, 125

Ataturk in, 37, 117, 121

CAS and, 128

Central Asian policy by, 124–28, 126*t*, 138, 141*n*36, 142*n*45

Cold War for, 121–22

constitution for, 118, 140*n*14

culture/identity debate in, 118, 127, 129

Cyprus and, 122

Directorate of Religious Affairs in, 133

ECO and, 124–25

economic development in, 127–28

EEC and, 121, 122

EU and, 119, 121, 138

foreign policy/state identity in, 118–28, 140*n*20

human rights in, 128

Islam in, 118, 120, 133

Islamization Project in, 132–36

Israel and, 122

MHP in, 118, 123, 139

military in, 37

National Front coalitions in, 123

nationalism in, 118, 123, 139

NATO and, 121, 122

Ottoman Empire in, 117, 119, 120, 121, 122

religious education in, 111

Russian ties with, 128–29

secularism in, 117

Sufism in, 129, 130, 134–35, 143*n*59

TDV in, 133, 143*n*60

TIKA and, 125

USSR and, 123

U.S. ties with, 120

War of Liberation in, 117

Westernization of, 117, 121–22

Turkish International Co-operation Agency (TIKA), 125

Turkistan, 115

Turkmenistan, 111, 112, 124, 126*t*, 133, 134*t*

Twin Towers. *See* World Trade Center

UAE. *See* United Arab Emirates

Uddin, Sufia M., 65

Uighur Muslims, 6, 7, 197–98, 199, 207, 208, 209, 217, 221*n*1, 222*n*5, 225*n*27, 226*n*31. *See also* China

ulama (religious scholars), 11–12, 15–16, 19, 26, 27, 29*n*1, 33, 35, 41, 51, 55, 57, 68, 112, 151

ummah (Islamic world community), 15–16, 28, 52, 54, 81, 89, 211, 231, 237, 256. *See also* Islam

Umm al-Qura, 254, 255

UMNO. *See* United Malays National Organization (UMNO)

United Arab Emirates (UAE), 54

United Malays National Organization (UMNO), 36, 83, 90, 94, 95, 96, 97–99, 102

United Nations, 250

United States (U.S.), 16–17

attack by, on Afghanistan, 17, 38, 65, 245, 251–53, 255

China and, 206–7, 225*nn*29–30

globalization and, 85

Guantanamo and, 207

Indonesia's fear of, 17

in Iraq, 5, 16, 17, 245, 253

Pakistan ties with, 38

radicalization and, 16–17

in support of Israel, 17

Turkish ties with, 120

war on terror by, 11, 16, 17, 27, 28, 38, 39, 42, 65, 207, 230, 240, 252–53, 255, 256

U.S. *See* United States

U.S. Bureau of Democracy, Human Rights and Labor, 254

U.S. Central Intelligence Agency (CIA), 27, 120, 253

USSR. *See* Soviet Union

Uzbekistan, 111, 112, 117, 124, 126*t*, 134*t*, 137. *See also* Central Asia

Veli, Haci Bektas(A!)i, 129–30

violence

in China, 201, 202–3, 209, 214–15, 218, 221, 223*n*15

in India, 178, 182, 183, 184–85, 186*t*, 189–90, 190*f*, 191, 192–93

between Indian Hindu/Muslim, 178, 182–85

in Indonesia, 4, 18, 19

by Muslim extremists, 4, 18, 19

against Muslim sects, 20

Votes and Violence: Electoral Competition and Ethnic Riots in India (Wilkinson), 189, 189f, 192f

waaf foundation, 112–13, 212
Waemahadi, Wae-dao, 253–54
Wahdah (unity) group, 248
Wahhabism, 14, 20, 24, 25, 54, 68–69, 116–17, 135, 136–37, 249, 252, 254
Wahid, Abdurrahman, 3, 16, 19, 24–25, 27
Wahid, Solahuddin, 27
Wall Street Journal, 50
Wan Azizah, 96–97, 98
war on Muslims. *See* war on terror
war on terror, 11, 16, 27, 28, 39, 42, 207, 230, 240, 256. *See also* September 11, 2001; United States
Wazed, Hasina, 62
Went, Alexander, 119
Wilkinson, Steven I., 188, 189f, 192f
Winbush, S. Enders, 110
Wirayuda, Hassan, 17
women
    in China, 217–21
    divorce from, 162, 172n35
    education for, 156–58
    gender separation for, 156
    in government, 13, 16, 22
    honor killings of, 160
    in Indonesia, 12, 19, 20, 21–22
    Islamic image of, 150
    Islamic intolerance towards, 4, 20
    legal rights for, 161
    as Muslims, 4, 20
    Muslim Women Act, 1986 for, 182–83
    Pakistani penal code for, 149
    practice of *swara* on, 160, 166
    in prostitution, 218, 219, 221
    Protection of Women Act for, 167, 173n46
    rights of, 12, 19, 160, 171n28
    trafficking in, 160, 218, 219, 221
Wood, Leonard, 232–33
Woodward, Mark, 25
World Bank, 155, 167
World Trade Center, 245, 250
World War II (WW II), 18, 113, 232

Yahya, Ahmad, 254
Yesevi, Ahmet, 129–30, 136, 142n51
Yilmaz, Mehmet N., 133, 143n59
Yongle, 200
Yorac, Heidi, 235
Yugoslavia, 118, 143n62
Yuldashev, Akram, 137

Zafarullah Khan Jamali, 43
Zakat Fund, 53
Zheng He, 200, 223n10
Zia. *See* Rahman, Ziaur
Zia, Khalida, 56, 61, 62
Zia ul-Haq, 32, 33, 34, 147, 149–51, 157
ziyaret (pilgrimage), 115, 140n9